THE
PUBLIC GENERAL ACTS
AND GENERAL SYNOD MEASURES
1978

[IN THREE PARTS]

PART III

TABLES AND INDEX

LONDON
HER MAJESTY'S STATIONERY OFFICE
£48 net.

H.M.SO
£48 per set
10.79

ISBN 0 11 840185 8

THIS PUBLICATION
relates to
the Public General Acts
and General Synod Measures
which received the Royal Assent in 1978
in which year ended the Twenty-Sixth
and began the Twenty-Seventh Year
of the Reign of Her Majesty
Queen Elizabeth the Second
and
ended the Fourth Session
and began the Fifth Session
of the Forty-Seventh Parliament of the
United Kingdom of Great Britain
and Northern Ireland.

e

CONTENTS

PART I

PART II

PART III

TABLE I

Alphabetical List of

the Public General Acts of 1978

TABLE II

Chronological List of

the Public General Acts of 1978

* Consolidation Act.

* **Consolidation Act.**

TABLE III

Alphabetical List of

the Local and Personal Acts of 1978

TABLE IV

Chronological List of

the General Synod Measures of 1978

---

*Measure passed by the General Synod of the Church of England
which received the Royal Assent during the year* 1978

		Part	Page
No. 1.	Dioceses Measure	II	1483
No. 2.	Parochial Registers and Records Measure	II	1507
No. 3.	Church of England (Miscellaneous Provisions) Measure.	II	1529

TABLE V

Tables of the Derivations and Destinations of the Consolidation Acts of 1978

These Tables have no official status. They are intended only as a help in tracing the derivations of the Consolidation Acts and the destinations of the enactments consolidated.

CONTENTS

ADOPTION (SCOTLAND) ACT 1978 (c. 28)

TABLE OF DERIVATIONS

Note:—The following abbreviations are used in this Table:—

1958	= The Adoption Act 1958 (7 & 8 Eliz. 2. c. 5)
1960	= The Adoption Act 1960 (1960 c. 59)
1964	= The Adoption Act 1964 (1964 c. 57)
1968 (c. 49)	= The Social Work (Scotland) Act 1968 (1968 c. 49)
1968	= The Adoption Act 1968 (1968 c. 53)
1975	= The Children Act 1975 (1975 c. 72)
1976	= The Adoption Act 1976 (1976 c. 36)
1978	= The Domestic Proceedings and Magistrates' Courts Act 1978 (1978 c. 22)
R (followed by a number)	= The recommendation set out in the paragraph of that number in the Appendix to the Report of the Scottish Law Commission (Cmnd. 7187).

Section of 1978 Act	Derivation
1	1975 s. 1.
2	1975 s. 2.
3	1975 s. 4.
4	1975 s. 5.
5	1975 s. 6.
6	1975 s. 3.
7	1975 s. 13.
8	1975 s. 7.
9(1), (2) (3) (4) (5)	1958 s. 32(1), (1A), subst. 1975 Sch. 3 para. 27(*a*). 1958 s. 32(3); rep. in part 1975. 1958 s. 32(2), am. 1975 Sch. 3 para. 27(*b*); 1978 Sch. 2 para. 17. 1958 s. 32(4); 1975 Sch. 3 para. 27(*c*).
10	1958 s. 33; am. 1975 Sch. 3 paras. 21, 28.
11	1958 s. 29; am. 1975 s. 28.
12(1), (2) (3) (4) (5) (6), (7) (8)	1975 s. 8(1), (2). 1975 s. 8(3); 1976 Sch. 3 para. 37; R. 1. 1975 s. 8(4); R. 1. 1975 s. 8(5). 1975 s. 8(7), (8). 1975 s. 8(6).

ADOPTION (SCOTLAND) ACT—*cont.*

Section of 1978 Act	Derivation
13	1975 s. 9.
14	1975 s. 10.
15	1975 s. 11.
16	1975 s. 12; 1976 Sch. 3 para. 38.
17	1975 s. 24.
18	1975 s. 14.
19	1975 s. 15.
20	1975 s. 16; 1976 Sch. 3 para. 39.
21	1975 s. 23; 1976 Sch. 3 para. 40.
22(1), (2), (3) (4)	1975 s. 18; 1976 s. 22. 1958 s. 36(3), subst. 1975 Sch. 3 para 30(*b*).
23	1975 s. 22(3); 1976 s. 23.
24	1975 s. 22(4), (5), (6).
25	1975 s. 19.
26	1975 s. 17(1), (2), (4).
27	1958 s. 34, subst. 1975 s. 29; 1976 Sch. 3 para. 29.
28	1958 s. 34A add. 1975 s. 29; 1958 s. 57(1); 1976 Sch. 3 para. 30; 1978 Sch. 2 para. 18.
29	1975 s. 30.
30	1958 s. 35, am. 1975 s. 31, Sch. 3 para. 29.
31(1) (2), (3)	1958 s. 36(1), am. 1975 Sch. 3 para. 30(*a*). 1958 s. 36(2), 1968 (c. 49) Sch. 8 para. 39.
32(1), (2) (3) (4)	1958 s. 37(1), am. 1975 Sch. 3 para. 31(*a*). 1958 s. 37(3); Mental Health Act 1959 (c. 72) Sch. 7 Part II; Mental Health (Scotland) Act 1960 (c. 61) Sch. 5; 1968 (c. 49) Sch. 9 Part I. 1958 s. 37(4), subs. 1975 Sch. 3 para. 31(*b*).
33(1) (2)	1958 s. 38. 1958 s. 39.
34	1958 s. 43.
35(1) (2)	1958 s. 40(4), (6), am. 1975 Sch. 3 para. 32. 1958 s. 40(5).
36(1)(*a*), (*b*) (1)(*c*) (2)	1958 s. 44(1)(*a*), (*b*). 1958 s. 44(1)(*d*). 1958 s. 44(2), am. 1975 Sch. 3 para. 33.
37(1) (2)	1958 s. 45. 1958 s. 46.

ADOPTION (SCOTLAND) ACT—*cont.*

Section of 1978 Act	Derivation
38	1975 Sch. 2 para. 7.
39(1), (2) (3) (4) (5)	1975 Sch. 2 para. 1(1), (2). 1975 Sch. 2 para. 1(5). 1975 Sch. 2 para. 1(6), (7). 1975 Sch. 2 para. 5(1).
40(1) (2) (3)	1958 s. 19. 1958 s. 19; 1964 s. 1(3). 1968 s. 9(5), am. 1975 Sch. 3 paras. 63, 64.
41(1), (2) (3)–(5)	1975 Sch. 2 para. 1(3), (4). 1975 Sch. 2 para. 4(1)–(3).
42	1975 Sch. 2 para. 2.
43	1975 Sch. 2 para. 3.
44	1975 Sch. 2 para. 5(1).
45(1), (2) (3) (4) (5) (6), (7) (8) (9)	1958 s. 22(1), (2). 1958 s. 22(3); R. 2. 1958 s. 22(4) (part). 1958 s. 22(4) (part); 1975 s. 27(*a*). 1958 ss. 20A(3), 22(4A), (4B); 1975 ss. 26(2), 27(*b*); 1976 s. 51(3). 1958 s. 22(6). —
46(1) (2)	1958 s. 26(1A); 1975 Sch. 2 para. 6(1). 1968 ss. 6(2), 11(1).
47(1) (2), (3), (4), (5)	1968 ss. 6(1), 11(1); 1978 s. 74(1). 1968 ss. 6(3), (4), (4A), (5), 11(1); 1976 Sch. 3 para. 35.
48	1968 ss. 7, 11(1).
49	1975 s. 25; 1976 Sch. 3 para. 41.
50	1958 s. 52, am.; 1975 Sch. 3 para. 36; 1976 Sch. 3 para. 32; 1958 s. 57(2)(*b*), (3).
51	1958 s. 50; 1975 s. 32, Sch. 3 para. 34; Criminal Law Act 1977 (c. 45) Sch. 12.
52	1958 s. 51; 1975 Sch. 3 para. 35.
53(1) (2) (3)	1968 s. 5(1). 1975 ss. 14(6), 16(3)(*c*). 1964 s. 1(5), subst. 1975 Sch. 3 para. 44.
54	1964 s. 2; Northern Ireland Constitution Act 1973 (c. 36) Sch. 5 para. 1(1).
55	1975 s. 102(1)(*a*), (2), (3)(*b*).
56(1), (2) (3), (4) (5)	1975 s. 100(1), (3). 1975 s. 100(4)(*b*), (5). 1975 s. 100(9).
57	1975 s. 21(4).
58	1975 s. 20.

ADOPTION (SCOTLAND) ACT—*cont.*

Section of 1978 Act	Derivation
59(1), (4)	1958 s. 11(2); 1975 Sch. 3 para. 23.
(2), (3)	1975 s. 22(1), (2).
60(1), (2)	1958 s. 56(1) subst. 1975 Sch. 3 para. 38; 1968 s. 12(2); 1975 s. 106(1).
(3)	1958 s. 34A(7), added 1975 s. 29; 1958 s. 50(9)(*b*), added 1975 s. 32.
(4)	1968 s. 12(3); 1975 s. 106(3).
(5)	1968 s. 12(4); 1975 s. 106(1).
(6)	1958 s. 56(2); subst. 1975 Sch. 3 para. 38.
(7)	1958 s. 56(4); subst. 1975 Sch. 3 para. 38.
61	1958 s. 54(1).
62	1958 s. 55; 1975 Sch. 3 para. 37
63	1968 s. 9(1)-(4); 1975 s. 24(9).
64(1)	1968 s. 11(1).
(2)	1968 s. 10(1); 1975 s. 24(9).
65(1)	1958 ss. 28(1), 57(1); am. 1975 Sch. 3 para. 39; 1968 s. 11(1); 1975 s. 107(1); 1976 Sch. 3 para. 43(*a*).
(2)	1968 s. 4(3).
(3)	1958 s. 57(2)(*a*).
(4)	1958 s. 57(4); 1968 s. 11(2).
(5)	—
66	—
67(1), (2), (4)	—
(3)	1975 s. 108(5).
Schedule 1	
para. 1(1)	1958 s. 23(1).
(2)	1968 s. 8(1).
(3)–(7)	1958 s. 23(2)–(6).
2(1)	1958 s. 24(5).
(2)	1964 s. 3(1).
(3)	1958 s. 24(5), (6); 1964 s. 3(2).
(4)	1964 s. 3(3); am. 1975 Sch. 3 para. 45.
3	1968 s. 8(2), am. 1975 Sch. 3 para. 61.
4(1)–(3)	1958 s. 24(1)–(3).
(4)	1968 s. 8(3).
5	1958 s. 27; 1964 s. 3(4); 1968 s. 8(4).
6	1958 s. 26(2), am. 1975 Sch. 3 para. 26; 1978 s. 74(3).
7	—
Schedule 2	
para. 1–3	1958 Sch. 5 paras. 9, 11.
4	1958 Sch. 5 para. 10.
5(1)	
(2), (3)	1958 Sch. 5 para. 6.
(4)	1958 Sch. 5 para. 7.
6	—
7	1958 Sch. 5 para. 5.
8	1975 s. 108(8)
Schedule 3	—
Schedule 4	—

ADOPTION (SCOTLAND) ACT 1978 (c. 28)

TABLE OF DESTINATIONS

Note: The abbreviations used in this Table are set out on page ii above

Section of Act	Subject Matter	Section of 1978 Act	Remarks
	ADOPTION ACT 1958 (7 & 8 Eliz. 2. c. 5)		
1–8	Adoption orders.	—	Rep. 1975.
9	—	—	Not applicable to Scotland.
10	—	—	Rep. 1975.
11(2)	Procedure.	59(1), (4)	Remainder rep 1975.
12–17	—	—	Rep. 1975.
18(1) (2)–(4)	Scottish intestacies, etc. —	— —	Rep. 1975. Rep. 1964 (c. 41)
19	Citizenship.	40	
20	—	—	Not applicable to Scotland.
20A(3)	Provision of counselling.	45(6)	Remaining subsections not applicable to Scotland.
21	—	—	Not applicable to Scotland.
22	Adopted Children Register.	45	Spent in part.
23(1) (2), (3) (4), (5), (6)	Registration of adoption orders. — —	Sch. 1 para. 1(1) para. 1(3)(4) para. 1(5)–(7)	
24(1)–(3) (4) (5) (6) (7)	Amendment of orders etc. — — — —	Sch. 1 para. 4(1)–(3) — para. 2(1), (3) para. 2(3) —	Not applicable to Scotland. Not applicable to Scotland.
25	—	—	Rep. 1975.

ADOPTION (SCOTLAND) ACT—*cont.*

Section of Act	Subject Matter	Section of 1978 Act	Remarks
	ADOPTION ACT 1958—*continued*		
26(1)	Legitimation: revocation of orders etc.	—	Not applicable to Scotland.
(1A)	—	46(1)	
(2)	—	Sch. 1 para. 6	
(3)	—	—	Not applicable to Scotland.
27	Legitimation: re-registration of births.	Sch. 1 para. 5	
28(1)	Local authorities.	65(1)	
(2)	—	—	Rep. 1975.
29(1)	Restrictions on adoptions etc.	11(1)	Subs. 1975 s. 28(*a*).
(2)	—	11(2)	Subs. 1975 s. 28(*b*).
(3), (4)	—	11(3), (4)	Am. 1975 s. 28(*c*), Sch. 3 para. 21.
(5)	—	11(5)	Subs. 1975 s. 28(*d*).
30, 31		—	Rep. 1975.
32(1), (1A)	Regulation of adoption agencies.	9(1), (2)	Subs. 1975 Sch. 3 para. 27(*a*).
(2)	—	9(4)	Am. 1975 Sch. 3 para. 27(*b*); 1978 Sch. 2 para. 16.
(3)	—	9(3)	Rep. in part 1975.
(4)	—	9(5)	Add. 1975 Sch. 3 para. 27(*c*).
33	Inspection of books etc.	10	Am. 1975 Sch. 3 para. 28.
34	Restriction on removal of child.	27	Subs. 1975 s. 29.
34A(1)–(3)	Further restrictions on removal of child.	28(1)–(3)	Add. 1975 s. 29; am. 1978 Sch. 2 para. 17.
(4)	—	28(5)	Add. 1975 s. 29.
(5), (6)	—	28(6), (7)	Add. 1975 s. 29.
(7)	—	28(10)	
(8)	—	28(4)	
35(1)–(5)	Return of children.	30(1)–(5)	Am. 1975 Sch. 3 para. 21.
(5A)	—	30(6)	Add. 1975 s. 31.
(6)	—	30(7)	Am. 1975 Sch. 3 para. 29.
36(1)	Return of children.	31(1)	Am. 1975 Sch. 3 paras. 21, 30(*a*).
(2)(*a*)	—	31(2), (3)	
(*b*)	—	—	Rep. 1965 (c. 55).
(3)	—	22(4)	Subs. 1975 Sch. 3 para. 30(*b*).
37(1)(*a*)	Protected children.	—	Rep. 1975.
(*b*)	—	32(1), (2)	Rep. in part 1975; am. 1975 Sch. 3 para. 31(*a*).
(2)	—	—	Rep. 1975.
(3)	—	32(3)	Rep. in part 1960 (c. 61). Sch. 5; 1968 (c. 49) Sch. 9, Part I.
(4)	—	—	Not applicable to Scotland.
(4A)	—	32(4)	Subs. 1975 Sch. 3 para. 31(*b*).
(5)	—	—	Rep. 1975.
38	Wellbeing of protected children.	33(1)	

ADOPTION (SCOTLAND) ACT—*cont.*

Section of Act	Subject Matter	Section of 1978 Act	Remarks
	ADOPTION ACT 1958—*continued*		
39	Visiting of protected children.	33(2)	
40(1)–(3)	Notices etc. to be given to local authorities.	—	Rep. 1975.
(4)	—	35(1)	
(5)	—	35(2)	
(6)	—	35(1)	Am. 1975 Sch. 3 para. 32.
41, 42	Further provisions relating to protected children.	—	Rep. 1975.
43	Removal of child from unsuitable surroundings.	34	Rep. in part 1975.
44(1)(*a*), (*b*), (*d*)	Offences relating to protected children.	36(1)	
(2)	—	36(2)	
(1)(*c*)	—	—	Spent.
45	Extension of power to issue warrant for child.	37(1)	
46	Life assurance.	37(2)	
47	—	—	Not applicable to Scotland.
48	—	—	Not applicable to Scotland.
49	—	—	Rep. 1975.
50(1)–(3)	Prohibition of certain payments.	51(1)–(3)	Am. 1975 Sch. 3 para. 34.
(3A)	—	51(4)	Add. Criminal Law Act 1977 (c. 45) Sch. 12.
(4)–(10)	—	51(5)–(11)	Add. 1975 s. 32.
51	Restrictions on advertisements.	52	Am. 1975 Sch. 3 para. 35.
52	Restriction on removal of child outside U.K. and Islands.	50	Am. 1975 Sch. 3 para. 36; rep. in part 1975.
53	Provisional adoption orders.	—	Rep. 1975.
54(1)	Offences.	61	
(2)	—	—	Not applicable to Scotland.
55	Service of notices.	62	Am. 1975 Sch. 3 para. 37.
56	Rules and regulations.	60(1), (6), (7)	Subs. 1975 Sch. 3 para. 38.
57(1), (1A)	Interpretation.	65(1)	Am. 1975 Sch. 3 paras. 39, 40; rep. in part 1975.
(2)(*a*)	—	65(3)	
(*b*)	—	50(3)	
(3)	—	50(1)	
(4)	—	65(4)	
58	Amendments and adaptation of enactments.	—	Rep. in part 1975.

ADOPTION (SCOTLAND) ACT—*cont.*

Section of Act	Subject Matter	Section of 1978 Act	Remarks
	ADOPTION ACT 1958—*continued*		
59	Transitional provisions and repeals.	—	
60	Short title, extent and commencement.	—	
Schs. 1 to 3	—	—	Rep. 1975.
Sch. 4	Consequential amendments of enactments.	—	
Sch. 5 para. 1–4	Transitional provisions. —	—	Rep. 1975.
5	—	Sch. 2 para. 7	
6, 7	—	Sch. 2 paras. 4, 5	
8	—	—	Spent.
9	—	Sch. 2 para. 1	
10	—	Sch. 2 para. 4	
11	—	Sch. 2 para. 1	
Sch. 6	Enactments repealed.	—	Spent.
	ADOPTION ACT 1960 (1960 c. 59)		
1(1)	Revocation of orders on legitimation.	—	Not applicable to Scotland.
(2)	—	—	Rep. 1975.
(3)	—	—	Not applicable to Scotland.
2	Short title and extent.	—	
	SUCCESSION (SCOTLAND) ACT 1964 (1964 c. 41)		
24(4)	Supplementary provision.	—	Spent.
	ADOPTION ACT 1964 (1964 c. 57)		
1(1), (2)	Extension of enactments referring to adoption.	—	Rep. 1975.
(3)	—	40(2),	
(4)	—	—	Rep. 1975.
(5)	—	53(3)	Subs. 1975 Sch. 3 para. 44.
2	Evidence of adoption.	54	
3(1)–(3)	Registration of adoptions outside Great Britain.	Sch. 1 para. 2(2)–(4)	Am. 1975 Sch. 3 para. 45.
(4)	—	para. 5	
4	Short title, etc.	—	

ADOPTION (SCOTLAND) ACT—*cont.*

Section of Act	Subject Matter	Section of 1978 Act	Remarks
	REGISTRATION OF BIRTHS, DEATHS AND MARRIAGES (SCOTLAND) ACT 1965 (1965 c. 49)		
Sch. 1 paras. 7 to 10	Consequential amendments.	—	See amended provisions.
	SOCIAL WORK (SCOTLAND) ACT 1968 (1968 c. 49)		
Sch. 8 paras. 37 to 41	Consequential amendments.	—	See amended provisions.
	ADOPTION ACT 1968 (1968 c. 53)		
1–3	Convention adoption orders.	—	Rep. 1975.
4(1), (2)	Extension of enactments to overseas adoptions.	—	Rep. 1975.
(3)	Interpretation.	65(2)	
5(1)	Recognition of overseas determinations.	53(1)	
(2)	Interpretation.	65(1)	
6(1)	Annulment etc. of overseas adoptions.	47(1)	
(2)	—	46(2)	
(3), (4), (4A), (5)	—	47(2), (3), (4), (5)	
7	Supplementary provisions.	48	
8(1)	Registration.	Sch. 1 para. 1(2)	
(2)	—	Sch. 1 para. 3	Am. 1975 Sch. 3 para. 61.
(3)	—	Sch. 1 para. 4(4)	
(4)	—	Sch. 1 para. 5	
(5)	—	Sch. 1	Am. 1975 Sch. 3 para. 62.
9(1)–(4)	Nationality.	63	
(5)	—	40(3)	Am. 1975 Sch. 3 para. 63; rep. in part 1975.
10(1)	Internal law.	64	
(2), (3)	—	—	Rep. 1975.
11(1)	Interpretation.	65(1)	Am. 1975 Sch. 3 para. 64 rep. in part 1975.
(2)	—	65(4)	
12(1)	Rules and orders.	59(1)	Rep. in part 1975.
(2)	—	60(1), (2)	
(3)	—	60(4)	
(4)	—	60(5)	
(5)	—	—	Unnecessary.
13	Powers of Parliament of Northern Ireland.	—	Rep. Northern Ireland Constitution Act 1973.
14	Short title, etc.	—	Spent.

ADOPTION (SCOTLAND) ACT—*cont.*

Section of Act	Subject Matter	Section of 1978 Act	Remarks
	CHILDREN AND YOUNG PERSONS ACT 1969 (1969 c. 54)		
Sch. 5 paras. 33 and 35	Amends 1958.	—	
	LOCAL GOVERNMENT (SCOTLAND) ACT 1973 (1973 c. 65)		
Sch. 27 para. 142	Amends 1958 s. 28(1).	—	
	CHILDREN ACT 1975 (1975 c. 72)		
1	The Adoption Service.	1	
2	Local authorities' social services.	2	
3	Duty to promote welfare of child.	6	
4	Approval of adoption societies.	3	
5	Withdrawal of approval.	4	
6	Procedure on refusal to approve or withdrawal of approval from societies.	5	
7	Inactive or defunct societies.	8	
8(1)–(5) (6) (7), (8) (9), (10)	Adoption orders. — — —	12(1)–(5) 12(8) 12(6), (7) —	Spent.
9	Child to live with adopters before order made.	13	
10	Adoption by married couple.	14	
11	Adoption by one person.	15	
12	Parental agreement.	16	
13	Religious upbringing.	7	
14	Freeing child for adoption.	18	
15	Progress reports to former parents.	19	
16	Revocation of s. 14 order.	20	
17(1), (2) (3) (4)	Care etc. of child on refusal of adoption order. — —	26(1), (2) — 26(3)	Not applicable to Scotland.
18	Need to notify local authority of adoption application.	22(1)–(3)	
19	Interim orders.	25	
20	Guardians ad litem and reporting officers.	58	

ADOPTION (SCOTLAND) ACT—*cont.*

Section of Act	Subject Matter	Section of 1978 Act	Remarks
	CHILDREN ACT 1975—*continued*		
21(1)–(3)	Hearings of applications in private.	—	Not applicable to Scotland
(4)	—	57	
22(1)	Making of orders.	59(2)	
(2)	—	59(3)	
(3)	—	23	
(4)–(6)	—	24	
23	Transfer of parental rights.	21	
24(1)–(8)	Convention adoption orders.	17	
(9)	—	63, 64	
25	Adoption of children abroad.	49	
26	Insertion of 1958 s. 20A(3).	45(6)	
27	Amendment of 1958 s. 22.	45(5)–(7)	
28	Amendment of 1958 s. 29.	11	
29	Substitution of ss. 34 and 34A for 1958 s. 34.	27, 28	
30	Return of children unlawfully taken away.	29	
31	Amendment of 1958 s. 35.	30(6)	
32	Amendment of 1958 s. 50.	51(5)–(11)	
100(4)	Courts.	56(3)	
(5)	—	56(4)	
(9)	—	56(5)	
102(1)(*a*)	Evidence of agreement and consent.	55	
107(1)	Interpretation.	65(1)	In part.
(2A)	—	—	Spent.
108(5)	Transitory provisions.	67(3)	
(6)	—	—	Spent.
Sch. 1	—	—	Not applicable to Scotland.
Sch. 2	Status conferred by adoption.		
para. 1(1), (2)	—	39(1), (2)	
(3), (4)	—	41(1), (2)	
(5)	—	39(3)	
(6), (7)	—	39(4)	
2	Pensions.	42	
3	Insurance.	43	
4(1)–(3)	Social Security.	41(3)–(5)	
5(1)	Succession and property.	44	
(2), (4)	—	Sch. 3 paras. 5, 6	
6(1)	Adoption and legitimation.	46(1)	
(3)	—	Sch. 3 para. 7	
7	Interpretation.	38	
Sch. 3	Consequential amendments.	—	See amended provisions.

ADOPTION (SCOTLAND) ACT—*cont.*

Section of Act	Subject Matter	Section of 1978 Act	Remarks
	ADOPTION ACT 1976 (1976 c. 36)		
22	Notification to local authority.	22	
23	Reports.	23	
51(3)	Provision of counselling.	45(6)	
73(2)	Amendments.	—	Spent.
74(3)	Extent, etc.	—	Words repealed spent.
Sch. 3 paras. 25 to 44	Consequential amendments.	—	See amended provisions
	CRIMINAL LAW ACT 1977 (1977 c. 45)		
Sch. 12	Amendment of 1958 s. 50.	51(4)	
	DOMESTIC PROCEEDINGS AND MAGISTRATES' COURTS ACT 1978 (1978 c. 22)		
74(1)	Amendment of 1975 s. 24.	47(1)	
(3)	Amendment of 1975 Sch. 3 para. 26.	Sch. 1 para 6	
90(2)	Short title and extent.	—	Words repealed spent.
Sch. 2	Amendment of enactments.	—	
para. 17	Amendment of 1958 s. 32 (2).	9(4)	
18	Amendment of 1958 s. 34A(3).	28(3)	

COMMONWEALTH DEVELOPMENT CORPORATION
ACT 1978 (c. 2)
TABLE OF DERIVATIONS

Note: The following abbreviations are used in this table:—

1959 = The Overseas Resources Development Act 1959 c. 23.
1963 = The Commonwealth Development Act 1963 c. 40.
1966 = The Overseas Aid Act 1966 c. 21.
1968 = The National Loans Act 1968 c. 13.
1969 = The Overseas Resources Development Act 1969 c. 36.
1977 = The International Finance, Trade and Aid Act 1977 c. 6.

M followed by a number indicates an amendment proposed in the Memorandum under the Consolidation of Enactments (Procedure) Act 1949.

By section 3(3) of and Part I of Schedule 1 to the Ministers of the Crown Act 1974 c. 21 (now section 7(2) of and Part I of Schedule 2 to the Ministers of the Crown Act 1975 c. 26), the functions conferred on the Secretary of State under 1959 and 1963 were transferred to the Minister of Overseas Development. The effect of this transfer of functions has not been acknowledged against each of the enactments affected.

Section of 1978 Act	Derivation
1	1959 s. 1, Sch. 1 para. 1; 1963 s. 1(1) and (2); 1969 s. 2(3).
2	1959 ss. 1(1) and 2(1); 1969 s. 2(1) and (2) .
3	1959 ss. 2(2) and (6)(*a*) and (*b*), 3.
4	1959 s. 2(3), (4), (5) and (6)(*c*) and (*d*); 1969 s. 2(1) and (4).
5	1959 ss. 10(1), 11 and 15(2)(*b*).
6	1959 s. 10(2)—(4).
7	1959 s. 9(1), (2)(*a*).
8	1959 ss. 8, 9(2)(*b*); 1969 s. 2(3).
9	1959 s. 12; 1977 s. 5(2) and (3).
10	1959 s. 13(1); 1968 s. 10(3); 1977 s. 5(4) and (5).
11	1959 ss. 13(2)—(4), 18(2).
12	1959 ss. 14(1) and (3), 19(1); 1968 s. 1(8).
13	1959 s. 14(2); 1966 s. 4.
14	1959 s. 15.
15	1959 s. 16.
16	1959 s. 17.
17	1959 s. 20(*a*); 1963 s. 1(1) and (2); 1969 s. 2(1); M1.
18	1959 ss. 4(2), 5(2); M2.
19	—
Sch. 1	1959 Sch. 1 paras. 2–9, s. 10(1); S.I. 1968/1656; M3.
Sch. 2	—

COMMONWEALTH DEVELOPMENT CORPORATION
ACT 1978 (c. 2)

TABLE OF DESTINATIONS

Note:—The abbreviations used in this Table are as set out on page xiv above, and in addition—

1960 = The Charities Act 1960 c. 58.
1972 = The Superannuation Act 1972 c. 11.
1974 = The Statute Law (Repeals) Act 1974 c. 22.
1976 = The Statute Law (Repeals) Act 1976 c. 16.

Section of Act	Subject Matter	Section of 1978 Act	Remarks
	OVERSEAS RESOURCES DEVELOPMENT ACT 1959 c. 23		
1	The Corporation and its purpose.	1, 2(1)	Amendment of s. 1(3) by 1963 s. 1(1) saved by 1969 s. 2(3).
2	Powers of Corporation.	2, 3(1) and (2), 4	Amended: 1969 s. 2(4).
3	Extension of powers of Corporation to additional enterprises.	3(3)–(5)	
4	Removal of doubts as to original purpose, and powers, of Corporation.	18(5)(*a*)	Spent in part.
5	Special provisions as to the Federation of Rhodesia and Nyasaland.	18(5)(*b*)	Repealed in part: 1963 s. 1(5).
6	Exercise of powers of Corporation where country or territory ceases to be within the Commonwealth.	—	Omitted under Consolidation of Enactments (Procedure) Act 1949.
7	Powers of Corporation as to Commonwealth countries which are not colonial territories.	—	Already repealed: 1969 s. 3(3)(*a*).
8	Local interests to be consulted.	8	Repealed in part: 1969 s. 3(3)(*a*); spent in part.
9	Interests of employees to be consulted.	7, 8(5)	
10	Powers of the Minister of Overseas Development.	5(1), 6 and Sch. 1 para. 10	
11	Disposal of capital assets.	5(2), (3)	
12	Borrowing powers.	9	Amended: 1977 s. 5(2), (3).
13	Advances, and guarantee of borrowings, by the government of the United Kingdom.	10(1) and (2), 11(1)–(3)	Amended: 1977 s. 5(4), (5).
14	Repayment of, and interest on, advances and sums issued to meet guarantees.	12(1)–(3) and (5), 13(3)	

COMMONWEALTH DEVELOPMENT CORPORATION
ACT—*cont.*

Section of Act	Subject Matter	Section of 1978 Act	Remarks
	OVERSEAS RESOURCES DEVELOPMENT ACT 1959—*continued*		
15	Reserve fund.	5(2) and (3), 14	
16	Balancing of revenue account, and surplus revenue.	15	
17	Accounts and audit.	16	
18	Issues out of the Consolidated Fund.	11(4)	Repealed in part: 1968 s. 24(2), Sch. 6 Part I.
19	Accounting for receipts of the Secretary of State.	12(4)	Repealed in part: 1968 s. 24(2), Sch. 6 Part I.
20	Interpretation.	17	
21	Repeal and savings.	—	Repealed in part: 1974 s. 1 and Sch. Part XI.
22	Short title.	—	Spent.
Sch. 1 para. 1	Corporation to be body corporate.	1	Repealed in part: 1960 s. 48(2), Sch. 7 Part II.
para. 2–9	Provisions relating to constitution etc. of Corporation.	Sch. 1 paras. 1–9, 11	References to the Treasury in para. 4 now references to Minister for the Civil Service: S.I. 1968/1656; para. 6 repealed in part: 1972 s. 29(4) and Sch. 8.
Sch. 2	Enactments repealed.	—	Already repealed: 1974 s. 1 and Sch. Part XI.
	COMMONWEALTH DEVELOPMENT ACT 1963 c. 40		
1(1), (3)–(5)	—	—	Already repealed: 1969 s. 3(3)(*b*).
(2)	Name of Corporation changed to " Commonwealth Development Corporation ".	1(1)	
2	—	—	Already repealed: 1965 c. 38 s. 3(3), Sch., and 1976 s. 1 and Sch. 1 Part XIII.
3(1), (2)	Short title and citation.	—	Spent.
(3)	—	—	Already repealed: 1976 s. 1 and Sch. 1 Part XIII.
	OVERSEAS AID ACT 1966 c. 21		
4	Power to remit payment of interest on certain advances to Corporation.	13(1) and (2)	

COMMONWEALTH DEVELOPMENT CORPORATION
ACT—*cont.*

Section of Act	Subject Matter	Section of 1978 Act	Remarks
	NATIONAL LOANS ACT 1968 c. 13		
10(3)	Sums required by Minister for advances under 1959 s. 13(1) to be paid out of money provided by Parliament.	10(3)	Repealed in part: 1976 s. 1 and Sch. 1 Part XIII.
	OVERSEAS RESOURCES DEVELOPMENT ACT 1969 c. 36		
1	Raising of limits on borrowings and advances.	—	Already repealed: 1977 s. 8(3) and Sch. 2.
2(1)	Extension of area of operation of Corporation.	2, 4	
(2)	Directions.	2(5)	Saving for directions under 1963 s. 1(3) repeated by clause 18(2) of 1978 Act.
(3)	Savings for 1959 ss. 1(3), 4, 6, 8 and 9(2)(*b*).	1(3), 8, 18(5)(*a*)	Saving for 1959 s. 6 spent.
(4)	Amendment of 1959 s. 2(4)(*a*).	4(3)(*a*)	
3	Citation, interpretation and repeals.	—	Repealed in part: 1977 s. 8(3) and Sch. 2; spent.
	MINISTERS OF THE CROWN ACT 1975 c. 26		
Sch. 2 Part I (part)	Functions under 1959 and 1969 transferred to Minister of Overseas Development.	—	Consequential repeal of references to 1959 and 1969.
	INTERNATIONAL FINANCE, TRADE AND AID ACT 1977 c. 6		
5	Raising of limits on borrowing by and advances to Corporation.	9(4)(*b*) and (6), 10(1) and (2)	S. 5(1) spent.
6	Power to free Corporation from obligations in respect of deferred liability account.	—	Spent.

EMPLOYMENT PROTECTION (CONSOLIDATION) ACT 1978 (c. 44)

TABLE OF DERIVATIONS

Notes

(1) The following abbreviations are used in this Table:—

1965 = The Redundancy Payments Act 1965
(1965 c. 62)

1972 = The Contracts of Employment Act 1972
(1972 c. 53)

1974 = The Trade Union and Labour Relations Act 1974
(1974 c. 52)
(The reference to " para." indicates a paragraph of Schedule 1 to the Act.)

1975 = The Employment Protection Act 1975
(1975 c. 71)

1977 = Redundancy Rebates Act 1977
(1977 c. 22)

1977 Order = Redundancy Payments (Variation of Rebates) Order 1977
(S.I. 1977/1321)

1977 Order (No. 2) = Employment Protection (Variation of Limits) Order 1977
(S.I. 1977/2031)

(2) This Table does not acknowledge the Secretary of State for Employment and Productivity Order 1968 (S.I. 1968/729) by virtue of which the functions of the Minister of Labour were transferred to the Secretary of State.

Section of 1978 Act	Derivation
1	1972 s. 4(1), (2)(2A); 1975 Sch. 16 Part II para. 4, 5, 6; Social Security Pensions Act 1975 (c. 60) s. 30(5).
	1972 s. 4(3) to (6).
3	1972 s. 4(7) to (10); 1975 Sch. 16 Part II para. 7, 8.
4	1972 s. 5; 1975 Sch. 16 Part II para. 9; House of Commons (Administration) Act 1978 (c. 36) Sch. 2 para. 4.
5	1972 s. 6.
6	1972 s. 7(1), (2).
7	1972 s. 10(1), (4); 1975 Sch. 16 Part II para. 11.
8	1975 s. 81.
9	1975 s. 82.
10	1975 s. 83.

EMPLOYMENT PROTECTION (CONSOLIDATION) ACT—*cont.*

Section of 1978 Act	Derivation
11	1972 s. 8; 1975 s. 84; Social Security Pensions Act 1975 (c. 60) s. 30(5).
12	1975 s. 22(1), (2).
13	1975 s. 23.
14	1975 s. 24(1), (2), (4).
15	1975 s. 25; 1977 Order (No. 2) Art. 2.
16	1975 s. 26.
17	1975 s. 27.
18	1975 s. 28.
19	1975 s. 29(1) to (3).
20	1975 s. 30(2), (3).
21	1975 s. 31(1), (3), (4).
22	1975 s. 32.
23	1975 s. 53.
24	1975 s. 54.
25	1975 s. 55(1), (2).
26	1975 s. 56.
27	1975 s. 57(1), (2), (4) to (8).
28	1975 s. 58(1) to (3), (5).
29	1975 s. 59.
30	1975 s. 60.
31	1975 s. 61(1) to (4), (7) to (13).
32	1975 s. 62(*a*)(*b*), 126(1).
33	1975 s. 35, s. 50(2).
34	1975 s. 36.
35	1975 s. 37(1) to (4).
36	1975 s. 38.
37	1975 s. 39.
38	1975 s. 41.
39	1975 s. 42.
40	1975 s. 43.
41	1975 s. 44.
42	1975 s. 45.

EMPLOYMENT PROTECTION (CONSOLIDATION) ACT—*cont.*

Section of 1978 Act	Derivation
43	1975 s. 46.
44	1975 s. 47.
45	1975 s. 48(1), (2), (4), (5).
46	1975 s. 48(6).
47	1975 s. 49.
48	1975 Sch. 3 para. 5.
49	1972 s. 1(1) to (4), (6); 1975 Sch. 16 Part II para. 1. 2, 3.
50	1972 s. 2(1) to (3); 1975 Sch. 16 Part II para. 1.
51	1972 s. 3.
52	1972 s. 11(2).
53	1975 s. 70(1) to (5).
54	1974 para. 4.
55	1974 para. 5(1) to (3), (5), (6); 1975 Sch. 16 Part III para. 8, 9, 10.
56	1975 s. 50(1).
57	1974 para. 6(1) to (3), (8), (9)(*a*)(*b*); 1974 s. 30(1).
58	1974 para. 6(4) to (6), (9); 1975 Sch. 16 Part III para. 11, 12; Trade Union and Labour Relations (Amendment) Act 1976 (c. 7) s. 1(*e*), s. 3(5), (6).
59	1974 para. 6(7).
60	1975 s. 34(1) to (5).
61	1975 ss. 33, 51.
62	1974 para. 7(1) to (3), (5); 1975 Sch. 16 Part III para. 13.
63	1974 para. 15.
64	1974 para. 10; 1975 s. 29(4); 1974 para. 11(1); 1975 Sch. 16 Part III para. 15.
65	1974 para. 13; 1975 s. 34(7).
66	1974 para. 14.
67	1974 paras. 17(1), 21(4), (4A), 7(4); 1975 Sch. 16 Part III paras. 13, 16, 20, 21.
68	1975 s. 71(1), s. 72(5).
69	1975 s. 71(2) to (7).
70	1975 s. 71(8), (9).
71	1975 s. 72(1) to (4), (6); Race Relations Act 1976 (c. 74) Sch. 3 para. 1(2).

EMPLOYMENT PROTECTION (CONSOLIDATION) ACT—*cont.*

Section of 1978 Act	Derivation
72	1975 s. 73.
73	1975 s. 74(1) to (3), (5) to (7); s. 75(7), (8).
74	1975 s. 76.
75	1974 para. 20; 1975 Sch. 16 Part III para. 17.
76	1975 s. 77; Race Relations Act 1976 (c. 74) Sch. 3 para. 1(3).
77	1975 s. 78.
78	1975 s. 79.
79	1975 s. 80(1) to (3).
80	1974 para. 27; 1975 Sch. 16 Part III para. 26, 27.
81	1965 s. 1, 48(3), 25(3), 8(1); 1975 Sch. 16 Part I para. 1, 5(1), 18.
82	1965 ss. 2, 48(1); 1975 Sch. 16 Part I para. 2, 18.
83	1965 s. 3(1), (2); 1975 Sch. 16 Part I para. 3.
84	1965 ss. 3(3) to (8), 48(1); 1975 Sch. 16 Part I para. 3, 18.
85	1965 s. 4.
86	1975 s. 50(1).
87	1965 s. 5(1), (2); 1975 Sch. 16 Part I para. 4.
88	1965 s. 6(1), (3) to (5).
89	1965 s. 7.
90	1965 s. 3(9), s. 4(2), s. 6(2) s. 3(10); 1975 Sch. 16 Part I para. 3.
91	1965 s. 9(1), (2)(*b*), (3).
92	1965 s. 10, s. 56(1).
93	1965 s. 22; 1975 Sch. 16 Part I para. 10.
94	1965 s. 13, 48(2); 1975 Sch. 16 Part I para. 7, 18.
95	1965 s. 13A; 1975 s. 120(2).
96	1965 s. 11.
97	1965 s. 12; 1975 Sch. 16 Part I para. 6.
98	1965 s. 14.
99	1965 s. 16(4), (5); Superannuation Act 1972 (c. 11) Sch. 6 para. 54.
100	1965 s. 19.
101	1965 s. 21; 1975 Sch. 16 Part I para. 9.
102	1965 s. 18.
103	1965 s. 26; Social Security Act 1973 (c. 38) Sch. 27 para. 55.

EMPLOYMENT PROTECTION (CONSOLIDATION) ACT—*cont.*

Section of 1978 Act	Derivation
104	1965 s. 30; 1975 Sch. 16 Part I para. 12; Criminal Procedure (Scotland) Act 1975 (c. 21) s. 289B(1); Criminal Law Act 1977 (c. 45) s. 28(2), Sch. 11 para. 5.
105	1965 s. 31; Social Security Act 1973 Sch. 27 para. 56; Social Security (Consequential Provisions) Act 1975 (c. 18) Sch. 2 para. 21; 1975 Sch. 16 Part I para. 13; Dock Work Regulation Act 1976 (c. 79) s. 14(4).
106	1965 s. 32; 1975 Sch. 16 Part I para. 14. 15.
107	1965 s. 33; Criminal Procedure (Scotland) Act 1975 (c. 21) s. 289B(1); Criminal Law Act 1977 (c. 45) s. 28(2), Sch. 11 para. 5.
108	1965 s. 34; 1975 Sch. 16 Part I para. 16.
109	1965 s. 35(1), (2), (4), (7); National Loans Act 1968 (c. 13) s. 5(1), Sch. 1; 1975 Sch. 16 Part I para. 17.
110	1965 s. 40; s. 56(1).
111	1965 s. 41; Superannuation Act 1972 (c. 11) Sch. 6 para. 55; Minister for the Civil Service Order 1968 (S.I. 1968/1656).
112	1965 s. 42.
113	1965 s. 43(1) to (5); Social Security Act 1973 (c. 38) Sch. 27 para. 58; Social Security (Consequential Provisions) Act 1975 (c. 18) Sch. 2 para. 22.
114	1965 s. 43(6).
115	1965 s. 49; Social Security Act 1973 Sch. 27 para. 59; Social Security (Consequential Provisions) Act 1975 Sch. 2 para. 23.
116	1965 s. 50.
117	1965 s. 51.
118	1965 s. 47.
119	1965 s. 53.
120	1965 s. 52.
121	1975 s. 63.
122	1975 s. 64; 1977 Order (No. 2) Art. 2.
123	1975 s. 65.
124	1975 s. 66.
125	1975 s. 67.
126	1975 s. 68.
127	1975 s. 69.
128	1974 para. 16; Industrial Training Act 1964 (c. 16) s. 12(1). 1965 s. 9(1), 34(2); 1972 s. 8(7), (8); 1975 s. 108(1).
129	1975 s. 108(1); 1974 para. 4(3).

EMPLOYMENT PROTECTION (CONSOLIDATION)
ACT—*cont.*

Section of 1978 Act	Derivation
130	1965 s. 44.
131	1975 s. 109(1) to (5), (7) to (9).
132	1975 s. 112(2), (3), (5) to (8); Supplementary Benefits Act 1976 (c. 71) Sch. 7 para. 40; Social Security (Miscellaneous Provisions) Act 1977 (c. 5) s. 16.
133	1975 s. 108(2) to (8).
134	1974 para. 26(2), (3), (4), (4A), (5); 1975 Sch. 16 Part III para. 24, 25.
135	1975 s. 87.
136	1975 s. 88; Race Relations Act 1976 (c. 74) Sch. 3 para. 1(4).
137	1975 s. 127(1)(c) to (*g*), (2) to (4).
138	1974 para. 33; 1975 s. 121, Sch. 16 Part III para. 33, 34.
139	1975 s. 122(1), (3) to (8); House of Commons (Administration) Act 1978 (c. 36) Sch. 2 para. 5.
140	1965 s. 25(4)(5); 1972 s. 2(4); 1974 para. 32; 1975 s. 118.
141	1972 s. 12(1); 1974 para. 9(2), (3); 1975 s. 119(5), (6); 1965 s. 17(1), (2).
142	1974 para. 12(*b*); 1965 s. 15(2) to (4).
143	1975 s. 22(3), s. 30(1), s. 119(7); 1972 s. 9(2A); 1975 Sch. 16 Part II para. 10(*a*).
144	1972 s. 9(2); 1975 s. 119(4); 1974 para. 9(1)(*d*); 1965 s. 16(2), 20; 1975 s. 119(12), (13).
145	Dock Work Regulation Act 1976 (c. 79) s. 14(1) to (3), (5), (6), (8), s. 15(1).
146(1)	1972 s. 9(3); 1975 s. 119(2), Sch. 16 Part II para. 10(*b*), Part III para. 14(*b*); 1974 para. 9(1)(*b*); 1965 s .16(3).
(2), (3)	1974 s. 30(1); 1975 s. 126(1).
(4) to (7)	1975 s. 119(8) to (11).
147	1972 s. 4(7), 9(4).
148	1975 s. 86.
149	1965 s. 16(6), (8); 1972 s. 9(5), (7); 1974 para. 11(2), (3); 1975 s. 119(15). (16); Dock Work Regulation Act 1976 (c. 79) s. 14(7).
150	1965 s. 23; 1975 s. 110.
151	1965 s. 8(2), s. 9(2)(*a*); 1972 s. 1(5); 1974 para. 30(1), (2); 1975 s. 126(5); Dock Work Regulation Act 1976 (c. 79) s. 14(3).
152	1972 Sch. 2 para. 1(1)(*b*); 1975 s. 62(*c*), 85, Sch. 5 para. 1(1)(*b*).

EMPLOYMENT PROTECTION (CONSOLIDATION)
ACT—*cont.*

Section of 1978 Act	Derivation
153	1965 s. 5(3), 25(1), (2), 36(5), (6), 48(4), 56, Sch. 1 para. 9, Sch. 4 para. 11, Sch. 6 para. 3; 1972 s. 11(1), 12(2), Sch. 1 para. 10(2); 1974 s. 30, Sch. 1 para. 6(9)(*c*); 1975 s. 24(5), 31(5), 48(2), (3), 52, 61(6), 126, Sch. 4 para. 8(*b*), Sch. 16 Part I para. 18, Part II para. 19, Part III para. 7(2), (3), (4); Trade Union and Labour Relations (Amendment) Act 1976 (c. 7) s. 3(3), (4).
154	1965 s. 11(4), s. 16(7), (8), s. 35(6), (7); Sch. 1 para. 5(5), (6), Sch. 4 para. 21A(3); Superannuation (Miscellaneous Provisions) Act 1967 (c. 28) s. 9(4); 1972 s. 7(2), (3), s. 9(6), (7), s. 10(3), (4); 1974 s. 26, Sch. 1 para. 20(4); 1975 s. 123, Sch. 16 Part I para. 21, 34, Part II para. 11; 1977 s. 1(3).
155	1975 s. 117.
156	1975 s. 124(3), (4); 1965 s. 55(5), (6); National Loans Act 1968 (c. 13) Sch. 1.
157	1975 s. 128; 1965 s. 58.
158	1965 s. 57.
159	—
160	—
Sch. 1	1975 Sch. 2.
Sch. 2	1975 Sch. 3 paras. 1 to 4, 6, 7.
Sch. 3	1972 Sch. 2, subst. 1975 Sch. 5.
Sch. 4	1965 Sch. 1 paras. 1 to 4, 6 to 9; 1975 Sch. 16 Part I paras. 19, 20, 22.
Sch. 5	1965 Sch. 3; National Health Service Reorganisation Act 1973 (c. 32) Sch. 4 para. 106; National Health Service (Scotland) Act 1972 (c. 58) Sch. 6 para. 130.
Sch. 6 para. 1, 2	1965 Sch. 5 paras, 2, 3; 1977 Order Art. 3.
3 to 7	1965 Sch. 5 paras. 4 to 8.
8	1965 Sch. 5 para. 9; 1977 Order Art. 3.
9, 10	1965 Sch. 5 paras. 10, 11.
11	1965 Sch. 5 para. 12; 1977 Order Art. 3.
12	1977 Order Art. 4.
13	1977 s. 1(1), (2), (4), Sch.
Sch. 7	1965 Sch. 6 paras. 1, 2.
Sch. 8	1965 Sch. 8.
Sch. 9 para. 1	1974 para. 21(1) to (3A), (5), (5A), (6); 1975 s. 109(6), Sch. 16 Part III para. 18, 19, 22, 23.
2	1975 s. 55(3), (4); 1974 para. 18.
3	1965 s. 46(6).
4	1974 para. 22.
5	1974 para. 23.
6	1974 para. 24.
7	1974 para. 25.
8	1975 s. 80(4).

EMPLOYMENT PROTECTION (CONSOLIDATION)
ACT—*cont.*

Section of 1978 Act	Derivation
9, 10	Industrial Training Act 1964 (c. 16) s. 12(2B), (3); 1965 s. 46(5); Employment and Training Act 1973 (c. 50) Sch. 2 Part I para. 15; Minister for the Civil Service Order 1971 (S.I. 1971/2099).
11	Superannuation (Miscellaneous Provisions) Act 1967 (c. 28) s. 9; Minister for the Civil Service Order 1968 (S.I. 1968/1656).
Sch. 10	1965 Sch. 7.
Sch. 11	1975 Sch. 6.
Sch. 12	1975 Sch. 12; 1965 Sch. 4, am. 1975 Sch. 16 Part I paras. 23 to 34.
para. 1	—
2	1975 Sch. 12 para. 2.
3	1975 Sch. 12 para. 3; 1965 Sch. 4 para. 21A(1), (2).
4	1975 Sch. 12 para. 4; 1965 Sch. 4 paras. 14, 21.
5	1975 Sch. 12 para. 5; 1965 Sch. 4 para. 22(1).
6	1975 Sch. 12 para. 6; 1965 Sch. 4 para. 15.
7 to 11	1975 Sch. 12 paras. 8 to 12.
12 to 21	1965 Sch. 4 paras. 1 to 5, 7 to 10, 13.
22 to 28	1965 Sch. 4 paras. 16 to 20, 22(2).
Sch. 13	1972 Sch. 1, am. 1975 Sch. 16 Part II paras. 12 to 19.
paras. 1 to 7	1972 Sch. 1 paras. 1 to 4C.
8	1972 s. 10(2).
9	1972 Sch. 1 para. 5(1), (2).
10	1972 Sch. 1 para. 5A.
11	1974 Sch. 1 para. 30(1A); 1975 s. 74(4); 1965 s. 8(3), (3A), (4), Sch. 1 para. 1(1)(*b*)(*c*); 1975 Sch. 16 Part I paras. 5, 19, 20, Part III para. 29.
12	1965 s. 24, s. 24A; 1975 s. 120(3).
13	1965 Sch. 1 para. 1(1)(*a*).
14	1965 s. 17(3) to (8), 20(1), (3); 1975 Sch. 16 Part I para. 8.
15	1972 Sch. 1 para. 6, 7.
16	1972 Sch. 1 para. 8.
17	1972 Sch. 1 para. 9.
18	1972 Sch. 1 para. 10.
19	1972 Sch. 1 para. 10A; 1975 s. 120(1).
20	1974 para. 30(3), (4); 1975 Sch. 16 Part III para. 30.
21	Contracts of Employment Act 1963 (c. 49) Sch. 1 para. 1(2); 1972 s. 13(5).
22	Contracts of Employment Act 1963 (c. 49) Sch. 1 para. 6; 1972 s. 13(5).
23	1972 s. 13(5).
24	1972 Sch. 1 para. 11.
Sch. 14	
para. 1 to 6	1975 Sch. 4 para. 1 to 6.
7(1)	1975 s. 24(3), (4), s. 31(2), s. 37(5), s. 61(5); 1972 Sch. 2 para. 1(2); 1975 s. 75(3), s. 75(1), s. 70(6), s. 72(7); 1965 s. 5(2A), Sch. 1 para. 5(1), (3); 1975 Sch. 5 para. 1(2), Sch. 16 Part I paras. 4, 21.
(2)	1975 s. 75(2); 1965 Sch. 1 para. 5(2); 1975 Sch. 16 Part I para. 21.
8	1975 s. 75(4) to (6), s. 72(8), s. 86; 1965 Sch. 1 para. 5(4), (5), (7); 1975 Sch. 16 Part I para. 21; 1977 Order (No. 2) Art. 2.
9	1975 Sch. 4 para. 7.
10	1975 Sch. 4 para. 8(*a*).
11, 12	1975 Sch. 4 para. 9, 10.

EMPLOYMENT PROTECTION (CONSOLIDATION)
ACT—*cont.*

Section of 1978 Act	Derivation
Sch. 15	
para. 1 to 3	—
4	1975 Sch. 17 para. 18; 1974 Sch. 4 para. 7; 1972 s. 13(6).
5	—
6	1977 Order (No. 2) Art. 3(1).
7	Employment Protection Act 1975 (Commencement No. 4) Order 1976 (S.I. 1976/530); Employment Protection Act 1975 (Commencement No. 5) Order 1976 (S.I. 1976/1379).
8	1972 s. 13(2).
9	1975 Sch. 17 para. 7.
10(1)	1974 para. 12(*a*).
(2)	1975 s. 34(6).
11	1975 Sch. 17 para. 16.
12	1965 s. 15(1).
13	—
14	National Health Service (Preservations of Boards of Governors) Order 1974 (S.I. 1974/281).
15(1)	1975 Sch. 17 para. 8.
(2)	1977 Order (No. 2) Art. 3(2).
16	1977 Order (No. 2) Art. 3(3), (4), (5).
17	1975 Sch. 17 para. 17.
18	—
Sch. 16	—
Sch. 17	—

EMPLOYMENT PROTECTION (CONSOLIDATION) ACT 1978 (c. 44)

TABLE OF DESTINATIONS

Note: The abbreviations used in this Table are on page xviii above.

Section of Act	Subject Matter	Section of 1978 Act	Remarks
	INDUSTRIAL TRAINING ACT 1964 (1964 c. 16)		
12(2B)	Industrial tribunals.	Sch. 9 para. 9	Added Employment and Training Act 1973 (c. 50) Sch. 2 Part I para. 15.
(3)	—	Sch. 9 para. 10	Am. 1965 s. 46(5); Minister for the Civil Service Order 1971 (S.I. 1971/2099).
(4)	—	154(2)	
	REDUNDANCY PAYMENTS ACT 1965 (1965 c. 62)		
1	Right to redundancy payment.	81(1)(2)	Am. 1975 Sch. 16 **Part I** para. 1.
2	Exclusions.	82(1)–(6)	Am. ibid. para. 2.
3(1)(2)	Dismissal by employer.	83	
(3)–(8)	—	84(1)–(6)	Sub. ibid. para. 3.
(9)(10)	—	90(1)(3)	
4(1)	Anticipation of expiry of notice.	85(1)	
(2)	—	85(2), 90(1)(*e*)	
(3)–(5)	—	85(3)–(5)	
5(1)(2)	Lay-off and short time.	87(1)(2)	Am. ibid. para. 4.
(2A)	—	Sch. 14 para. 7(1)(*j*)	Added ibid. para. 4.
(3)	—	153(1)	
6(1)	—	88(1)	
(2)	—	90(2)	
(3)–(5)	—	88(2)–(4)	
7	—	89	
8(1)	Continuous employment.	81(4)	Am. ibid. para. 5.
(2)	—	151(1)	
(3)(3A)	—	Sch. 13 para. 11(2)(3)	Am. ibid. para. 5.
(4)	—	Sch. 13 para. 1(2)	Am. ibid. para. 5.
9(1)	References to tribunals.	91(1)	
(2)(*a*)	—	151(2)	
(2)(*b*)(3)	—	91(2)(3)	
10	Misconduct etc.	92(1)–(4)	
11	Exemption orders.	96, 154(1)	

EMPLOYMENT PROTECTION (CONSOLIDATION) ACT—*cont.*

Section of Act	Subject Matter	Section of 1978 Act	Remarks
	REDUNDANCY PAYMENTS ACT 1965—*continued*		
12	Extension of terms or conditions.	97	Sub. ibid. para. 6.
13	Change of ownership.	94(1)–(5), (7)	Am. ibid. para. 7.
13A	Transfer to Crown employment	95	Sub. 1975 s. 120(2).
14	Pension rights.	98	
15(1)	Fixed term contracts	Sch. 15 para. 12	
(2)–(4)	—	142(2)–(4)	
(5)	—	144(3)	
16(1)	Exclusions.	—	Rep. Dockwork Regulation Act 1976 (c. 79) Sch. 6.
(2)	—	144(2)	
(3)	—	146(1)	
(4)(5)	—	99	Am. Superannuation Act 1972 (c. 11) Sch. 6 para. 54.
(6)(a)	—	149 (1)(a)(b), (2)	
(6)(b)	—	149(1) (c)(d)	
(7)	—	154(3)(4)	
(8)	—	154(1), 149(4)	
17(1)(2)	Employment abroad.	141(3)(4)	Sub. 1975 Sch. 16 **Part I** para. 8.
(3)–(6)	—	Sch. 13 para. 14 (1)–(4)	
(7)(8)	—	Sch. 13 para. 14(5)(6)	
18	Written particulars of payments.	102	
19	Domestic servants.	100	
20(1)	Mariners.	Sch. 13 para. 14(6)	
(2)	—	144(3)	
(3)	—	144(3), Sch. 13 para.14(6)	
21	Claims.	101	Am. ibid. para. 9.
22	Termination of contract.	93	Am. ibid. para. 10.
23	Death.	150	
24(1)	Previous redundancy payment.	Sch. 13 para. 12(2)(a)	
(2)	—	Sch. 13 para. 12(1)(a)	
(3)	—	Sch. 13 para. 12(3)	

EMPLOYMENT PROTECTION (CONSOLIDATION) ACT—*cont.*

Section of Act	Subject Matter	Section of 1978 Act	Remarks
	REDUNDANCY PAYMENTS ACT 1965—*continued*		
24A(1)	Equivalent payments.	Sch. 13 para. 12(2)(*b*)	⎫ Added 1975 s. 120(3).
(2)	—	Sch. 13 para. 12(1)(*a*)(*b*)	⎭
25(1)(2)	Interpretation.	153(1)	Am. 1975 Sch. 16 Part I para. 11.
(3)	—	81(3)	
(4)(5)	—	140(1)(2) (*f*) (*h*)	
26(1)	Redundancy Fund.	103(1)	Rep. in part Social Security Act 1973 (c. 38) Sch. 28.
(2)(3)	—	103(2)(3)	Am. ibid. Sch. 27 para. 55.
27, 28, 29	—	—	Rep. ibid. Sch. 28.
30(1)(2)	—	104(1)(2)	Am. 1975 Sch. 16 Part I para. 12(1).
(2A)	—	104(3)	Added ibid. para. 12(2).
(3)–(8)	—	104(4)–(10)	Am. Criminal Procedure (Scotland) Act 1975 (c. 21) s. 289B(1); Criminal Law Act 1977 (c. 45) s. 28(2), Sch. 11 para. 5.
31(1)	—	105(1)	Rep. in part Social Security Act 1973 (c. 38) Sch. 28.
(2)(3)	—	105(2)(3)	
(4)	—	105(4)	Am. ibid. Sch. 27 para. 56; Social Security (Consequential Provisions) Act 1975 (c. 18) Sch. 2 para. 21; 1975 Sch. 16 Part I para. 13.
32	—	106	Am. 1975 Sch. 16 Part I paras. 14, 15.
33	—	107	Am. Criminal Procedure (Scotland) Act 1975 (c. 21) s. 289B(1); Criminal Law Act 1977 (c. 45) s. 28(2), Sch. 11 para. 5.
34(1)(2)	—	108(1)(2) (3)	
(3)	—	108(3) 128(4) 151(2)	
(3A)	—	108(4)	Added ibid. para. 16.
(4)	—	108(5)	
35(1)(2)(4)	—	109(1)(2) (3)	Am. National Loans Fund Act 1968 (c. 13) s. 2, Sch. 1; 1975 Sch. 16 Part I para. 17.
(3)(5)	—	—	Rep. National Loan Funds Act 1968 Sch. 6 Part I.
(6)(7)	—	154(4), 154(1), 109(4)	

EMPLOYMENT PROTECTION (CONSOLIDATION) ACT—*cont.*

Section of Act	Subject Matter	Section of 1978 Act	Remarks
		REDUNDANCY PAYMENTS ACT 1965—*continued*	
36(1)–(4)	—	—	Rep. Social Security Act 1973 (c. 38) Sch. 28.
(5)(6)		153(1)	Am. ibid. Sch. 27 para. 57.
37, 38, 39	—	—	Rep. 1972 Sch. 3.
40	Miscellaneous.	110	
41(1)(2)	—	111(1)(2)	Am. Superannuation Act 1972 (c. 11) Sch. 6 para. 55.
(3)	—	111(3)	Am. Minister for the Civil Service Order 1968 (S.I. 1968/1656); Superannuation Act 1972 (c. 11) Sch. 6 para. 55.
(4)–(6)	—	111(4)–(6)	Am. Superannuation Act 1972 Sch. 6 para. 55; rep. in part Post Office Act 1969 (c. 48) Sch. 11 Part II.
42	—	112	
43(1)	—	113(1)	Am. Social Security Act 1973 (c. 38) Sch. 27 para. 58.
(1A)	—	113(2)	Added ibid.; am. Social Security (Consequential Provisions) Act 1975 (c. 18) Sch. 2 para. 22.
(2)–(5)	—	113(3)–(6)	
(6)		114	
44	—	130	
46(1)–(4)	—	Sch. 9 paras. 1, 7(1)	Rep. in part Industrial Relations Act 1971 (c. 72) Sch. 9.
(5)	—	Sch. 9 para. 10	
(6)	—	Sch. 9 para. 3	
(7)	—	—	Unnecessary.
47	—	118	
48(1)	—	82(7), 84(7),	Sub. 1975 Sch. 16 Part I para. 18.
(2)	—	94(6)	
(3)	—	81(2)	
(4)	—	153(4)	
49(1)	—	115(1)	Am. Social Security Act 1973 (c. 38) Sch. 27 para. 59; Social Security (Consequential Provisions) Act 1975 (c. 18) Sch. 2 para. 23.
(2)(3)	—	115(2)(3)	
50	—	116	
51	—	117	

EMPLOYMENT PROTECTION (CONSOLIDATION) ACT—*cont.*

Section of Act	Subject Matter	Section of 1978 Act	Remarks
	REDUNDANCY PAYMENTS ACT 1965—*continued*		
52	—	120	
53	—	119	
54(1)	—	154(1)(3)	
(2)	—	154(2)	
55(1)–(3)	—	—	Unnecessary.
(4)	—	—	Rep. Post Office Act 1969 (c. 48) Sch. 11.
(5)(6)	—	156(2)(3)	Rep. in part ibid. Sch. 11; Social Security Act 1975 (c. 38) Sch. 28.
56(1)	—	153(1)	
(2)	—	—	Unnecessary.
(3)	—	114	
(4)	—	153(5)	
(5)	—	153(7)	
57	—	158	
58(1)–(3)	—	157(1)–(3)	
(4)	—	—	Rep. Northern Ireland Constitution Act 1973 (c. 36) Sch. 6.
(5)	—	157(4)	
59(2)	Repeals.	—	
Schedule 1. para. 1	Calculation of redundancy payments. —	Sch. 4 para. 1, Sch. 13 paras. 13, 11(2)(3)	Am. 1975 Sch. 16 Part I paras. 19, 20.
2, 3, 4	—	Sch. 4 paras. 2, 3, 4	
5(1)	—	Sch. 14 para. 7(1) (*l*)	
(2)	—	Sch. 14 para. 7(2)	⎫ Sub. ibid. para. 21.
(3)	—	Sch. 14 para. 7(1) (*k*)	⎭
(4)	—	Sch. 14 para. 8(1)(*c*)	Sub. ibid. para. 21; am. 1977 Order (No. 2) Art. 2.
5(5)	—	Sch. 14 para. 8(2), 154(1)	⎫
(6)	—	154(3)(4)	Sub. ibid. para. 21.
(7)	—	Sch. 14 para. 8(4)	⎭
6, 7, 8	—	Sch. 4 paras. 5, 6, 7	
9	—	Sch. 4 para. 2	Am. ibid. para. 22.

EMPLOYMENT PROTECTION (CONSOLIDATION) ACT—*cont.*

Section of Act	Subject Matter	Section of 1978 Act	Remarks
	REDUNDANCY PAYMENTS ACT 1965—*continued*		
Schedule 2	—	—	Rep. 1975 Sch. 18.
Schedule 3 para. 1	National Health Service Employees. —	Sch. 5 para. 1	Sub. National Health Service Reorganisation Act 1973 (c. 32) Sch. 4 para. 106.
2	—	—	Rep. ibid. Sch. 5.
3	—	—	Rep. National Health Service (Scotland) 1972 (c. 58) Sch. 7 Part II.
4	—	para. 2	
5	—	—	Rep. ibid.
6	—	—	Rep. National Health Service Reorganisation Act 1973 (c. 32) Sch. 5; National Health Service (Scotland) Act 1972 (c. 58) Sch. 7 Part II.
7	—	para. 3	Am. National Health Service (Scotland) Act 1972 Sch. 6 para. 130; rep. in part National Health Service Reorganisation Act 1973 Sch. 5.
8	—	para. 4	
Schedule 4 para. 1, 2	Death of employer or employee. —	Sch. 12 paras. 12, 13	
3, 4	—	paras. 14, 15	Sub. 1975 Sch. 16 Part I para. 23.
5	—	para. 16	Am. ibid. para. 24.
6	—	—	Rep. ibid. para. 25.
7–10	—	paras. 17–20	Am. ibid. para. 26.
11	—	153(1)	
12	—	—	Rep. ibid. para. 27.
13	—	Sch. 12 para. 21	
14	—	Sch. 12 para. 4(1)	
15	—	Sch. 12 para. 6	
16	—	Sch. 12 para. 22	Am. ibid. para. 28.
17	—	Sch. 12 para. 23	Am. ibid. paras. 29–31.
17A	—	Sch. 12 para. 24	Added ibid. para. 32.
18	—	Sch. 12 para. 25	
19	—	Sch. 12 para. 26	
20	—	Sch. 12 para. 27	Am. ibid. para. 33.
21	—	Sch. 12 para. 4(1)	

EMPLOYMENT PROTECTION (CONSOLIDATION) ACT—*cont.*

Section of Act	Subject Matter	Section of 1978 Act	Remarks
REDUNDANCY PAYMENTS ACT 1965—*continued*			
para. 21A(1)(2)	—	Sch. 12 para. 3	⎫
(3)	—	154	⎬ Added ibid. para. 34.
22(1)	—	Sch. 12 para. 5	⎭
(2)	—	Sch. 12 para. 28	
Schedule 5	Calculation of rebates.		
para. 1	—	153, Sch. 13 para. 1(1)	Rep. in part 1975 Sch. 18.
2, 3	—	Sch. 6 para. 1, 2	Am. 1977 Order Art. 3.
4–6	—	Sch. 6 para. 3–5	
7	—	153, Sch. 6 para. 6	
8	—	Sch. 6 para. 7	
9	—	Sch. 6 para. 8	Am. ibid.
10, 11	—	Sch. 6 para. 9, 10	
12	—	Sch. 6 para. 11	Am. ibid.
13	—	—	Rep. 1975 Sch. 18.
Schedule 6	Calculation of certain payments.		
para. 1, 2	—	Sch. 7 para. 1, 2	
3	—	153	
Schedule 7	Statutory provisions relating to referees.	Sch. 10	Rep. in part Post Office Act 1969 (c. 48) Sch. 8 Part I.
Schedule 8	Employees not paid by employer.	Sch. 8	
Schedule 9	Repeals.	—	
IRON AND STEEL ACT 1967 **(1967 c. 17)**			
31(3)(c) to end of subsection	Amends Iron and Steel Act 1949 (c. 72).	Sch. 16 para. 3(1)	
31(4)(b)	—	Sch. 16 para. 3(2)	
31(6)	Money.	—	Unnecessary.
SUPERANNUATION (MISCELLANEOUS PROVISIONS) ACT 1967 **(1967 c. 28)**			
9	Pensions.	154, Sch. 9 para. 11	Am. Minister for the Civil Service Order 1968 (S.I. 1968/1656).

EMPLOYMENT PROTECTION (CONSOLIDATION) ACT—_cont._

Section of Act	Subject Matter	Section of 1978 Act	Remarks
	NATIONAL LOANS ACT 1968 (1968 c. 13)		
In Schedule 1, the paragraph relating to the 1965 Act	Amends 1965 s. 35.	109(1), (3)	
	REDUNDANCY REBATES ACT 1969 (1969 c. 8)		
1	Reduction of redundancy rebates.	Sch. 6 paras. 1, 2, 8, 11	Partly spent.
2	Short title.	—	
	POST OFFICE ACT 1969 (1969 c. 48)		
Schedule 9 para. 34	Continuity of employment.	Sch. 16 para. 8	
	EQUAL PAY ACT 1970 (1970 c. 41)		
2(7)	Industrial tribunals.	—	Unnecessary. Rep. in part Sex Discrimination Act 1975 (c. 65) Sch. 1 para. 2(5).
	CIVIL AVIATION ACT 1971 (1971 c. 75)		
Schedule 9 para. 2	Continuity of employment.	Sch. 16 para. 11	
	SUPERANNUATION ACT 1972 (1972 c. 11)		
Schedule 6 paras. 54 55	Amends 1965 s. 16, 41.	99, 111	
	CONTRACTS OF EMPLOYMENT ACT 1972 (1972 c. 53)		
1(1)–(4), (6).	Minimum period of notice.	49	Am. 1975 Sch. 16 Part II paras. 1–3.
(5)	—	151(1)	
2(1)–(3)	Rights of employees.	50	Am. ibid. para. 1.
(4)	—	140(1)	
3	Measure of damages.	51	
4(1)	Written particulars of terms of employment.	1(1), (2), (3)	Am. ibid. para. 4.

EMPLOYMENT PROTECTION (CONSOLIDATION) ACT—*cont.*

Section of Act	Subject Matter	Section of 1978 Act	Remarks
	CONTRACTS OF EMPLOYMENT ACT 1972—*continued*		
4(2)	—	1(4)	Am. Social Security Pensions Act 1975 (c. 60) s. 30(5); 1975 Sch. 16 Part II para. 5.
(2A)	—	1(5)	Added 1975 Sch. 16 Part II para. 6.
(3)–(6)	—	2	
(7)	—	3(1), 147	Am. 1975 Sch. 16 Part II para. 7.
(8)–(10)	—	3(2)–(4)	Am. ibid. para. 8.
5	Changes in terms of employment.	4	Am. ibid. para. 9.
6	Excluded contracts.	5	
7(1)	Further particulars.	6	
(2)	—	6, 154 (3), (4)	
(3)	—	154(1), (2)	
8(1)–(3)	References to tribunals.	11(1)–(3)	
(4)–(6)	—	11(5)–(7)	
(7)	—	128(4)	
(8)	—	11(9), 128(4)	
(9)	—	—	Unnecessary.
9(1)	Exclusions.	—	Rep. Dock Work Regulation Act 1976 (c. 79) Sch. 6.
(2)(*a*)	—	144(1)(*a*)	
(2)(*b*)	—	—	Spent.
(2)(*c*)	—	144(1)(*b*)	
(2A)	—	143(3)(*b*), (4)	Added 1975 Sch. 16 Part II para. 10(*a*).
(3)	—	146(1)	Am. ibid. para. 10(*b*).
(4)	—	147	
(5)	—	149(1)(*a*), (*c*), (2)	
(6)	—	154(3), (4)	
(7)	—	149(4), 154(1)	
10(1)	Power to vary hours.	7(1)	
(2)	—	Sch. 13 para. 8	Substituted ibid. para. 11.
(3)	—	154(3), (4)	
(4)	—	154(1), 7(2)	
11(1)	Interpretation.	153(1)	Rep. in part 1974 Sch. 3 para. 16.
(2)	—	52	
12(1)	Work abroad.	141(1)	
(2)	—	153(5)	
13(1)	Repeals.	—	
(2)	Transitionals.	Sch. 15 para. 8	
(3), (4)	—	Sch. 15 para. 1, 2	

EMPLOYMENT PROTECTION (CONSOLIDATION) ACT—*cont.*

Section of Act	Subject Matter	Section of 1978 Act	Remarks
	CONTRACTS OF EMPLOYMENT ACT 1972—*continued*		
13(5)	—	Sch. 13 para. 23	
(6)	—	Sch. 15 para. 4(*a*)	
(7)	—	159(1)	
14(1)	Short title.	—	
(2)	Extent.	160(3)	
Schedule 1	Computation of period of employment.	Sch. 13	
para. 1(1)	—	para. 1(1)	Sub. 1975 Sch. 16 Part II para. 12.
(2)	—	para. 1(2)	
2	—	para. 2	
3, 4	—	para. 3, 4	Am. ibid. para. 13.
4A, 4B, 4C	—	paras. 5 6, 7	Added ibid. para. 14.
5(1), (2)	—	para. 9(1), (2)	Am. ibid. para. 15, 16.
(3)	—	—	Unnecessary.
5A	—	para. 10	Added 1975 Sch. 16 Part II para. 17.
6, 7	—	para. 15	Am. ibid. para. 18.
8, 9	—	paras. 16, 17	
10(1)	—	para. 18	⎱ Sub. ibid. para. 19.
(2)	—	153(4)	⎰
10A	—	para. 19	Added ibid. section 120(1).
11	—	para. 24, clause 153(1)	
Schedule 2	Rights of employee in period of notice.	Sch. 3	Sub. 1975 s. 85(2), Sch. 5.
para. 1(1)(*a*)	—	para. 1	
(1)(*b*)	—	clause 152	
(2)	—	Sch. 14 para. 7(1)(*e*)	
2–7	—	Sch. 3 paras. 2–7	
Schedule 3	Repeals.	—	
	BRITISH LIBRARY ACT 1972 (1972 c. 54)		
In the Schedule, para. 13(2) so far as it refers to the 1963 Act	Interpretation.	—	Unnecessary.
	NATIONAL HEALTH SERVICE (SCOTLAND) ACT 1972 (1972 c. 58)		
Schedule 6 para. 130	Amends 1965 Sch. 3.	Sch. 5, para. 3	

EMPLOYMENT PROTECTION (CONSOLIDATION) ACT—*cont.*

Section of Act	Subject Matter	Section of 1978 Act	Remarks
	NATIONAL HEALTH SERVICE REORGANISATION ACT 1973 (1973 c. 32)		
Schedule 4 para. 106	Amends 1965 Sch. 3.	Sch. 5 para. 1	
	SOCIAL SECURITY ACT 1973 (1973 c. 38)		
Schedule 27 para. 54	Amends 1965 s. 17.	Sch. 13 para. 14	
55	Amends 1965 s. 26.	103(3)	
56	Amends 1965 s. 31.	105	
57	Amends 1965 s. 36.	153(1)	
58	Amends 1965 s. 43.	113	
59	Amends 1965 s. 49.	115	
	EMPLOYMENT AND TRAINING ACT 1973 (1973 c. 50)		
Schedule 2, in Part I, para. 15	Amends Industrial Training Act 1964 (c. 16).	Sch. 9 para. 9	
	TRADE UNION AND LABOUR RELATIONS ACT 1974 (1974 c. 52)		
1(2)(*b*)(*c*)	Re-enactment of Industrial Relations Act 1971.	—	Unnecessary.
Schedule 1 para. 4(1)	Re-enacted provisions of 1971 Act. Unfair dismissal.	54(1), 129	
(2)	—	54(2)	
5(1)(2)	Meaning of dismissal.	55(1)(2)	
(3)	—	55(3)	Am. 1975 Sch. 16 Part III para. 8.
(4)	—	—	Rep. ibid. para. 9.
(5)	—	55(4)	
(6)	—	55(5)	Added ibid. para. 10.
6(1)(2)(3)	Fair and unfair dismissal.	57(1)(2)(3)	
(4)	—	58(1)	
(4A)	—	58(2)	Added ibid. para. 11.
(5)	—	58(3)	Am. Trade Union and Labour Relations (Amendment) Act 1976 (c. 7) s. 3(5); rep. in part ibid. s. 1(*e*).
(5A)	—	58(4)	Added 1975 Sch. 16 Part III para. 12.
(6)	—	58(5)	
(7)	—	59	
(8)	—	57(3)	
(9)	—	57(4), 58(6), 153(2)	Am. Trade Union and Labour Relations (Amendment) Act 1976 (c. 7) s. 3(6).
7(1)(2)(3)	Industrial action.	62(1), (2), (3)	Subst. 1975 Sch. 16 Part III para. 13.
(4)	—	67(3)	
(5)	—	62(4)	
8	—	—	Rep. ibid. para. 13.

EMPLOYMENT PROTECTION (CONSOLIDATION) ACT—*cont.*

Provision of Act	Subject Matter	Section of 1978 Act	Remarks
	TRADE UNION AND LABOUR RELATIONS ACT 1974—*continued*		
para. 9(1)(*a*)	Exclusions.	—	Rep. ibid. para. 14(1).
(*b*)		146(1)	Am. ibid. para. 14(1).
(*c*)		—	Rep. Dock Work Regulation Act 1976 (c. 79) Sch. 6.
(*d*)		144(2)	
(*e*)(*f*)		—	Rep. 1975 Sch. 16 Part III para. 14(1).
(2)(3)		141(2), (5)	
(4)		—	Rep. ibid. para. 14(2).
(5)		—	Unnecessary.
10	Qualifying period.	64(1)	
11(1)		64(3)	Am. ibid. para. 15.
(2)(3)		149(1)(4)	
12(*a*)	Fixed term contracts.	Sch. 15 para. 10(1)	
(*b*)		142(1)	
13	Dismissal procedures agreements.	65	
14		66	
15	Pressure on employer.	63	
16	Industrial tribunals.	128(1)(2)	
17(1)	Complaint to tribunal.	67(1)	Rep. in part ibid. para. 16.
(2)(3)		—	Rep. 1975 Sch. 18.
18	National security.	Sch. 9 para. 2	Partly unnecessary.
20(1)(2)(3)	Limit on compensation	75	Subst. 1975 Sch. 16 Part III para. 17.
(4)		154	
21(1)	Regulations for tribunal procedure.	Sch. 9 para. 1(1)	
(2)(*a*)		Sch. 9 para. 1(2)(*a*)	
(*b*)–(*i*)		Sch. 9 para. 1(2)(*c*)–(*j*)	
(3)		Sch. 9 para. 1(3)	Am. 1975 Sch. 16 Part III para. 18.
(3A)		Sch. 9 para. 1(4)	Added ibid. para. 19.
(4)		67(2)	Am. ibid. para. 20.
(4A)		67(4)	Added ibid. para. 21.
(5)		Sch. 9 para. 1(5)	Am. ibid. para. 22.
(5A)		Sch. 9 para. 1(6)	Added ibid. para. 23.
(6)		Sch. 9 para. 1(7)	
22, 23, 24, 25		Sch. 9 paras. 4–7	
26	Conciliation officers.	134	Rep. in part 1975 Sch. 18; am. 1975 Sch. 16 Part III paras. 24, 25.
27	Teachers in aided schools.	80	Am. ibid. paras. 26, 27.
30(1)	Continuous employment.	151(1)	
(1A)		Sch. 13 para. 11(1)	Added ibid. para. 29.
(2)		151(2)	
(3)(4)		Sch. 13 para. 20	Am. ibid. para. 30.

EMPLOYMENT PROTECTION (CONSOLIDATION) ACT—*cont.*

Section of Act	Subject Matter	Section of 1978 Act	Remarks
	TRADE UNION AND LABOUR RELATIONS ACT 1974—*continued*		
32(1)(*b*)	Contracting out.	140(1)(*b*)	
(2)(*b*)-(*e*)	—	140(2)(*c*) (*d*)(*g*)(*h*)	
Schedule 3 para. 16.	—	—	Unnecessary.
Schedule 4	Transitionals.	—	
para. 1	—	—	
3	—	—	
6(4)	—	Sch. 15 para. 1	
	SOCIAL SECURITY (CONSEQUENTIAL PROVISIONS) ACT 1975 (1975 c. 18)		
Schedule 2			
para. 19	Amends 1965 s. 43.	113(2)	Rep. in part 1975 Sch. 18.
21, 22, 23	Amend 1965 ss. 31, 43, 49.	105, 113, 115	
	SOCIAL SECURITY PENSIONS ACT 1975 (1975 c. 60)		
30(5)	Amends 1972 s. 4.	2(1)(*d*), 11(4)	
	EMPLOYMENT PROTECTION ACT 1975 (1975 c. 71)		
22(1) (2)	Guarantee payments.	12	
(3)	—	143(1)	
23	—	13	
24(1)(2)	—	14(1)(2)	
(3)	—	Sch. 14 para. 7 (1)(*a*)	
(4)	—	14(3)	
(5)	—	153(1)	
25	—	15	Am. 1977 Order (No. 2) Art. 2.
26–28	—	16–18	
29(1)–(3)	Suspension on medical grounds.	19(1)–(3)	
(4)	—	64(2)	
30(1)	—	143(2)	
(2)(3)	—	20	
31(1)	—	21(1)	
(2)	—	Sch. 14 para. 7 (1)(*b*)	
(3)(4)	—	21(2)(3)	
(5)	—	153(1)	
32	—	22	
33	—	61(2)	

B

EMPLOYMENT PROTECTION (CONSOLIDATION) ACT—*cont.*

Section of Act	Subject Matter	Section of 1978 Act	Remarks
	EMPLOYMENT PROTECTION ACT 1975—*continued*		
34(1)–(5)	Dismissal on ground of pregnancy.	60	
(6)	—	Sch. 15 para. 10(2)	
(7)	—	65(4)	
35(1)	Rights of employee.	33(1)	
(2)–(5)	—	33(3)–(6)	
36	Maternity pay.	34	
37(1)–(4)	—	35	
(5)	—	Sch. 14 para. 7 (1)(*d*)	
38, 39	—	36, 37	
41–47	—	38–44	
48(1)	Right to return to work.	45(1)	
(2)(*a*)	—	153(1)	
(2)(*b*)	—	45(2)	
(3)	—	153(3)	
(4)(5)	—	45(3)(4)	
(6)	—	46	
49	—	47	
50(1)	—	56, 86	
(2)	—	33(2)	
51	—	61(1)	
52	—	153(1), 33(3)(*c*), 47(1)	
53	Trade union membership etc.	23	
54	—	24	
55(1)(2)	—	25(1)(2)	
(3)(4)	—	Sch. 9 para. 2	
56	—	26	
57(1)(2)	Time off work.	27(1)(2)	
(3)	—	Sch. 16 para. 23(2)(*b*)	
(4)–(8)	—	27(3)–(7)	
58(1)–(3)	—	28(1)–(3)	
(4)	—	Sch. 16 para. 23(2)(*c*)	
(5)	—	28(4)	

EMPLOYMENT PROTECTION (CONSOLIDATION) ACT—*cont.*

Section of Act	Subject Matter	Section of 1978 Act	Remarks
	EMPLOYMENT PROTECTION ACT 1975—*continued*		
59, 60	—	29, 30	
61(1)–(4)	—	31(1)–(4)	
(5)	—	Sch. 14 para. 7 (1)(*c*)	
(6)	—	153(1)	
(7)–(13)	—	31(5)–(11)	
62(*a*)(*b*)	—	32	
(*c*)	—	152	
63	Insolvency of employers.	121	
64	—	122	Am. 1977 Order (No. 2) Art. 2.
65–69	—	123–127	
70(1)–(5)	Written statements on dismissal.	53	
(6)	—	Sch. 14 para. 7(1) (*f*)(*g*)	
71(1)	Remedies for unfair dismissal.	68(1)	
(2)–(7)	—	69	
(8)(9)	—	70	
72(1)–(4)	—	71(1)–(4)	Am. Race Relations Act 1976 (c. 74) Sch. 3 para. 1(2).
72(5)	—	68(2)	
(6)	—	71(5)	
(7)	—	Sch. 14 para. 7(1) (*f*)(*g*)	
(8)	—	Sch. 14 para. 8 (1)(*a*)	Am. 1977 Order (No. 2) Art. 2.
73	Compensation.	72	
74(1)	Basic awards.	73(1)	
(2)(*a*)	—	73(2)	
(2)(*b*)	—	73(8)	
(3)	—	73(3)	
(4)	—	Sch. 13 para. 11(1)	
(5)–(7)	—	73(4)–(6)	
75(1)	—	Sch. 14 para. 7 (1)(*i*)	
(2)	—	Sch. 14 para. 7(2)	
(3)	—	Sch. 14 para. 7 (1)(*h*)	
(4)–(6)	—	Sch. 14 para. 8(1) (*b*), (2)(3)	Am. 1977 Order (No. 2) Art. 2.
(7)	—	73(7)	
(8)	—	73(9)	

EMPLOYMENT PROTECTION (CONSOLIDATION) ACT—*cont.*

Section of Act	Subject Matter	Section of 1978 Act	Remarks
	EMPLOYMENT PROTECTION ACT 1975—*continued*		
76	Compensatory awards.	74	
77	—	76	Sub. Race Relations Act 1976 (c. 74) Sch. 3 para. 1(3).
78, 79	Interim relief.	77, 78	
80(1)–(3)	—	79	
(4)		Sch. 9 para. 8	
81–83	Statements relating to pay.	8–10	
84(1)–(3)	—	11(1)(2)(4)	
(4)	—	11(9)	
(5)	—	11(8)	
85(1)	Normal working hours and a week's pay.	152	
(2)	—	—	Unnecessary.
86	Review of limits.	148	
87, 88	Employment Appeal Tribunal.	135, 136	Am. Race Relations Act 1976 (c. 74) Sch. 3 para. 1(4).
108(1)	References to tribunals.	129	
(2)–(8)	Conciliation officers.	133	
109(1)–(5)	Jurisdiction of tribunals.	131(1)–(5)	
(6)	—	Sch. 9 para. 1 (2)(*b*)	
(7)–(9)	—	131(6)–(8)	
112(1)	Regulations under Social Security Act 1975.	Sch. 16 para.19(2)	
112(2)(3)(5)–(8)	Recoupment of benefits.	132	Am. Supplementary Benefits Act 1976 (c. 71) Sch. 7 para. 40; Social Security (Miscellaneous Provisions) Act 1977 (c. 5) s. 16.
(4)	—	Sch. 16 para.19(1)	
118(2)(*b*	Contracting out of Act.	140(2) (*b*)(i)	
118(2)(*c*)	—	140(2)(*e*)	
119(2)	Exclusions.	146(1)	
(8)–(11)	—	146(4)–(7)	
120(1)	—	Sch. 13 para. 19	
(2)	—	95	
(3)	—	Sch. 13 para. 12	
121(8)	—	138(8)	

EMPLOYMENT PROTECTION (CONSOLIDATION) ACT—*cont.*

Section of Act	Subject Matter	Section of 1978 Act	Remarks
	[EMPLOYMENT PROTECTION ACT 1975—*continued*		
124(2)	—	—	Unnecessary.
(3)(4)	—	156(1)(2)	
126(3)	—	153	
(5)	—	151	
127(1)(*c*)(*d*)	—	137(1)(*a*)	
(3)(*g*)(i)–(iii)	—	137(3)(*g*)	
128(2)	—	157(2)	
129(2)	—	—	Unnecessary.
Schedule 2	Suspension on medical grounds.	Sch. 1	
Schedule 3	Maternity.	Sch. 2	
para. 1	—	para. 1, 3	
2	—	para. 2	
3	—	para. 4	
4	—	para. 6	
5	—	clause 48	
6	—	Sch. 2 para. 5	
7	—	para. 7	
Schedule 4	Normal working hours etc.	Sch. 14	
para. 1–6	—	paras. 1–6	
7–10	—	paras. 9–12	
Schedule 5	—	—	Replaces 1972 Sch. 2.
Schedule 6	Employment Appeal Tribunal.	Sch. 11	
Schedule 12	Death of employer or employee.	Sch. 12	
paras. 8–12	—	paras. 7–11	
Schedule 16 Parts I and II and paras. 8–30, 33 and 34 in Part III.	—	—	These paras. amend provisions repealed by the 1978 Act.
Schedule 17	Transitionals.	Sch. 15	
para. 7	—	para. 9	
8	—	para. 15	
9, 10	—	—	Unnecessary.
16	—	para. 11	
17	—	para. 17	
	SUPPLEMENTARY BENEFITS ACT 1976 (1976 c. 71)		
Schedule 7 para. 40	Amends 1975 s. 112.	132	
	RACE RELATIONS ACT 1976 (1976 c. 74)		
In Schedule 3 para. 1(2)–(4).	Am. 1975 ss. 72, 77, 88.	71, 76, 136	

EMPLOYMENT PROTECTION (CONSOLIDATION) ACT—*cont.*

Section of Act	Subject Matter	Section of 1978 Act	Remarks
	DOCK WORK REGULATION ACT 1976 (1976 c. 79)		
14(1)–(5)	Dock workers.	145	
Schedule 1 para. 17 (2).	Continuous employment.	—	Unnecessary.
	SOCIAL SECURITY (MISCELLANEOUS PROVISIONS) ACT 1977 (1977 c. 5)		
16	Amends 1975 s. 112.	132	
	REDUNDANCY REBATES ACT 1977 (1977 c. 22)		
1(1), (2), (4)	Variation of rebates.	Sch. 6 para. 13	
(3)	—	154(3), (4)	
2	—	—	Northern Irish provision.
3	—	—	Unnecessary.
Schedule	—	Sch. 6 para. 13	
	ADMINISTRATION OF JUSTICE ACT 1977 (1977 c. 38)		
6	Amends 1975 Sch. 6.	Sch. 11 paras. 8, 10, 26	
32(11)	—	—	Unnecessary.

EXPORT GUARANTEES AND OVERSEAS INVESTMENT ACT 1978 (c. 18)

TABLE OF DERIVATIONS

Note: The following abbreviations are used in this Table:

1972 = The Overseas Investment and Export
Guarantees Act 1972
(1972 c. 40)

1975 = The Export Guarantees Act 1975
(1975 c. 38)

1977 = The International Finance, Trade and
Aid Act 1977
(1977 c. 6)

Section of 1978 Act	Derivation
1–4	1975 ss. 1–4.
5(1), (2)	1975 s. 5(1), (2).
(3)	1975 s. 5(3); Export Guarantees (Extension of Period) (No. 2) Order 1978.
(4)	1975 s. 5(4).
6	1975 s. 6(1)–(4); 1977 s. 4, Sch. 1 para. 1.
7, 8	1975 ss. 6A, 6B; 1977 s. 4 Sch. 1 para. 1.
9	1975 s. 7; 1977 s. 4 Sch. 1 para. 2.
10	1975 s. 8.
11(1)–(3)	1972 s. 1(1)–(3).
(4), (5)	1972 s. 2(3), (4).
(6), (7)	1972 s. 1(5), (6).
12	1975 s. 9.
13	1972 s. 2(4); 1975 ss. 5(5), 6(5); 1977 s. 4 Sch. 1 para. 1.
14(1)	1972 ss. 2(1), 5(3); 1975 s. 10(1).
(2)	1972 s. 2(2); 1975 s. 10(2).
15(1)	1972 s. 5(2)(*a*), 1975 s. 11(1), (definition of " business "); 1975 s. 11(1), (definition of " export contracts "); 1975 ss. 6(6), 11(1); 1975 s. 6(6); 1977 s. 4 Sch. 1 para. 1 (definition of " foreign currency "); 1977 s. 4 Sch. 1 para. 1, (definition of " foreign currency liabilities "); 1975 s. 11(1), (definition of " guarantee "); 1975 s. 11(1); 1977 s. 4 Sch. 1 para. 4, (definition of " quarter "); 1975 ss. 6A(6), 11(1); 1977 s. 4 Sch. 1 para. 1, 4, (definition of " quarterly revaluation "); 1975 s. 4(4), (definition of " securities "); 1975 ss. 6(6), 11(1); 1977 s. 4 Sch. 1 paras. 1, 4, (definition of " sterling liabilities "); 1975 s. 11(1), (definition of " trade with other countries ").
(2)	1975 s. 6(7); 1977 s. 4 Sch. 1 para. 1.
(3)	1975 s. 6(6); 1977 s. 4 Sch. 1 para. 1.
(4)	1975 s. 8; 1972 s. 5(2)(*b*).
(5), (6)	1975 s. 11(2), (3).
(7)	1975 s. 11(5).
16	[Short title, repeals, revocation, commencement and extent.]
Sch.	[Enactments repealed.]

EXPORT GUARANTEES AND OVERSEAS INVESTMENT ACT 1978 (c. 18)

TABLE OF DESTINATIONS

The abbreviations used in this Table are set out on page xlv above.

The effect of the order revoked by Section 16(3) of the Act (the Export Guarantees (Extension of Period) (No. 2) Order 1978) is reproduced in Section 5(3).

Section of Act	Subject Matter	Section of 1978 Act	Remarks
	THE OVERSEAS INVESTMENT AND EXPORT GUARANTEES ACT 1972 (1972 c. 40)		
1(1)–(3)	Investment overseas: arrangements for meeting non-commercial risks.	11(1)–(3)	
(4)	—	12(1)	
(5), (6)	—	11(6), (7)	
2(1)	Arrangements for meeting non-commercial risks: financial provisions.	14(1)(a)	
(2)	—	14(2)(b)	
(3)	—	11(4)	
(4)	—	11(5), 13	
5(1)	Short title and supplemental provisions.	—	
(2)	—	15(1), (4)	
(3)	—	14(1)(b)	
	THE EXPORT GUARANTEES ACT 1975 (1975 c. 38)		
1	Export guarantees.	1	
2	Guarantees and other arrangements in national interest.	2	
3	Loans and interest grants.	3	
4(1)–(3)	Securities.	4(1)–(3)	
(4)	—	15(1)	
5(1)–(4)	Payments to exporters in respect of cost increases.	5(1)–(4)	
(5)	—	13	
6(1)–(4)	Limits on commitments.	6(1)–(4)	Section subst. 1977 s. 4, Sch. 1 para. 1.
(5)	—	13	
(6)	—	15(1), (3)	
(7)	—	15(2)	
6A	Application of limit on foreign currency transactions.	7	Section inserted by 1977 s. 4 Sch. 1 para. 1.
6B	Circumstances in which limit on commitments under section 6(2) may be exceeded.	8	Section inserted by 1977 s. 4 Sch. 1 para. 1.

EXPORT GUARANTEES AND OVERSEAS INVESTMENT
ACT—*cont.*

Section of Act	Subject Matter	Section of 1978 Act	Remarks
	THE EXPORT GUARANTEES ACT 1975—*continued*		
7	Returns.	9	Section subst. 1977 s. 4 Sch. 1 para. 2.
8	Controlled companies.	10	See also Section 15(4).
9	The Export Credits Guarantee Department and the Export Guarantees Advisory Council.	12	
10	Expenses and receipts.	14(1), (2)(*a*)	
11(1)	Interpretation.	15(1)	Am. 1977 s. 4 Sch. 1 para. 4.
(2), (3)	—	15(5), (6)	
(4)	—	—	Unnecessary.
(5)	—	15(7)	
12	[Short title, repeals and commencement.]	—	
	THE INTERNATIONAL FINANCE, TRADE AND AID ACT 1977 (1977 c. 6)		
4(1)	Amendments of Export Guarantees Act 1975.	6, 7, 8, 9, 12(1), 15(1)–(3)	
(2), (3)	—	—	Unnecessary.
Sch. 1	Amendments of Export Guarantees Act 1975.		
para. 1	—	6, 7, 8	
2	—	9	
3	—	12(1)	
4	—	15(1)	

INTERPRETATION ACT 1978 (c. 30)

TABLE OF DERIVATIONS

Note: The following abbreviations are used in this Table:—

1889 = The Interpretation Act 1889
(52 & 53 Vict. c. 63)

R (followed by a number) = The recommendation set out in the paragraph of that number in the Appendix to the Report of the Law Commission and the Scottish Law Commission (Cmnd. 7235).

Section of 1978 Act	Derivation
1	1889 s. 8.
2	1889 s. 10.
3	1889 s. 9.
4	Acts of Parliament (Commencement) Act 1793 (c. 13); 1889 s. 36(2); R.1.
5	—
6	1889 s. 1(1); R.2.
7	1889 s. 26.
8	1889 s. 34.
9	Statutes (Definition of Time) Act 1880 (c. 9) s. 1; Summer Time Act 1972 (c. 6) s. 1.
10	1889 s. 30.
11	1889 s. 31.
12(1)	1889 32(1).
(2)	1889 32(2).
13	1889 s. 37; R.3.
14	1889 s. 32(3); R.4.
15	1889 s. 11(1).
16(1)	1889 s. 38(2).
(2)	R.5.
17(1)	1889 s. 11(2).
(2)	1889 s. 38(1); R.6.
18	1889 s. 33.
19(1)	1889 s. 35(2); R.7.
(2)	Short Titles Act 1896 (c. 14) s. 3.
20(1)	1889 s. 35(3).
(2)	R.8.
21(1)	1889 s. 39.
(2)	1889 s. 30.

INTERPRETATION ACT—*cont.*

Section of 1978 Act	Derivation
22(1)(2) (3)	— Interpretation Measure 1925 (No. 1) s. 1; Synodical Government Measure 1969 (No. 2) s. 2(2).
23(1)(2) (3) (4)	R.9. See derivation of provisions referred to; R.6. R.9.
24(1) (2) (3) (4) (5)	— R.10. R.4. See derivation of provisions referred to. —
25(1)(2) (3)	— 1889 s. 40.
26	—
27	—
Sch. 1	" Associated state ": West Indies Act 1967 (c. 4) s. 1(3). " Bank of England ": 1889 s. 12(18). " Bank of Ireland ": 1889 s. 12(19). " British Islands ": 1889 s. 18(1); Irish Free State (Consequential Adaptation of Enactments) Order 1923 (No. 405) Art. 2, Sch. " British possession ": 1889 s. 18(2). " British subject " and " Commonwealth citizen ": British Nationality Act 1948 (c. 56) s. 1. " Building regulations ": Public Health Act 1936 (c. 49) s. 61; Health and Safety at Work etc. Act 1974 (c. 37) s. 61. " Central funds ": Costs in Criminal Cases Act 1973 (c. 14) s. 13(1). " Charity Commissioners ": 1889 s. 12(14); Charities Act 1960 (c. 58) s. 1. " Church Commissioners ": 1889 s. 12(15)(16); Church Commissioners Measure 1947 (No. 2). " Colonial legislature " and " legislature ": 1889 s. 18(7). " Colony ": 1889 s. 18(3); Statute of Westminster 1931 (c. 4) s. 11; Independence Acts from 1947 to date; West Indies Act 1967 (c. 4) s. 3(5). " Commencement ": 1889 s. 36(1). " Committed for trial ": 1889 s. 27; Magistrates' Courts Act 1952 (c. 55) s. 131, Sch. 5; Bail Act 1976 (c. 63) s. 12, Sch. 2; R.11. " The Communities ", " the Treaties " and " the Community Treaties ": European Communities Act 1972 (c. 68) s. 1(2). " Comptroller and Auditor General ": Revenue Act 1884 (c. 62) s. 14. " Consular officer ": 1889 s. 12(20); Consular Relations Act 1968 (c. 18) s. 1, Sch. 1. " The Corporation Tax Acts ": Income and Corporation Taxes Act 1970 (c. 10) s. 526(1)(a). " County court ": 1889 ss. 6, 29; County Courts Act 1959 (c. 22) s. 205(4); County Courts Act (Northern Ireland) 1959 (c. 25) s. 152(3). " Court of Appeal ": 1889 s. 13(3). " Court of summary jurisdiction ", " summary conviction " and " Summary Jurisdiction Acts ": Northern Ireland Act 1962 (c. 30) s. 27. " Crown Court ": 1889 s. 13(4); Courts Act 1971 (c. 23) ss. 1(2), 6(1); Northern Ireland (Judicature) Act 1978 (c. 23) ss. 1, 4(1). " Crown Estate Commissioners ": 1889 s. 12(12); Crown Estate Act 1961 (c. 55) s. 1. " England ": Local Government Act 1972 (c. 70) s. 269. " Financial year ": 1889 s. 22; National Loans Act 1968 (c. 13) s. 1(6).

INTERPRETATION ACT—*cont.*

Section of 1978 Act	Derivation
	" Governor-General ": 1889 s. 18(6).
	" High Court ": 1889 s. 13(3).
	" The Income Tax Acts ": Income and Corporation Taxes Act 1970 (c. 10) s. 526(1)(6).
	" Land ": 1889 s. 3; R.12.
	" Lands Clauses Acts ": 1889 s. 23; Interpretation Act (Northern Ireland) 1954 (c. 33) s. 46(1).
	" Local land charges register " and " appropriate local land charges register ": Local Land Charges Act 1975 (c. 76) s. 4.
	" London borough ": 1889 s. 15(4); London Government Act 1963 (c. 33) s. 1.
	" Lord Chancellor ": 1889 s. 12(1).
	" Magistrates' Court ": 1889 s. 13(11); Magistrates' Courts Act 1952 (c. 55) s. 124; Magistrates Courts Act (Northern Ireland) 1964 (c. 21) s. 1.
	" Month ": 1889 s. 3.
	" National Debt Commissioners ": 1889 s. 12(17).
	" Northern Ireland legislation ": R.10.
	" Oath " and " Affidavit ": 1889 s. 3; Administration of Justice Act 1977 (c. 38) s. 8, Sch. 5 Part III.
	" Ordnance Map ": 1889 s. 25.
	" Parliamentary Election ": 1889 s. 17(1).
	" Person ": 1889 s. 19.
	" Police area ", " police authority " and other expressions relating to the police: Police Act 1964 (c. 48) s. 62; Police (Scotland) Act 1967 (c. 77) ss. 50 and 51(4).
	" The Privy Council ": 1889 s. 12(5).
	" Registered medical practitioner ": Medical Act 1956 (c. 76) s. 52(3); Medical Act 1978 (c. 12) Sch. 6, para. 48(*b*).
	" Rules of Court ": 1889 s. 14.
	" Secretary of State ": 1889 s. 12(3).
	" Sheriff ": 1889 s. 28; Sheriff Courts (Scotland) Act 1971 (c. 58) s. 4(3).
	" Statutory declaration ": 1889 s. 21.
	" Supreme Court ": 1889 s. 13(1); Courts Act 1971 (c. 23) s. 1(1).
	" The Tax Acts ": Income and Corporation Taxes Act 1970 (c. 10) s. 526(2).
	" The Treasury ": 1889 s. 12(2).
	" United Kingdom ": Royal and Parliamentary Titles Act 1927 (c. 4) s. 2(2).
	" Wales ": Local Government Act 1972 (c. 70) s. 269.
	" Water authority " and " water authority area ": Water Act 1973 (c. 37) s. 2(3).
	" Writing ": 1889 s. 20.
	Construction of certain expressions relating to children: 1889 s. 19A: Children Act 1975 (c. 72) s. 89.
	Construction of certain expressions relating to offences: Criminal Law Act 1977 (c. 45) s. 64(1)(2).
Sch. 2 paras.	
1–3	See derivation of provisions referred to.
4(1)	See derivation of provisions referred to.
(2)	Irish Free State (Consequential Adaptation of Enactments) Order 1923 (No. 405) Art. 2, Sch.
(3)	1889 s. 18(3); Statute of Westminster 1931 (c. 4) s. 11; Independence Acts from 1947 to date; West Indies Act 1967 (c. 4) s. 3(5).
(4)	1889 s. 12(1); General Adaptation of Enactments (Northern Ireland) Order 1921 (No. 1804) Art. 5.
(5)	1889 s. 2(1).
(6)	National Health Service Reorganisation Act 1973 (c. 32) s. 55(2); Water Act 1973 (c. 37) s. 38(2).

INTERPRETATION ACT—*cont.*

Section of 1978 Act	Derivation
5	Wales and Berwick Act 1746 (c. 42) s. 3; 1889 ss. 3, 13(8); Criminal Procedure (Scotland) Act 1975 (c. 21) Sch. 9 para. 6.
6	See derivation of provisions referred to.
7	1889 s. 6.
Sch. 3	—

INTERPRETATION ACT 1978 (c. 30)

TABLE OF DESTINATIONS

Notes:

1. The effect of the enactments specified in column 1 in their application to enactments passed before the Act comes into force is preserved by Schedule 2. That Schedule is not referred to in column 3, except where the Act differentiates between past and future enactments.

2. The abbreviations used in this Table are set out on page xlviii above.

Section of Act	Subject Matter	Section of 1978 Act	Remarks
	WALES AND BERWICK ACT 1746 (20 Geo. 2. c. 42)		
3	England includes Wales and Berwick upon Tweed.	Sch. 1, Sch. 2 para. 5(a)	Act repealed except s. 3, 43 Geo. 3, c. 161 s. 84; s. 3 repealed (Wales) Welsh Language Act 1967 (c. 66) s. 4, superseded (Berwick) Local Government Act 1972 (c. 70) s. 1.
	ACTS OF PARLIAMENT (COMMENCEMENT) ACT 1793 (33 Geo. 3. c. 13)		
1	Endorsement of date of Royal Assent: commencement on endorsed date.	4(b)	See R.1.
	STATUTES (DEFINITION OF TIME) ACT 1880 (43 & 44 Vict. c. 9)		
1	Expressions relating to time of day construed as referring to Greenwich mean time.	9	Act repealed and revived British Standard Time Act 1968 (c. 45) ss. 4(2), 5(2), Schedules 1, 2. 1968 c. 45 repealed, revival saved Summer Time Act 1972 (c. 6) s. 6(3).
	REVENUE ACT 1884 (47 & 48 Vict. c. 62)		
14	Vouching of payments out of money granted for army and navy services; definition of Comptroller and Auditor-General.	Sch. 1	
	INTERPRETATION ACT 1889 (52 & 53 Vict. c. 63)		
1	Rules as to gender and number.	6	See R.2.
2	Application of penal Acts to bodies corporate.		
(1)	Person.	Sch. 1, Sch. 2 para. 4(5)	
(2)	Party aggrieved.	—	Obsolete. See Justices of the Peace Act 1949 (c. 101) s. 27(1), Common Informers Act 1951 (c. 93) s. 1(1).

INTERPRETATION ACT—*cont.*

Section of Act	Subject Matter	Section of 1978 Act	Remarks
3	" Month ", " land ", " oath " etc.	Sch. 1, Sch. 2 para. 5(*b*)	
4	" County " (county of a city or town).	—	Obsolete.
5	" Parish ".	—	Repealed Rating and Valuation Act 1925 (c. 90) s. 69(1), Sch. 8, London Government Act 1963 (c. 33) s. 93(1), Sch. 18.
6	" County court ".	Sch. 1	Reference to County Courts Act 1888 translated by 1889 s. 38(1). See also Sch.2 para. 7.
7	Scottish definitions: " sheriff clerk ", " shire ", " sheriffdom " and " county ".	—	Obsolete.
8	Sections to be substantive enactment.	1	
9	Acts to be Public Acts.	3	
10	Amendment and repeal in same session.	2	
11(1) (2)	Repeal of repeals: non-reviver. Repeal and substitution: simultaneous operation.	15 17(1)	
12 (1)	Official definitions— Lord Chancellor.	Sch. 1	Amended S.R. & O. 1921 No. 1802 art. 2, S. R. & O. 1921 No. 1804 art 5; see Sch. 2 para. 4(5).
(2)	Treasury.	Sch. 1	References to Lord High Treasurer omitted.
(3)	Secretary of State.	Sch. 1	
(4)	Admiralty.	—	Repealed S.I. 1964/488.
(5)	Privy Council.	Sch. 1	References to Ireland omitted.
(6)	Education Department.	—	Now Secretary of State. See S.I. 1964/490.
(7)	Scottish Education Department.	—	Now Secretary of State. See Reorganisation of Offices (Scotland) Act 1939 (c. 20) s. 1(1)).
(8)	Board of Trade.	—	Obsolete. See S.I. 1971/1537.
(9)	Lord Lieutenant (Ireland).	—	Now Secretary of State. See Northern Ireland Constitution Act 1973 (c. 36) s. 7.
(10)	Chief Secretary (Ireland).	—	Now head of appropriate Northern Ireland Department. See Northern Ireland Constitution Act 1973 (c. 36) s. 7.

INTERPRETATION ACT—*cont.*

Section of Act	Subject Matter	Section of 1978 Act	Remarks
12(11)	Postmaster General.	—	Abolished Post Office Act 1969 (c. 48) s. 1(1).
(12)	Commissioners of Woods.	Sch. 1	Now Crown Estate Commissioners. Crown Estate Act 1956 (c. 73) s. 1 repealed Crown Estate Act 1961 (c. 55) s. 1.
(13)	Commissioners of Works.	—	Now Secretary of State. See S.I. 1970/1681.
(14)	Charity Commissioners.	Sch. 1	Reconstituted Charities Act 1960 (c. 58) s. 1, Sch. 1.
(15)	Ecclesiastical Commissioners.	—	Dissolved C.A.M. 1947 No. 2 s. 2. Reference to Church Commissioners (ibid. s. 1) substituted in 1978 Act Sch. 1.
(16)	Queen Anne's Bounty.	—	See note on Ecclesiastical Commissioners above.
(17)	National Debt Commissioners.	Sch. 1	
(18)	Bank of England.	Sch. 1	Constitution amended Bank of England Act 1946 (c. 27) s. 3.
(19)	Bank of Ireland.	Sch. 1	
(20)	Consular officer.	Sch. 1	See now Consular Relations Act 1968 (c. 18) Sch. 1.
13	Judicial definitions—		
(1)	Supreme Court.	Sch. 1	Supreme Court (E.) redefined Courts Act 1971 (c. 23) s. 1.
(2)	Court of Appeal.	Sch. 1	
(3)	High Court.	Sch. 1	
(4)	Court of Assize.	—	Repealed (E.) Courts Act 1971 (c. 23) s. 56(4), Sch. 11 Pt. IV. Not repealed (N.I.) by 1978 Act but repealed prospectively Judicature (Northern Ireland) Act 1978 (c. 23) s. 122(2), Sch. 7.
(5)	Assizes.	—	See note on s. 13(4) above.
(6)	Summary Jurisdiction Act 1848.	—	Obsolete. Short title enacted Short Titles Act 1896 (c. 14); whole Act except s. 30 repealed Magistrates' Courts Act 1952 (c. 55) s. 132, Sch. 6.
(7)	Summary Jurisdiction (England) Acts.	—	See note on s. 13(6) above. Summary Jurisdiction Act 1879 repealed Courts Act 1971 (c. 23) Sch. 11 Pt. IV. Otherwise obsolete.
(8)	Summary Jurisdiction (Scotland) Acts.	Sch. 2 para. 5(c)	
(9)	Summary Jurisdiction (Ireland) Acts.	—	Repealed Northern Ireland Act 1962 (c. 30) s. 30, Sch. 4 Pt. IV.
(10)	Summary Jurisdiction Acts.	—	See notes on s. 13(7), (8) and (9) above. As to N.I. see now 1962 c. 30 s. 27.

INTERPRETATION ACT—*cont.*

Section of Act	Subject Matter	Section of 1978 Act	Remarks
13(11)	Court of Summary Jurisdiction.	—	Obsolete (E.). Definition of " magistrates' court " substituted in 1978 Act Sch. 1. Repealed (N.I.) 1962 c. 30 s. 30, Sch. 4 Pt. IV.
(12)	Petty sessional court (E.).	—	Words repealed Justices of the Peace Act 1968 (c. 69) s. 8(2), Sch. 5 Pt. II. Obsolete.
(13)	Petty sessional court-house (E.).	—	See note on s. 13(12) above.
(14)	Court of quarter session.	—	See note on s. 13(4) above.
14	Rules of Court.	Sch. 1	
15	Boroughs—		
(1)	Municipal borough (E.).	—	Obsolete.
(2)	Municipal borough (I.).	—	Obsolete.
(3)	Parliamentary borough.	—	Repealed Representation of the People Act 1948 (c. 65) s. 80(7), Sch. 13.
(4)	Borough (local government).	—	Boroughs outside London abolished Local Government Act 1972 (c. 70) s. 1. Definition of London borough substituted in 1978 Act Sch. 1.
16	Board of guardians and Poor law union.	—	Poor law abolished (E.) National Assistance Act 1948 (c. 29) s. 1 and (N.I.) National Assistance Act (N.I.) 1948 (c. 13) s. 1.
17	Expressions relating to elections—		
(1)	Parliamentary election.	Sch. 1	Words repealed Representation of the People Act 1948 (c. 65) s. 80(7), Sch. 13.
(2)	Parliamentary register of electors.	—	Repealed Representation of the People Act 1948 (c. 65) s. 80(7), Sch. 13.
(3)	Local government register of electors.	—	See note on s. 17(2) above.
18	Geographical and colonial—		
(1)	British Islands.	Sch. 1, Sch. 2 para. 4(2)	
(2)	British possessions.	Sch. 1	
(3)	Colony.	Sch. 1, Sch. 2 para. 4(3)	S. 18(3) restricted— 1931 c. 4 s. 11. 1947 c. 7 s. 4(2). 1957 c. 6 s. 4(1). 1960 c. 55 s. 3(1). 1961 c. 16 s. 3(1). 1961 c. 1 s. 3(1). 1962 c. 40 s. 3(1). 1962 c. 54 s. 3(1). 1962 c. 57 s. 3(1). 1963 c. 54 s. 4(1). 1964 c. 46 s. 4(1). 1964 c. 86 s. 4(1). 1964 c. 93 s. 4(1). 1966 c. 14 s. 5(1).

INTERPRETATION ACT—*cont.*

Section of Act	Subject Matter	Section of 1978 Act	Remarks
18(3)	Colony.	Sch. 1	1966 c. 37 s. 4(1). 1967 c. 4 s. 3(5). 1968 c. 8 s. 4(1). 1970 c. 50 s. 4(1). 1973 c. 27 s. 4(1).
(4)	British India.	—	Repealed S.R. & O. 1937 No. 230 Art. 2, Sch. Pt. I.
(5)	India.	—	See note on s. 18(4) above.
(6)	Governor.	Sch. 1	Amended (India) S.R. & O. 1937 No. 230.
(7)	Colonial legislature.	Sch. 1	
18A	Special definitions relating to India.	—	Inserted S.R. & O. 1937 No. 230. Obsolete.
19	Person.	Sch. 1	Saved Town and Country Planning Act 1971 (c. 78) s. 204(4); Town and Country Planning (Scotland) Act 1972 (c. 52) s. 193(4).
19A	Parental rights and duties (E.).	Sch. 1	Inserted Children Act 1975 (c. 72) s. 89.
20	Writing.	Sch. 1	
21	Statutory declaration.	Sch. 1	
22	Financial year.	Sch. 1	Amended National Loans Act 1968 (c. 13) s. 1(6).
23	Lands Clauses Acts.	Sch. 1	Saved Administration of Justice Act 1965 (c. 2) s. 17(2).
24	Irish Valuation Acts.	—	Obsolete. But see " Valuation Acts " in Interpretation Act (Northern Ireland) (c. 33) s. 46(1).
25	Ordnance map.	Sch. 1	
26	Service by post.	7	S. 26 applied with modifications— 1946 c. 35 s. 6(3). 1946 c. 49 s. 1. Sch. 1 Pt. I para. 19(3). 1947 c. 39 s. 12(3). 1947 c. 42 s. 1, Sch. 1 para. 19. 1947 c. 48 s. 107(3). 1958 c. 24 s. 12(3). 1958 c. 30 s. 23(3), S.I. 1958/956, 957. 1960 c. 66 s. 13(2). 1962 c. 58 s. 49(3). 1963 c. 38 s. 120(3). 1964 c. 26 s. 33(2). 1964 c. 89 s. 11(2). 1964 c. 40 s. 48(3).

INTERPRETATION ACT—*cont.*

Section of Act	Subject Matter	Section of 1978 Act	Remarks
26	Service by post.	7	1965 c. 19 s. 13. 1965 c. 46 s. 15(3). 1967 c. 1 s. 96(4). 1967 c. 10 s. 30(3). 1967 c. 72 s. 4(1). 1967 c. 79 s. 16(2). 1968 CAM No. 1 s. 83(5). 1969 c. 10 s. 30(3). 1969 c. 27 s. 35. 1969 c. 40 s. 14(1). 1969 c. 49 s. 24(2). 1970 c. 30 s. 12(3). 1971 c. 10 s. 25(2). 1971 c. 38 s. 29(3). 1971 c. 40 s. 38(3). 1972 c. 20 s. 109, 140(2), 161(6). 1972 GSM No. 2 s. 27(3). 1974 c. 23 s. 2(4). 1974 c. 37 s. 46(4), (5) 1974 c. 40 s. 95(3). 1974 c. 49 s. 67(4). 1974 c. 50 s. 5(6). 1975 c. 35 s. 17. S. 26 excluded— 1951 c. 23 s. 2(4). 1965 c. 66 ss. 12(5), 59. 1965 c. 67 ss. 12(5), 55.
27	Committed for trial (E.).	Sch. 1	Amended Magistrates' Court Act 1952 (c. 55) Sch. 5; Bail Act 1976 (c. 63) s. 12, Sch. 2. See R.11.
28	Scottish definitions, " Sheriff " etc.	Sch. 1	Amended Sheriff Courts (Scotland) Act 1971 (c. 58) s. 4(3). Definitions of " felony " and " misdemeanour " obsolete.
29	Irish county court.	Sch. 1	County Courts Act (Northern Ireland) 1959 (c. 25) s. 152(3).
30	References to Crown.	10, 21(2)	
31	Construction of statutory rules.	11	
32	Exercise of powers and duties.		
(1)	—	12(1)	
(2)	—	12(2)	
(3)	—	14	See R.4.
33	Offences under two or more laws.	18	S. 33 saved— 1960 c. 34 s. 19(5). 1961 c. 47 s. 3(6). 1963 c. 38 s. 135(8). 1965 c. 24 s. 22(4). 1968 c. 67 s. 133(2). 1973 c. 53 s. 20(4). 1974 c. 20 s. 13(2). 1975 c. 74 s. 48(3).
34	Measurement of distance.	8	

INTERPRETATION ACT—*cont.*

Section of Act	Subject Matter	Section of 1978 Act	Remarks
35	Citation of Arts.		
(1)	—	—	See R.7.
(2)	—	19(1)	
(3)	—	20(1)	
36	Commencement.	—	S. 36 modified 1959 c. 24 s. 32(3); excluded— 1959 c. 70 s. 56(4). 1960 c. 16 s. 270(1). 1964 c. 53 s. 36(3). 1971 c. 25 s. 14(2).
(1)	—	Sch. 1	
(2)		4(*a*), 23(1)	
37	Exercise of statutory powers between passing and commencement of enabling Act.	13	S. 37 saved— 1946 c. 36 s. 10(1). 1954 c. 57 s. 13(4). 1964 c. 53 s. 36(4). 1965 c. 67 s. 55, 57. 1968 c. 37 s. 4(2). 1969 c. 48 s. 132(2). 1971 c. 10 s. 39(3). 1971 c. 42 s. 4(4). 1971 c. 78 s. 294(5). 1972 c. 52 s. 280(5). 1972 G.S.M. No. 2 s. 32(2). See R.3.
38	Effect of repeal.	—	S. 38 applied by some 30 enactments listed on the Chronological Table (1977 edn. at page 570) saved by enactments too numerous to list there; excluded by the following— 1948 c. 63 s. 100(8), (12). 1949 c. 36 s. 9(2). 1953 c. 36 s. 63(7). 1957 c. 20 s. 14(2). 1973 c. 52 s. 16(3). and modified by— 1965 c. 52 s. 87(7). 1965 c. 53 s. 23(4).
(1)	—	17(2)	See R.6.
(2)	—	16(1)	See R.5.
39	Definition of "Act".	21(1)	Internal.
40	Saving for past Acts.	25(3)	
41	Repeals.	—	
42	Commencement of Act.	—	
43	Short title.	—	

INLAND REVENUE REGULATION ACT 1890
(53 & 54 Vict. c. 21)

38(1)	England includes Wales.	—	Impliedly repealed by Local Government Act 1972 (c. 70) s. 269.

INTERPRETATION ACT—*cont.*

Section of Act	Subject Matter	Section of 1978 Act	Remarks
	SHORT TITLES ACT 1896 (59 & 60 Vict. c. 14)		
3	Repeal of short title.	19(2)	
	IRISH FREE STATE (CONSEQUENTIAL ADAPTATION OF ENACTMENTS) ORDER 1923 (S.R. & O. 1923 No. 405)		
Sch.	British Islands.	Sch. 1, Sch. 2 para. 4(2)	
	INTERPRETATION MEASURE 1925 (15 & 16 Geo. 5. No. 1)		
1	Application of 1889 to Church Measures.	22(3)	Amended Synodical Government Measure 1969 (No. 2).
	ROYAL AND PARLIAMENTARY TITLES ACT 1927 (17 & 18 Geo. 5. c. 4)		
2(2)	United Kingdom.	Sch. 1, Sch. 2 para. 6	
	STATUTE OF WESTMINSTER 1931 (22 & 23 Geo. 5. c. 4)		
11	Colony.	Sch. 1, Sch. 2 para. 4(3)	
	CEYLON INDEPENDENCE ACT 1947 (11 & 12 Geo. 6. c. 7)		
4(2)	Colony.	Sch. 1, Sch. 2 para. 4(3)	
	BRITISH NATIONALITY ACT 1948 (11 & 12 Geo. 6. c. 56)		
1(2)	British subject/Commonwealth citizen.	Sch. 1, Sch. 2 para. 6, clause 24(4)	
	MAGISTRATES' COURTS ACT 1952 (15 & 16 Geo. 6 & 1 Eliz. 2. c. 55)		
Sch. 5	Amendment of 1889 s. 27 (Committed for trial).	Sch. 1	
	MEDICAL ACT 1956 (4 & 5 Eliz. 2. c. 76)		
52(3)	Meaning of "registered medical practitioner".	Sch. 1	Inserted by Medical Act 1978 (c. 12) Sch. 5, para. 48(*b*).
	GHANA INDEPENDENCE ACT 1957 (5 & 6 Eliz. 2. c. 6)		
4(1)	Colony.	Sch. 1, Sch. 2 para. 4(3)	

INTERPRETATION ACT—*cont.*

Section of Act	Subject Matter	Section of 1978 Act	Remarks
	NIGERIA INDEPENDENCE ACT 1960 (8 & 9 Eliz. 2. c. 55)		
3(1)	Colony.	Sch. 1, Sch. 2 para. 4(3)	
	SIERRA LEONE INDEPENDENCE ACT 1961 (9 & 10 Eliz. 2. c. 16)		
3(1)	Colony.	Sch. 1, Sch. 2 para. 4(3)	
	TANGANYIKA INDEPENDENCE ACT 1961 (10 & 11 Eliz. 2. c. 1)		
3(1)	Colony.	Sch. 1, Sch. 2 para. 4(3)	
	NORTHERN IRELAND ACT (10 & 11 Eliz. 2. c. 30)		
27	Court of Summary Jurisdiction, Summary Conviction, Summary Jurisdiction Acts.	Sch. 1	
	JAMAICA INDEPENDENCE ACT 1962 (10 & 11 Eliz. 2. c. 40)		
3(1)	Colony.	Sch. 1, Sch. 2 para. 4(3)	
	TRINIDAD AND TOBAGO INDEPENDENCE ACT 1962 (10 & 11 Eliz. 2. c. 54)		
3(1)	Colony.	Sch. 1, Sch. 2 para. 4(3)	
	UGANDA INDEPENDENCE ACT 1962 (10 & 11 Eliz. 2. c. 57)		
3(1)	Colony.	Sch. 1, Sch. 2 para. 4(3)	
	LONDON GOVERNMENT ACT 1963 (1963 c. 33)		
1(1)	Inner and outer London boroughs.	Sch. 1	1978 Act also defines "London borough".
(6)	Application of certain Acts to London boroughs.	—	Words repealed refer to 1889 s. 15, which is not re-enacted by 1978 Act.
	KENYA INDEPENDENCE ACT 1963 (1963 c. 54)		
4(1)	Colony.	Sch. 1, Sch. 2 para. 4(3)	

INTERPRETATION ACT—*cont.*

Section of Act	Subject Matter	Section of 1978 Act	Remarks
	MALAWI INDEPENDENCE ACT 1964 (1964 c. 46)		
4(1)	Colony.	Sch. 1, Sch. 2 para. 4(3)	
	POLICE ACT 1964 (1964 c. 48)		
62	Police area etc.	Sch. 1	
	MALTA INDEPENDENCE ACT 1964 (1964 c. 86)		
4(1)	Colony.	Sch. 1, Sch. 2 para. 4(3)	
	GAMBIA INDEPENDENCE ACT 1964 (1964 c. 93)		
4(1)	Colony.	Sch. 1, Sch. 2 para. 4(3)	
	GUYANA INDEPENDENCE ACT 1966 (1966 c. 14)		
5(1)	Colony.	Sch. 1, Sch. 2 para. 4(3)	
	BARBADOS INDEPENDENCE ACT 1966 (1966 c. 37)		
4(1)	Colony.	Sch. 1, Sch. 2 para. 4(3)	
	WEST INDIES ACT 1967 (1967 c. 4)		
3(5)	Colony.	Sch. 1, Sch. 2 para. 4(3)	
	POLICE (SCOTLAND) ACT 1967 (1967 c. 77)		
50	Police area etc.	Sch. 1, Sch. 2 para. 6	
51(4)	Constable.	Sch. 1, Sch. 2 para. 6	
	MAURITIUS INDEPENDENCE ACT 1968 (1968 c. 8)		
4(1)	Colony.	Sch. 1, Sch. 2 para. 4(3)	
	NATIONAL LOANS ACT 1968 (1968 c. 13)		
1(6)	Financial year.	Sch. 1	

INTERPRETATION ACT—*cont.*

Section of Act	Subject Matter	Section of 1978 Act	Remarks
	INCOME AND CORPORATION TAXES ACT 1970 (1970 c. 10)		
526(1)	Corporation Tax Acts, Income Tax Acts.	Sch. 1, clause 24(4)	
(2)	Tax Acts.	Sch. 1, clause 24(4)	
	FIJI INDEPENDENCE ACT 1970 (1970 c. 50)		
4(1)	Colony.	Sch. 1, Sch. 2 para. 4(3)	
	SHERIFF COURTS (SCOTLAND) ACT 1971 (1971 c. 58)		
4(3)	Sheriff and sheriff principal.	Sch. 1	
	EUROPEAN COMMUNITIES ACT 1972 (1972 c. 68)		
1(2)	The Communities, the Treaties etc.	Sch. 1, clause 24(4)	
	LOCAL GOVERNMENT ACT 1972 (1972 c. 70)		
269	England, Wales.	Sch. 1, Sch. 2 paras. 4(6), 5(a) and 6, clause 23(1)	Applied National Health Service Reorganisation Act 1973 (c. 32) s. 55(2); Water Act 1973 (c. 37) s. 38(2).
	COSTS IN CRIMINAL CASES ACT 1973 (1973 c. 14)		
13(1)	Central funds (payment of costs out of).	Sch. 1	
	BAHAMAS INDEPENDENCE ACT 1973 (1973 c. 27)		
4(1)	Colony.	Sch. 1, Sch. 2 para. 4(3)	
	NATIONAL HEALTH REORGANISATION ACT 1973 (1973 c. 32)		
55(2)	England, Wales.	Sch. 2 para. 4(6)	
	WATER ACT 1973 (1973 c. 37)		
2(3)	Water authority; Water authority area.	Sch. 1	
38(2)	England, Wales.	Sch. 2 para. 4(6)	

INTERPRETATION ACT—*cont.*

Section of Act	Subject Matter	Section of 1978 Act	Remarks
	CRIMINAL PROCEDURE (SCOTLAND) ACT 1975 (1975 c. 21)		
Sch. 9 para. 6	Amendments of other enactments.	Sch. 2 para. 5(*c*)	
	CHILDREN ACT 1975 (1975 c. 72)		
89	Expressions relating to children.	Sch. 1	
	LOCAL LAND CHARGES ACT 1975 (1975 c. 76)		
4	Appropriate local land charges register.	Sch, 1, Sch. 2 para. 6	
	CRIMINAL LAW ACT 1977 (1977 c. 45)		
64(1)	Construction of certain expressions relating to offences.	Sch. 1	Explained s. 64(2) of that Act.
	MEDICAL ACT 1978 (1978 c. 12)		
Sch. 6 para. 48(*b*)	Meaning of " registered medical practitioner ".	Sch. 1	
	SOLOMON ISLANDS ACT 1978 (1978 c. 15)		
7(1)	Colony.	Sch. 2 para. 4(3)	
	TUVALU ACT 1978 (1978 c. 20)		
4(1)	Colony.	Sch. 2 para. 4(3)	

NATIONAL HEALTH SERVICE (SCOTLAND)
ACT 1978 (c. 29)

TABLE OF DERIVATIONS

Note :—The following abbreviations are used in this Table:—

1947	=	National Health Service (Scotland) Act 1947 (c. 27)
1949	=	National Health Service (Amendment) Act 1949 (c. 93)
1951	=	National Health Service Act 1951 (c. 31)
1952	=	National Health Service Act 1952 (c. 25)
1953	=	Hospital Endowments (Scotland) Act 1953 (c. 41)
1961	=	National Health Service Act 1961 (c. 19)
1966	=	National Health Service Act 1966 (c. 8)
1968	=	Health Services and Public Health Act 1968 (c. 46)
1971	=	Hospital Endowments (Scotland) Act 1971 (c. 8)
1972	=	National Health Service (Scotland) Act 1972 (c. 58)
1973	=	National Health Service Reorganisation Act 1973 (c. 32)
1976A	=	National Health Service (Vocational Training) Act 1976 (c. 59)
1976B	=	Health Services Act 1976 (c. 83)

Section of 1978 Act	Derivation
1(1)	1947 s. 1(1); 1972 s. 1, Sch. 6 para. 1.
(2)	1947 s. 1(2); 1972 Sch. 6 Part I; 1976B s. 23(3).
2(1)	1972 s. 13(1).
(2)	1972 s. 13(2).
(3)	1972 s. 13(3).
(4)	1972 s. 13(4).
(5)	1972 s. 13(5).
(6)	1972 s. 13(6).
(7)	1972 s. 13(7).
(8)	1972 s. 13(9).
(9)	1972 s. 13(10).
(10)	1972 s. 13(1) and (11).
(11)	1972 s. 13(8).
3(1)	1947 s. 35(2); 1972 Sch. 6 para. 4.
(2)	1947 s. 35(5).
4(1)	1947 s. 39(2)(*d*).
(2)	1947 s. 39(2)(*e*); 1972 Sch. 6 para. 6.
5(1)	1972 s. 17(1).
(2)	1972 s. 17(1).
(3)	1972 s. 17(2).
(4)	1972 s. 17(3).
6	1972 s. 18.

NATIONAL HEALTH SERVICE (SCOTLAND)
ACT—*cont.*

Section of 1978 Act	Derivation
7(1)	1972 s. 14(1).
(2)	1972 s. 14(2).
(3)	1972 s. 14(4).
(4)	1972 s. 14(5).
(5)	1972 s. 14(3).
(6)	1972 s. 14(6).
(7)	1972 s. 14(7).
(8)	1972 s. 14(8).
(9)	1972 s. 14(9).
8	1972 s. 15.
9	1972 s. 16.
10(1)	1972 s. 19(1).
(2)	1972 s. 19(1).
(3)	1972 s. 19(2).
(4)	1972 s. 19(5).
(5)	1972 s. 19(6).
(6)	1972 s. 19(7).
(7)	1972 s. 19(8).
(8)	1972 ss. 13(9), 19(9).
(9)	1972 ss. 13(10), 19(9).
11(1)	1971 s. 1(1).
(2)	1971 s. 1(1).
(3)	1971 s. 1(2).
(4)	1971 s. 1(3).
(5)	1971 s. 1(4).
(6)	1971 s. 1(4), proviso; 1972 Sch. 6 para. 147.
(7)	1971 s. 1(5).
12(1)	1953 s. 1(1).
(2)	1953 s. 1(1).
(3)	1953 s. 1(2).
(4)	1953 s. 1(3).
(5)	1953 s. 1(4).
(6)	1953 s. 1(5).
(7)	1953 s. 1(6).
13	1972 s. 20.
14	1972 s. 21.
15(1), (2)	1972 s. 22.
(3)	1973 Sch. 4 para. 138.
16(1)	1972 s. 23(1).
(2)	1973 Sch. 4 para. 139.
(3)	1972 s. 23(2).
17	1972 s. 55.
18	1972 s. 3.
19(1)	1947 s. 34(1); 1972 Sch. 6 para. 3.
(2)	1947 s. 34(2); 1949 s. 14(1), Sch. Part II.
(3)	1947 s. 34(1), proviso; 1949 s. 10.
20(1)	1947 s. 35(2); 1972 Sch. 6 para. 4.
(2)	1947 s. 35(2).

Part III   C

NATIONAL HEALTH SERVICE (SCOTLAND)
ACT—*cont.*

Section of 1978 Act	Derivation
21(1)	1976A s. 1(1), (2).
(2)	1976A ss. 1(3), 4(1).
22(1)	1976A s. 2(1), (4).
(2)	1976A s. 2(2).
(3)	1976A s. 2(3).
23(1)	1947 s. 35(3).
(2)	1947 s. 35(3).
(3)	1947 s. 35(3); 1972 Sch. 6 para. 4.
(4)	1947 s. 35(4); 1972 Sch. 6 para. 4; 1976A s. 3(1).
(5)	1947 s. 35(6); 1976A s. 3(2).
(6)	1947 s. 35(7).
(7)	1947 s. 35(7).
(8)	1947 s. 35(9).
24	1949 s. 15; 1947 s. 35(8); 1972 Sch. 6 para. 4.
25(1)	1947 s. 39(1); 1972 Sch. 6 para. 6.
(2)	1947 s. 39(2); 1949 s. 14(3).
(3)	1949 s. 11.
26(1)	1947 s. 42(1); 1968 s. 19(1); 1972 Sch. 6 para. 9.
(2)	1947 s. 42(3); 1949 s. 14(4); 1968 s. 19(1).
(3)	1949 s. 21; 1968 s. 38.
27(1)	1947 s. 40(1); 1968 s. 23(1), (2); 1973 Sch. 4 para. 42(1).
(2)	1947 s. 40(2); 1949 s. 14(2); 1973 Sch. 4 para. 42(2).
28(1)	1947 s. 41(1); 1972 Sch. 6 para. 8.
(2)	1947 s. 41(2); 1968 (c. 67) s. 135(1) and Sch. 5 para. 12.
29(1)	1947 s. 43(1); 1968 s. 19(1); 1972 Sch. 6 para. 10.
(2)	1947 s. 43(2).
(3)	1947 s. 43(3); 1972 Sch. 6 para. 10.
(4)	1947 s. 43(4).
(5)	1947 s. 43(5); 1972 Sch. 6 para. 10.
(6)	1972 Sch. 6 para. 10.
30(1)	1947 s. 43(5).
(2)	1968 s. 26.
31	1947 s. 43(6); 1968 s. 25(2).
32	1947 s. 43(7); 1968 s. 26.
33	1947 s. 44; 1968 s. 19(4); 1972 Sch. 6 para. 11.
34	1947 s. 46.
35(1)	1947 s. 36(1).
(2)	1947 s. 36(1); 1972 Sch. 6 para. 5.
(3)	1949 s. 8; 1972 Sch. 6 para. 20.
36(1)	1972 s. 2(1).
(2)	1972 s. 2(2).
37	1972 s. 4(1).
38	1972 s. 5(1).
39	1972 s. 6.

NATIONAL HEALTH SERVICE (SCOTLAND)
ACT—*cont.*

Section of 1978 Act	Derivation
40	1972 s. 7.
41	1972 s. 8(1).
42	1972 s. 10.
43	1947 s. 18(1); 1972 s. 12(4).
44(1)	1947 s. 19; 1972 s. 12(5); 1976B s. 7(1), Sch. 3 para. 2.
(2)	1976B s. 7(2).
45	1947 s. 16(1); 1972 s. 12(2).
46(1)	1968 ss. 33(1), 43(3).
(2)	1968 ss. 33(2), 43(3).
(3)	1968 ss. 33(3), 43(3).
(4)	1968 ss. 33(5), 43(3).
(5)	1968 s. 33(7).
47(1)	1972 s. 9.
(2)	1947 s. 17(1); 1972 s. 12(3).
48	1972 s. 11.
49(1)	Emergency Laws (Re-enactments and Repeals) Act 1964 (c.60) s. 5(1); 1973 s. 57 and Sch. 4 para. 104.
(2)	1964 (c. 60) s. 5(2).
(3)	1964 (c. 60) ss. 5(3), 15.
50(1)	1968 ss. 31, 43(3); 1972 Sch. 6 para. 34; 1976B s. 7 and Sch. 3 para. 3.
(2)	1976B s. 7(2).
51(1)–(4)	1976B s. 8(1)–(4).
52(1)	1976B s. 8(5).
(2)	1976B s. 8(6).
(3)	1976B s. 8(7).
(4)	1976B s. 8(8), (10).
(5)	1976B s. 8(9), (10).
(6)	1976B s. 8(10).
53(1), (2)	1968 s. 32(1), 43(3); 1972 Sch. 6 para. 35.
(3)	1976B s. 7(2).
54	1976B s. 7(2).
55(1)	1947 s. 4; 1968 s. 4(1), (4); 1972 s. 12(1) and Sch. 7.
(2)	1968 s. 4(2).
56	1949 s. 28; 1972 Sch. 6 para. 22.
57(1)	1968 ss. 1(1), 43(3); 1972 Sch. 6 para. 30; 1976B s. 5(1).
(2)	1968 ss. 1(2), 43(3); 1972 Sch. 7.
(3)	1968 ss. 1(3), 43(3); 1972 Sch. 7.
(4)	1968 ss. 1(4), 43(3).
(5)	1968 ss. 1(5), 43(3).
(6)	1968 s. 1(6).
58(1)	1968 ss. 2(1), 43(3); 1972 Sch. 6 para. 31; 1976B s. 5(2).
(2)	1968 ss. 2(2), 43(3).
(3)	1968 s. 2(3).
59(1), (2)	1976B s. 2 (1), (2).

C 2

NATIONAL HEALTH SERVICE (SCOTLAND)
ACT—*cont.*

Section of 1978 Act	Derivation
60(1)	1976B s. 4(1).
(2)	1976B s. 4(2).
(3)	1976B s. 4(3).
(4)	1976B s. 4(7).
61(1)	1976B s. 4(4).
(2)	1976B s. 4(5).
(3)	1976B s. 4(6).
62	1976B s. 4(8).
63(1)	1976B s. 5(2), (3).
(2), (3)	1976B s. 5(4).
(4)	1976B s. 5(5).
(5)	1976B s. 5(6).
64(1)–(4)	1976B s. 9(1)–(4).
(5)	1976B s. 9(6).
(6)	1976B s. 9(7).
65	1976B s. 4(9).
66	1976B s. 10(1).
67(1)	1976B s. 10(2).
(2)	1976B s. 10(3).
68(1)	1976B s. 6(1).
(2)	1976B s. 6(1), (2).
69(1)	1947 s. 40(3); 1949 s. 16; 1952 s. 1(1), (3); 1972 Sch. 6 para. 25
(2)	1968 s. 30(1); 1972 Sch. 6 para. 33.
(3)	1947 s. 40(3); 1949 s. 16; 1952 ss. 1(1), 7(4).
70(1)	1951 s. 1(1); 1972 Sch. 6 para. 23.
(2)	1952 s. 4(1), (2).
(3)	1951 s. 1 and Sch.; 1961 ss. 1 to 3.
71(1)	1952 s. 2(1), (2), (4).
(2)	1947 s. 45(2).
72	1972 ss. 4(2), 5(2), 8(2).
73	1947 ss. 3(3)(*a*), 45(1)(*a*); 1968 ss. 19(1), 33(4), (8); 1972 s. 12(1) and Sch. 6 para. 2.
74	1947 ss. 3(3)(*b*), 45(1)(*b*); 1968 ss. 19(1), 33(4), (8), 39.
75	1951 s. 1(4); 1952 s. 7(6); 1961 s. 2(3); 1968 s. 19(1); 1972 Sch. 6 para. 26.
76	1947 s. 69; 1972 Sch. 6 para. 13.
77	1947 s. 56; 1972 Sch. 6 para. 12.
78	1972 s. 54.
79	1972 s. 58.
80(1)	1947 s. 6(4).
(2)	1947 s. 60.
81	1949 s. 23(1); 1972 Sch. 6 para. 21.

NATIONAL HEALTH SERVICE (SCOTLAND)
ACT—*cont.*

Section of 1978 Act	Derivation
82(1)	1972 s. 37(1), (3).
(2)	1972 s. 39(1), (3).
(3)	1972 ss. 37(3), 39(3).
(4)	1972 ss. 37(1), 39(1).
83	1972 s. 41.
84	1972 s. 40.
85(1)	1972 s. 60(3).
(2)	1972 s. 60(4).
(3)	1972 s. 60(5).
(4)	1972 s. 60(6).
(5)	1947 s. 3(4); 1972 Sch. 6 para. 2(*b*).
(6)	1947 s. 52(2); 1949 s. 30(2); 1951 s. 4(3); 1952 s. 7(3); 1972 s. 60(2); 1976B ss. 8(8), 21.
86	1972 s. 57.
87(1)	1968 ss. 29(1), (3), 43; 1972 Sch. 6 para. 32.
(2)	1968 ss. 29(1), 43.
(3)	1968 ss. 29(2), 43.
88(1)	1968 s. 37(1), 43; 1976A s. 3(3).
(2)	1968 s. 37(2), 43; 1976A s. 3(3).
(3)	1968 s. 37(3), 43.
(4)	1968 s. 37(4), 43.
89(1)	1949 s. 18(1), (5); Superannuation Act 1972 c. 11 s. 29 and Sch. 6 para. 27.
(2)	1949 s. 18(3).
(3)	1949 s. 18(4), (5); Superannuation Act 1972 c. 11 s. 29 and Sch. 6 para. 27; 1973 Sch. 4 para. 149.
90	1972 s. 42.
91(1)	1972 s. 43(1); Parliamentary and other Pensions and Salaries Act 1976 c. 48 s. 7 (2).
(2)	1972 s. 43(2); 1973 Sch. 4 para. 142.
(3)	1972 s. 43(3); Parliamentary and other Pensions and Salaries Act 1976 s. 7(3) and Schedule.
(4)	1972 s. 43(3A); Parliamentary and other Pensions and Salaries Act 1976 s. 7(3).
(5)	1973 s. 32(4).
(6)	1973 s. 32(5).
(7)	1973 s. 32(6).
(8)	1972 s. 43(5); 1973 s. 32(7).
92(1)	1972 s. 44(1).
(2)	1972 s. 44(4); 1973 Sch. 4 para. 143.
(3)	1972 s. 44(3).
(4)	1972 s. 44(4).
93(1)	1972 s. 45(1); 1976B Sch. 1 para. 30(1).
(2)	1972 s. 45(2); 1973 Sch. 4 para. 144.
(3)	1972 s. 45(3).
(4)	1972 s. 45(4).
(5)	1972 s. 45(5).
(6)	1972 s. 45(6).
94(1)	1972 s. 46(1).
(2)	1972 s. 46(2); 1973 Sch. 4 para. 145(1).
(3)	1972 s. 46(3).
(4)	1972 s. 46(4); 1973 Sch. 4 para. 145(2).
(5)	1972 s. 46(5).
95	1972 s. 47; 1973 s. 36 and Sch. 4 para. 146, Sch. 5

C 3

NATIONAL HEALTH SERVICE (SCOTLAND)
ACT—*cont.*

Section of 1978 Act	Derivation
96(1)	1972 s. 48(1); 1976B Sch. 1 para. 31(*a*)(i).
(2)	1976B Sch. 1 para. 31(*a*)(i).
(3)	1972 s. 48(2).
(4)	1972 s. 48(3); 1976B Sch. 1 para. 31(*a*)(ii).
(5)	1972 s. 48(4); 1976B Sch. 1 para. 31(*b*).
(6)	1976B Sch. 1 para. 32.
(7)	1972 s. 48(5); 1973 s. 37(5).
97	1972 ss. 45(1), 50.
98	1949 s. 17; 1976B Sch. 5.
99	1952 s. 6.
100	1968 s. 40; 1972 Sch. 6 para. 36.
101	1947 s. 70; 1976 Sch. 6 para. 14; Law Reform (Limitation of Actions) Act 1954 (c. 36) s. 6(4)(*d*) and Sch.
102	1972 s. 51.
103	1947 s. 77; 1972 Sch. 6 para. 16.
104	1972 s. 59.
105(1)	Statutory Instruments Act 1946 (c. 36) s 1(2) 1947 s. 73(1); 1952 ss. 4(3), 7(27); 1971 s. 11(1); 1972 s. 62(1).
(2)	Statutory Instruments Act 1946 (c. 36) s. 5(2); 1951 s. 1(1); 1952 s. 7(7); 1961 s. 1(6); Emergency Laws (Re-enactments and Repeals) Act 1964 (c. 60) s. 7(1); 1968 s. 42(1); 1971 s. 11(3); 1972 s. 62(2); 1976A s. 2(3)(*c*).
(3)	1971 s. 11(2).
(4)	1972 s. 62(2), (3).
(5)	1947 s. 73(3); 1951 s. 1(1); 1968 s. 42(2); 1972 s. 62(5); **1976A** s. 2.
(6)	1947 s. 73(4); 1952 s. 4(2); 1968 s. 42(3); 1972 s. 62(6).
(7)	1972 s. 62(4).
106	1947 s. 72; 1972 Sch. 6 para. 15.
107	1972 s. 62(7) to (9).
108(1)	1947 s. 80(1); 1949 s. 31(2); 1952 s. 8(1); 1968 ss. 20(1), 43(3); Local Government (Scotland) Act 1973 (c.65) Sch. 27 para. 1(2); 1972 s. 63(1); 1976A s. 4(1); 1976B ss. 1(1), (3), 23(1).
(2)	1947 s. 80(2); 1968 s. 43(3); 1972 s. 63(1).
(3)	1947 s. 80(4); 1972 s. 63(2).
(4)	[Internal reference].
109	[Transitional provisions and savings, consequential amendments and repeals].
110	[Citation, extent and commencement].
Schedule 1 para. 1	1972 Sch. 1 Part I para. 1.
2	1972 Sch. 1 Part I para. 2.
3	1972 Sch. 1 Part I para. 3; Local Government (Scotland) Act 1973 (c. 65) Part I Sch. 27 para. 1(2).
4	1972 Sch. 1 Part I para. 5.
5	1972 Sch. 1 Part I para. 7.
6	1972 Sch. 1 Part I para. 8.

NATIONAL HEALTH SERVICE (SCOTLAND) ACT—*cont.*

Section of 1978 Act	Derivation
para. 7	1972 Sch. 1 Part I para. 9.
8	1972 Sch. 1 Part I para. 10.
9	1972 Sch. 1 Part I para. 11.
10	1972 Sch. 1 Part I para. 12.
11	1972 Sch. 1 Part III para. 1.
12	1972 Sch. 1 Part III para. 2.
13	1972 Sch. 1 Part III para. 3.
14	1972 Sch. 1 Part III para. 4.
15	1972 Sch. 1 Part III para. 5.
16	1971 s. 5(1); 1972 Sch. 6 para. 149.
17	1971 s. 6(1); 1972 Sch. 6 para. 150.
18	1972 s. 56.
19	1972 s. 61(5).
Schedule 2	
para. 1	1947 Sch. 7 para. 1.
2	1947 Sch. 7 para. 2.
3	1947 Sch. 7 para. 3(*a*).
4	1947 Sch. 7 para. 4.
5	1947 Sch. 7 para. 5.
Schedule 3	1972 Sch. 2.
Schedule 4	1972 Sch. 1 Part II.
Schedule 5	1972 Sch. 3; s. 61(5).
Schedule 6	
paras. 1–3	1971 Sch.
4	1971 s. 3; 1972 Sch. 6 para. 148.
5	1971 s. 4.
6(1)	1971 s. 5(2); 1972 Sch. 6 para. 149.
(2)	1971 s. 6(2); 1972 Sch. 6 para. 150.
7(1)	1971 s. 7(1); 1972 Sch. 6 para. 151.
(2)	1971 s. 7(2); 1972 Sch. 6 para. 151.
(3)	1971 s. 7(3); 1972 s. 38(5), Sch. 6 para. 151.
(4)	1972 s. 38(3), (4).
(5)	1971 s. 7(4).
8	1971 s. 8(1).
9	1971 s. 8(2).
10(1)	1971 s. 9(1).
(2)	1971 s. 9(2).
Schedule 7	
para. 1	1953 Sch. para. 1.
2	1953 Sch. para. 2.
3	1953 s. 3(1).
4	1953 Sch. para. 3; 1971 s. 10.
5	1953 Sch. para. 4.
6	1953 Sch. para. 5.
7	1953 Sch. para. 6.
Schedule 8	
para. 1	1947 Sch. 8 para. 1.
2	1947 Sch. 8 para. 2.
3	1947 Sch. 8 para. 3; 1972 Sch. 6 para. 18.
4	1947 Sch. 8 para. 4; 1949 s. 20.
5	1947 Sch. 8 para. 4; 1949 s. 20.
6	1947 Sch. 8 para. 5; 1949 s. 20.
7	1947 Sch. 8 para. 6; 1968 Sch. 4.

NATIONAL HEALTH SERVICE (SCOTLAND)
ACT—*cont.*

Section of 1978 Act	Derivation
Schedule 9	
para. 1(1)	1947 s. 36(2).
(2)	1947 s. 36(9).
(3)	1947 s. 36(9).
(4)–(6)	1947 s. 36(10).
(7)	1947 s. 36(11).
(8)	1947 s. 36(12).
2(1)	1947 s. 36(3).
(2)	1947 s. 36(4).
(3)	1947 s. 36(5).
(4)	1947 s. 36(6).
(5)	1947 s. 36(6) proviso.
(6)	1947 s. 36(7).
(7)	1947 s. 36(8).
Schedule 10	
para. 1(1)	Emergency Laws (Re-enactments and Repeals) Act 1964 (c. 60) s. 7(3).
(2)	1964 (c. 60) s. 7(4).
(3)	1964 (c. 60) s. 7(5).
(4)	1964 (c. 60) s. 7(7).
2(1)–(3)	1964 (c. 60) s. 8(1)–(3).
(4), (5)	1964 (c. 60) s. 8(4).
3	1964 (c. 60) s. 9(1), (2).
4	1964 (c. 60) s. 10.
5	1964 (c. 60) s. 11.
6	1964 (c. 60) s. 12.
7(1), (2)	1964 (c. 60) s. 13(1).
(3)	1964 (c. 60) s. 13(2).
8(1)–(3)	1964 (c. 60) Sch. 1 para. 1(1)–(3).
9(1)–(4)	1964 (c. 60) Sch. 1 para. 2(1)–(5).
Schedule 11	
para. 1(1)	1952 s. 1(2); 1972 Sch. 6 para. 25.
(2)	1947 s. 40(3); 1949 s. 16.
2(1)	1951 s. 1 and Sch.; 1961 s. 3(1); 1972 Sch. 6 para. 29; 1973 Sch. 4 para. 59(1).
(2)	1951 s. 1(3); 1961 s. 2(1), (2); 1972 Sch. 6 para. 23.
(3)	1951 s. 1(2); 1973 Sch. 4 para. 58(2).
(4)	1961 ss. 1(3), 3(1), (2).
(5)	1961 s. 1(4); 1972 Sch. 6 para. 28.
(6)	1961 s. 1(5).
(7)	1961 s. 3(1); 1972 Sch. 6 para. 29.
(8)	1951 s. 1(6); 1961 s. 3(2).
3(1)	1952 s. 2(2), (5); 1961 s. 2(1).
(2)	1961 s. 2(1), (2).
(3)	1952 s. 2(2); 1961 s. 2(1).
(4)	1952 s. 2(4); 1961 ss. 1(3), 3(1).
(5)	1961 s. 1(3), (5).
4	1952 s 7(4); 1972 Sch. 6 para. 26.
5	1973 s. 50(1).
6	1952 s. 5(1).
Schedule 12	1947 Sch. 10; 1972 Sch. 6 para. 19.
Schedule 13	1947 Sch. 3; 1972 Sch. 6 para. 17.
Schedule 14	1972 Sch. 5.
Schedule 15	[Transitional and savings].
Schedule 16	[Consequential amendments].
Schedule 17	[Repeals].

NATIONAL HEALTH SERVICE (SCOTLAND) ACT 1978 (c. 29)

TABLE OF DESTINATIONS

Note: The abbreviations used in this Table are set out on page lxiv above.

Section of Act	Subject Matter	Section of 1978 Act	Remarks
	THE NATIONAL HEALTH SERVICE (SCOTLAND) ACT 1947 (10 & 11 Geo. 6. c. 27)		
1(1)	Duty of Secretary of State.	1(1)	Amended 1972 Sch. 6 Pt. I.
(2)		1(2)	Amended 1972 Sch. 6 Pt. I; 1976B s. 23(3).
2	Scottish Health Services Council and Standing Advisory Committees.	—	Repealed 1972 Sch. 7.
3(1), (2)	Provision of hospital and specialist services.	—	Repealed 1972 Sch. 7.
(3)		73, 74	Amended 1968 s. 33(4), (8), 39(1), (2); 1972 Sch. 6 para. 2; Repealed in part 1972 Sch. 7.
(4)		85(5)	Amended 1972 Sch. 6 para. 2.
4	Accommodation available on part payment.	55 Saved Sch. 15 para. 7.	Amended 1968 s. 4. Repealed in part 1972 Sch. 7.
5	Accommodation for private patients.	—	Repealed 1968 Sch. 4 (with saving 1968 s. 3).
6(1) to (3)	Transfer of hospital to Secretary of State.	—	Repealed 1972 Sch. 7.
(4)		80(1)	
(5) to (8)			Repealed 1972 Sch. 7.
7	Endowments of voluntary Hospitals.	—	Repealed 1972 Sch. 7.
8	Hospital Endowments Commission.	—	Repealed 1971 s. 13(1)(b).
9	Supplementary provisions relating to transfer of hospital property and liabilities.	—	Repealed 1972 Sch. 7.
10	Power to acquire hospital equipment.	—	Repealed 1972 Sch. 7.
11	Regional Hospital Boards etc.	—	Repealed 1972 Sch. 7.
12	Functions of Regional Hospital Boards etc.	—	Repealed 1972 Sch. 7.
13	Legal status of Regional Hospital Boards etc.	—	Repealed 1972 Sch 7.
14	Conditions of Service and appointment of officers.	—	Repealed 1972 Sch. 7.

NATIONAL HEALTH SERVICE (SCOTLAND) ACT—*cont.*

Section of Act	Subject Matter	Section of 1978 Act	Remarks
15	Health Centres.	—	Repealed 1972 Sch. 7.
16(1)	Ambulances.	45	Repealed in part Mental Health (Scotland) Act 1960 (c. 61). Sch. 5; Amended 1972 s. 12(2).
(2)		—	Repealed 1972 Sch. 7.
17(1)	Research.	47(2)	Repealed in part Mental Health (Scotland) Act 1960 (c. 61). Sch. 5; Amended 1972 s. 12(3).
(2)		—	Repealed 1972 Sch. 7.
18(1)	Bacteriological service.	43	Repealed in part 1972 s. 12(4), Sch. 7.
(2)		—	Repealed 1972 Sch. 7.
19	Blood transfusion and other services.	44(1)	Repealed in part 1972 Sch. 7; amended 1972 s. 12(5); 1976B s. 7(1) and Sch. 3.
20	Local health authorities.	—	Repealed 1972 Sch. 7.
21	Proposals for provision of services by local health authorities.	—	Repealed 1972 Sch. 7.
22	Care of mothers and young children.	—	Repealed 1972 Sch. 7.
23	Midwifery.	—	Repealed 1968 s. 78(2) Sch. 4.
24	Health visiting.	—	Repealed 1972 Sch. 7.
25	Home nursing.	—	Repealed 1972 Sch. 7.
26	Vaccination and immunisation.	—	Repealed 1972 Sch. 7.
27(1)	Prevention of illness, care and after-care.	Saving Sch. 15 para. 15	Repealed in part 1972 Sch. 7.
(2)		Saving Sch. 15 para. 15	Repealed in part 1972 Sch. 7.
(3)		—	Repealed 1968 Sch. 4.
(4)		Saving Sch. 15 para. 15	Added Social Work (Scotland) Act 1968 (c. 49), Sch. 8, para. 12.
28(1)	Domestic help.	—	Repealed 1968 Sch. 4.
(2)		—	Repealed 1968 Sch. 4 (with saving).
29	Research.	—	Repealed 1972 Sch. 7.
30	Power of local health authorities to contribute to expenditure on co-ordination.	—	Repealed 1972 Sch. 7.
31	Appointed day.	—	Repealed 1972 Sch. 7.

NATIONAL HEALTH SERVICE (SCOTLAND) ACT—*cont.*

Section of Act	Subject Matter	Section of 1978 Act	Remarks
32	Executive Councils.	—	Repealed 1972 Sch. 7.
33	Local representative committees.	—	Repealed 1972 Sch. 7.
34(1)	Arrangements for general medical services.	19(1), (3)	Amended 1949 s. 10; 1972 Sch. 6 para. 3.
(2)		19(2)	Amended 1949 s. 14(1). Sch. Pt. II.
35(1)	Distribution of medical practitioners.	—	Repealed 1972 Sch. 7.
(2)		3(1), 20(1), (2)	Amended 1972 Sch. 6 para. 4. Repealed in part 1972 Sch. 7.
(3)		23(1), (2), (3)	Amended 1972 Sch. 6 para. 4.
(4)		23(4)	Amended 1972 Sch. 6 para. 4. 1976A s. 3(1).
(5)		3(2)	
(6)		23(5)	Amended 1976A s. 3(2).
(7)		23(6), (7)	
(8)		24	Modified 1949 s. 15. Amended 1972 Sch. 6 para. 4.
(9)		23(8)	
36(1)	Prohibition of sale of medical practices.	35(1), (2)	Amended 1972 Sch. 6 para. 5.
(2)		Sch. 9, para. 1(1)	
(3)		Sch. 9 para. 2(1)	
(4)		Sch. 9 para. 2(2)	
(5)		Sch. 9 para. 2(3)	
(6)		Sch. 9 para. 2(4), (5)	
(7)		Sch. 9 para. 2(6)	
(8)		Sch. 9 para. 2(7)	
(9)		Sch. 9 para. 1(2), (3)	
(10)		Sch. 9 para. 1(4), (5), (6)	
(11)		Sch. 9 para. 1(7)	
(12)		Sch. 9 para. 1(8)	
37(1)	Compensation for loss of right to sell practice.	Saving Sch. 15 para. 4.	Spent.
(2) (3) (3A)			
38	Practitioners dying or retiring before appointed day.	—	Repealed 1972 Sch. 7.
39(1)	Arrangements for general dental services.	25(1), (3)	Amended 1949 s. 11; 1972 Sch. 6 para. 6.

NATIONAL HEALTH SERVICE (SCOTLAND) ACT—*cont.*

Section of Act	Subject Matter	Section of 1978 Act	Remarks
39(2)		25 (2), 4(1), (2)	Repealed in part 1968 Sch. 4; amended 1949 s. 14(3); 1972 Sch. 6 para. 6.
40(1)	Arrangements for pharmaceutical services.	27(1)	Substituted 1973 Sch. 4 para. 42.
(2)		27(2)	Amended 1949 s. 14(2); 1973, Sch. 4, para. 42(2).
(3)		69(1), (3) Sch. 11 para. 1(2)	Added 1949 s. 16.
41(1)	Persons authorised to provide pharmaceutical services.	28(1)	Amended 1972 Sch. 6 para. 8.
(2)		28(2), Saving Sch. 15 para. 5	Amended Medicines Act 1968 (c. 67) s. 135(1) and Sch. 5 para. 12.
42(1)	Supplementary ophthalmic services.	26(1)	Amended 1968 s. 19; 1972 Sch. 6 para. 9; repealed in part 1972 Sch. 7.
(2)		—	Repealed 1972 Sch. 7.
(3)		26(2)	Amended 1949 s. 14(4); 1968 s. 19.
(4)		—	Repealed 1968 Sch. 4.
43(1)	Disqualification of persons providing services.	29(1), (2)	Amended 1968 s. 19; 1972 Sch. 6 para. 10.
(2)		29(2)	
(3)		29(3)	Amended 1972 Sch. 6 para. 10.
(4)		29(4)	
(5)		29(5), 30(1)	Amended 1972 Sch. 6 para. 10.
(6)		31	Amended 1968 s. 25(2).
(7)		32	Amended 1968 s. 26.
(8)		Saving Sch. 15 para. 6	Substituted 1972 Sch. 6 para. 10.
(9)		29(6)	Added 1972 Sch. 6 para. 10.
44	Powers of Secretary of State where services are inadequate.	33	Amended 1968 s. 19(4); 1972 Sch. 6 para. 11.
45(1)	Recovery of charges in respect of certain appliances and dental treatment.	73(*b*), 74(*b*)	Amended 1968 ss. 19, 39.
(2)		71(2)	
46	Exercise of choice of medical practitioner etc.	34	
47	Decision of disputes.	—	Repealed 1972 Sch. 7.
48	Provision of courses.	—	Repealed 1968 Sch. 4.
49 to 51	Provisions as to mental health services.	—	Repealed Mental Health (Scotland) Act 1960 (c. 61) Sch. 5.

NATIONAL HEALTH SERVICE (SCOTLAND) ACT—*cont.*

Section of Act	Subject Matter	Section of 1978 Act	Remarks
52(1)	Expenses and receipts of Secretary of State.	—	Unnecessary.
(2)		85(6)	
53(1) to (3)	Grants to local health authorities.	—	Repealed Local Government and Miscellaneous Financial Provisions (Scotland) Act 1958 (c. 64) Sch. 6.
(4) (5)		—	Repealed Local Government Act 1948 (c. 26) Sch. 2.
(6)		—	Repealed Local Government (Scotland) Act 1947 (c. 43) Sch. 14.
(7)		—	Repealed 1972 Sch. 7.
54	Payment to Regional Hospital Boards etc.	—	Repealed 1972 Sch. 7.
55	Accounts of local health authorities etc.	—	Repealed 1972 Sch. 7.
56(1)	Default powers of Secretary of State.	77(1)	Amended 1972 Sch. 6 para. 12.
(2)		77(2)	Amended 1972 Sch. 6 para. 12.
(3)		—	Repealed 1972 Sch. 7.
(4)		77(3)	
57	Purchase of land.	—	Repealed 1972 Sch. 7.
58	Power of Boards to hold property on trust.	—	Repealed 1972 Sch. 7.
59	Power of trustees to pay to Boards.	—	Repealed 1972 Sch. 7.
60	Preservation of associations of denominational hospitals.	80(2)	Repealed in part, 1972.
61	Special educational treatment in hospitals.	—	Repealed 1972 Sch. 7.
62	Supply of goods by local health authorities	—	Repealed 1972 Sch. 7.
63	Use of premises and equipment by other authorities.	—	Repealed 1972 Sch. 7.
64	Residential accommodation for staff.	—	Repealed 1972 Sch. 7.
65	Qualifications. remuneration and conditions of service of officers.	—	Repealed 1972 Sch. 7.
66	Superannuation of officers.	—	Repealed Superannuation Act 1972 (c. 11) Sch. 8.
67	Regulations as to transfer and compensation of officers.	Saving Sch. 15 para. 8	Repealed, with partial saving 1972 s. 61(4) and Sch. 7.
68	Consequential provisions on transfer of functions.	—	Repealed 1972 Sch. 7.

NATIONAL HEALTH SERVICE (SCOTLAND) ACT—*cont.*

Section of Act	Subject Matter	Section of 1978 Act	Remarks
69	Inquiries.	76	Amended 1972 Sch. 6 para. 13.
70	Protection of certain bodies and their officers.	101	Amended 1972 Sch. 6 para. 14; repealed in part Law Reform (Limitation of Actions) Act 1954 (c. 36) s. 6(4)(d) and Sch.
71	Exemptions from stamp duty.	—	Repealed 1972 Sch. 7.
72	Miscellaneous administrative matters.	106	Amended 1972 Sch. 6 para. 15.
73(1)	Regulations and orders.	105(1), (2)	Repealed in part, 1972.
(2)		—	Repealed 1972 Sch. 7.
(3)		105(5)	
(4)		105(6)	
74	Consequential amendments and repeals.	Part saving Sch. 15 para. 10	Repealed in part, 1972.
75	Amendment and repeal of local Acts and charters.	—	Repealed 1972 Sch. 7.
76	Provision for winding up certain bodies.	—	Repealed 1972 Sch. 7.
77	Arbitration.	103	Amended 1972 Sch. 6 para. 16.
78	Repeal of s. 2(3) of Nurses (Scotland) Act 1943.	—	Repealed 1972 Sch. 7.
79	Expression " asylum " to cease to be used.	Saving Sch. 15 para. 10	
80(1)	Interpretation.	108(1)	Amended Mental Health (Scotland) Act 1960 (c. 61) Schs. 4, 5; 1968 s. 20(1); 1973 Sch. 4; 1973 Sch. 4 para. 43. Repealed in part Pharmacy Act 1953 (c. 19) Sch. 2; Mental Health (Scotland) Act 1960 (c. 61) Sch. 5; 1972 Sch. 7.
(2)		108(2)	
(3)		—	Repealed 1972 Sch. 7.
(4)		108(3)	
81(1) (2)	Short title and extent.	—	Unnecessary.
Sch. 1	Scottish Health Services Council and Advisory Committees.	—	Repealed 1972 Sch. 7.
Sch. 2	Hospital Endowments Commission.	—	Repealed 1971 s. 13(1)(*a*).

NATIONAL HEALTH SERVICE (SCOTLAND) ACT—*cont.*

Section of Act	Subject Matter	Section of 1978 Act	Remarks
Sch. 3	Acquisition of Property other than Land.	Sch. 13	Amended 1972 Sch. 6 para. 17.
Sch. 4	Regional Hospital Boards etc.	—	Repealed 1972 Sch. 7.
Sch. 5	Health Committees.	—	Repealed Local Government and Miscellaneous Financial Provisions (Scotland) Act 1958 (c. 64) Sch. 6.
Sch. 6	Executive Councils.	—	Repealed 1972 Sch. 7.
Sch. 7	Scottish Medical Practices Committee.	Sch. 2	Repealed in part, 1968 Sch. 4.
Sch. 8	Constitution of Tribunal.	Sch. 8	Amended 1949 s. 20; 1972 Sch. 6 para. 18; Repealed in part, 1968 Sch. 4.
Sch. 9	Amendment and Repeal of Enactments relating to Lunatics and Mental Defectives. Repeal	— —	Repealed Mental Health (Scotland) Act 1960 (c. 61) Sch. 5. Spent.
Sch. 10	Provisions as to Inquiries.	Sch. 12	Amended 1972 Sch. 6 para. 19.
Sch. 11 Pt. I	Consequential Amendments.	Saved in part Sch. 15 para 10.	Repealed in part, 1972.
Pt. II	Consequential Repeals.		Spent.

THE NATIONAL HEALTH SERVICE (AMENDMENT) ACT 1949
(12, 13 & 14 Geo. 6 c. 93)

1–7	Medical partnerships	—	Not consolidated.
8	Removal of doubts as to operation of 1947 s. 36.	35(3)	Amended 1972 Sch. 6 para. 20.
9	Application of Pt. I to Scotland.	—	Not consolidated
10	Prohibition of full-time salaried practitioner service.	19(3)	
11	Prohibition of full-time salaried dental practitioner service.	25(3)	
12	Regulations not to require specialists to be employed whole time.	—	Repealed 1972 Sch. 7.
13	Reference of disputes as to conditions of service.	—	Repealed Employment Protection Act 1975 (c. 71) Sch. 18.
14(1)	Removal from lists of persons who do not provide services under 1947.	19(2)	
(2)		27(2)	
(3)		25(2)	
(4)		26(2)	

NATIONAL HEALTH SERVICE (SCOTLAND) ACT—*cont.*

Section of Act	Subject Matter	Section of 1978 Act	Remarks
15	Additional functions of Scottish Medical Practices Committee.	24	
16	Recovery of charges in respect of pharmaceutical services.	69(1) Sch. 11 para. 1(2)	
17	Recovery of charges from persons resident outside Great Britain.	98	Repealed in part, 1976B Sch. 5.
18(1)	Superannuation of officers of certain hospitals.	89(1)	Amended Superannuation Act. 1972 (c. 11) Sch. 6 para. 27.
(2)		—	Repealed Superannuation (Miscellaneous Provisions) Act 1967 (c. 28) s. 6(4).
(3)		89(2)	
(4)		89(3)	Amended 1973 Sch. 4 para. 52(2).
(5)		89	Repealed in part Superannuation Act 1972 (c. 11) Sch. 6 para. 27. Amended 1973 Sch. 4 para. 149.
19	Superannuation of certain officers.	—	Repealed Superannuation (Miscellaneous Provisions) Act 1967 (c. 28), s. 7(6).
20(1)	Appointment of practitioner members of Tribunal.	Sch. 8 para. 4,5,6	
(2)		—	Repealed 1972 Sch. 7.
(3)		Sch. 8	
21	Removal of doubts as to power to prescribe certain qualifications.	26(3)(*a*)	Repealed in part, 1968 Sch. 4.
22	Removal of doubts as to powers of local health authorities in connection with midwifery.	—	Repealed 1968 Sch. 4.
23(1)	Power of voluntary organisations to transfer property to local health authorities.	81	Amended 1972 Sch. 6 para. 21.
(2)		Saving Sch. 14 para. 11	
24	Cost of conveyance.	—	Not applicable to Scotland.
25	Payment of certain remuneration and expenses.	—	Not applicable to Scotland.
26	Validation of certain orders.	—	Not applicable to Scotland.
27	Reception of certain persons into mental hospitals.	—	Repealed, Mental Health (Scotland) Act 1960 Sch. 5.
28	Recovery of expenses from in-patients engaged in remunerative employment.	56	Amended 1972 Sch. 6 para. 22.

NATIONAL HEALTH SERVICE (SCOTLAND) ACT—*cont.*

Section of Act	Subject Matter	Section of 1978 Act	Remarks
29	Minor amendments and repeals.	—	Spent.
30(1)	Expenses and receipts.	—	Unnecessary.
(2)		85(6)	Not repealed.
31(1)	Interpretation.	—	
(2)		108(1)	Not repealed.
(3)		108(3)	Not repealed.
32	Short title and extent.	—	Spent in part, otherwise unnecessary.
Sch. Pt. I	Minor amendments of National Health Service Act 1946.	—	Not applicable to Scotland.
Pt. II	Minor amendments of 1947	19(2)(*d*)	Repealed in part 1968 Sch. 4; 1971 s. 13(1)(*a*); 1972 Sch. 7; Superannuation Act 1972 (c. 11) Sch. 8.

THE NATIONAL HEALTH SERVICE ACT 1951
(14 & 15 Geo. 6, c. 31)

Section of Act	Subject Matter	Section of 1978 Act	Remarks
1(1)	Charges in respect of certain dental and optical appliances.	70(1)	Amended 1972 Sch. 6 para. 23(*a*).
(2)		Sch. 11 para. 2(3)	Amended 1973 Sch. 4 para. 58(2); Repealed in part 1972 Sch. 7.
(3)		Sch. 11 para. 2(2)	Amended 1972 Sch. 6 para. 23.
(4)		Sch. 11 para. 2(2) 75(*b*)	Amended 1968 s. 19; 1972 Sch. 6 para. 23.
(5)		—	Unnecessary.
(6)		Sch. 11 para. 2(8)	
2	Power to amend Schedule.	—	Repealed 1952 s. 3(1).
3	Provisions of treatment abroad for respiratory tuberculosis.	—	Repealed 1971 Sch. 7.
4(1)	Consequential provisions.	—	Repealed Finance Act 1970 (c. 24) Sch. 8 Pt. V.
(2)		—	Repealed Ministry of Social Security Act 1966 (c. 20) Sch. 8.
(3)		85(6)	Repealed in part Ministry of Social Security Act 1966 (c. 20) Sch. 8; in part unnecessary.
5	Duration of certain provisions.	—	Repealed 1952 s. 3(4).
6(1)	Short title, citation and extent.	—	Spent.
(2), (3)		—	Unnecessary.
Sch.	Charges for dental and optical appliances.	Sch. 11 para. 2(1)	Amended 1961 s. 1; Decimal Currency Act 1969 (c. 19), s. 10; 1972 Sch. 6 para. 24; 1973 Sch. 4 para. 59.

NATIONAL HEALTH SERVICE (SCOTLAND) ACT—*cont.*

Section of Act	Subject Matter	Section of 1978 Act	Remarks
	THE NATIONAL HEALTH SERVICE ACT 1952 (15 & 16 Geo. 6 & 1 Eliz. 2 c. 25)		
1(1)	Charges for certain drugs etc.	69(1), (3)	Amended 1972 Sch. 6 para. 25.
(2)		Sch. 11 para. 1(1)	
(3)		69(1)	
2(1)	Charges for dental treatment.	71(1)	
(2)		Sch. 11 para. 3(1), (3)	
(3)		Sch. 11 para. 3(2)	
(4)		Sch. 11 para. 3(4)	
(5)		Sch. 11 para. 3(1)	
3	Power to vary or abolish certain charges.	—	Repealed 1961 s. 2(4).
4(1), (2)	Power to remit charges for dentures supplied by teaching hospitals.	70(2)	
(3)		105(1)	
5(1)	Miscellaneous amendments	Sch. 11 para. 6	
(2) & (3)		—	Repealed 1968 Sch. 4.
6	Evasion of charges.	99	Repealed in part, Theft Act 1968 (c. 60) Sch. 3 Pt. I.
7(1)	Supplementary and consequential provisions.	—	Repealed Finance Act 1970 (c. 24) Sch. 8 Pt. V.
(2)		—	Repealed Ministry of Social Security Act 1966 (c. 20) Sch. 8.
(3)		85(6)	Repealed in part Ministry of Social Security Act 1966 (c. 20) Sch. 8.
(4)		Sch. 11 para. 4	Amended 1972 Sch. 6 para. 26.
(5)		—	Unnecessary.
(6)		75	Amended 1972 Sch. 6 para. 26.
(7)		105 (1), (2)	
8(1)	Interpretation.	108(1)	Amended 1972 Sch. 6 para. 27.
(2)		108(3)	
9	Short title, citation etc.	—	Unnecessary.
	THE HOSPITAL ENDOWMENTS (SCOTLAND) ACT 1953 (1 & 2 Eliz. 2 c. 41)		
1(1)	Scottish Hospital Endowments Research Trust.	12(1), (2)	
(2)		12(3)	
(3)		12(4)	

NATIONAL HEALTH SERVICE (SCOTLAND) ACT—*cont.*

Section of Act	Subject Matter	Section of 1978 Act	Remarks
1(4) (5) (6)		12(5) 12(6) 12(7)	
2	Additional power of Hospital Endowments Commission.	—	Repealed 1971 s. 13.
3(1)	Regulations.	Sch. 7 para. 3	
(2)		105(1), (2)	
4(1) (2)	Extent, citation, and construction.	110(2) 108(1)	
Sch.	Scottish Hospital Endowments Research Trust.	Sch. 7	Amended 1971 s. 10.

THE NATIONAL HEALTH SERVICE ACT 1961
(9 & 10 Eliz. 2 c. 19)

Section of Act	Subject Matter	Section of 1978 Act	Remarks
1(1)	Increase of, and exemptions from charges for dental and optical appliances.	—	Spent.
(2)		—	Spent.
(3)		Sch. 11 paras. 2(4), 3(4)	
(4)		Sch. 11 para. 2(5)	Amended 1972 Sch. 6 para. 28.
(5)		Sch. 11 paras. 2(6), 3(5)	
(6)		105(1), (2)	
2(1), (2)	Variation of charges for dental and optical appliances and dental treatment.	Sch. 11 paras. 2(2), 3(2)	
(3)		75, 105(1), (2)	
(4)		—	Spent.
3(1)	Interpretation.	Sch. 11 paras. 2(1), (7), 7	Amended 1972 Sch. 6 para. 29.
(2)		Sch. 11 para. 2(8)	
4(1) (2)	Expenses and receipts.	— 85(6)	Unnecessary.
5	Short title, commencement and extent.	—	Unnecessary.

EMERGENCY LAWS (RE-ENACTMENTS AND REPEALS) ACT 1964
(1964 c. 60)

Section of Act	Subject Matter	Section of 1978 Act	Remarks
5(1)–(3) (4)	Medical supplies.	49(1)–(3) —	Repealed S. I 1968/1699.

NATIONAL HEALTH SERVICE (SCOTLAND) ACT—*cont.*

Section of Act	Subject Matter	Section of 1978 Act	Remarks
	THE HEALTH SERVICES AND PUBLIC HEALTH ACT 1968 (1968 c. 46)		
1(1)	Accommodation and treatment of private resident patients.	57(1)	Amended 1972 Sch. 6 para. 30.
(2)		57(2)	Repealed in part 1972 Sch. 7.
(3)		57(3)	Repealed in part 1972 Sch. 7.
(4)–(6)		57(4)–(6)	
2(1)	Accommodation and treatment of private non-resident patients.	58(1)	Amended 1972 Sch. 6 para. 31.
(2), (3)		58(2),(3)	
3	Certain transitional provisions.	—	Not applicable to Scotland.
4(1)	Fixing of charges for accommodation	55(1) Sch. 15 para. 7	
(2)		55(2)	
(3)			Not applicable to Scotland.
(4)		55(1)	Spent in part.
5 to 7		—	Not applicable to Scotland.
8	Association with universities.	—	Repealed 1972 Sch. 7.
9(1)	Appointment of officers.	—	Not applicable to Scotland.
(2)		—	Repealed 1972 Sch. 7.
10	Midwifery services.	—	Repealed 1972 Sch. 7.
11	Health visiting and district nursing.	—	Repealed 1972 Sch. 7.
12		—	Not applicable to Scotland.
13	Home help and laundry facilities.	—	Repealed Social Work (Scotland) Act 1968 (c. 49) Sch. 9.
14(1)	Amendments as to certain charges.	—	Not applicable to Scotland.
(2)		—	Repealed 1972 Sch. 7
15	Provision of advice etc. for family planning.	—	Repealed 1972 Sch. 7.
16 to 18	—	—	Not applicable to Scotland.
19(1)	General ophthalmic services.	Passim	
(2)		—	Repealed 1972 Sch. 7.
(3)		—	Repealed 1972 Sch. 7.
(4)		33	
(5)–(7)		—	Repealed 1972 Sch. 7.
(8)		—	Unnecessary.
20(1)	Amendment of definitions in 1947 s. 80(1) of " dispensing optician " and " ophthalmic optician ".	108(1)	
(2)		—	Unnecessary.
21(1) to (3)		—	Not applicable to Scotland.
(4)	Amends 1947 s. 15(6).	—	Repealed 1972 Sch. 7.
22		—	Not applicable to Scotland.

NATIONAL HEALTH SERVICE (SCOTLAND) ACT—*cont.*

Section of Act	Subject Matter	Section of 1978 Act	Remarks
23	Amends 1947 s. 40.	27(1)	
24	Power of Executive Councils to supply goods in certain cases.	—	Repealed 1972 Sch. 7.
25(1)		—	Not applicable to Scotland.
(2)		31	
26	Amends 1947 provisions as to enquiries.	30(2), 32	
27(1)	Amendments of provisions as to approval of certain expenditure (E & W).	—	Not applicable to Scotland.
(2)	Amendments of provisions as to approval of certain expenditure (E & W) (S).	—	Repealed 1972 Sch. 7.
28	Accounts of Regional Hospital Boards etc.	—	Repealed 1972 Sch. 7.
29(1)	Financial arrangements of hospital authorities etc.	87(1), (2)	Amended 1972 Sch. 6 para. 32.
(2)		87(3)	
(3)		87(1)	Amended 1972 Sch. 6 para. 32. Repealed in part 1972 Sch. 7.
30(1)	Certificates for exemption from prescription charges.	69(2)	Amended 1972 Sch. 6 para. 33.
(2)		—	Repealed 1972 Sch. 7.
31	Services otherwise than for purposes of hospital and specialist services.	50(1)	Amended 1972 Sch. 6 para. 34.
32(1)	Disposal of goods and production otherwise than for purposes of hospital and specialist services.	53(1), (2)	Amended 1972 Sch. 6 para. 35.
(2)		—	Amended 1972 Sch. 6 para. 35.
33(1)	Provision of vehicles for persons suffering from disability.	46(1)	
(2)		46(2)	
(3)		46(3)	
(4)		73, 74	Repealed in part, 1972 Sch. 7.
(5)		46(4)	
(6)		Saving Sch. 15 para. 9	Repealed 1972 Sch. 7.
(7)		46(5)	
(8)		—	Scottish application.
34	Superannuation of certain officers in England and Wales.	—	Not applicable to Scotland.
35	Compensation for loss of employment.	—	Repealed Superannuation Act 1972 (c. 11) Sch. 8.
36	Allowances etc. (England and Wales).	—	Not applicable to Scotland.

NATIONAL HEALTH SERVICE (SCOTLAND) ACT—*cont.*

Section of Act	Subject Matter	Section of 1978 Act	Remarks
37(1)	Allowances etc. (Scotland)	88(1)	Repealed in part 1972 Sch. 7.
(2) to (4)		88(2)–(4)	
(5)		110(2)	
38(1)	Appeals from determinations as to medical practitioners qualifications.	26(3)(*b*)	
(2)		—	Spent.
(3)		26(3)(*b*)	
39	Power to recover cost of replacement of appliances in certain cases.	74	Repealed in part, 1972 Sch. 7.
40	Accommodation for persons displaced.	100	Amended 1972 Sch. 6 para. 36.
41	Provision of practice accommodation.	—	Repealed 1972 Sch. 7.
42	Orders and regulations.	105	
43(1)	Interpretation of Pt. I etc.	—	Unnecessary.
(2)		—	Not applicable to Scotland.
(3)		108(1)	Spent in part.
(4) and Sch. 2 Pt. II		76, 77, 101	Repealed in part, 1972 Sch. 7.

THE HOSPITAL ENDOWMENTS (SCOTLAND) ACT 1971
(1971 c. 8)

Section of Act	Subject Matter	Section of 1978 Act	Remarks
1(1)	Scottish Hospital Trust.	11(1), (2)	
(2)		11(3)	
(3)		11(4)	
(4)		11(5), (6)	Amended 1972 Sch. 6 para. 147.
(5)		11(7)	
2	Transference of endowments to Trust.	—	Spent.
3	Powers of Trusts.	Sch. 6 para 4	Amended 1972 Sch. 6 para. 148.
4	Duty of Trust to obtain advice on investment.	Sch. 6 para. 5	
5(1)	Further provisions relating to transference of funds from Boards.	Sch. 1 para. 16	Amended 1972 Sch. 6 para. 149.
(2)		Sch. 6 para. 6(1)	Amended 1972 Sch. 6 para. 149.
6(1)	Borrowing by Boards.	Sch. 1 para. 17	Amended 1972 Sch. 6 para. 150.
(2)		Sch. 6 para. 6(2)	Amended 1972 Sch. 6 para. 150. Spent in part.
(3)		Saving Sch. 15 para. 14	Spent.

NATIONAL HEALTH SERVICE (SCOTLAND) ACT—*cont.*

Section of Act	Subject Matter	Section of 1978 Act	Remarks
7	Distribution of income of endowments.	Sch. 6 para. 7	Amended 1972 s. 38(5) Sch. 6 para. 151.
8(1)	Administration of trust.	Sch. 6 para. 8.	
(2)		Sch. 6 para. 9	
9	Audit of Trust accounts.	Sch. 6 para. 10	
10	Extension of powers of investment of Scottish Hospital Endowments Research Trust.	Sch. 7 para. 4	
11(1)	Regulations.	105(1)	
(2)		105(3)	
(3)		105(2)	
12(1)	Interpretation.	108(1)	
(2)		108(3)	
13(1)	Repeals.	—	Spent.
(2)			
14(1)	Short title and extent.	—	Unnecessary.
(2)		110(2)	
Sch.	Scottish Hospital Trust.	Sch. 6 Pt. I	

THE NATIONAL HEALTH SERVICE (SCOTLAND) ACT 1972
(1972 c. 58)

Section of Act	Subject Matter	Section of 1978 Act	Remarks
1(1)	General duty of Secretary of State.	1(1)	
(2)		1(1)	
2(1)	Provision of accommodation and medical services etc.	36(1)	
(2)		36(2)	
(3), (4)		—	Repealed 1976B Sch. 5.
3	Provision of medical dental etc. services.	18	
4(1)	Prevention of illness and after-care.	37	
(2)		72(*a*), 75	
(3)		108(1)	
5(1)	Care of mothers and young children.	38	
(2)		72(*b*)	
6	Medical and dental inspection. Supervision and treatment of pupils and young persons.	39	
7	Vaccination and immunisation.	40	
8(1)	Family planning.	41	
(2)		72(*c*)	

NATIONAL HEALTH SERVICE (SCOTLAND) ACT—*cont.*

Section of Act	Subject Matter	Section of 1978 Act	Remarks
9	Educational and research facilities.	47(1)	
10	Health education.	42	
11	Residential and practice accommodation.	48	
12(1)	Amendments of 1947 Pt. II and 1968 Pt. I.	55, 73, 74, 85(5)	
(2)		45	Spent in part.
(3)		47(2)	Spent in part.
(4)		—	Spent.
(5)		44(1)	Spent in part.
13(1)	Health Boards.	2(1), (10)	
(2)		2(2)	
(3)		2(3)	
(4)		2(4)	
(5)		2(5)	
(6)		2(6)	
(7)		2(7)	
(8)		2(11)	
(9)		2(8)	
(10)		2(9)	
(11)		2(10)	
14(1)	Local Health Councils.	7(1)	
(2)		7(2)	
(3)		7(5)	
(4)		7(3)	
(5)		7(4)	
(6)		7(6)	
(7)		7(7)	
(8)		7(8)	
(9)		7(9)	
15(1)	University Liaison Committees.	8(1)	
(2)		8(2)	
16	Local Consultative Committees	9	
17(1)	Scottish Health Service Planning Council.	5(1) (2)	
(2)		5(3)	
(3)		5(4)	
18	National Consultative Committees.	6	
19(1)	Common Services Agency.	10(1) (2)	
(2)		10(3)	
(3)		—	Spent.
(4)		—	Spent.
(5)		10(4)	
(6)		10(5)	
(7)		10(6)	
(8)		10(7)	
(9)		10(8) (9)	
20	Co-operation between Health Boards and local authorities.	13	
21	Designated medical officers.	14	

NATIONAL HEALTH SERVICE (SCOTLAND) ACT—*cont.*

Section of Act	Subject Matter	Section of 1978 Act	Remarks
22(1)	Supply of goods and services to local authorities etc.	15(1)	
(2)		15(2)	
(3)		15(3)	
23(1)	Assistance to voluntary organisations.	16(1)	Added 1973 Sch. 4 para. 138.
(1A)		16(2)	Added 1973 Sch. 4 para. 139.
(2)		16(3)	
24(1)	Dissolution of Boards etc.	—	Spent.
(2)		—	Not consolidated.
(3)		—	Spent.
25	Rights and liabilities of Regional Hospital Boards and Boards of Management.	—	Spent.
26	Transfer of property etc. of Executive Councils and the Scottish Dental Estimates Board.		Not consolidated.
27	Transfer of property etc. of local authorities.	—	Not consolidated.
28	Staff Commission.	—	Not consolidated.
29	Transfer of staff of Regional Hospital Boards and Boards of Management.	—	Spent.
30	Transfer of staff of Executive Councils etc.	—	Spent.
31	Transfer of staff of local health and education authorities.	—	Spent.
32	Transfer of staff employed for purposes of public health.	—	Not consolidated.
33	Transfer of certain staff to Agency.	—	Not consolidated.
34(1)	Transfer of other staff.	—	Not consolidated.
(2)		—	Amended 1973 Sch. 4 para. 140. Not consolidated.
34A	Provision for early retirement in lieu of compensation for loss of office.	—	Added 1973 Sch. 4 para. 141; not consolidated.
35	Supplementary order-making powers.	—	Not consolidated.
36	Representations to Staff Commission.	—	Not consolidated.
37(1)	Transfer of endowments and income held under s. 7(1) or 58 of Act of 1947.	82(1)	
(2)		—	Spent.
(3)		82(1), (3) (4)	

NATIONAL HEALTH SERVICE (SCOTLAND) ACT—*cont.*

Section of Act	Subject Matter	Section of 1978 Act	Remarks
38(1)	Transfer of rights held under Hospital Endowments (S) Act 1971.	—	Spent.
(2)		—	Spent.
(3)		Sch. 6 para. 7(4)	
(4)		Sch. 6 para. 7(4)	
(5)		Sch. 6 para. 7(3)	
39(1)	Transfer of property held on trust by local health authorities.	82(2) (4)	
(2)		—	Spent.
(3)		82(3) (4)	
40	Power of trustees to make payments to Health Boards.	84	
41	Power of Health Boards and local councils to hold property on trust.	83	
42	Appointment of Health Service Commissioner and tenure of office.	90	
43(1)	Salary and pension.	91(1)	Amended Parliamentary and other Pensions and Salaries Act 1976 (c. 48) s. 7(2).
(2)		91(2)	Amended 1973 Sch. 4 para. 142.
(3)		91(3)	Repealed in part 1976 (c. 48) s. 7(3) and Sch.
(3A)		91(4)	Added 1976 (c. 48) s. 7(3).
(4)		—	Repealed 1973 Sch. 5.
(5)		91(8)	
44(1)	Administrative provisions.	92(1)	
(2)		92(2)	Substituted 1973 Sch. 4 para. 143.
(3)		92(3)	
(4)		92(4)	
45(1)	Bodies and action subject to investigation.	93(1)	Amended 1976B Sch. 1 para. 30(1).
(2)		93(2)	Substituted 1973 Sch. 4 para. 144.
(3)		93(3)	
(4)		93(4)	Amended 1973 Sch. 4 para. 145.
(5)		93(5)	
(6)		93(6)	
46(1)	Provisions relating to complaints.	94(1)	
(2)		94(2)	Amended 1973 Sch. 4 para. 145.
(3)		94(3)	
(4)		94(4)	Amended 1973 Sch. 4 para. 145.
(5)		94(5)	

NATIONAL HEALTH SERVICE (SCOTLAND) ACT—*cont.*

Section of Act	Subject Matter	Section of 1978 Act	Remarks
47	Application of certain provisions of the Parliamentary Commissioner Act 1967.	95	Amended 1973 Sch. 4 para. 146; repealed in part 1973 Sch. 5.
48(1)	Reports by Commissioner.	96(1) (2)	Amended 1976B Sch. 1 para. 31(*a*)(i).
(2)		96(3)	
(3)		96(4)	Amended 1976B Sch. 1 para. 31(*a*)(ii).
(4)		96(5) (6)	Amended 1976B Sch. 1 paras. 31(*b*), 32.
(5)		96(7)	
49	Transitional provisions.	Saving Sch. 15 para. 12	
50	Interpretation of Part VI	97	
51	State hospitals.	102	
52(1)	The Mental Welfare Commission for Scotland.	—	Not consolidated.
(2) (3) (4) (5) (6)			
53	Extension of definition of infectious diseases.	—	Not consolidated.
54	Power of Secretary of State in an emergency.	78	
55	Furnishing of overseas aid by Health Boards and the Agency.	17	
56	Transfer of functions under the Nursing Homes Registration (Scotland) Act 1938 (c. 73).	Sch. 1 para. 18	
57	Accounts of Health Boards and the Agency.	86	
58	Purchase of land and moveable property.	79	
59(1) (2)	Exemption from stamp duty.	104	
60(1)	Expenses.	—	Unnecessary.
(2)		85(6)	
(3)		85(1)	
(4)		85(2)	
(5)		85(3)	
(6)		85(4)	
(7)–(9)		—	Spent.
61(1)	Supplementary and transitional.	—	Not consolidated.
(2)		—	Not consolidated.
(3)		—	Not consolidated.

NATIONAL HEALTH SERVICE (SCOTLAND) ACT—*cont.*

Section of Act	Subject Matter	Section of 1978 Act	Remarks
(4)		Saving Sch. 15 para. 8	
(5)		Sch. 1 para. 19 Sch. 5 para. 12	
62(1)	Regulations, orders and legal enactments.	105(1)	
(2)		105(2)	
(3)		105(4)	
(4)		105(7)	
(5)		105(5)	
(6)		105(6)	
(7)		107(1)	
(8)		107(2)	
(9)		107(3)	
63(1)	Interpretation.	108(1)	
(2)		108(3)	
64(1)	Minor and consequential amendments and repeals.	Saving Sch. 15 para. 10 Sch. 16	
(2)		—	Spent.
65(1)	Commencement, short title and extent.	—	Spent.
(2)		—	Unnecessary.
(3)		—	Subst. 1973 Sch. 4 para. 147.
(4)		—	Added 1973 Sch. 4 para. 148.
Sch. 1	Health Boards and University Liaison Committees.	Sch. 1, 4	
Sch. 2	Scottish Health Service Planning Council.	Sch. 3	
Sch. 3	The Common Services Agency for the Scottish Health Service.	Sch. 5	
Sch. 4	Public Health functions.	—	Not consolidated.
Sch. 5	Action not subject to investigation.	Sch. 14	
Sch. 6	Minor and consequential amendments and enactments.	Saving Sch. 15 para. 10 Sch. 16	
Sch. 7	Repeal of enactments.	—	Spent.

NATIONAL HEALTH SERVICE (SCOTLAND) ACT—*cont.*

Section of Act	Subject Matter	Section of 1978 Act	Remarks
	NATIONAL HEALTH RE-ORGANISATION ACT 1973 (c. 32)		
32(4) (5) (6) (7)	Salaries and pensions.	91(5) 91(6) 91(7) 91(8)	
36	Application of certain provisions of Parliamentary Commissioner Act 1967 (c. 13).	95	
37(5)	Reports by Commissioners.	96(7)	
39(1)	Interpretation of Part III.	97(1)	
50	Remission of charges and consequential adaptation of 1966 Act (c. 20) s. 6.	Sch. 11 para. 5	
51	Compensation for loss of rights to sell medical practices.	Saving Sch. 15 para. 4	
57(1)	Minor and consequential amendments and repeals.	Saving Sch. 15 para. 10	Spent in part.
Sch. 4	Minor and consequential amendments of enactments.	Saving Sch. 15 para. 10	
Sch. 5	Repeals.	—	Spent.
	NATIONAL HEALTH SERVICE (VOCATIONAL TRAINING) ACT 1976 (c. 59)		
1(1)	Experience required by medical practitioners seeking to provide general medical services.	21(1)	
(2) (3)		21(1) 21(2)	
2(1)–(3)	Regulations in connection with s. 1.	22(1)–(3), 105(2), (5)	
(4)		22(1)	
3(1)	Minor and consequential amendments.	23(4)	
(2) (3) (4)		23(5) 88(1), (2) —	Spent.
4(1)	Interpretation etc.	21(2) 108(1)	
(3)		—	
5	Citation and extent.	—	
	HEALTH SERVICES ACT 1976 (c. 83)		
2(1), (2)	Purpose of ss. 3 to 5 of Health Services Act 1976.	59(1), (2)	

NATIONAL HEALTH SERVICE (SCOTLAND) ACT—_cont._

Section of Act	Subject Matter	Section of 1978 Act	Remarks
4(1)	Functions of Health Services Board as regards withdrawal of NHS facilities from private patients.	60(1)	Spent in part.
(2)		60(2)	Spent in part.
(3)		60(3)	
(4)		61(1)	
(5)		61(2)	Spent in part.
(6)		61(3)	
(7)		60(4)	
(8)		62	
(9)		65	
5(1)	Restrictions on Secretary of State's powers under ss. 1 and 2 of 1968 Act.	—	Spent.
(2)		63(1)	
(3)		63(1)	Spent in part.
(4)		63(2), (3)	Spent in part.
(5)		63(4)	
(6)		63(5)	
6(1), (2)	Recommendations on arrangements for securing use of NHS facilities on basis of medical priority.	68(1), (2)	Not repealed.
7(1)	Secretary of State's powers to provide services etc. otherwise than for purposes of services under National Health Service Acts.	44, 50	
(2)		54	
8(1), (2)	Restrictions on power under s. 31 of 1968 Act to allow use of NHS facilities by private patients.	51(1), (2)	
(3), (4)		51(3), (4)	
(5)		52(1)	
(6)		52(2)	
(7)		52(3)	
(8)		52(4), 85(6)	
(9)		52(5)	
(10)		52(6)	
9(1)–(4)	Use by general practitioners etc. of NHS accommodation and facilities for private practice.	64(1)–(4)	
(5)		Sch. 15 para. 13	
(6)		64(5)	
(7)		64(6)	
10(1)	Publication of proposals and preparation of annual reports by Secretary of State.	66	
(2)		67(1)	
(3)		67(2)	
11	Interpretation of Pt. II.	—	In part spent; in part unnecessary.

NATIONAL HEALTH SERVICE (SCOTLAND) ACT—*cont.*

Section of Act	Subject Matter	Section of 1978 Act	Remarks
23(1), (2)	General interpretation, amendments and repeals.	108(1)	
(3)		1(2)	
(4), (5)		—	Spent.
(6)		—	
Sch. 1, Pt. VI	Liability of Scottish Committee to investigation by Health Service Commissioner for Scotland.		
para. 30(1)		109, 93	
(2)		110, 96	
31		96(2), (4), (5), (7)	
32		96(6)	
Sch. 4 Pt. II	Provisions of 1947 Act applied.	76, 77, 101	

NORTHERN IRELAND (EMERGENCY PROVISIONS) ACT 1978 (c. 5)

TABLE OF DERIVATIONS

Note:—The following abbreviations are used in this table:—

1973 c. 36	= The Northern Ireland Constitution Act 1973 (c. 36).
1973	= The Northern Ireland (Emergency Provisions) Act 1973 (c. 53).
S.I. 1973	= The Northern Ireland (Emergency Provisions) Act Proscribed Organisations (Amendment) Order 1973 (S.I. 1973/1880).
S.I. 1973/2163	= The Northern Ireland (Modification of Enactments—No. 1) Order 1973 (S.I. 1973/2163).
1974	= The Northern Ireland (Young Persons) Act 1974 (c. 33).
S.I. 1974	= The Northern Ireland (Emergency Provisions) Act 1973 (Amendment) Order 1974 (S.I. 1974/864).
1975 CJ	= The Criminal Jurisdiction Act 1975 (c. 59).
1975	= The Northern Ireland (Emergency Provisions) (Amendment) Act 1975 (c. 62).
S.I. 1975	= The Northern Ireland (Emergency Provisions) Act 1973 (Amendment) Order 1975 (S.I. 1975/1609).
1976	= The Prevention of Terrorism (Temporary Provisions) Act 1976 (c. 8).
1977 D	= The Criminal Damage (Northern Ireland) Order 1977 (S.I. 1977/426 (N.I. 4)).
1977	= The Northern Ireland (Emergency Provisions) (Amendment) Act 1977 (c. 34).
S.I. 1977	= The Northern Ireland (Various Emergency Provisions) (Continuance) (No.2) Order 1977 (S.I. 1977/2142)
1977 AO	= The Northern Ireland (Emergency Provisions) Act 1973 (Amendment) Order 1977 (S.I. 1977/1265).

Section of 1978 Act	Derivation
1	1975 s. 2.
2(1)	1973 s. 3(1) (substituted by 1975 s. 4(1)).
(2)	1973 s. 3(2).
(3)–(5)	1973 s. 3(3)–(5).
(6)	1973 s. 3(6) (inserted by 1975 s. 4(2)).
3	1975 s. 5; S.I. 1977/1252 (N.I. 19) art. 4(*d*).
4(1)	1974 s. 1(3).
(2)	1974 s. 1(4).
(3)	1974 s. 1(5).
(4)	1974 s. 1(1).
(5)	1974 s. 1(2).
5	1974 s. 2.
6(1)	1973 s. 4(1); 1975 s. 6(1).
(2)	1973 s. 4(2); 1975 ss. 3(2), 6(1).
(3)	1973 s. 4(3) (repealed in part: 1975 Sch. 3).
(4)	1973 s. 4(4).
7(1)	1973 s. 2(1).
(2)	1973 s. 2(2).
(3)	1973 s. 2(3) (substituted by 1975 s. 3(1))
(4)–(7)	1973 s. 2(4)–(7).
8(1)	1973 s. 6(1); 1975 s. 3(2).
(2)	1973 s. 6(2).
(3)	1975 s. 8 (part).

NORTHERN IRELAND (EMERGENCY PROVISIONS) ACT—*cont.*

Section of 1978 Act	Derivation
9(1)–(4) (5)	1973 s. 7(1)–(4). 1975 s. 8 (part).
10	1973 s. 8.
11	1973 s. 10(1)–(4).
12	1975 s. 9(1).
13	1973 s. 11; 1975 s. 22(1).
14	1973 s. 12.
15	1973 s. 13; 1975 s. 11(1)–(4)(6).
16	1973 s. 14.
17	1973 s. 15.
18(1) (2)	1973 s. 16(1); 1975 s. 10. 1973 s. 16(2).
19	1973 s. 17.
20	1973 s. 18; 1975 s. 11(5)
21(1) (2)–(9)	1973 s. 19(1); 1975 s. 12; 1977 s. 1. 1973 s. 19(2)–(8); S.I. 1977/1248 (N.I. 15) art. 3(4).
22(1)(2) (3) (4) (5)(6)	1973 s. 20(1)(1A) (part) (substituted by 1975 s. 13(1)). 1973 s. 20(3). 1973 s. 20(1A) (part); 1977 s. 1. 1973 s. 20(2)(4).
23	1975 s. 15; 1977 s. 1.
24	1973 s. 21.
25	1973 s. 23.
26	1975 s. 16.
27	1973 s. 24
28(1) (2) (3) (4)	1973 s. 25(1); 1975 s. 11(5) (part); S.I. 1973/2163 art. 2(1), Sch. 1 1973 s. 25(2) (part). 1973 s. 25(2) (part). 1973 s. 25(3).
29(1) (2)	1973 s. 26(1); 1975 s. 17(1). 1973 s. 26(2); 1975 s. 17(2).
30(1) (2) (3)	1973 s. 27(1); 1975 CJ Sch. 2 para. 3(2). 1973 s. 27(2). 1973 s. 27(3); 1975 CJ Sch. 2 para. 3(3).
31(1) (2) (3)	1973 s. 28(1); 1973 c. 36 Sch. 5 para. 1(1). 1973 s. 28(2); 1975 s. 20(2). 1975 s. 20(3).
32(1) (2) (3) (4)	1973 s. 29(1); 1974 s. 3(3). 1973 s. 29(2). 1973 s. 29(3); 1974 s. 3(4); 1975 s. 21(4). 1973 s. 29(4); 1974 s. 3(5): 1975 s. 21(5).

Part III

D

NORTHERN IRELAND (EMERGENCY PROVISIONS) ACT—*cont.*

Section of 1978 Act	Derivation
33(1)	Commencement.
(2)	1973 s. 30(2); 1974 s. 3(1); 1975 s. 21(2); 1975 CJ Sch. 2 para. 2(1); S.I. 1977, art. 3.
(3)	1973 s. 30(3); 1974 s. 3(2); 1975 ss. 21(3), 22(3) (part).
(4)	1973 s. 30(4).
(5)	1973 s. 30(5); 1975 s. 6.
(6)	1973 s. 30(6) (part).
(7)	1973 s. 30(6) (part).
(8)	1973 s. 30(7); 1975 s. 21(6).
34	Consequential amendments.
35(1)	1973 s. 31(7).
(2)(3)	Transitionals, repeals.
36(1)	Short title.
(2)	1973 s. 31(8); 1974 s. 4 (part); 1975 s. 23(3).
Sch. 1	1975 Sch. 1 Part I.
Sch. 2	1973 Sch. 2; S.I. 1973; S.I. 1974; S.I. 1975.
Sch. 3	1973 Sch. 3.
Sch. 4	
para. 1–3	1973 Sch. 4 paras. 1, 2, 4.
4, 5	1973 Sch. 4 paras. 4A, 4B (inserted by 1975 CJ Sch. 2 para. 1(2)).
6	1973 Sch. 4 para. 4C (inserted by 1975 Sch. 2 para. 2).
7	1973 Sch. 4 para. 5; 1975 CJ Sch. 2 para. 1(3); 1975 Sch. 2 para. 3; 1977 Sch. 2.
8	1973 Sch. 4 para. 6; 1975 Sch. 2 para. 4; 1977 AO.
9	1973 Sch. 4 para. 7.
10	1973 Sch. 4 para. 7A (inserted by 1975 Sch. 2 para. 5).
11	1973 Sch. 4 para. 9; 1975 Sch. 2 para. 6.
12	1973 Sch. 4 para. 10.
13	1973 Sch. 4 para. 11.
14, 15	1973 Sch. 4 paras. 11A, 11B (inserted by 1975 CJ Sch. 2 para. 1(4)).
16	1973 Sch. 4 para. 13A (inserted by 1976 Sch. 3 para. 8).
17	1973 Sch. 4 para. 13B (inserted by 1977 D art. 13(5)(*b*)).
18	1977 Sch. 4 para. 13C (inserted by 1977 AO).
19	1973 Sch. 4 para. 12; 1975 Sch. 2 para. 7.
Note 1	1973 Sch. 4 Note 1; 1975 Sch. 2 para. 8.
Note 2	1973 Sch. 4 Note 2; 1975 Sch. 2 para. 10; 1977 D art. 13(5)(*d*); 1977 AO.
Note 3	1973 Sch. 4 Note 3 (substituted by 1975 Sch. 2 para. 11).
Note 4	1973 Sch. 4 Note 4; 1975 Sch. 2 para. 12.
para. 20	1973 Sch. 4 para. 13.
21	1973 Sch. 4 para. 14 (inserted by 1975 CJ s. 4(1)); 1977 AO.
Sch. 5	Transitionals.
Sch. 6	Repeals.

NORTHERN IRELAND (EMERGENCY PROVISIONS) ACT 1978
(c. 5)

TABLE OF DESTINATIONS

Note: The abbreviations used in this Table are set out on page xcvi above.

Section of Act	Subject Matter	Section of 1978 Act	Remarks
	NORTHERN IRELAND (EMERGENCY PROVISIONS) ACT 1973 (c. 53)		
2(1)	Mode of trial on indictment of scheduled offences.	7(1)	
(2)	—	7(2)	
(3)	—	7(3)	Substituted: 1975 s. 3(1).
(4)–(7)	—	7(4)–(7)	
3(1)	Limitation of power to grant bail in case of scheduled offences.	2(1)	Substituted: 1975 s. 4(1).
(2)	—	2(2)	
(3)	—	2(3)	
(4)	—	2(4)	Repealed in part: 1975 Sch. 3.
(5)	—	2(5)	
(6)	—	2(6)	Inserted: 1975 s. 4(2).
4(1)	Court of trial for scheduled offences.	6(1)	Repealed in part: 1975 Sch. 3.
(2)	—	6(2)	Amended: 1975 s. 3(2); repealed in part: 1975 Sch. 3.
(3)	—	6(3)	Repealed in part: 1975 Sch. 3.
(4)	—	6(4)	
6(1)	Admissions by persons charged with scheduled offences.	8(1)	Amended: 1975 ss. 3(2), 8.
(2)	—	8(2)	
7	Onus of proof in relation to offences of possession.	9	Amended: 1975 s. 8.
8	Treatment of young persons convicted of scheduled offences.	10	
10(1)–(4)	Arrest and detention of terrorists.	11(1)–(4)	
(5)	—	—	Repealed: 1975 Sch. 3.
11	Constables' general power of arrest and seizure.	13	Applied: 1975 s. 22(1).
12	Powers of arrest of members of Her Majesty's forces.	14	
13	Power to search for munitions.	15	
14	Powers of explosives inspectors.	16	
15	Entry to search for persons unlawfully detained.	17	
16(1)	Power to stop and question.	18(1)	Amended: 1975 s. 10.
(2)	—	18(2)	

NORTHERN IRELAND (EMERGENCY PROVISIONS) ACT—*cont.*

Section of Act	Subject Matter	Section of 1978 Act	Remarks
	NORTHERN IRELAND (EMERGENCY PROVISIONS) ACT 1973—*continued*		
17	General powers of entry and interference with rights of property and with highways.	19	
18	Supplementary provisions.	20	Applied: 1975 s. 11(5).
19(1) (2)–(7)	Proscribed organisations. —	21(1) 21(2)–(8)	Amended: 1975 s. 12; 1977 s. 1. SI 1973, SI 1975.
20(1) (1A) (2) (3) (4)	Unlawful collection, etc. of information. — — — —	22(1)(4) 22(2) 22(5) 22(3) 22(6)	Substituted: 1975 s. 13; amended 1977 s. 1. Inserted: 1975 s. 13.
21	Failure to disperse when required to do so.	24	
23	Dressing or behaving in a public place like a member of unlawful organisation.	25	
24	Supplementary regulations for preserving the peace, etc.	27	
25	Provisions as to compensation.	28	Applied: 1975 s. 11(5); functions transferred to Secretary of State: S.I. 1973/2163.
26	Restriction of prosecutions.	29	
27(1) (2) (3)	The scheduled offences. — —	30(1) 30(2) 30(3)	Amended: 1975 CJ Sch. 2 para. 3(2). Substituted: 1975 CJ Sch. 2 para. 3(3).
28(1)	Interpretation.	31(1)	" enactment " amended: 1973 c. 36 Sch. 5 para. 1; " imitation firearm " and " offensive weapon " repealed: 1975 Sch. 3; " Ministry " unnecessary: S.I. 1973/2163.
29	Orders and regulations.	32	
30(1) (2) (3) (4) (5) (6) (7)	Commencement, duration, expiry and revival of Act. — — — — — —	33(1) 33(2) 33(3) 33(4) 33(5) 33(6)(7) 33(8)	Amended: 1975 CJ Sch. 2 para. 2(1). Provisions of Act continued S.I. 1977. Amended: 1975 s. 22(3). Impliedly repealed in part by repeal of 1973 s. 5. Repealed in part only. Amended: 1975 s. 6. Repealed in part only. Repealed in part: 1975 Sch. 3.

NORTHERN IRELAND (EMERGENCY PROVISIONS) ACT—*cont.*

Section of Act	Subject Matter	Section of 1978 Act	Remarks
	NORTHERN IRELAND (EMERGENCY PROVISIONS) ACT 1973—*continued*		
31(2)	Repeal of Special Powers Act etc.	—	Spent.
(3)	Other repeals.	—	Spent.
(5)	—	Sch. 5 para. 1(3)	
(7)	—	35(1)	Repealed in part only, as unnecessary for unrepealed provisions of 1973.
Sch. 2	Proscribed organisations.	Sch. 2	Amended: S.I. 1973, S.I. 1974, S.I. 1975.
Sch. 3	The Northern Ireland (Emergency Provisions) Regulations 1973.	Sch. 3	
Sch. 4	Scheduled offences.	Sch. 4	
para. 1	—	para. 1	
2	—	para. 2	
3	—	—	Repealed: 1977 Sch. 2.
4	—	para. 3	
4A	—	para. 4	Inserted: 1975 CJ Sch. 1 para. 1(2).
4B	—	para. 5	Inserted: 1975 CJ Sch. 2 1(2).
4C	—	para. 6	Inserted: 1975 Sch. 2 para. 2.
5	—	para. 7	Amended: 1975 CJ Sch. 2 para. 1(3), 1975 Sch. 2 para. 3, 1977 Sch. 2.
6	—	para. 8	Amended: 1975 Sch. 2 para. 4; 1977 AO.
7	—	para. 9	
7A	—	para. 10	Inserted: 1975 Sch. 2 para. 5.
8	—	—	Repealed: 1975 Sch. 3.
9	—	para. 11	Amended: 1975 Sch. 2 para. 6.
10	—	para. 12	
11	—	para. 13	
11A	—	para. 14	Inserted: 1975 CJ Sch. 2 para. 1(4).
11B	—	para. 15	Inserted: 1975 CJ Sch. 2 para. 1(4).
12	—	para. 19	
13	—	para. 19	Inserted: 1975 Sch. 2 para. 7.
13A	—	para. 16	Inserted: 1976 Sch. 3 para. . 8
13B	—	para. 17	Inserted: 1977 D art. 13(5)(*b*).
13C	—	para. 18	Inserted: 1977 AO.
NOTE		NOTE	
1	—	1	Amended: 1975 Sch. 2 para. 8.
1A	—	—	Repealed: 1977 Sch. 2.
2	—	2	Amended: 1975 Sch. 2 para. 10; 1977 AO.
3	—	3	Substituted: 1975 Sch. 2 para. 11.
4	—	4	Amended: 1975 Sch. 2 para. 12.
5	—	2	Inserted: 1977 D art. 13(5)(*d*); amended: 1977 AO.
para. 13	—	para. 20	Amended: 1977 AO.
14	—	para. 21	Inserted: 1975 CJ s. 4(1).
Sch. 5	Repeals.	—	Spent.

NORTHERN IRELAND (EMERGENCY PROVISIONS) ACT—*cont.*

Section of Act	Subject Matter	Section of 1978 Act	Remarks
	NORTHERN IRELAND (YOUNG PERSONS) ACT 1974 (c. 33)		
1(1)	Holding in custody of young persons charged with certain offences.	4(4)	
(2)	—	4(5), 31(1)	
(3)	—	4(1)	
(4)	—	4(2)	
(5)	—	4(3)	
(6)	—	31(1)	
2	Directions under s. 1.	5	
3(1)	Duration, expiry and revival of s. 1.	33(2)	Duration of s. 1 extended: S.I. 1977.
(2)	—	33(3)	Amended: 1975 s. 22(3).
(3)	—	32(1)	
(4)	—	32(3)	
(5)	—	32(4)	
4	Short title and extent.	36(2)	Part unnecessary.
	CRIMINAL JURISDICTION ACT 1975 (c. 59)		
4(1)	Insertion of Part III in 1973 Sch. 4.	Sch. 4 Part III	Repealed in part only.
Sch. 2 para. 1(1)	Amendment of 1973 Sch. 4.	—	Introductory.
(2)	—	Sch. 4 paras. 4, 5	
Sch. 2 para. 1(3)	—	Sch. 4 para. 7	
(4)	—	Sch. 4 paras. 14, 15	
2(1)	Duration of 1973 Sch. 4, Part III etc.	33(2)	
3(1)	Amendment of 1973 s. 27.	—	Introductory.
(2)	—	30(1)	
(3)	—	30(3)	
	NORTHERN IRELAND (EMERGENCY PROVISIONS) (AMENDMENT) ACT 1975 (c. 62)		
2	Preliminary enquiry into scheduled offences.	1	
3(1)	Trial of scheduled and non-scheduled offences together.	7(3)	
(2)	—	6(2), 8(1)	
4(1)	Removal of certain limitations to grant bail.	2(1)	
(2)	—	2(6)	

NORTHERN IRELAND (EMERGENCY PROVISIONS) ACT—*cont·*

Section of Act	Subject Matter	Section of 1978 Act	Remarks
	NORTHERN IRELAND (EMERGENCY PROVISIONS) (AMENDMENT) ACT 1975—*continued*		
5	Legal aid to applicants for bail.	3	
6(1)	Court of trial for scheduled offences.	—	Effected repeals in 1973 s. 4: spent.
(2)	—	33(5)	Repealed in part only.
8	Exclusion of summary proceedings from 1973 ss. 6, 7.	8(3), 9(5)	
9(1)	Detention of terrorists etc.	12(1)	
(3)	Repeal of 1973 Sch. 1.	—	Spent.
10	Power to stop and question.	18(1)	
11(1)	Power to search for radio transmitters.	15(1)	
(2)	—	15(2)	
(3)	—	15(3)	
(4)	—	15(4)	
(5)	—	20, 28	
(6)	—	15(5)	
12	Invitation to join etc. proscribed organisations.	21(1)	
13	Extension of classes of information in 1973 s. 20.	22(1)(2)(4)	Amended: 1977 AO.
14	Repeal of 1973 s. 22 (part) and declaratory provision.	—	Repealed in part only.
15	Training in making or use of firearms etc.	23	Amended: 1977 s. 1.
16	Wearing of hoods etc. in public places.	26	
17	Prosecutions.	29	
18	Amendments to list of scheduled offences.	—	Established Sch. 2.
19	Expenses.	—	Unnecessary.
21(1)	Commencement, duration, expiry, revival of certain provisions.	—	Commencement: unnecessary.
(2)	—	33(2)	
(3)	—	33(3)	
(4)	—	32(3)	
(5)	—	32(4)	
(6)	—	33(8)	
22(1)	Consequential amendments.	13	
(2)	—	—	Amendments consequential on repeal of 1973 Sch. 1: unnecessary.
(3)	—	33(3)	

NORTHERN IRELAND (EMERGENCY PROVISIONS) ACT—*cont.*

Section of Act etc.	Subject Matter	Section of 1978 Act	Remarks
NORTHERN IRELAND (EMERGENCY PROVISIONS) (AMENDMENT) ACT 1975—*continued*			
23(2)	Repeals.	—	Spent.
Sch. 1 Part I	Detention of terrorists.	Sch. 1	
Sch. 2	Amendments of Part I of 1973 Sch. 4.		
para. 1	—	—	Introductory: unnecessary.
2	—	Sch. 4 para. 6	
3	—	—	Repealed: 1977 Sch. 2.
4	—	para. 8(*a*)	
5	—	para. 10	
6	—	para. 11	
7	—	para. 18	
8	—	Note 1	
9	—	—	Repealed: 1977 Sch. 2.
10	—	Note 2	
11	—	Note 3	
12	—	Note 4	
Sch. 3	Repeals.	—	Spent.
PREVENTION OF TERRORISM (TEMPORARY PROVISIONS) ACT 1976 (c. 8)			
Sch. 3 para. 8	Insertion of para. 13A in 1973 Sch. 4.	Sch. 4 para. 16	Repealed in part only.
CRIMINAL DAMAGE (NORTHERN IRELAND) ORDER 1977 (S.I. 1977/426 (N.I. 4))			
Art. 13(5)(*b*)	Insertion of para. 13B in 1973 Sch. 4.	Sch. 4 para. 17	
13(5)(*d*)	Insertion of Note 5 in 1973 Sch. 4.	Sch. 4 Note 2.	
NORTHERN IRELAND (EMERGENCY PROVISIONS) (AMENDMENT) ACT 1977 (c. 34)			
1	Increase in penalties under 1973 ss. 19, 20, 1975 s. 15.	21(1), 22(4), 23(1)	
	Short title etc.	—	Unnecessary.
ORDERS			
NORTHERN IRELAND (EMERGENCY PROVISIONS) ACT PROSCRIBED ORGANISATIONS (AMENDMENT) ORDER 1973 (S.I. 1973/1880)			
Art. 1	Short title etc.	—	Unnecessary.
2	Addition of UFF, Red Hand Commando to 1973 Sch. 2.	Sch. 2	

NORTHERN IRELAND (EMERGENCY PROVISIONS) ACT—*cont.*

Section of Act etc.	Subject Matter	Section of 1978 Act	Remarks
NORTHERN IRELAND (EMERGENCY PROVISIONS) ACT 1973 (AMENDMENT) ORDER 1974 (S.I. 1974/864)			
Art. 3	Removal of Sinn Fein, UVF from 1973 Sch. 2.	—	Repealed in part only.
NORTHERN IRELAND (EMERGENCY PROVISIONS) ACT 1973 (CONTINUANCE) ORDER 1974 (S.I. 1974/1212)			
—	Continuance of temporary provisions in 1973.	33(2)	
NORTHERN IRELAND (VARIOUS EMERGENCY PROVISIONS) (CONTINUANCE) ORDER 1974 (S.I. 1974/2162)			
—	Continuance of temporary provisions.	33(2)	
NORTHERN IRELAND (VARIOUS EMERGENCY PROVISIONS) (CONTINUANCE) ORDER 1975 (S.I. 1975/1059)			
—	Continuance of temporary provisions.	33(2)	
NORTHERN IRELAND (EMERGENCY PROVISIONS) ACT 1973 (AMENDMENT) ORDER 1975 (S.I. 1975/1609)			
Art. 1	Short title etc.	—	Unnecessary.
2	Interpretation.	—	Unnecessary.
3	Addition of UVF to 1973 Sch. 2.	Sch. 2	
NORTHERN IRELAND (VARIOUS EMERGENCY PROVISIONS) (CONTINUANCE) (No. 2) ORDER 1975 (S.I. 1975/2214)			
—	Continuance of temporary provisions.	33(2)	
NORTHERN IRELAND (VARIOUS EMERGENCY PROVISIONS) (CONTINUANCE) ORDER 1976 (S.I. 1976/1090)			
—	Continuance of temporary provisions.	33(2)	
NORTHERN IRELAND (VARIOUS EMERGENCY PROVISIONS) (CONTINUANCE) (No. 2) ORDER 1976 (S.I. 1976/2238)			
—	Continuance of temporary provisions.	33(2)	
NORTHERN IRELAND (VARIOUS EMERGENCY PROVISIONS) (CONTINUANCE) (No. 2) ORDER 1977 (S.I. 1977/2142)			
—	Continuance of temporary provisions.	33(2)	

NORTHERN IRELAND (EMERGENCY PROVISIONS) ACT—*cont.*

Section of Act etc.	Subject matter	Section of 1978 Act	Remarks
	NORTHERN IRELAND (EMERGENCY PROVISIONS) ACT 1973 (AMENDMENT) ORDER 1977 (S.I. 1977/1265)		
Art. 1	Short title etc.	—	Unnecessary.
2	Interpretation.	—	Unnecessary.
3	Amendment of 1973 Sch. 4 paras. 6, 13, 13C, notes 2, 5.	Sch. 4 paras. 8, 18, 20, note 2 Sch. 5 para. 5	

OATHS ACT 1978 (c. 19)

TABLE OF DERIVATIONS

Note:—The following abbreviations are used in this Table:—

1838 = The Oaths Act 1838
(1 & 2 Vict. c. 105)

1888 = The Oaths Act 1888
(51 & 52 Vict. c. 46.)

1909 = The Oaths Act 1909
(9 Edw. 7 c. 39)

1961 = The Oaths Act 1961
(9 & 10 Eliz. 2 c. 21)

1977 = The Administration of Justice Act 1977
(1977 c. 38).

Section of 1978 Act	Derivation
1	1909 ss. 1–3.
2	[Consequential amendments.]
3	1888 s. 5.
4(1)	1838.
(2)	1888 s. 3.
5(1)	1888 s. 1; 1977 s. 8(1).
(2), (3)	1961 s. 1(1), (2).
(4)	1888 s. 1; 1977 s. 8(1).
6(1)	1888 s. 2.
(2)	1888 s. 4.
7	[Repeals and savings.]
8	[Short title, extent and commencement.]
Sch.	[Enactments repealed.]

OATHS ACT 1978 (c. 19)

TABLE OF DESTINATIONS

The abbreviations used in this Table are set out on page cvii above.

Section of Act	Subject matter	Section of 1978 Act	Remarks
	THE OATHS ACT 1838 (1 & 2 Vict. c. 105)		
[1]	All persons to be bound by an oath administered in the form &c. which such persons may declare binding.	4(1)	Rep. in part by Perjury Act 1911 s. 17 and False Oaths (Scotland) Act 1933 s. 8, Sch.
	THE OATHS ACT 1888 (51 & 52 Vict. c. 46)		
1	When affirmation may be made instead of oath.	5(1), (4)	A new section substituted by 1977 s. 8.
2	Form of affirmation.	6(1)	
3	Validity of oath not affected by absence of religious belief.	4(2)	
4	Form of affirmation in writing.	6(2)	
5	Swearing with uplifted hand.	3	
6	Repeals.	—	Repealed Statute Law Revision Act 1908 (c. 49).
7	Short Title.	—	
Sch.	Repeals.	—	Repealed Statute Law Revision Act 1908 (c. 49).
	THE OATHS ACT 1909 (9 Edw. 7. c. 39)		
1	Short Title.	—	
2(1)	Manner of administration of oaths.	1(1)	
(2)	—	1(2), (3)	
3	Definition.	1(4)	
4	Extent.	—	Repealed in part Statute Law Revision Act 1909.
	THE OATHS ACT 1961 (9 & 10 Eliz. 2. c. 21)		
1(1), (2)	Making of affirmations instead of oaths.	5(2), (3)	
(3)	—	—	See section 7(4), (5).
2	Short title, citation and extent.	—	

OATHS ACT—*cont.*

Section of Act	Subject matter	Section of 1978 Act	Remarks
	THE ADMINISTRATION OF JUSTICE ACT 1977 (1977 c. 38)		
8(1)	Oaths and affirmations.	5(1), (4)	
(2)	—	—	See Section 8(3).
(3)	—	—	
32(2)	Citation.	—	

REFUSE DISPOSAL (AMENITY) ACT 1978 (c. 3)

Note: The following abbreviations are used in this Table:—

1967	=	Civic Amenities Act 1967 (c. 69).
1969	=	Vehicle and Driving Licences Act 1969 (c. 27).
1971	=	Town and Country Planning Act 1971 (c. 78).
1972(S)	=	Town and Country Planning (Scotland) Act 1972 (c. 52).
1972	=	Local Government Act 1972 (c. 70).
1973	=	Local Government (Scotland) Act 1973 (c. 65).
1974	=	Control of Pollution Act 1974 (c. 40).

This Table does not acknowledge the transfer of the functions of the Minister of Housing and Local Government and the Minister of Transport to the Secretary of State (Secretary of State for the Environment Order 1970, S.I. 1970/1681).

Section of 1978 Act	Derivation
1(1)–(3)	1967 s. 18(1)–(3).
(4)	1967 s. 18(4); 1972 Sch. 30.
(5), (6)	1967 s. 18(5).
(7)	1967 s. 18(6); 1972 Sch. 14 para. 45.
(8)	1967 s. 18(1); 1974 Sch. 3 para. 25(1).
2	1967 s. 19.
3(1)–(3)	1967 s. 20(1), (2).
(4)	1967 s. 20(7)(*a*).
(5), (6)	1967 s. 20(3), (4).
(7)	1967 s. 20(4A); 1972 Sch. 19 para. 33(1).
(8)	1967 s. 20(5); 1972 Sch. 19 para. 33(2).
(9)	1967 s. 20(6).
4(1)	1967 s. 21(1); 1972 Sch. 19 para. 34.
(2)	1969 s. 29(3).
(3)–(7)	1967 s. 21(2)–(5).
(8)	1967 s. 21(1); 1972 Sch. 19 para. 34.
5(1)–(3)	1967 s. 22(1), (2).
(4), (5)	1967 s. 22(3); 1972 Sch. 19 para. 35.
(6)	1967 s. 22(4).
6(1), (2)	1967 s. 23(1), (2).
(3)	1967 s. 23(3); 1972 Sch. 30.
(4), (5)	1967 s. 23(4).
(6)	1967 s. 23(5).
(7)	1967 s. 23(6).
(8)	1974 Sch. 3 para. 25(2), Sch. 4.
7	1967 s. 24; 1972 Sch. 19 para. 36.
8(1)	1967 s. 28(1); 1971 Sch. 25; 1972(S) Sch. 23.
(2), (3)	1967 s. 28(2), (3); 1971 Sch. 23 Pt. II.
(4)	1967 s. 28(4); 1972(S) Sch. 21 Pt. II.
9	1967 s. 29(1).

REFUSE DISPOSAL (AMENITY) ACT—*cont.*

Section of 1978 Act	Derivation
10(1), (2)	1967 ss. 27(2), 29(2).
(3)	1974 s. 109(2)(*b*).
(4), (5)	1967 ss. 27(3), 29(2); 1969 s. 34(1); 1974 s. 104(1).
11(1)	1967 ss. 27(1), 30(1); 1972 Sch. 30; 1973 Sch. 27 Pt. II para. 169.
(2)	1967 s. 30(2).
12	—
13(1), (2)	—
(3), (4)	1969 s. 38(2); 1974 s. 109(2)(*a*).
(5)	1967 s. 32(3).
Sch. 1	—
Sch. 2	—

REFUSE DISPOSAL (AMENITY) ACT 1978 (c. 3)

TABLE OF DESTINATIONS

Note: The abbreviations used in this Table are as set out on page cx above, and in addition—

1975 = Airports Authority Act 1975 (c. 78)

This Table does not acknowledge the transfer of the functions of the Minister of Housing and Local Government and the Minister of Transport to the Secretary of State (Secretary of State for the Environment Order 1970, S.I. 1970/1681).

Section of Act	Subject Matter	Section of 1978 Act	Remarks
	CIVIC AMENITIES ACT 1967 (c. 69)		
18(1)	Provision of refuse dumps.	1(1), (8)	Amended 1974 Sch. 3 para. 25(1).
(2), (3)	—	1(2), (3)	
(4)	—	1(4)	Repealed in part (England and Wales) 1972 Sch. 30; superseded in part (Scotland) 1973 s. 56(5).
(5)	—	1(5), (6)	
(6)	—	1(7)	Amended 1972 Sch. 14 para. 45.
(7)	—	—	Repealed in part 1973 Sch. 29; remainder spent.
(8)	—	—	Repealed 1973 Sch. 29.
(9)	—	—	Repealed in part 1973 Sch. 29; remainder spent.
19	Penalty for unauthorised dumping.	2	
20(1), (2)	Removal of abandoned vehicles.	3(1)–(3)	Applied 1975 s. 14(1).
(3), (4)	—	3(5), (6)	
(4A)	—	3(7)	Added 1972 Sch. 19 para. 33(1).
(5)	—	3(8)	Amended 1972 Sch. 19 para. 33(2).
(6)	—	3(9)	
(7)	—	3(4)	Para. (*b*) unnecessary.
(8), (9)	—	—	Spent.
21(1)	Disposal of removed vehicles.	4(1), (8)	Applied 1975 s. 14(1); amended 1969 s. 29(3), 1972 Sch. 19 para. 34.
(2)–(5)	—	4(3)–(7)	
(6)	—	—	Unnecessary.
22(1), (2)	Recovery of expenses connected with removed vehicles.	5(1)–(3)	Applied 1975 s. 14(1).
(3)	—	5(4), (5)	Amended 1972 Sch. 19 para. 35.
(4)	—	5(6)	

REFUSE DISPOSAL (AMENITY) ACT—*cont.*

Section of Act	Subject Matter	Section of 1978 Act	Remarks
	CIVIC AMENITIES ACT 1967—*continued*		
23(1)	Removal and disposal etc. of other refuse.	6(1)	
(2)	—	6(2)	Part unnecessary.
(3)	—	6(3), (8)	Repealed in part 1972 Sch. 30; substituted 1974 Sch. 3 para. 25(2).
(4)	—	6(4), (5)	
(5)	—	6(6)	
(6)	—	6(7), (8)(*b*)	Repealed in part 1974 Sch. 4.
24	Acquisition of land.	7	Amended 1972 Sch. 19 para. 36.
27(1)	Interpretation etc.	11(1)	Repealed in part 1972 Sch. 30; amended 1973 Sch. 27 Pt. II para. 169; part unnecessary.
(2)	—	10(1), (2)	
(3)	—	10(4), (5)	
28(1)	Rights of entry etc.	8(1)	Applied 1975 s. 14(1); repealed in part 1971 Sch. 25, 1972(S) Sch. 23; para. (*b*) spent.
(2)	—	8(2)	Amended 1971 Sch. 23 Pt. II.
(3)	—	8(3)	Amended 1971 Sch. 23 Pt. II; part unnecessary.
(4)	—	8(4)	Amended 1972(S) Sch. 21 Pt. II; para. (*a*) unnecessary—local planning authorities irrelevant to Bill; provisions in para. (*b*) relating to disputed compensation superseded in part 1972(S) s. 266(5), remainder spent.
30(1) the definitions of " the Common Council ", " local authority ", " local planning authority " and ' owner ".	Interpretation.	11(1)	Definitions of " local authority ", " local planning authority " and " owner " spent.
	VEHICLE AND DRIVING LICENCES ACT 1969 (c. 27)		
29(3)	Amendment of 1967 s. 21(1).	4(2)	
	TOWN AND COUNTRY PLANNING ACT 1971 (c. 78)		
Sch. 23, in Pt. II the entry relating to 1967 s. 28.	Amendment of 1967 s. 28.	8(2), (3)	

REFUSE DISPOSAL (AMENITY) ACT—*cont.*

Section of Act	Subject Matter	Section of 1978 Act	Remarks
	TOWN AND COUNTRY PLANNING (SCOTLAND) ACT 1972 (c. 52)		
Sch. 21, in Pt. II the entry relating to 1967 s. 28(4).	Amendment of 1967 s. 28(4).	8(4)	
	LOCAL GOVERNMENT ACT 1972 (c. 70)		
186(2)	Local authority functions.	—	
Sch. 14, para. 45	Amendment of 1967 s. 18(6).	1(7)	
Sch. 19, para. 33	Amendment of 1967 ss. 20–22 and 24.	3(7), (8)	
34	—	4(1), (8)	
35	—	5(4), (5)	
36	—	7	
	LOCAL GOVERNMENT (SCOTLAND) ACT 1973 (c. 65)		
Sch. 27, in Pt. II,	Amendment of 1967 ss. 27(1) and 30(1).		
para. 169	—	11(1)	
para. 170	—	—	Spent.
	CONTROL OF POLLUTION ACT 1974 (c. 40)		
Sch. 3, para. 25(1)	Amendment of 1967 ss. 18 and 23.	1(8)	
25(2)	—	6(8)	

TABLE VI

Effect of Legislation

Acts and Measures (in chronological order)
repealed, amended or otherwise affected
by those Acts, Measures and Statutory Instruments
which received the Royal Assent or were made during 1978

LIST OF ABBREVIATIONS

am.	... ...	amended	mod.	modified
appl.	... ...	applied	(mods.) ...	with modifications
C.A.M. ...	...	Church Assembly Measure	(prosp.) ...	prospectively
cont.	... ...	continued	rep.	repealed
excl.	... ...	excluded	restr.	restricted
expld.	... ...	explained	(retrosp.)	retrospectively
ext.	... ...	extended	S.I.	Statutory Instrument
G.S.M. ...	...	General Synod Measure	S.L.(R.) ...	Statute Law (Repeals)
incorp. ...	...	incorporated	subst.	substituted

Session and Chap. or No. of Measure	Short title or Subject	How affected	Chapter of 1978 Act or number of Measure or Statutory Instrument
Statutes of uncertain date	Of the King's Prerogative [Crown grants].	Chapter 17 rep. (N.I.) ...	S.I. No. 459.
9 Hen. 5, St. 2: c. 11	Repair of roads and bridges between Abingdon and Dorchester [1421].	Rep.	45, S.L. (R.), s. 1(1), sch. 1 Pt. XI.
11 Hen. 7: c. 34	Lands assured to Prince of Wales [1495].	Rep.	45, S.L. (R.), s. 1(1), sch. 1 Pt. IV.
c. 35	Lands assured to Duke of York [1495].	Rep.	45, S.L. (R.), s. 1(1), sch. 1 Pt. XIV.
c. 36	Estates of Duchess of Bedford [1495].	Rep.	45, S.L. (R.), s. 1(1), sch. 1 Pt. XIV.
c. 37	Estates of Marquis of Dorset and wife [1495].	Rep.	45, S.L. (R.), s. 1(1), sch. 1 Pt. XIV.
c. 39	Estates of Earl of Suffolk [1495].	Rep.	45, S.L. (R.), s. 1(1), sch. 1 Pt. XIV.
c. 40	Estates of Earl of Surrey [1495].	Rep.	45, S.L. (R.), s. 1(1), sch. 1 Pt. XIV.
12 Hen. 7: c. 8	Feoffments made by the King [1496].	Rep.	45, S.L. (R.), s. 1(1), sch. 1 Pt. XIV.

Session and Chap. or No. of Measure	Short title or Subject	How affected				Chapter of 1978 Act or number of Measure or Statutory Instrument
19 Hen. 7:						
c. 26	Prince of Wales [1503].	Rep.	...	...	...	45, S.L. (R.), s. 1(1), sch. 1 Pt. XIV.
c. 29	Monastery of Syon [1503]	Rep.	...	...	...	45, S.L. (R.), s. 1(1), sch. 1 Pt. XIV.
c. 30	Partition of Lands: Barkley and Earl of Surrey [1503].	Rep.	...	...	...	45, S.L. (R.), s. 1(1), sch. 1 Pt. XIV.
c. 33	Estates of Lord Wells [1503].	Rep.	...	...	...	45, S.L. (R.), s. 1(1), sch. 1 Pt. XIV.
3 Hen. 8:						
c. 16	Estates of Earl of Surrey [1511].	Rep.	...	...	...	45, S.L. (R.), s. 1(1), sch. 1 Pt. XIV.
c. 18	Grant to William Compton [1511].	Rep.	...	...	...	45, S.L. (R.), s. 1(1), sch. 1 Pt. XIV.
4 Hen. 8:						
c. 10	Grant to Earl and Countess of Devon [1512].	Rep.	...	...	...	45, S.L. (R.), s. 1(1), sch. 1 Pt. XIV.
c. 11	Countess of Devon and Hugh Conway [1512].	Rep.	...	...	...	45, S.L. (R.), s. 1(1), sch. 1 Pt. XIV.
c. 12	Countess of Devon and William Knyvett [1512].	Rep.	...	...	...	45, S.L. (R.), s. 1(1), sch. 1 Pt. XIV.
c. 13	Estates of Earl of Surrey [1512].	Rep.	...	...	...	45, S.L. (R.), s. 1(1), sch. 1 Pt. XIV.
5 Hen. 8:						
c. 9	Creation of Duke of Norfolk [1513].	Rep.	...	...	...	45, S.L. (R.), s. 1(1), sch. 1 Pt. XIV.
c. 10	Creation of Duke of Suffolk [1513].	Rep.	...	...	...	45, S.L. (R.), s. 1(1), sch. 1 Pt. XIV.
c. 11	Creation of Earl of Surrey [1513].	Rep.	...	...	...	45, S.L. (R.), s. 1(1), sch. 1 Pt. XIV.
c. 14	Dowry of Countess of Oxford [1513].	Rep.	...	...	...	45, S.L. (R.), s. 1(1), sch. 1 Pt. XIV.
c. 18	Sir Edward Poynyngs [1513]	Rep.	...	...	...	45, S.L. (R.), s. 1(1), sch. 1 Pt. XIV
6 Hen. 8:						
c. 19	Grant to Duke of Norfolk [1514].	Rep.	...	...	...	45, S.L. (R.), s. 1(1), sch. 1 Pt. XIV.
c. 20	Letters patent to Duke of Suffolk [1514].	Rep.	...	...	...	45 S.L. (R.), s. 1(1), sch. 1 Pt. XIV.
c. 23	Assurance of Manor of Hanworth [1514].	Rep.	...	...	...	45, S.L. (R), s. 1(1), sch. 1 Pt. XIV.

Session and Chap. or No. of Measure	Short title or Subject	How affected	Chapter of 1978 Act or number of Measure or Statutory Instrument
14 & 15 Hen. 8:			
c. 18	Royal Manor of Beaulieu [1523].	Rep.	45, S.L. (R), s. s. 1(1), sch. Pt. XIV.
c. 24	Sale of land to Sir William Compton [1523].	Rep.	45, S.L. (R), s. 1(1), sch. 1 Pt. XIV.
c. 25	Sale of land to Thomas Kitson [1523].	Rep.	45, S.L. (R), s. 1(1), sch. 1 Pt XIV.
c. 26	Sale of land to Sir Richard Sacheverell [1523].	Rep.	45, S.L. (R), s. 1(1), sch. 1 Pt. XIV.
c. 27	Grant to Lord Marny [1523].	Rep.	45, S.L. (R), s. 1(1), sch. 1 Pt. XIV.
c. 30	Grant to Earl of Northumberland [1523].	Rep.	45, S.L. (R), s. 1(1), sch. 1 Pt. XIV.
c. 31	Grants to Sir Andrew Windsor and Anthony Windsor [1523].	Rep.	45, S.L. (R), s. 1(1), sch. 1 Pt. XIV.
c. 33	Grant to Earl of Shrewsbury [1523].	Rep.	45, S.L. (R), s. 1(1), sch. 1 Pt. XIV.
c. 34	Jointure of Elizabeth Talboys [1523].	Rep.	45, S.L. (R), s. 1(1), sch. 1 Pt. XIV.
21 Hen. 8:			
c. 22	Assurance to Duke of Norfolk [1529].	Rep.	45, S.L. (R), s. 1(1), sch. 1 Pt. XIV.
c. 26	Assurance of Duchess of Norfolk [1529].	Rep.	45, S.L. (R), s. 1(1), sch. 1 Pt. XIV.
22 Hen. 8:			
c. 17	Duke of Richmond [1530]	Rep.	45, S.L. (R), s. 1(1), sch. 1 Pt. XIV.
c. 19	Assurance to heirs of Sir William Fyloll [1530].	Rep.	45, S.L. (R), s. 1(1), sch. 1 Pt. XIV.
c. 21	Exchange between King and heirs of Lord Montague [1530].	Rep.	45, S.L. (R), s. 1(1), sch. 1 Pt. XIV.
c. 22	Annuities granted out of Bishopric of Winchester [1530].	Rep.	45, S.L. (R), s. 1(1), sch. 1 Pt. XIV.
c. 23	Jointure of Countess of Derby [1530].	Rep.	45, S.L. (R), s. 1(1), sch. 1 Pt. XIV.
23 Hen. 8:			
c. 8	Maintenance of ports in Devon and Cornwall [1531].	Rep.	45, S.L. (R), s. 1(1), sch. 1 Pt. X.
c. 21	Exchange of lands, King and Abbot of Westminster [1531].	Rep.	45, S.L. (R), s. 1(1), sch. 1 Pt. XIV.

Session and Chap. or No. of Measure	Short title or Subject	How affected	Chapter of 1978 Act or number of Measure or Statutory Instrument
23 Hen. 8:—*cont.*			
c. 22	Exchange of lands, King and Christ's College Cambridge [1531].	Rep.	45, S.L. (R), s. 1(1), sch. 1 Pt. XIV.
c. 23	Exchange of lands, King and Abbot of Waltham [1531].	Rep.	45, S.L. (R), s. 1(1), sch. 1 Pt. XIV.
c. 24	Exchange of lands, King and Provost of Eton [1531].	Rep.	45, S.L. (R), s. 1(1), sch. 1 Pt. XIV.
c. 25	Exchange of lands, King and Abbot of St. Albans [1531].	Rep.	45, S.L. (R), s. 1(1), sch. 1 Pt. XIV.
c. 26	Exchange of lands, King and Prior of St. John of Jerusalem. [1531].	Rep.	45, S.L. (R.), s. 1(1), sch. 1 Pt. XIV
c. 27	Exchange of lands, King and Prior of Sheene [1531].	Rep.	45, S.L. (R.), s. 1(1), sch. 1 Pt. XIV.
c. 28	Exchange of lands, King, Duke of Richmond and Lord Lumley [1531].	Rep.	45, S.L. (R.), s. 1(1), sch. 1 Pt. XIV.
c. 29	Lands of Earl of Surrey [1531].	Rep.	45, S.L. (R.), s. 1(1), sch. 1 Pt. XIV.
c. 30	Manor of Hunsdon [1531].	Rep.	45, S.L. (R.), s. 1(1), sch. 1 Pt. XIV.
c. 31	Jointure of Countess of Wiltshire [1531].	Rep.	45, S.L. (R.), s. 1(1), sch. 1 Pt. XIV.
c. 32	Award to heirs of Earl of Oxford [1531].	Rep.	45, S.L. (R.), s. 1(1), sch. 1 Pt. XIV.
c. 33	Jointure of Dowager Countess of Oxford and Countess of Oxford [1531].	Rep.	45, S.L. (R.), s. 1(1), sch. 1 Pt. XIV.
24 Hen. 8:			
c. 14	Lands of Walter Walsh [1532].	Rep.	45, S.L. (R.), s. 1(1), sch. 1 Pt. XIV.
25 Hen. 8:			
c. 23	Town of Plymouth [1533].	Rep.	45, S.L. (R.), s. 1(1), sch. 1 Pt. XIV.
c. 24	Exchange of lands, Duke of Norfolk and Earl of Oxford [1533].	Rep.	45, S.L. (R.), s. 1(1), sch. 1 Pt. XIV.
c. 26	Exchange of lands, King and Abbot of Waltham [1533]	Rep.	45, S.L. (R.), s. 1(1), sch. 1 Pt. XIV.
c. 30	Exchange between King, Duke of Richmond and Lord Lumley [1533].	Rep.	45. S.L. (R.), s. 1(1), sch. 1 Pt. XIV.
c. 31	Assurance of Manor of Pyssowe [1533].	Rep.	45, S.L. (R.), s. 1(1), sch. 1 Pt. XIV.

Session and Chap. or No. of Measure	Short title or Subject	How affected	Chapter of 1978 Act or number of Measure or Statutory Instrument
25 Hen. 8:—*cont.*			
c. 33	Assurance of Christchurch, London to the King [1533].	Rep.	45, S.L. (R.), s. 1(1), sch. 1 Pt. XIV.
26 Hen. 8:			
c. 14	Suffragan Bishops Act 1534.	Ss. 2 rep in pt (saving), 4 rep. in pt., 6 am.	G.S.M. No. 1 s. 15.
c. 20	Assurance of lands to Duke of Norfolk [1534].	Rep.	45, S.L. (R.), s. 1(1), sch. 1 Pt. XIV.
c. 21	Assurance of lands to Duke of Richmond [1534].	Rep.	45, S.L. (R.), s. 1(1), sch. 1 Pt. XIV.
c. 24	Exchange, King and Abbot of Waltham [1534].	Rep.	45, S.L. (R.), s. 1(1), sch. 1 Pt. XIV.
27 Hen. 8:			
c. 23	Preservation of ports in Devon and Cornwall [1535].	Rep.	45, S.L. (R.), s. 1(1), sch. 1 Pt. X.
c. 29	Assurance of Manor of Grenes Norton [1535].	Rep.	45, S.L. (R.), s. 1(1), sch. 1 Pt. XIV.
c. 30	Jointure of Lady Elizabeth Vaux [1535].	Rep.	45, S.L. (R.), s. 1(1), sch. 1 Pt. XIV.
c. 31	Lands of Lord Audley [1535].	Rep.	45, S.L. (R.), s. 1(1), sch. 1 Pt. XIV.
c. 32	Agreement, Earl of Rutland and City of York [1535].	Rep.	45, S.L. (R.), s. 1(1), sch. 1 Pt. XIV.
c. 33	Exchange of lands, King, Duke of Norfolk and Prior of Thetford [1535].	Rep.	45, S.L. (R.), s. 1(1), sch. 1 Pt. XIV.
c. 34	Exchange of lands, King and Archbishop of Canterbury [1535].	Rep.	45, S.L. (R.), s. 1(1), sch. 1 Pt. XIV.
c. 36	Jointure of Lady Clifford [1535].	Rep.	45, S.L. (R.), s. 1(1), sch. 1 Pt. XIV.
c. 37	Pardon to Duke of Suffolk [1535].	Rep.	45, S.L. (R.), s. 1(1), sch. 1 Pt. XIV.
c. 38	Exchange of lands, King, Duke of Suffolk and Earl of Northumberland [1535].	Rep.	45, S.L. (R.), s. 1(1), sch. 1 Pt. XIV.
c. 39	Assurance of lands to King and Duke of Suffolk [1535].	Rep.	45, S.L. (R.), s. 1(1), sch. 1 Pt. XIV.
c. 40	Agreement, Duke of Suffolk and Sir Christopher Willoughby [1535].	Rep.	45, S.L. (R.), s. 1(1), sch. 1 Pt. XIV.
c. 43	Award, Sir Piers Dutton and others [1535].	Rep.	45, S.L. (R.), s. 1(1), sch. 1 Pt. XIV.

Session and Chap. or No. of Measure	Short title or Subject	How affected	Chapter of 1978 Act or number of Measure or Statutory Instrument
27 Hen. 8:—*cont.*			
c. 44	Partition of lands between the heirs of Lord Broke [1535].	Rep.	45, S.L. (R.), s. 1(1), sch. 1 Pt. XIV.
c. 45	Assurance to King of temporalities of see of Norwich [1535].	Rep.	45, S.L. (R.), s. 1(1), sch. 1 Pt. XIV.
c. 46	Partition of lands, Lord Thomas Howard and Sir Thomas Poynyngs [1535].	Rep.	45, S.L. (R.), s. 1(1), sch. 1 Pt. XIV.
c. 47	Assurance to King of land of Earl of Northumberland [1535].	Rep.	45, S.L. (R.), s. 1(1), sch. 1 Pt. XIV.
c. 48	Assurance of lands to Lord Chancellor Audley [1535].	Rep.	45, S.L. (R.), s. 1(1), sch. 1 Pt. XIV.
c. 49	Assurance of lands in Cheape to City of London [1535].	Rep.	45, S.L. (R.), s. 1(1), sch. 1 Pt. XIV.
c. 50	Assurance of Manor of Halyng to King [1535].	Rep.	45, S.L. (R.), s. 1(1), sch. 1 Pt. XIV.
c. 51	Assurance of Manor of Collyweston to Queen [1535].	Rep.	45, S.L. (R.), s. 1(1), sch. 1 Pt. XIV.
c. 52	Exchange of lands, King and Corpus Christi College, Oxford [1535].	Rep.	45, S.L. (R.), s. 1(1), sch. 1 Pt. XIV.
c. 53	Exchange of lands, King and Prior of Marten Abbey [1535].	Rep.	45, S.L. (R.), s. 1(1), sch. 1 Pt. XIV.
c. 54	Assurance of lands to Sir Arthur Darcy [1535].	Rep.	45, S.L. (R.), s. 1(1), sch. 1 Pt. XIV.
c. 55	Assurance of lands to Anne Fitzwilliam [1535].	Rep.	45, S.L. (R.), s. 1(1), sch. 1 Pt. XIV.
c. 56	Assurance of lands to Lord William Howard [1535].	Rep.	45, S.L. (R.), s. 1(1), sch. 1 Pt. XIV.
c. 57	Assurance of lands to Thomas Pope [1535].	Rep.	45, S.L. (R.), s. 1(1), sch. 1 Pt. XIV.
c. 58	Annulment of feoffment by Sir Thomas More [1535].	Rep.	45, S.L. (R.), s. 1(1), sch. 1 Pt. XIV.
c. 61	Assurance of Manor of Bromhill to King [1535].	Rep.	45, S.L. (R.), s. 1(1), sch. 1 Pt. XIV.
28 Hen. 8:			
c. 19	Assurance of lands of St. Saviour's, Bermondsey to King [1536].	Rep.	45, S.L. (R.), s. 1(1), sch. 1 Pt. XIV.
c. 20	Assurance of lands to Dame Grace Parker [1536].	Rep.	45, S.L. (R.), s. 1(1), sch. 1 Pt. XIV.
c. 21	Exchange of lands, King and Prior of St. John of Jerusalem [1536].	Rep.	45, S.L. (R.), s. 1(1), sch. 1 Pt. XIV.

Session and Chap. or No. of Measure	Short title or Subject	How affected	Chapter of 1978 Act or number of Measure or Statutory Instrument
28 Hen. 8:—*cont.*			
c. 22	Assurance of lands of Earl of Warwick to King [1536].	Rep.	45, S.L. (R.), s. 1(1), sch. 1 Pt. XIV.
c. 25	Assurance of lands to Lord Beauchamp [1536].	Rep.	45, S.L. (R.), s. 1(1), sch. 1 Pt. XIV.
c. 26	Assurance of lands at Kew to Lord Beauchamp [1536].	Rep.	45, S.L. (R.), s. 1(1), sch. 1 Pt. XIV.
c. 28	Assurance of Richard's Castle to John Onley [1536].	Rep.	45, S.L. (R.), s. 1(1), sch. 1 Pt. XIV.
c. 29	Exchange of lands, King and Abbot of Westminster [1536].	Rep.	45, S.L. (R.), s. 1(1), sch. 1 Pt. XIV.
c. 30	Assurance of Stanton Barrey to King [1536].	Rep.	45, S.L. (R.), s. 1(1), sch. 1 Pt. XIV.
c. 32	Assurance of lands to King from Sir William Essex and others [1536].	Rep.	45, S.L. (R.), s. 1(1), sch. 1 Pt. XIV.
c. 33	Exchange, King and Bishop of Durham [1536].	Rep.	45, S.L. (R.), s. 1(1), sch. 1 Pt. XIV.
c. 34	Assurance of Baynard's Castle to Duke of Richmond [1536].	Rep.	45, S.L. (R.), s. 1(1), sch. 1 Pt. XIV.
c. 35	Exchange of lands, King and Lord Sandys [1536].	Rep.	45, S.L. (R.), s. 1(1), sch. 1 Pt. XIV
c. 36	Award, Sir Adrian Fortescue and Sir Walter Stonor [1536].	Rep.	45, S.L. (R.), s. 1(1), sch. 1 Pt. XIV.
c. 37	Marriage of Richard Devereux [1536].	Rep.	45, S.L. (R.), s. 1(1), sch. 1 Pt. XIV.
c. 38	Assurance of Manors of Southwark and Paris Garden to Queen [1536].	Rep.	45, S.L. (R.), s. 1(1), sch. 1 Pt. XIV.
c. 39	Assurance of lands of Earldom of March to King [1536].	Rep.	45, S.L. (R.), s. 1(1), sch. 1 Pt. XIV.
c. 40	Assurance of Manor of Kirteling to Edward North [1536].	Rep.	45, S.L. (R.), s. 1(1), sch. 1 Pt. XIV.
c. 41	Assurance of Manor of Birmingham to King [1536].	Rep.	45, S.L. (R.), s. 1(1), sch. 1 Pt. XIV.
c. 42	Exchange of lands, King and Abbot of Abingdon [1536].	Rep.	45, S.L. (R.), s. 1(1), sch. 1 Pt. XIV.
c. 43	Assurance of lands to Thomas Jermyn [1536].	Rep.	45, S.L. (R.), s. 1(1), sch. 1 Pt. XIV.
c. 44	Assurance of Manor of Haslingfield to Prior of Charterhouse [1536].	Rep.	45, S.L. (R.), s. 1(1), sch. 1 Pt. XIV.

Session and Chap. or No. of Measure	Short title or Subject	How affected	Chapter of 1978 Act or number of Measure or Statutory Instrument
28 Hen. 8:—*cont.*			
c. 46	Assurance of lands to Thomas Hatcliffe [1536].	Rep.	45, S.L. (R.), s. 1(1), sch. 1 Pt. XIV.
c. 47	Assurance of lands to John Gostwick [1536].	Rep.	45, S.L. (R.), s. 1(1), sch. 1 Pt. XIV.
c. 48	Marriage of Lord Bulbeck [1536].	Rep.	45, S.L. (R.), s. 1(1), sch. 1 Pt. XIV.
c. 49	Exchange of lands, King and Abbot of Westminster [1536].	Rep.	45, S.L. (R.), s. 1(1), sch. 1 Pt. XIV.
c. 50	Exchange of lands, King, Archbishop of Canterbury and Thomas Cromwell [1536].	Rep.	45, S.L. (R.), s. 1(1), sch. 1 Pt. XIV.
c. 51	Assurance of lands to Duchess of Suffolk [1536].	Rep.	45, S.L. (R.), s. 1(1), sch. 1 Pt. XIV.
31 Hen. 8:			
c. 5	Manor of Hampton Court [1539].	Rep.	45, S.L. (R.), s. 1(1), sch. 1 Pt. XIV.
33 Hen. 8:			
c. 26	Conveyances by Sir John Shelton made void [1541].	Rep.	45, S.L. (R.), s. 1(1), sch. 1 Pt. XIV.
c. 35	Gloucester water supply [1541].	Rep.	45, S.L. (R.), s. 1(1), sch. 1 Pt. XVII.
c. 37	Honour of Ampthill [1541].	Rep.	45, S.L. (R.), s. 1(1), sch. 1 Pt. XIV.
c. 38	Honour of Grafton [1541].	Rep.	45, S.L. (R.), s. 1(1), sch. 1 Pt. XIV.
34 & 35 Hen. 8:			
c. 21	Confirmation of grants [1542].	Rep.	45, S.L. (R.), s. 1(1), sch. 1 Pt. XIV.
37 Hen. 8:			
c. 18	Honours of Westminster, Kingston, St Osyth's and Donington [1545].	Rep.	45, S.L. (R.), s. 1(1), sch. 1 Pt. XIV.
2 & 3 Edw. 6:			
c. 12	Assurance of lands of Duke of Somerset [1548].	Rep.	45, S.L. (R.), s. 1(1), sch. 1 Pt. XIV.
1 Mar. Sess. 3:			
c. 4	Lord Steward Act 1554...	Short title	45, S.L. (R.), s. 2. sch. 3 para 1,
21 Jas. 1: c. 30	Exchange of lands, King and Archbishop of York [1623].	Rep.	45, S.L. (R.), s. 1(1), sch. 1 Pt. XIV.
3 Chas. 1: ... c. 6	Lands at Bromfield and Yale, Denbighshire [1627].	Rep.	45, S.L. (R.), s. 1(1), sch. 1 Pt. XIV.

Session and Chap. or No. of Measure	Short title or Subject	How affected	Chapter of 1978 Act or number of Measure or Statutory Instrument
11 Will. 3: c. 2	Crown lands, forfeited estates [1698].	Rep.	45, S.L. (R.), s. 1(1), sch. 1 Pt. XIV.
3 & 4 Anne: c. 4	Grant to Duke of Marlborough [1704].	Rep.	45, S.L. (R.), s. 1(1), sch. 1 Pt. XIV.
6 Anne: c. 41 ...	Succession to the Crown Act 1707.	S. 26 rep.	45, S.L. (R.), s. 1(1), sch. 1 Pt. III.
7 Anne: c. 29	Earl of Clanriccard's estates [1708].	Rep.	45, S.L. (R), s. 1(1), sch. 1 Pt. XIV.
1 Geo. 1: Stat. 2: c. 10	Queen Anne's Bounty Act 1714.	S. 21 rep. in pt. ...	G.S.M. No. 3, s. 12.
10 Geo. 2: c. 19	Plays and Wine Licences [1736].	Rep.	45, S.L. (R), s. 1(1), sch. 1 Pt. V.
20 Geo. 2: c. 42	Wales and Berwick Act 1746.	Rep.	30, s. 25(1), sch. 3.
28 Geo. 2: c. 54	Dean's Yard Westminster [1755].	Rep.	45, S.L. (R), s. 1(1), sch. 1 Pt. XIV.
30 Geo. 2: c. 21	Medway Fisheries [1757]	Rep.	45, S.L. (R), s. 1(1), sch. 1 Pt. X.
31 Geo. 2: c. 16	Crown lands, forfeited estates [1757].	Rep.	45, S.L. (R), s. 1(1), sch. 1 Pt. XIV.
c. 25	Westminster corn and grain market [1757].	Rep.	45, S.L. (R), s. 1(1), sch. 1 Pt. XVII.
c. 22 (Pr.) ...	Leeds coal supply [1757]	Rep.	45, S.L. (R), s. 1(1), sch. 1 Pt. XV.
32 Geo. 2: c. 61	Manchester, School Mills [1758].	Rep.	45, S.L. (R), s. 1(1), sch. 1 Pt. XVII.
2 Geo. 3: c. 17	Crown lands, forfeited estates [1762].	Rep.	45, S.L. (R), s. 1(1), sch. 1 Pt. XIV.

Session and Chap. or No. of Measure	Short title or Subject	How affected	Chapter of 1978 Act or number of Measure or Statutory Instrument
10 Geo. 3:			
c. 13	Grant of Manor of Cosham to Paul Methuen [1770].	Rep.	45, S.L. (R), s. 1(1), sch. 1 Pt. XIV.
11 Geo. 3:			
c. 10	Morden College, Kent [1771].	Rep.	45, S.L. (R), s. 1(1), sch. 1 Pt. II.
c. 56	Crown lands in Meath to vest in Gerald Fitzgerald [1771].	Rep.	45, S.L. (R), s. 1(1), sch. 1 Pt. XIV.
12 Geo. 3:			
c. 19	Crown lands in Fenchurch Street, London [1772].	Rep.	45, S.L. (R), s. 1(1), sch. 1 Pt. XIV.
c. 35	Crown lands at Richmond, Surrey [1772].	Rep.	45, S.L. (R), s. 1(1), sch. 1 Pt. XIV.
c. 43	Crown lands in Holborn, London [1772].	Rep.	45, S.L. (R), s. 1(1), sch. 1 Pt. XIV.
c. 44	Crown lands, grant to James Archibald Stuart [1772].	Rep.	45, S.L. (R), s. 1(1), sch. 1 Pt XIV.
c. 59	Crown lands at Richmond, Surrey [1772].	Rep.	45, S.L. (R), s. 1(1), sch. 1 Pt. XIV.
13 Geo. 3:			
c. 52	Plate Assay (Sheffield and Birmingham) Act 1772.	Ss. 2 rep. in pt., 3, 6, 7 rep., 8 rep. in pt., 18, 28–30 rep.	S.I. No. 639.
17 Geo. 3:			
c. 17	Crown lands at Enfield, Middlesex [1776].	Rep.	45, S.L. (R), s. 1(1), sch. 1 Pt. XIV.
c. 24	York Buildings Company, sale of Scottish estates [1776].	Rep.	45, S.L. (R), s. 1(1), sch. 1 Pt. XVII.
18 Geo. 3:			
c. 61	Repeal of provisions in Acts relating to Crown lands, forfeited estates [1778].	Rep.	45, S.L. (R), s. 1(1), sch. 1 Pt. XIV.
19 Geo. 3:			
c. 11	Leeds coal supply [1779]	Rep.	45, S.L. (R), s. 1(1), sch. 1 Pt. XV.
23 Geo. 3:			
c. 61	Lands of Earl of Pembroke [1783].	Rep.	45, S.L. (R), s. 1(1), sch. 1 Pt. XIV.
24 Geo. 3 Sess. 1:			
c. 19	Isle of Wight, carriage rates [1783].	Rep.	45, S.L. (R), s. 1(1), sch. 1 Pt. XVII.

Session and Chap. or No. of Measure	Short title or Subject	How affected	Chapter of 1978 Act or number of Measure or Statutory Instrument
25 Geo. 3: c. 98	Crown lands at North Scotland Yard, Middle-sex [1785].	Rep.	45, S.L. (R), s. 1(1), sch. 1 Pt. XIV.
26 Geo. 3: c. 27	Forfeited estates, Scotland [1786].	Rep.	45, S.L. (R), s. 1(1), sch. 1 Pt. XIV.
28 Geo. 3: c. 63	Charles Radcliffe's estates [1788].	Rep.	45, S.L. (R), s. 1(1), sch. 1 Pt. XIV.
30 Geo. 3: c. 51	Crown lands at Catterick and Tunstall, York-shire [1790].	Rep.	45, S.L. (R), s. 1(1), sch. 1 Pt. XIV.
31 Geo. 3: c. 32	Roman Catholic Relief Act 1791.	Rep.	45, S.L. (R), s. 1(1), sch. 1 Pt. XVI.
32 Geo. 3: c. 24	Crown lands in Privy Garden, Westminster [1792].	Rep.	45, S.L. (R), s. 1(1), sch. 1 Pt. XIV.
33 Geo. 3: c. 13	Acts of Parliament (Commencement) Act 1793.	Rep. in pt.	30, s. 25(1), sch. 3.
c. 46	Crown lands, forfeited estates in Ireland [1793].	Rep.	45, S.L. (R), s. 1(1), sch. 1 Pt. XIV.
c. 86	Leeds coal supply [1793].	Rep.	45, S.L. (R), s. 1(1), sch. 1 Pt. XV.
35 Geo. 3: c. 40	Crown lands in North-amptonshire, grant to Earl of Upper Ossory [1795].	Rep.	45, S.L. (R), s. 1(1), sch. 1 Pt. XIV.
36 Geo. 3: c. 62	Crown lands in North-amptonshire, grant to Earl of Westmorland [1796].	Rep.	45, S.L. (R), s. 1(1), sch. 1 Pt. XIV.
c. 63	Crown lands in North-amptonshire, grant to Earl of Exeter [1796].	Rep.	45, S.L. (R), s. 1(1), sch. 1 Pt. XIV.
37 Geo. 3: c. 47	John Yeldham's estate [1797].	Rep.	45, S.L. (R), s. 1(1), sch. 1 Pt. XIV.

Session and Chap. or No. of Measure	Short title or Subject	How affected	Chapter of 1978 Act or number of Measure or Statutory Instrument
39 Geo. 3:			
c. 34	Partridges Act 1799. ...	Rep.	45, S.L. (R), s. 1(1), sch. 1 Pt. XVII.
39 & 40 Geo. 3:			
c. 67	Union with Ireland Act 1800.	S. 1 art. VIII rep. in pt. (*prosp*)	23, s. 122(2) sch. 7 Pt. I.
41 Geo. 3: **(U.K.):**			
c. 88	Judges' Lodgings (Ireland) Act 1801.	Rep. (*prosp*)	23, s. 122 (2), sch. 7 Pt. I.
c. 90	Crown Debts Act 1801.	S. 5 am. (*prosp*) ...	23, s. 122(1), sch. 5 Pt. II (1).
43 Geo. 3:			
c. xii	Leeds coal supply [1803].	Rep.	45, S.L. (R.), s. 1(1), sch. 1 Pt. XV.
44 Geo. 3:			
c. 25	Crown lands at Byfleet, Weybridge, Walton, Walton Leigh and Chertsey, Surrey [1804].	Rep.	45, S.L. (R.), s. 1(1), sch. 1 Pt. XIV.
c. 102 ...	Habeas Corpus Act 1804.	S. 1 rep. in pt. (*prosp*) ...	23, s. 122(2), sch. 7 Pt. I.
45 Geo. 3:			
c. 92	Writ of Subpoena Act 1805.	Ss. 3, 4 am. (*prosp*) ...	23, s. 122(1), sch. 5 Pt. II (1).
c. 116 ...	Crown lands at Shilston Bay, Devon [1805].	Rep.	45, S.L. (R.), s. 1(1), sch. 1 Pt. XIV.
47 Geo. 3 Sess. 2:			
c. 77	Crown lands, Exchange, King and David Jebb [1807].	Rep.	45, S.L. (R.), s. 1(1), sch. 1 Pt. XIV.
50 Geo. 3:			
c. 6	Cornwall duchy [1810].	Rep.	45, S.L. (R.), s. 1(1), sch. 1 Pt. IV.
52 Geo. 3:			
c. 11	House of Commons (Offices) Act 1812.	Rep.	36, s. 5(4), sch. 3.
c. 123 ...	Duchy of Cornwall Act 1812.	Short title	45, S.L. (R.), s. 2, sch. 3 para. 1
		Act (except ss. 6–9) rep.	45, S.L. (R), s. 1(1), sch. 1 Pt. IV.
c. 124 ...	Vesting in Crown of lands at Sandhurst, Berkshire [1812].	Rep.	45, S.L. (R.), s. 1(1), sch. 1 Pt. XIV.
c. 146 ...	Parochial Registers Act 1812.	Rep.	G.S.M. No. 2, s. 26(2) sch. 4.
55 Geo. 3:			
c. 157 ...	Evidence (Ireland) Act 1815.	Rep. (*prosp*) ...	23, s. 122(2), sch. 7 Pt. I.
c. 188 ...	Grant of feu duties to John Francis Erskine [1815].	Rep.	45, S.L. (R.), s. 1(1), sch. 1 Pt. XIV.

Session and Chap. or No. of Measure	Short title or Subject	How affected	Chapter of 1978 Act or number of Measure or Statutory Instrument
56 Geo. 3:			
c. 98	Consolidated Fund Act 1816.	S. 14 rep.	45, S.L. (R), s. 1(1), sch. 1 Pt. III.
		S. 18 rep.	45, S.L. (R.), s. 1(1), sch. 1 Pt. IX.
c. 136 ...	Lands of Hertford College [1816].	Rep.	45, S.L. (R.), s. 1(1), sch. 1 Pt. V.
c. lxxiii ...	Department of Customs in England Fund for Widows, children etc. [1816].	S. 16 proviso am. ...	iii, s. 4.
57 Geo. 3:			
c. 129 ...	Manor of Rialton and Retraighe, Cornwall [1817].	Rep.	45, S.L. (R.), s. 1(1), sch. 1 Pt. XIV.
60 Geo. 3 & 1 Geo. 4:			
c. 1	Unlawful Drilling Act 1819.	Saved (N.I.)	5, s. 23(4).
c. 4	Pleading in Misdemeanor Act 1819.	Rep. (N.I.) (*prosp.*) ...	23, s. 122(2), sch. 7 Pt. I.
1 Geo. 4:			
c. 5	Transfer of Stock (Ireland) Act 1820.	Rep. (*prosp.*)	23, s. 122(2), sch. 7 Pt. I.
1 & 2 Geo. 4:			
c. 53	Common Law Procedure (Ireland) Act 1821.	Rep. (*prosp.*)	23, s. 122(2), sch. 7 Pt. I.
c. 54	Clerk of Assize (Ireland) Act 1821.	Rep. (*prosp.*)	23, s. 122(2), sch. 7 Pt. I.
4 Geo. 4:			
c. 61	Court of Chancery (Ireland) Act 1823.	Rep. (*prosp.*)	23, s. 122(2), sch. 7 Pt. I.
c. 75	Land at Kew Green, Surrey [1823].	Rep.	45, S.L. (R.), s. 1(1), sch. 1 Pt. XIV.
c. 89	Law Costs (Ireland) Act 1823.	Rep. (*prosp.*)	23, s. 122(2), sch. 7 Pt. I.
5 Geo. 4:			
c. 111 ...	Crown Debts Act 1824	Rep. (N.I.) (*prosp.*) ...	23, s. 122(2), sch. 7 Pt. I.
6 Geo. 4:			
c. 51	Assizes (Ireland) Act 1825.	Rep. (*prosp.*)	23, s. 122(2), sch. 7 Pt. I.
c. 62	Poor Prisoners (Scotland) Act 1825.	Rep.	45, S.L. (R.), s. 1(1), sch. 1 Pt. I.
9 Geo. 4:			
c. 29	Circuit Courts (Scotland) Act 1828.	S. 13 rep.	19, s. 7(1), sch. Pt. II.
c. 54	Criminal Law (Ireland) Act 1828.	Ss. 22, 26, 27, 34 rep. (*prosp.*).	23, s. 122(2), sch. 7 Pt. I.

Session and Chap. or No. of Measure	Short title or Subject	How affected	Chapter of 1978 Act or number of Measure or Statutory Instrument
10 Geo. 4:			
c. 7	Roman Catholic Relief Act 1829.	Preamble, ss. 2, 5, 11 rep., 16 rep in pt., 23, 24 rep.	45, S.L. (R.), s. 1(1), sch. 1 Pt. XVI.
11 Geo. 4 & 1 Will. 4:			
c. 66	Forgery Act 1830 ...	S. 21 rep.	G.S.M. No. 2, s. 26(2), sch. 4.
c. cxxxii ...	Chapel of Ease, Parish of St. George Blooms-bury [1830].	Rep.	ix, s. 7, sch. 2.
1 & 2 Will. 4:			
c. 50	Fresh Wharf, London [1831].	Rep.	45, S.L. (R.), s. 1(1), sch. 1 Pt. XIV.
2 & 3 Will. 4:			
c. 48	Clerk of the Crown (Ire-land) Act 1832.	Rep. (*prosp.*)	23, s. 122(2), sch. 7 Pt. I.
c. 75	Anatomy Act 1832 ...	Devolved (S.) (*prosp.*) ...	51, s. 63, sch. 10 Pt. III.
3 & 4 Will. 4:			
c. 41	Judicial Committee Act 1833.	Appl. ... ... Appl. (mods.) ... ... Appl. (*prosp.*)	S.I. No. 1030. S.I. No. 182. 12, s. 11(6).
4 & 5 Will. 4:			
c. 70	House of Commons Officers Act 1834.	Rep.	36, s. 5(4), sch. 3.
c. 78	Chancery (Ireland) Act 1834.	Rep. (*prosp.*)	23, s. 122(2), sch. 7 Pt. I.
5 & 6 Will. 4:			
c. 16	Chancery (Ireland) Act 1835.	Rep. (*prosp.*)	23, s. 122(2), sch. 7 Pt. I.
c. 26	Assizes (Ireland) Act 1835	Rep. (*prosp.*)	23, s. 122(2), sch. 7 Pt. I.
6 & 7 Will. 4:			
c. 43	Judicial Ratifications (Scotland) Act 1836.	Rep.	45, S.L. (R), s. 1(1), sch. 1 Pt. I.
c. 74	Court of Chancery (Ire-land) Act 1836.	Rep. (*prosp.*)	23, s. 122(2), sch. 7 Pt. I.
c. 86	Births and Deaths Regis-tration Act 1836.	S. 35 appl. ... ... S. 35 (except as appl. by any enactment) rep.	G.S.M. No. 2, s. 26(1), sch. 3 paras. 1, 2. G.S.M. No. 2, s. 26(2), sch. 4.
7 Will. 4 & 1 Vict.:			
c. 83	Parliamentary Documents Deposit Act 1837.	Am. (N.I.) (*prosp.*) ...	23, s. 122(1), sch. 5 Pt. II(1).
c. xcix ...	Montrose Harbour Act 1837.	Ss. VII, VIII rep. ...	S.I. No. 919.

Session and Chap. or No. of Measure	Short title or Subject	How affected	Chapter of 1978 Act or number of Measure or Statutory Instrument
1 & 2 Vict.:			
c. 43	Dean Forest (Mines) Act 1838.	S. 56 rep. in pt. ...	45, S.L. (R), s. 1(1), sch. 1 Pt. XVII.
c. 101 ...	Duchies of Lancaster and Cornwall (Accounts) Act 1838.	Title rep. in pt., preamble, s. 1 rep.	45, S.L. (R), s. 1(1), sch. 1 Pt. IV.
c. 105 ...	Oaths Act 1838	Rep.	19, s. 7(1), sch. Pt. I.
2 & 3 Vict.:			
c. 47	Metropolitan Police Act 1839.	S. 10 rep.	45, S.L. (R), s. 1(1), sch. 1 Pt. XI.
c. 71	Metropolitan Police Courts Act 1839.	S. 37 rep.	45, S.L. (R), s. 1(1), sch. 1 Pt. VIII.
4 & 5 Vict.:			
c. 38	Schools Sites Act 1841 ...	Transfer of functions (*prosp.*).	52, s. 9(1), sch. 2 Pt. III.
		S. 14 am.	45, S.L. (R), s. 1(2), sch. 2 para. 1.
		Ss. 15, 19 rep. ...	45, S.L. (R), s. 1(1), sch. 1 Pt. V.
5 & 6 Vict.:			
c. 55	Railway Regulation Act 1842.	S. 20 rep.	45, S.L. (R), s. 1(1), sch. 1 Pt. XV.
c. 69	Perpetuation of Testimony Act 1842.	Rep. (N.I.) (*prosp.*) ...	23, s. 122(2), sch. 7 Pt. I.
c. 78	Exchange, Crown and Eton College [1842].	Rep.	45, S.L. (R), s. 1(1), sch. 1 Pt. XIV.
c. 94	Defence Act 1842 ...	S. 19 saved (N.I.) (*prosp.*)	S.I. No. 1050.
		S. 29 rep. (N.I.) (*prosp.*)	23, s. 122(2), sch. 7 Pt. I.
c. 97	Limitations of Actions and Costs Act 1842.	Rep. (N.I.) (*prosp.*) ...	23, s. 122(2), sch. 7 Pt. I.
6 & 7 Vict.:			
c. 19	Thatched House Court and Little St. James's St., Westminster [1843].	Rep.	45, S.L. (R.), s. 1(1), sch. 1 Pt. XIV.
c. 85	Evidence Act 1843 ...	S. 2 rep. (N.I.) (*prosp.*)...	23, s. 122(2), sch. 7 Pt. I.
c. 98	Slave Trade Act 1843 ...	S. 4(1) am. (N.I.) (*prosp.*)	23, s. 122(1), sch. 5 Pt. II(1).
		rep. in pt. (N.I.) (*prosp.*).	23, s. 122(2), sch. 7 Pt. I.
7 & 8 Vict.:			
c. 37	School Sites Act 1844 ...	Transfer of functions (*prosp.*).	52, s. 9(1), sch. 2 Pt. III.
c. 105 ...	Duchy of Cornwall (No. 2) Act 1844	Act (except ss. 39, 40, 53–70, 92, schs. 1, 2) rep. s. 92 rep. in pt. ...	45, S.L. (R.), s. 1(1), sch. 1 Pt. IV
c. 107 ...	Common Law Officers (Ireland) Act 1844.	Rep. (*prosp.*)	23, s. 122(2), sch. 7 Pt. I.

Session and Chap. or No. of Measure	Short title or Subject	How affected	Chapter of 1978 Act or number of Measure or Statutory Instrument
7 & 8 Vict.: *—cont.*			
c. xl.	Manchester Police Regulation Act 1844.	S. 187 am.	S.I. No. 844.
8 & 9 Vict:			
c. 16	Companies Clauses Consolidation Act 1845.	Act (except ss. 56–60, 161, 162) incorp.	S.I. No. 1482.
		(except ss. 56–60, 161, 162) incorp. (mods.).	S.I. No. 986.
c. 18	Lands Clauses Consolidation Act 1845.	Ss. 3 (definition of " Supreme Court ") added (*prosp.*), 9, 69–71, 73, 76, 78, 84, 85 mod. (*prosp.*), 86 replaced (*prosp.*), 89 mod. (*prosp.*).	23, s. 122(1), sch. 5 Pt. II(1).
		S. 91 saved (N.I.) (*prosp.*).	S.I. No. 1050.
		Ss. 99, 100, 107, 109, 111, 113, 117, Sch. A mod. (*prosp*)	23, s. 122(1), sch. 5 Pt. II(1).
c. 19	Lands Clauses Consolidation (Scotland) Act 1845.	Incorp.	29, s. 79(4).
c. 33	Railways Clauses Consolidation (Scotland) Act 1845.	Ss. 6, 70–78 incorp. ...	29, s. 79(4)
c. 104 ...	Darby Court, Westminster [1845].	Rep.	45, S.L. (R.), s. 1(1), sch. 1 Pt. XIV.
c. 115 ...	Chancery Taxing Master (Ireland) Act 1845.	Rep. (*prosp.*)	23, s. 122(2), sch. 7 Pt. I.
c. 118 ...	Inclosure Act 1845 ...	Transfer of certain functions (*prosp.*).	52, s. 9(1), sch. 2 Pt. VIII.
9 & 10 Vict: ...			
c. 70	Inclosure Act 1846.	Transfer of functions (*prosp.*).	52, s. 9(1), sch. 2. Pt. VIII.
c. 77	House of Commons Offices Act 1846.	Rep.	36, s. 5(4), sch. 3.
		S. 5 am.	44, s. 159(2), sch. 16 para. 1.
10 & 11 Vict:			
c. 14	Markets and Fairs Clauses Act 1847.	Transfer of functions (*prosp.*).	52, s. 9(1), sch. 2 Pt. II.
c. 27	Harbours Docks and Piers Clauses Act 1847.	S. 28 not devolved (S.) (*prosp.*).	51, s. 63, sch. 10. Pt. III.
		S. 52 am.	S.I. No. 647.
		S. 102 not devolved (S.) (*prosp.*).	51, s. 63, sch. 10 Pt. III.
c. 65	Cemeteries Clauses Act 1847.	S. 32 rep. in pt. (E., & W.).	G.S.M. No. 2 s. 26(2), sch. 4.
		S. 33 subst. (E. & W.) ...	G.S.M. No. 2, s. 26(1), sch. 3 para. 1.
c. 111 ...	Inclosure Act 1847 ...	Transfer of functions (*prosp.*).	52, s. 9(1), sch. 2 Pt. VIII.
11 & 12 Vict.:			
c. 42	Indictable Offences Act 1848.	Ss. 12, 14 am. (*prosp.*) ...	23, s. 122(1), sch. 5 Pt. II(1).

Session and Chap. or No. of Measure	Short title or Subject	How affected	Chapter of 1978 Act or number of Measure or Statutory Instrument
11 & 12 Vict.: *—cont.*			
c. 83	Assessionable Manors Award Act 1848.	Act (except ss. 6, 14) rep.	45, S.L. (R), s. 1(1), sch. 1 Pt. IV.
c. 99	Inclosure Act 1848 ...	Transfer of functions (*prosp.*).	52, s. 9(1), sch. 2 Pt. VIII.
c. 132 ...	Taxing Masters (Ireland) Act 1848.	Rep. (*prosp.*)	23, s. 122(2), sch. 7 Pt. I.
12 & 13 Vict.:			
c. 49	School Sites Act 1849 ...	Transfer of functions (*prosp.*).	52, s. 9(1), sch. 2 Pt. III.
c. 72	House of Commons Offices Act 1849.	Rep.	36, s. 5(4), sch. 3.
c. 83	Inclosure Act 1849 ...	Transfer of functions (*prosp.*).	52, s. 9(1), sch. 2 Pt. VIII.
13 & 14 Vict.:			
c. xliii ...	Montrose Harbour Act 1850.	Ss. III–VI, IX rep. ...	S.I. No. 919.
14 & 15 Vict.:			
c. 24	School Sites Act 1851 ...	Transfer of functions (*prosp.*).	52, s. 9(1), sch. 2 Pt. III.
c. 42	Crown Lands Act 1851...	S. 22 transfer of functions (S.) (*prosp.*).	51, s. 63, sch. 11 Group J.
c. 53	Inclosure Commissioners Act 1851.	Transfer of functions (*prosp.*).	52, s. 9(1), sch. 2 Pt. VIII.
c. 99	Evidence Act 1851 ...	S. 6 rep. (N.I.) (*prosp.*)...	23, s. 122(2), sch. 7 Pt. I.
c. 100 ...	Criminal Procedure Act 1851.	S. 27 rep. (N.I.) (*prosp.*)	23, s. 122(2), sch. 7 Pt. I.
c. *15* (personal)	St. George Bloomsbury and St. Matthew Oakley Square [1851].	Preamble rep. in pt., ss. I–III rep., IV rep. in pt., sch. Pt. I rep.	ix, s. 7 sch. 2.
15 & 16 Vict.:			
c. 28	Commissioners of Works Act 1852.	S. 2 mod. (*prosp.*) ... transfer of certain functions (*prosp.*). concurrent powers of Min. (*prosp.*).	51, s. 73. 52, s. 9(1), sch. 2 Pt. XVIII. 52, s. 9(2), sch. 3.
c. 49	School Sites Act 1852 ...	Transfer of functions (*prosp.*).	52, s. 9(1), sch. 2 Pt. III.
c. 79	Inclosure Act 1852 ...	Transfer of functions (*prosp.*).	52, s. 9(1), sch. 2 Pt. VIII.
16 & 17 Vict.:			
c. 59	Stamp Act 1853... ...	S. 20 rep.	45, S.L. (R), s. 1(1), sch. 1 Pt. IX.
c. 113 ...	Common Law Procedure Amendment Act (Ireland) 1853.	Rep. (*prosp.*)	23, s. 122(2), sch. 7 Pt. I.
c. 134 ...	Burial Act 1853 ...	Transfer of functions (*prosp.*). S. 1 mod. (*prosp.*) ...	52, s. 9(1), sch. 2 Pt. II. 52, s. 77(1), sch. 11 para. 1.
c. cliv ...	Lands Improvement Company's Act 1853.	Transfer of functions (W.)	S.I. No. 272.

Session and Chap. or No. of Measure	Short title or Subject	How affected	Chapter of 1978 Act or number of Measure or Statutory Instrument
17 & 18 Vict.:			
c. 34	Attendance of Witnesses Act 1854.	Rep. in pt. (N.I.) (*prosp.*)	23, s. 122(2), sch. 7 Pt. II.
c. 38	Gaming Houses Act 1854	S. 12 rep. (N.I.) (*prosp.*)	23, s. 122(2), sch. 7 Pt. I.
c. 93	Duchy of Cornwall Office Act 1854.	Short title	45, S.L. (R.), s. 2, sch. 3 para. 1.
c. 94	Public Revenue and Consolidated Fund Charges Act 1854.	Sch. (B) rep. in pt. (*prosp.*)	23, s. 122(2), sch. 7 Pt. I.
c. 97 ...	Inclosure Act 1854 ...	Transfer of functions (*prosp.*).	52, s. 9(1), sch. 2 Pt. VIII.
18 & 19 Vict.:			
c. 128 ...	Burial Act 1855 ...	Transfer of functions (*prosp.*).	52, s. 9(1), sch. 2 Pt. II.
		S. 1 mod. (*prosp.*) ...	52, s. 77(1), sch. 11 para. 1(1).
c. 131	School Grants Act 1855	Transfer of functions (*prosp.*).	52, s. 9(1), sch. 2 Pt. III.
		S. 1 am.	45, S.L. (R.), s. 1(2), sch. 2 para. 2.
c. lxxxiv ...	Lands Improvement Company's Amendment Act 1855.	Transfer of functions (W.)	S.I. No. 272.
c. xcviii ...	South Wales Railway Consolidation Act 1855.	S. LXXV rep.	xxi, ss. 29(2), 30, sch. 4.
19 & 20 Vict.:			
c. 77	Chancery Receivers (Ireland) Act 1856.	Rep. (*prosp.*)	23, s. 122(2), sch. 7 Pt. I.
c. 92	Chancery Appeal Court (Ireland) Act 1856.	Rep. (*prosp.*)	23, s. 122(2), sch. 7 Pt. I.
c. 102 ...	Common Law Procedure Amendment Act (Ireland) 1856.	Rep. (*prosp.*)	23, s. 122(2), sch. 7 Pt. I.
c. xvii ...	Cambridge Award Act 1856.	S. 11 rep. in pt. ...	45, S.L. (R.), s. 1(1), sch. 1 Pt. V.
20 & 21 Vict.:			
c. 31	Inclosure Act 1857 ...	Transfer of functions (*prosp.*).	52, s. 9(1), sch. 2 Pt. VIII.
c. 79	Probates and Letters of Administration Act (Ireland) 1857.	Ss. 6, 16–18, 23–29, 32, 34, 36, 41, rep. (*prosp.*).	23, s. 122(2), sch. 7 Pt. I.
		Ss. 55, 57 am.	23, s. 122(1), sch. 5 Pt. II(1).
		S. 69 rep. (*prosp.*) ...	23, s. 122(2), sch. 7 Pt. I.
		S. 71 am.	23, s. 122(1), sch. 5 Pt. II(1).
		Ss. 109, 114, 115 sch. (A) rep. (*prosp.*).	23, s. 122(2), sch. 7 Pt. I.
c. 81	Burial Act 1857 ...	Transfer of functions (*prosp.*).	52, s. 9(1), sch. 2 Pt. II.
		Ss. 10, 23 mod. (*prosp.*)	52, s. 77(1), sch. 11 para. 1.

Session and Chap. or No. of Measure	Short title or Subject	How affected	Chapter of 1978 Act or number of Measure or Statutory Instrument
21 & 22 Vict.:			
c. 27	Chancery Amendment Act 1858.	Rep. (N.I.) (*prosp.*) ...	23, s. 122(2), sch. 7 Pt. I.
c. 36	Lands of Commissioners for the Exhibition of 1851 [1858].	Rep.	45, S.L. (R.), s. 1(1), sch. 1 Pt. XIV.
c. 71	Bishops Trusts Substitution Act 1858.	Saved	G.S.M. No. 1, s. 3, sch. para. 15(2).
c. 109 ...	Cornwall Submarine Mines Act 1858.	Preamble, ss. 1, 2, 7, 9 rep.	45, S.L. (R) s. 1(1), sch. 1 Pt. IV.
22 Vict.:			
c. 1	Burial Act 1859 ...	Transfer of functions (*prosp.*).	52, s. 9(1), sch. 2 Pt. II.
c. 12	Defence Act 1859 ...	S. 6 rep. in pt. (*prosp.*)...	S.I. No. 1050.
c. iv	Kirkwall Harbour Act 1859.	Rep.	iv, s. 1 sch., s. 9 sch. 2.
22 & 23 Vict.:			
c. 21	Queen's Remembrancer Act 1859.	S. 15 rep.	45, S.L. (R), s. 1(1), sch. 1 Pt. IX.
		rep. (N.I.) (*prosp.*)	23, s. 122(2), sch 7 Pt. I.
		Sch. rep.	45, S.L. (R), s. 1(1), sch. 1 Pt. IX.
c. 29	Repeal of Nore Tolls [1859].	Rep.	45, S.L. (R), s. 1(1), sch. 1 Pt. X.
c. 31	Court of Probate Act (Ireland) 1859.	Ss. 1, 3, 4, 9, 20, 31 rep. (*prosp.*).	23, s. 122(2), sch. 7 Pt. I.
c. 35	Law of Property Amendment Act 1859.	S. 21 rep. (N.I.) ...	S.I. No. 459.
c. 43	Inclosure Act 1859 ...	Transfer of functions (*prosp.*).	52, s. 9(1), sch. 2 Pt. VIII.
c. lxxxii ...	Lands Improvement Company's Amendment Act 1859.	Transfer of functions (W.)	S.I. No. 272.
23 & 24 Vict.:			
c. 53	Duchy of Cornwall Act 1860.	Rep.	45, S.L. (R), s. 1(1), sch. 1 Pt. IV.
c. 112 ...	Defence Act 1860 ...	Ss. 21, 22 am. (*prosp.*) ...	23, s. 122(1), sch. 5 Pt. II(1).
24 & 25 Vict.:			
c. 45	General Pier and Harbour Act 1861.	Transfer of functions (W.)	S.I. No. 272.
c. 47	Harbours and Passing Tolls, &c. Act 1861.	Pts. II, III, ss. 21, 44, 48, 54, 56–64, schs. 1, 3 rep.	45, S.L. (R), s. 1(1), sch. 1 Pt. X.
25 & 26 Vict.:			
c. 19	General Pier and Harbour Act 1861 Amendment Act [1862].	Transfer of functions (W.)	S.I. No. 272.

Session and Chap. or No. of Measure	Short title or Subject	How affected	Chapter of 1978 Act or number of Measure or Statutory Instrument
26 & 27 Vict.:			
c. 50	Salmon Fisheries (Scotland) Act 1863.	S. 4 not devolved (*prosp.*)	51, s. 63, sch. 10 Pt. III.
c. 118 ...	Companies Clauses Act 1863.	Act (except Pt. IV, ss. 36–39) incorp. (mods).	S.I. Nos. 986, 1482.
c. cxl	Lands Improvement Company's Amendment Act 1863.	Transfer of functions (W.)	S.I. No. 272.
27 & 28 Vict.:			
c. 7	Bills of Exchange (Ireland) Act 1864.	Rep. (*prosp.*)	23, s. 122(2), sch. 7 Pt. I.
c. 97	Registration of Burials Act 1864.	S. 3 rep.	G.S.M. No. 2, s. 26(2), sch. 4.
		S. 6 subst.	G.S.M. No. 2, s. 26(1), sch. 3 para. 2.
c. 114 ...	Improvement of Land Act 1864.	Transfer of functions (W.)	S.I. No. 272.
28 & 29 Vict.:			
c. 63	Colonial Laws Validity Act 1865.	Excl. (Tuvalu)	20, s. 1(2), sch. 1 para. 1.
29 & 30 Vict.:			
c. 83	National Gallery Enlargement Act 1866.	Act (except ss. 1, 3, 16, 17, 20, 29) rep.	45, S.L. (R.), s. 1(1), sch. 1 Pt. XIII.
30 & 31 Vict.:			
c. 41	National Gallery Enlargement Act 1867.	Rep.	45, S.L. (R.), s. 1(1), sch. 1 Pt. XIII.
c. 44	Chancery (Ireland) Act 1867.	Rep. (*prosp.*)	23, s. 122(2), sch. 7 Pt. I.
c. 75	Office and Oath Act 1867	Rep.	45, S.L. (R.), s. 1(1), sch. 1 Pt. XVI.
c. 114	Court of Admiralty (Ireland) Act 1867.	Rep. (*prosp.*)	23, s. 122(2), sch. 7 Pt. I.
c. 129 ...	Chancery and Common Law Offices (Ireland) Act 1867.	Rep. (*prosp.*)	23, s. 122(2), sch. 7 Pt. I.
c. 144 ...	Policies of Assurance Act 1867.	Saved (*prosp.*)	23, s. 87(3).
c. xxxii ...	Hartlepool Gas and Water Act 1867.	Ss. 45 am., 50A, 50B added.	S.I. No. 1823.
31 & 32 Vict.:			
c. 20	Legitimacy Declaration Act (Irelano) 1868.	Ss. 3, 4, 5, 7 rep. (*prosp.*)	23, s. 122(2), sch. 7 Pt. I.
c. 37	Documentary Evidence Act 1868.	Appl. (N.I.)	5, s. 20(9).
c. 72	Promissory Oaths Act 1868.	S. 2 (definition of " oath of allegiance ") appl. (*prosp.*). S. 4 (definition of " judicial oath ") appl. (*prosp.*).	23, s. 13(2).

Session and Chap. or No. of Measure	Short title or Subject	How affected	Chapter of 1978 Act or number of Measure or Statutory Instrument
31 & 32 Vict.: *—cont.*			
c. 88	Court of Chancery and Exchequer Funds (Ireland) Act 1868.	Rep.	45, S.L. (R.), s. 1(1), sch. 1 Pt. IX.
c. 89	Inclosure, &c., Expenses Act 1868.	Transfer of functions (*prosp.*).	52, s. 9(1), sch. 2 Pt. VIII.
c. 123 ...	Salmon Fisheries (Scotland) Act 1868.	S. 34 rep. in pt. ...	45, S.L. (R.), s. 1(1), sch. 1 Pt. X.
c. 125 ...	Parliamentary Elections Act 1868.	Rep. (N.I.) (*prosp.*) ...	23, s. 122(2), sch. 7 Pt. I.
c. cxiii ...	Gun Barrel Proof Act 1868.	Ext. (S., N.I.)	9, s. 6.
		Ss. 4 am. (definitions of " the Permanent International Commission", " convention proof mark ") added (*prosp.*) (definition of " statutory maximum "), 6A added, 21 am.	9, s. 8(1), sch. 3 paras. 1–3.
		Ss. 21, 23 rep. in pt. ...	9, s. 8(2), sch. 4.
		Ss. 28, 30 am.	9, s. 8(1), sch. 3 paras. 4, 5.
		Ss. 38, 40, 56 rep. in pt.	9, s. 8(2), sch. 4.
		S. 87 rep.	9, ss. 2(2), 8(2), sch. 4.
		S. 89 rep. in pt. ...	9, s. 8(2), sch. 4.
		Ss. 90, 92, 95 am. ...	9, s. 8(1), sch. 3 paras. 6, 7.
		S. 100 rep.	9, ss. 2(2), 8(2), sch. 4.
		S. 101–105 rep.	9, ss. 4, 8(2), sch. 4.
		Ss. 106, 117, 119, 121 am.	9, s. 8(1), sch. 3 paras. 6, 8, 9
		S. 121 renumbered (*prosp.*), (2) added (*prosp.*).	9, s. 8(1), sch. 3 para. 10(2).
		S. 122 am.	9, s. 8(1), sch. 3 para. 11.
		rep. in pt. ...	9, s. 8(1)(2), sch. 3 para. 11, sch. 4.
		Ss. 123, 124 am. ...	9, s. 8(1), sch. 3 paras. 12, 13.
		Ss. 124 rep. in pt., 125, 126 rep., 127 rep. in pt.	9, s. 8(2), sch. 4.
		S. 127 am.	9, s. 8(1), sch. 3 para. 14.
		S. 128 rep. in pt. ...	9, s. 8(2), sch. 4.
		Ss. 129–137 replaced (*prosp.*).	9, s. 1, sch. 1.
		Ss. 138 am., renumbered (2)(3) added, 139 subst. (pt. *prosp.*), 140 subst., 141 am.	9, s. 8(1), sch. 3 paras. 15–18.
		S. 142 rep.	9, ss. 2(2), 8(2), sch. 4.
		S. 143 am.	9, s. 8(1), sch. 3 para. 19.
		S. 144 rep.	9, s. 8(2), sch. 4.

Session and Chap. or No. of Measure	Short title or Subject	How affected	Chapter of 1978 Act or number of Measure or Statutory Instrument
32 & 33 Vict.:			
c. 10	Colonial Prisoners Removal Act 1869.	S. 2 rep. in pt.	45, S.L. (R.), s. 1(1), sch. 1 Pt. XVII.
c. 68	Evidence Further Amendment Act 1869.	Rep. (E. & W.)	45, S.L. (R), s. 1(1), sch. 1 Pt. I.
33 & 34 Vict.:			
c. 52	Extradition Act 1870 ...	S. 3(1) mod.	26, s. 2(1).
		Ss. 17, 22 ext. (*prosp.*) ...	17, s. 4(1).
		Sch. 1 am.	26, s. 3(1).
		am.	37 s. 1(6).
		am. (*prosp.*) ...	17, s. 3(1).
		rep. in pt. ...	26, s. 9, sch. 2.
c. 56	Limited Owners Residences Act 1870.	Transfer of functions (W.)	S.I. No. 272.
c. 110 ...	Matrimonial Causes and Marriage Law (Ireland) Amendment Act 1870.	S. 7 am. (*prosp.*) ...	23, s. 122(1), sch. 5 Pt. II(1).
		Ss. 8, 10–12 rep. (*prosp.*)	23, s. 122(2), sch. 7 Pt. I.
		S. 13 am. (*prosp.*) ...	23, s. 122(1), sch. 5 Pt. II(1).
		Ss. 14–17, 23, 28, 29 rep. (*prosp.*).	23, s. 122(2), sch. 7 Pt. I.
34 & 35 Vict.:			
c. 12	Fairs Act 1871	Transfer of functions (*prosp.*).	52, s. 9(1), sch. 2 Pt. II.
c. 16	Anatomy Act 1871 ...	Devolved (S.) (*prosp.*) ...	51, s. 63, sch. 10 Pt. III.
c. 42	Citation Amendment (Scotland) Act 1871.	Rep.	45, S.L. (R), s. 1(1), sch. 1 Pt. I.
c. 49	Matrimonial Causes and Marriage Law (Ireland) Amendment Act 1871.	Ss. 3, 9, 11–14, 20 rep. (*prosp.*).	23, s. 122(2), sch. 7 Pt. I.
c. 63	College Charter Act 1871	Am.	ii, s. 8(2).
c. 70	Local Government Board Act 1871.	Ss. 2, 7 sch. Pt. I rep. in pt.	45, S.L. (R), s. 1(1), sch. 1 Pt. XII.
35 & 36 Vict.:			
c. 15	Parks Regulation Act 1872.	Transfer of functions (S.) (*prosp.*).	51, s. 63, sch. 11 Goup J.
c. 61	Steam Whistles Act 1872	Rep. (N.I.) (*prosp.*) ...	S.I. No. 1049.
c. 75	Commissioners for Oaths (Ireland) Act 1872.	Rep. (*prosp.*)	23, s. 122(2), sch. 7 Pt. I.
c. 94	Licensing Act 1872 ...	S. 39 rep.	45, S.L. (R), s. 1(1), sch. 1 Pt. XVII.
c. lxviii ...	Gill Pier Order (Pier and Harbour Order Confirmation) Act 1872.	Order rep.	iv, s. 1 sch., s. 9 sch. 2.
c. lxxvii ...	Orkney Piers and Harbours Act 1872.	Rep.	iv, s. 1 sch., s. 9 sch. 2.
36 & 37 Vict.:			
c. 19	Poor Allotments Management Act 1873.	S. 9 transfer of functions (*prosp.*).	52, s. 9(1), sch. 2 Pt. VIII.

Session and Chap. or No. of Measure	Short title or Subject	How affected	Chapter of 1978 Act or number of Measure or Statutory Instrument
36 & 37 Vict.: *—cont.*			
c. 37	Fairs Act 1873	Transfer of functions (*prosp.*).	52, s. 9(1), sch. 2 Pt. II.
c. 57	Consolidated Fund (Permanent Charges Redemption) Act 1873.	S. 3 am. (N.I.) (*prosp.*)...	23, s. 122(1), sch. 5 Pt. II(1).
c. 60	Extradition Act 1873 ...	Sch. am.	31, s. 5(3).
		rep. in pt.	26, s. 9, sch. 2.
c. xlii ...	Caterham Water Order (Water Orders Confirmation) Act 1873.	Order rep.	S.I. No. 1482.
38 & 39 Vict.:			
c. 17	Explosives Act 1875 ...	Ss. 15, 18 am.	S.I. No. 270.
		S. 66(1) am. (*prosp.*) ...	23, s. 122(1), sch. 5 Pt. II(1).
c. 55	Public Health Act 1875	S. 184 transfer of functions (*prosp.*). Pt. IX transfer of certain functions (*prosp.*).	52, s. 9(1), sch. 2 Pt. II.
		Sch. 5 Pt. III rep. in pt.	45, S.L. (R.), s. 1(1), sch. 1 Pt. XVII.
c. clxi ...	Manchester Corporation Waterworks and Improvement Act 1875.	S. 48 rep.	S..I. No. 739.
39 & 40 Vict.:			
c. 28	Court of Admiralty (Ireland) Amendment Act 1876.	Rep (*prosp*).	23, s. 122(2), sch. 7 Pt. I.
c. 56	Commons Act 1876 ...	Transfer of functions (*prosp.*).	52, s. 9(1), sch. 2 Pt. VIII.
c. 59	Appellate Jurisdiction Act 1876.	Ss. 4, 5 appl. (*prosp.*) ...	23, ss. 41(3), 42(3)(4).
		S. 11 ext. (*prosp.*) ...	23, s. 42(5).
		S. 25 am. (*prosp.*) ...	23, s. 122(1), sch. 5 Pt. II(1).
40 & 41 Vict.:			
c. 11	Jurisdiction in Rating Act 1877.	S. 3 rep. in pt. (*prosp*).	23, s. 122(2), sch. 7 Pt. I.
c. 18	Settled Estates Act 1877	S. 34 am. (*prosp*).	23, s. 122(1), sch. 5 Pt. II (1).
		S. 42 rep. (N.I.) ...	23, s. 122(2), sch. 7 Pt. I.
c. 43	Justices Clerks Act 1877	S. 10. rep.	45, S.L. (R.), s. 1(1), sch. 1 Pt. I.
c. 57	Supreme Court of Judicature Act (Ireland) 1877.	Rep. (*prosp.*)	23, s. 122(2), sch. 7 Pt. I.
		S. 41(5)(*b*) am. ...	5, s. 34(1).
c. 59	Colonial Stock Act 1877	S. 20 mod.	15, s. 7(4), sch. para. 7.
		mod.	20, s. 4(3), sch. 2 para. 7.
		mod.	S.I. Nos. 1030, 1899
c. cxxi ...	New Forest Act 1877	S. 2(a) (c) am.	S.I. No. 1277
		S. 38 sch. 3 am. ...	S.I. No. 440

Session and Chap. or No. of Measure	Short title or Subject	How affected	Chapter of 1978 Act or number of Measure or Statutory Instrument
41 & 42 Vict.:			
c. 56	Commons (Expenses) Act 1878.	Transfer of functions (*prosp.*).	52, s. 9(1), sch. 2 Pt. VIII.
c. 76	Telegraph Act 1878	S. 7(1)–(8) incorp (mods)	S.I. No. 647
c. 77	Highways and Locomotives (Amendment) Act 1878.	Transfer of functions (*prosp.*).	52, s. 9(1), sch. 2 Pt. XV.
c. cxv... ...	Montrose Harbour Order [Confirmation Act] 1878.	Ss. III–IX rep.	S.I. No. 919.
42 & 43 Vict.:			
c. 37	Commons Act 1879	Transfer of functions (*prosp.*).	52, s. 9(1), sch. 2 Pt. VIII.
c. 42	Valuation of Lands (Scotland) Amendment Act 1879.	Ss. 8 rep. 9 am. ...	S.I. No. 252.
c. 75	Parliamentary Elections and Corrupt Practices Act 1879.	Rep. (N.I.) (*prosp.*) ...	23, s. 122(2), sch. 7 Pt. I.
		S. 2 rep. in pt.	45, S.L. (R.), s. 1(1), sch. 1 Pt. VI.
c. lv	Whitehall (Stronsay) Pier and Harbour Order (Pier and Harbour Orders Confirmation) Act 1879.	Order rep.	iv, s. 1, sch., s. 9, sch. 2.
43 & 44 Vict.:			
c. 9	Statutes (Definition of Time) Act 1880.	Rep.	30, s. 25(1), sch. 3.
44 & 45 Vict.:			
c. 41	Conveyancing Act 1881	S. 48(5) rep. (N.I.) ...	23, s. 122(2), sch. 7 Pt. I.
		S. 50 rep. (N.I.) ...	S.I. No. 459.
		Ss. 69(3)(7), 72(3) rep. (N.I.) (*prosp.*), (5) rep. (N.I.).	23, s. 122(2), sch. 7 Pt. I.
c. ccvii ...	Caterham Spring Water Company's Act 1881.	Ss. 7, 8, 23–26 rep. ...	S.I. No. 1482.
45 & 46 Vict.:			
c. 15	Commonable Rights Compensation Act 1882.	Transfer of functions (*prosp.*).	52, s. 9(1), sch. 2 Pt. VIII.
c. 37	Corn Returns Act 1882	Transfer of functions (W.)	S.I. No. 272.
c. 38	Settled Land Act 1882	S. 2(11) added (*prosp.*)	23, s. 122(1), sch. 5 Pt. II(1).
		S. 65(3)(4) rep. (N.I.) (*prosp.*).	23, s. 122(2), sch. 7 Pt. I.
c. 42	Civil Imprisonment (Scotland) Act 1882.	S. 8 rep.	45, S.L. (R.), s. 1(1), sch. 1 Pt. I.
c. 61	Bills of Exchange Act 1882.	S. 70 rep. (N.I.) (*prosp.*)	23, s. 122(2), sch. 7 Pt. I.
c. 70	Supreme Court of Judicature (Ireland) Act 1882.	Rep. (*prosp.*)	23, s. 122(2), sch. 7 Pt. I.
c. 72	Revenue, Friendly Societies and National Debt Act 1882.	S. 25 rep. (N.I.) (*prosp.*)	23, s. 122(2), sch. 7 Pt. I.

Session and Chap. or No. of Measure	Short title or Subject	How affected	Chapter of 1978 Act or number of Measure or Statutory Instrument
45 & 46 Vict.: —*cont.*			
c. 75	Married Women's Property Act 1882.	S. 17 saved (*prosp.*) ...	23, s. 31(7).
c. xiii ...	King's College London Act 1882.	Rep.	xii, s. 19, sch. 2.
c. clxvii ...	Belfast Presbyterian College Act 1882.	Rep.	v, s. 19(3), sch. 4.
c. clxviii ...	Kettletoft Pier Order (Pier and Harbour Orders Confirmation) Act 1882.	Order rep.	iv, s. 1, sch., s. 9, sch. 2.
c. ccxliii ...	Blackburn Improvement Act 1882.	S. 197 rep.	S.I. No. 1595.
46 & 47 Vict.:			
c. 3	Explosive Substances Act 1883.	Ss. 3(1)(*b*), 4 am. (N.I.)	5, s. 9.
c. 18	Municipal Corporations Act 1883.	Ss. 12, rep., 25(2) rep. in pt., 27 rep.	45, S.L. (R.), s. 1(1), sch. 1 Pt. XII.
c. 34	Cheap Trains Act 1883	Rep.	45, S.L. (R.), s. 1(1), sch. 1 Pt. XV.
47 & 48 Vict.:			
c. 62	Revenue Act 1884 ...	S. 14 rep. in pt. ...	30, s. 25(1), sch. 3.
c. 70	Municipal Elections (Corrupt and Illegal Practices) Act 1884.	Rep.	45, S.L. (R), s. 1(1), sch. 1 Pt. VI.
c. cclvii ...	Barry Dock and Railways Act 1884.	Rep. (Barry Harbour) ...	xvii, s. 37, sch. 3.
48 & 49 Vict.:			
c. xxviii ...	East Surrey Water Act 1885.	Ss. 8, 20–23 rep. ...	S.I. No. 1482.
49 & 50 Vict.:			
c. 27	Guardianship of Infants Act 1886.	Ss. 9, 10 rep. in pt. (N.I.) (*prosp.*), 11 rep. (N.I.) (*prosp.*).	23, s. 122(2), sch. 7 Pt. I.
c. 57	Parliamentary Elections (Returning Officers) Act (1875) Amendment Act 1886.	Rep.	45, S.L. (R), s. 1(1), sch. 1 Pt. VI.
c. xxxix ...	Barry Dock and Railways Act 1886.	Rep. (Barry Harbour) ...	xvii, s. 37, sch. 3.
50 & 51 Vict.:			
c. 6	Supreme Court of Judicature (Ireland) Act 1887.	Rep. (*prosp.*)	23, s. 122(2), sch. 7 Pt. I.
c. 55	Sheriffs Act 1887 ...	Sch. 2 rep. in pt. ...	45, S.L. (R), s. 1(1), sch. 1 Pt. XII.
c. clii	Darwen Corporation Act 1887.	S. 110 rep.	S.I. No. 1595.
c. clxii ...	Orkney Harbours Act 1887.	Rep.	iv, s. 1 sch., s. 9, sch. 2.

Session and Chap. or No. of Measure	Short title or Subject	How affected	Chapter of 1978 Act or number of Measure or Statutory Instrument
51 & 52 Vict.:			
c. 27	Supreme Court of Judicature (Ireland) Amendment Act 1888.	Rep. (*prosp.*)	23, s. 122(2), sch. 7 Pt. I.
c. 41	Local Government Act 1888.	Ss. 79(3) rep. in pt., 82, 87(2)(4) rep., 100 rep. in pt., 109 rep.	45, S.L. (R), s. 1(1), sch. 1 Pt. XII.
c. 46	Oaths Act 1888	Rep.	19, s. 7(1), sch. Pt. I.
c. 56	Suffragans Nomination Act 1888.	Am.	G.S.M. No. 1, s. 18.
52 & 53 Vict.:			
c. 25	National Portrait Gallery Act 1889.	Rep.	45, S.L. (R), s. 1(1), sch. 1 Pt. XIII.
c. 30	Board of Agriculture Act 1889.	S. 2(3) transfer of functions (W.).	S.I. No. 272.
		Sch. 1 Pt. II rep. in pt....	45, S.L. (R), s. 1(1), sch. 1 Pt. XVII.
c. 48	County Court Appeals (Ireland) Act 1889.	Rep. (*prosp.*)	23, s. 122(2), sch. 7 Pt. I.
c. 63	Interpretation Act 1889...	Rep. (except s. 13(4) (5) (14) (N.I.)).	30, s. 25(1), sch. 3.
		Saved (N.I.)	5, ss. 22(6), 23(4).
		S. 13(4) (5) (14) rep. (N.I.) (*prosp.*).	23, s. 122(2), sch. 7 Pt. I.
53 & 54 Vict.:			
c. 21	Inland Revenue Regulation Act 1890.	Ss. 10, 14, 15, 23, 33 rep., 35(1) rep. in pt.	45, S.L. (R), s. 1(1), sch. 1 Pt. IX.
		S. 38(1) rep. in pt.... ...	30, s. 25(1), sch. 3.
		Ss. 38(2), 40 rep. ...	45, S.L. (R), s. 1(1), sch. 1 Pt. IX.
c. 27	Colonial Courts of Admiralty Act 1890.	Ss. 4 excl., 7 restr. ...	20, s. 1(2), sch. 1 para. 4(*b*).
54 & 55 Vict.:			
c. clxxxiv ...	Barry Dock and Railways Act 1891.	Rep. (Barry Harbour) ...	xvii, s. 37, sch. 3.
55 & 56 Vict.:			
c. 29	Technical and Industrial Institutions Act 1892.	Transfer of functions (*prosp.*).	52, s. 9(1), sch. 2 Pt. III.
c. 55	Burgh Police (Scotland) Act 1892.	Ss. 270, 271, sch. 5 restr.	S.I. Nos. 584, 585.
c. 64	Witnesses (Public Inquiries) Protection Act 1892.	S. 3 am. (N.I.) (*prosp.*)...	23, s. 122(1), sch. 5 Pt. II(1).
56 & 57 Vict.:			
c. 57	Law of Commons Amendment Act 1893.	Transfer of functions (*prosp.*).	52, s. 9(1), sch. 2 Pt. VIII.
c. 73	Local Government Act 1894.	Ss. 21(1), 25(1) rep., 26(7) rep. in pt., 32, 35, 66, 71 rep., 75(2) rep. in pt., 84 rep.	45, S.L. (R), s. 1(1), sch. 1 Pt. XII.

Session and Chap. or No. of Measure	Short title or Subject	How affected	Chapter of 1978 Act or number of Measure or Statutory Instrument
57 & 58 Vict.:			
c. 60	Merchant Shipping Act 1894.	S. 427(2) am.	15, s. 7(4), sch. para. 4.
		am.	20, s. 4(3), sch. 2 para. 4.
		am.	S.I. Nos. 1030, 1899.
		Ss. 735, 736 excl. ...	20, s. 1(2), sch. 1 para. 4(a).
c. cxix ...	East Surrey Water Order (Water Orders Confirmation) Act 1894.	Order rep.	S.I. No. 1482.
c. clxvii ...	Barry Railway Act 1894	Rep. (Barry Harbour) ...	xvii, s. 37, sch. 3.
c. clxxxix ...	Great Western and Midland Railway Companies (Severn and Wye and Severn Bridge Railway) Act 1894.	S. 22(1) rep.	xiv, s. 16.
58 & 59 Vict.:			
c. 16	Finance Act 1895 ...	S. 12 excl. (S.)	29, s. 104(2).
59 & 60 Vict.:			
c. 8	Life Insurance Companies (Payment into Court) Act 1896.	S. 3 am. (N.I.) (*prosp.*)	23, s. 122(1), sch. 5 Pt. II(1).
		S. 4 rep. in pt. (N.I.) (*prosp.*).	23, s. 122(2), sch. 7 Pt. I.
c. 14	Short Titles Act 1896 ...	S. 3 rep.	30, s. 25(1), sch. 3.
		Sch. 1 col. 3 am. ...	45, S.L. (R.), s. 2, sch. 3 para. 2.
c. xiv ...	Customs' Annuity and Benevolent Fund Act 1896.	S. 5 am.	iii, s. 5.
c. cxxvii ...	East Surrey Water Act 1896.	Ss. 38, 42–44, 46 rep. ...	S.I. No. 1482.
c. cxciii ...	Barry Railway Act 1896	Rep. (Barry Harbour) ...	xvii, s. 37, sch. 3.
60 & 61 Vict.:			
c. 17	Supreme Court of Judicature (Ireland) Act 1897.	Rep. (*prosp.*)	23, s. 122(2), sch. 7 Pt. I.
c. 38	Public Health (Scotland) Act 1897.	Ss. 6, 8, 32(1)–(3), 36(1), 146(1), 148, 149 transfer of certain functions (*prosp.*).	51, s. 63, sch. 11 Group F.
		S. 166 appl. (mods.) ...	29, s. 101.
		S. 178 transfer of certain functions (*prosp.*).	51, s. 63, sch. 1 Group F.
c. 44	District Councils (Water Supply Facilities) Act 1897.	Transfer of functions (W.)	S.I. No. 272.
c. 53	Congested Districts (Scotland) Act 1897.	S. 4(1)(e) devolved in pt. (*prosp.*).	51, s. 63, sch. 10 Pt. III.
c. 66	Supreme Court of Judicature (Ireland) (No. 2) Act 1897.	Rep. (*prosp.*)	23, s. 122(2), sch. 7 Pt. I.
c. cxxxi ...	Stromness Harbour Act 1897.	Rep.	iv, s. 1, sch., s. 9, sch. 2.

Session and Chap. or No. of Measure	Short title or Subject	How affected	Chapter of 1978 Act or number of Measure or Statutory Instrument
61 & 62 Vict.:			
c. 29	Locomotives Act 1898	Transfer of functions (*prosp.*).	52, s. 9(1), sch. 2 Pt. XV.
c. 36	Criminal Evidence Act 1898.	S. 1 saved	37, s. 2(1).
62 & 63 Vict.:			
c. 30	Commons Act 1899 ...	Transfer of functions (*prosp.*).	52, s. 9(1), sch. 2 Pt. VIII.
c. 44	Small Dwellings Acquisition Act 1899.	Transfer of certain functions (*prosp.*).	52, s. 9(1), sch. 2 Pt. IV.
c. 46	Improvement of Land Act 1899.	Transfer of functions (W.)	S.I. No. 272.
63 & 64 Vict.:			
c. 15	Burial Act 1900 ...	Rep.	45, S.L. (R.), s. 1(1), sch. 1 Pt. XVII.
c. clxxiii ...	East Surrey Water Order (Water Orders Confirmation) Act 1900.	Order rep.	S.I. No. 1482.
1 Edw. 7:			
c. 16	National Gallery (Purchase of Adjacent Land) Act 1901.	Rep.	45, S.L. (R.), s. 1(1), sch. 1 Pt. XIII.
2 Edw. 7:			
c. 8	Cremation Act 1902	Transfer of certain functions (*prosp*). Ss. 2, 3 rep. in pt. ...	52. s. 9(1), sch. 2. Pt. II. 45, S.L. (R.), s. 1(1), sch. 1 Pt. XVII.
3 Edw. 7:			
c. 31	Board of Agriculture and Fisheries Act 1903.	S. 1(5) rep.	45, S.L. (R.), s. 1(1), sch. 1 Pt. X.
c. xcii ...	King's College London Act 1903.	Rep.	xii, s. 19 sch. 2.
5 Edw. 7			
c. 23	Provisional Order (Marriages) Act 1905.	Transfer of functions (*prosp.*).	52, s. 9(1), sch. 2 Pt. XVII.
6 Edw. 7:			
c. 14	Alkali &c. Works Regulation Act 1906.	Transfer of functions (S.) (*prosp.*). Transfer of functions (*prosp.*).	51, s. 63, sch. 11 Group F. 52, s. 9(1) sch. 2 Pt. VII.
c. ix	Sheffield Assay Act 1906	Ss. 2 rep. 3(1) rep. in pt. (2) rep (3) am. 4 rep in pt., 5 am., 7–12 rep.	S.I. No. 639.
c. cxiii ...	Newlyn Pier and Harbour Order (Pier and Harbour Orders Confirmation (No. 1)) Act 1906.	Sch., s. 34 rep. (saving)...	S.I. No. 427.
7 Edw. 7:			
c. 43	Education (Administrative Provisions) Act 1907.	Rep.	45, S.L. (R), s. 1(1), sch. 1 Pt. V.
c. 51	Sheriff Courts (Scotland) Act 1907.	S. 5(2) am. (*prosp*) (2A) added (*prosp.*), proviso am. (*prosp.*).	22, s. 89 sch. 2 para. 1. ...
c. 53	Public Health Acts Amendment Act 1907.	S. 82 transfer of f unctions (*prosp.*).	52. s. 9(1) sch. 2 Pt. II.

Session and Chap. or No. of Measure	Short title or Subject	How affected	Chapter of 1978 Act or number of Measure or Statutory Instrument
8 Edw. 7:			
c. 36	Small Holdings and Allotments Act 1908.	Transfer of certain functions (W.).	S.I. No. 272.
		Transfer of functions (*prosp.*).	52. s. 9(1) sch. 2 Pt. VIII.
c. 44	Commons Act 1908	Transfer of functions (*prosp.*).	52, s. 9(1), sch. 2 Pt. VIII.
c. xxxix ...	King's College London (Transfer) Act 1908.	Ss. 2 rep. in pt., 3–21, 36–43, Sch. 1 rep.	xii, s. 19, sch. 2.
9 Edw. 7:			
c. 30	Cinematograph Act 1909	Transfer of functions (*prosp.*).	52, s. 9(1), sch. 2 Pt. II.
		S. 2(5) am.	S.I. No. 1387
		am. (S)	S.I. No. 1545
c. 39	Oaths Act 1909 ...	Rep.	19, s. 7(1) sch. Pt. I.
c. 47	Development and Road Improvement Funds Act 1909	Pt. I (ss. 1–6) not devolved (S.) (*prosp.*).	51, s. 63, sch. 10 Pt. III.
10 Edw. 7 & 1 Geo. 5:			
c. 7	Development and Road Improvement Funds Act 1910.	S. 3 rep.	45, S.L. (R.), s. 1(1), sch. 1 Pt. XI.
c. cviii ...	Cambridge University and Town Waterworks Act 1910.	Ss. 27, 29, 33 rep. ...	S.I. No. 986.
1 & 2 Geo. 5:			
c. 28	Official Secrets Act 1911	Saved (N.I.)	5 s. 22(6)
2 & 3 Geo. 5:			
c. 30	Trade Union Act 1913...	S. 5A am.	44, s. 159(2), sch. 16 para. 2.
c. clxiii ...	East Surrey Water Order (Water Orders Confirmation) Act 1912.	Sch., ss. 23, 24 rep. ...	S.I. No. 1482.
3 & 4 Geo. 5:			
c. 20	Bankruptcy (Scotland) Act 1913.	S. 118 am.	44, s. 121.
c. 32	Ancient Monuments Consolidation and Amendment Act 1913.	Transfer of functions (*prosp.*).	52, s. 9(1), sch. 2 Pt. XII.
		Ss. 14(4), 15(2) mod. (*prosp.*).	52, s. 77(1), sch. 11 para. 2.
c. clxv ...	Pilotage Order (London) Confirmation Act 1913.	Sch. para. 4(1)(3), Appendix paras. 1–10 subst.	S.I. No. 1540.
4 & 5 Geo. 5:			
c. 31	Housing Act 1914 ...	Transfer of functions (*prosp.*).	52, s. 9(1), sch. 2 Pt. IV.
c. 59	Bankruptcy Act 1914 ...	S. 33 am.	44, s. 121.
5 & 6 Geo. 5:			
c. 48	Fishery Harbours Act 1915.	Transfer of functions (W.)	S.I. No. 272.
6 & 7 Geo. 5:			
c. 58	Registration of Business Names Act 1916.	Not devolved (S.) (*prosp.*)	51, s. 63, sch. 10 Pt. III.
7 & 8 Geo. 5:			
c. 31	Finance Act 1917 ...	S. 34 rep.	45, S.L. (R.), s. 1(1), sch. 1 Pt. IX.

Session and Chap. or No. of Measure	Short title or Subject	How affected	Chapter of 1978 Act or number of Measure or Statutory Instrument
7 & 8 Geo. 5: —*cont.*			
c. 64	Representation of the People Act 1918.	Ss. 21(3) rep. in pt., 42, sch. 6 rep.	45, S.L. (R.), s. 1(1), sch. 1 Pt. VI.
8 & 9 Geo. 5:			
c. 15	Finance Act 1918 ...	S. 42 rep.	45, S.L. (R.), s. 1(1), sch. 1 Pt. IX.
c. 59	Termination of the Present War (Definition) Act 1918.	Rep.	45, S.L. (R.), s. 1(1), sch. 1 Pt. XVII.
9 & 10 Geo. 5:			
c. 20	Scottish Board of Health Act 1919.	Sch. 1 paras. 2, 3 rep. ...	45, S.L. (R.), s. 1(1), sch. 1 Pt. XVII.
c. 32	Finance Act 1919 ...	Ss. 8, 38(1) rep. ...	42, s. 80(5), sch. 13 Pt. I.
c. 37	War Loan Act 1919 ...	S. 3(1) rep.	45, S.L. (R.), s. 1(1), sch. 1 Pt. IX.
c. 50	Ministry of Transport Act 1919.	Ss. 11, 20 transfer of functions (*prosp.*).	52, s. 9(1), sch. 2 Pt. XV.
c. 59	Land Settlement (Facilities) Act 1919.	Transfer of certain functions (W.).	S.I. No. 272.
		Transfer of functions (*prosp.*).	52, s. 9(1), sch. 2 Pt. VIII.
c. 75	Ferries (Acquisition by Local Authorities) Act 1919.	Transfer of certain functions (*prosp.*).	52, s. 9(1), sch. 2 Pt. XV.
10 & 11 Geo. 5:			
c. 5	War Emergency Laws (Continuance) Act 1920.	Rep.	45, S.L. (R.), s. 1(1), sch. 1 Pt. XVII.
c. 33	Maintenance Orders (Facilities for Enforcement) Act 1920.	S. 3(4) am. (*prosp.*) ...	22, s. 89, sch. 2 para. 2.
c. 41	Census Act 1920 ...	S. 2(2) transfer of certain functions (*prosp.*).	52, s. 9(1), sch. 2 Pt. XVII.
c. 54	Seeds Act 1920 ...	Transfer of functions (W)	S.I. No. 272.
c. 65	Employment of Women, Young Persons, and Children Act 1920	Preamble ss. 1(3) rep. in pt. (6) (e) rep. 3(1), 4 rep. in pt. sch. Pt. III rep.	45 S.L. (R), s. 1(1), sch. 1 Pt. VIII.
c. 67	Government of Ireland Act 1920	Ss. 38, 40, 41(1) proviso 44, 46, 50 sch. 7 rep. (*prosp.*).	23, s. 122(2) sch. 7 Pt. I.
c. 72	Roads Act 1920 ...	S. 3 transfer of functions (*prosp.*).	52, s. 9(1) sch. 2 Pt. XV.
c. 75	Official Secrets Act 1920	Saved (N.I.)	5, s. 22(6)
c. 81	Administration of Justice Act 1920	Ss. 11, 12(2) rep. (N.I.)	23, s. 122(2) sch. 7 Pt. I.
c. xi	Lands Improvement Company's Amendment Act 1920	Transfer of functions (W)	S.I. No. 272.
11 & 12 Geo. 5:			
c. 35	Corn Sales Act 1921	Transfer of functions (W)	S.I. No. 272.
c. 55	Railways Act 1921	Ss. 14, 68(1) proviso, (3), 70(2), 71(1) proviso, 86(2) schs. 3, 9 rep.	45, S.L. (R.), s. 1 (1), sch. 1 Pt. XV.

Session and Chap. or No. of Measure	Short title or Subject	How affected	Chapter of 1978 Act or number of Measure or Statutory Instrument
11 & 12 Geo. 5: *—cont.*			
c. xliii	East Surrey Water Act 1921	Ss. 26, 28 rep.	S.I. No. 1482.
12 & 13 Geo. 5:			
c. 16	Law of Property Act 1922	S. 144A saved	G.S.M. No. 2 s. 8(2).
		(6) (definition of 'manorial documents') appl.	GSM No 2 s. 8(1).
c. 51	Allotments Act 1922	Transfer of certain functions (W)... ...	S.I. No. 272.
		Transfer of functions (*prosp*).	52, s. 9(1) sch. 2 Pt. VIII.
13 Geo. 5 Sess. 2:			
c. 2	Irish Free State (Consequential Provisions) Act 1922	Sch. 1 para. 6 rep. (*prosp*).	23, s. 122(2) sch. 7 Pt. I.
13 & 14 Geo. 5:			
c. 4	Fees (Increase) Act 1923	S. 7 transfer of functions (*prosp*).	52, s. 9(1) sch. 2 Pt. II.
c. 27	Railway Fires Act (1905) Amendment Act 1923	S. 4 rep.	45, S.L. (R.), s. 1(1), sch. 1 Pt. XV.
c. 33	Universities of Oxford and Cambridge Act 1923	Ss. 2–4 rep.	45, S.L. (R.), s. 1(1), sch. 1 Pt. V.
c. 34	Agricultural Credits Act 1923	Transfer of functions (W).	S.I. No. 272.
14 & 15 Geo. 5:			
c. 20	Marriages Validity (Provisional Orders) Act 1924	Transfer of functions (*prosp*).	52, s. 9(1), sch. 2 Pt. XVII.
15 & 16 Geo. 5:			
c. 19	Trustee Act 1925 ...	S. 69(3) sch. 1 rep. ...	45, S.L. (R.), s. 1(1), sch. 1 Pt. XVII.
c. 20	Law of Property Act 1925	Ss. 193, 194 transfer of functions (*prosp*). ...	52, s. 9(1), sch. 2 Pt. VIII.
c. 24	Universities and College Estates Act 1925.	Ss. 10(1) (i) (iii), 15(1) am.	S.I. No. 443.
c. 33	Church of Scotland (Property and Endowments) Act 1925.	Ss. 34(1) (g) am., rep. in pt. 36 am.	i s. 2 sch.
c. 49	Supreme Court of Judicature (Consolidation) Act 1925.	S. 49 appl. (*prosp*). ...	12, s. 14 sch. 4 para. 2(2).
		Sch. 4 rep. in pt. ...	45, S.L. (R), s. 1(1), sch. 1 Pt. I.
c. 50	Theatrical Employers Registration Act 1925.	Transfer of functions (*prosp*.). ...	52, s. 9(1), sch. 2 Pt. II.
c. 61	Allotments Act 1925	Transfer of certain functions (W)	S.I. No. 272.
		Transfer of functions (*prosp*). ...	52, s. 9(2), sch. 2 Pt. VIII.
		S. 3(2) rep.	45, S.L. (R.), s. 1(1), sch. 1 Pt. XVII.
c. 73	National Library of Scotland Act 1925.	Devolved in pt. (*prosp*.)	51, s. 63, sch. 10 Pt. III.

Session and Chap. or No. of Measure	Short title or Subject	How affected	Chapter of 1978 Act or number of Measure or Statutory Instrument
15 & 16 Geo. 5: —*cont.*			
c. xvii ...	Imperial Institute Act 1925.	S. 8(2) am.	15, s. 7(4), sch. para. 8.
		am.	20, s. 4(3), sch. 2 para. 8.
		am.	S.I. Nos. 1030, 1899
C.A.M. No. 1... ...	Interpretation Measure 1925.	S.1. rep.	30, s. 25(1), sch. 3.
16 & 17 Geo. 5:			
c. 36	Parks Regulation (Amendment) Act 1926.	Transfer of functions (S.) (*prosp.*).	51, s. 63, sch. 11 Group J.
c. 44	Supreme Court of Judicature of Northern Ireland Act 1926.	Rep. (*prosp.*).	23, s. 122(2) sch. 7 Pt. I.
c. 46	University of London Act 1926.	Rep.	ii, s. 10 sch. 2
c. 48	Births and Deaths Registration Act 1926.	Ss. 1, 3 am. (*prosp.*) ...	52, s. 77(1), sch. 11 para. 3.
		S. 12 transfer of certain functions (*prosp.*).	52, s. 9(1), sch. 2 Pt. XVII.
c. 51	Electricity (Supply) Act 1926.	Sch. 6 rep. in pt. ...	45, S.L. (R.), s. 1(1), sch. 1 Pt. VII.
c. 52	Small Holdings and Allotments Act 1926.	Transfer of certain functions (W.).	S.I. No. 272.
c. 59	Coroners (Amendment) Act 1926.	S. 6(1), sch. 1 excl. ...	S.I. No. 374.
c. xlvii ...	Shoreham Harbour Act 1926.	Ss. 57, 58 rep. 72 am. ...	S.I. No. 647.
17 & 18 Geo. 5:			
c. 4	Royal and Parliamentary Titles Act 1927.	S. 2(2) rep. in pt. ...	30, s. 25(1) sch. 3.
c. 36	Landlord and Tenant Act 1927.	S. 20 transfer of functions (*prosp.*).	52, s. 9(1), sch. 2 Pt. IV.
c. civ ...	East Surrey Water Act 1927.	Ss. 5–8, 32–34 rep. ...	S.I. No. 1482
C. A.M. No. 3... ...	New Dioceses (Transitional Provisions) Measure 1927.	Rep.	G.S.M. No. 1, s. 9(8).
18 & 19 Geo. 5:			
c. 32	Petroleum (Consolidation) Act 1928.	Sch. 1 subst.	S.I. No. 635.
c. 43	Agricultural Credits Act 1928.	S. 4 transfer of functions (W.).	S.I. No. 272.
19 & 20 Geo. 5:			
c. lxix ...	Iveagh Bequest (Kenwood) Act 1929.	S. 3(2)(*aa*) added ...	xiii, s. 7.
C.A.M. No. 1... ...	Parochial Registers and Records Measure 1929.	Rep.	G.S.M. No. 2 s. 26(2), sch. 4.
20 & 21 Geo. 5:			
c. 20	Land Drainage (Scotland) Act 1930.	Ss. 7 devolved in pt. (*prosp.*), 8 not devolved (*prosp.*).	51, s. 63, sch. 10 Pt. III.
c. lxi	East Surrey Water Act 1930.	Ss. 5–8, 47 rep.	S.I. No. 1482.
c. lxvii ...	Portsmouth Water Act 1930.	S. 46 rep.	S.I. No. 1932.

Session and Chap. or No. of Measure	Short title or Subject	How affected	Chapter of 1978 Act or number of Measure or Statutory Instrument
21 & 22 Geo. 5:			
c. 16	Ancient Monuments Act 1931.	Transfer of functions (*prosp.*).	52, s. 9(1), sch. 2 Pt. XII.
c. 41	Agricultural Land (Utilisation) Act 1931.	Transfer of certain functions (W.).	S.I. No. 272.
		Pt. II transfer of certain functions (*prosp.*).	52, s. 9(1), sch. 2 Pt. VIII.
c. 43	Improvement of Live Stock (Licensing of Bulls) Act 1931.	Transfer of functions (W.)	S.I. No. 272.
c. lx	West Ham Corporation Act 1931.	S. 31(1)(*b*) rep. in pt. (street trading) (Gtr. London).	xiii, s. 10(5), sch. 2.
		S. 32 subst. (street trading) (Gtr. London).	xiii, s. 10(1)(2), sch. 1 Pt. I.
c. xcv... ...	Dagenham Urban District Council Act 1931.	S. 119(1)(*f*) rep. (street trading) (Gtr. London).	xiii, s. 10(5), sch. 2.
		S 120 subst. (street trading) (Gtr. London).	xiii, s. 10(1)(2), sch. 1 Pt. II.
22 & 23 Geo. 5:			
c. 4	Statute of Westminster 1931.	S. 11 rep.	30, s. 25(1), sch. 3.
c. 11	Northern Ireland (Miscellaneous Provisions) Act 1932.	S. 5 rep. (*prosp.*). ...	23, s. 122(2), sch. 7 Pt. I.
		S. 9(3) am. (*prosp.*). ...	23, s. 122(1), sch. 5 Pt. II(1).
c. 12	Destructive Imported Animals Act 1932.	Ss. 3–8 transfer of functions (W.).	S.I. No. 272.
c. 34	British Museum Act 1932.	S. 2(2) rep.	45, S.L. (R), s. 1(1), sch. 1 Pt. XIII.
c. 39	Extradition Act 1932 ...	S. 1 rep. in pt.	26, s. 9, sch. 2.
c. 51	Sunday Entertainments Act 1932.	S. 2 rep.	45, S.L. (R), s. 1(1), sch. 1 Pt. IX.
23 & 24 Geo. 5:			
c. 6	Visiting Forces (British Commonwealth) Act 1933.	S. 4 appl.	15, s. 7(4), sch. para. 2.
		appl.	20, s. 4(3), sch. 2 para. 2.
		appl.	S.I. Nos. 1030, 1899.
c. 12	Children and Young Persons Act 1933.	Ss. 10(4), 18, 27 transfer of functions (*prosp.*).	52, s. 9(1), sch. 2 Pt. VI.
		Ss. 87(1)(4), 88(1)(2)(4) am. (*prosp.*).	22, s. 89, sch. 2 paras. 3, 4.
		Ss. 93, 103 transfer of functions (*prosp.*).	52, s. 9(1), sch. 2 Pt. VI.
		S. 107(1) (definition of " commission area ") added (*prosp.*).	22, s. 89, sch. 2 para. 5.
		Sch. 1 am. (except for purposes of ss. 15, 99).	37, s. 1(5).
c. 13	Foreign Judgments (Reciprocal Enforcement) Act 1933.	S. 13(*b*) am.	23, s. 122(1), sch. 5 Pt. II(1).
c. 21	Solicitors (Scotland) Act 1933.	Ss. 37–39 am. (1.3.1979)	S.I. No. 1910.

Session and Chap. or No. of Measure	Short title or Subject	How affected	Chapter of 1978 Act or number of Measure or Statutory Instrument
23 & 24 Geo. 5: —*cont.*			
c. 44	Church of Scotland (Property and Endowments) Amendment Act 1933.	Ss. 3(2), 4, 5, 6, 8(1)(2)(3) am., rep. in pt.	i, s. 2, sch.
c. lxvii ...	Wimbledon Corporation Act 1933.	S. 98(1)(*b*) rep. in pt. (street trading) (Gtr. London).	xiii, s. 10(5), sch. 2.
		S. 99 subst. (street trading) (Gtr. London).	xiii, s. 10(1)(2), sch. 1 Pt. I.
c. lxviii ...	Barking Corporation Act 1933.	S. 198(1)(*b*) rep. in pt. (street trading) (Gtr. London).	xiii, s. 10(5), sch. 2.
		S. 199 subst. (street trading) (Gtr. London).	xiii, s. 10(1)(2), sch. 1, Pt. I.
24 & 25 Geo. 5:			
c. 36	Petroleum (Production) Act 1934.	Sch. rep. pt.	45, S. L.(R.), 1(1), sch. 1 Pt. XVII.
c. 49	Whaling Industry (Regulation) Act 1934.	S. 17(1) (definition of " British ships to which this Act applies ") am.	15, s. 7(4), sch. para. 5.
		am.	20, s. 4(3), sch. 2 para. 5.
		am.	S.I. Nos. 1030, 1899.
25 & 26 Geo. 5:			
c. 8	Unemployment Insurance Act 1935.	Rep.	45, S.L. (R.), s. 1(1), sch. 1 Pt. VIII.
c. 21	Northern Ireland Land Purchase (Winding Up) Act 1935.	Ss. 2, 6(3), 7(1)(*a*), 8, 9(4) rep. (*prosp.*).	23, s. 122(2), sch. 7 Pt. I.
c. 25	Counterfeit Currency (Convention) Act 1935.	S. 4 rep.	26, s. 9, sch. 2.
c. 30	Law Reform (Married Women and Tortfeasors) Act 1935.	S. 6 rep.	47, s. 9(2), sch. 2.
c. lxx ...	East Surrey Water Order (Ministry of Health Provisional Order Confirmation) Act 1935.	Sch., s. 9 rep. in pt., ss. 10, 12, 14 rep.	S.I. No. 1482.
c. xcii ...	London Building Act (Amendment) Act 1935.	S. 5 am.	xvi, s. 7(1).
		S. 9(8) am.	xvi, s. 7(2).
26 Geo. 5 & 1 Edw. 8:			
c. 22	Hours of Employment (Conventions) Act 1936.	S. 1(3) rep.	45, S.L. (R.), s. 1(1), sch. 1 Pt. VIII.
c. 27	Petroleum (Transfer of Licences) Act 1936.	S. 1(4) am.	S.I. No. 635.
c. 43	Tithe Act 1936	S. 36(2) saved	G.S.M. No. 2 s. 8(2).
c. 49	Public Health Act 1936	Transfer of certain functions (*prosp.*).	52, s. 9(1), sch. 2 Pt. VII.
		Ss. 2, 6 consent of Min. required (*prosp.*).	52, s. 36(1), sch. 4.
		S. 76 (except s. 76(3)(*a*)) appl.	3, s. 6(3).
		S. 143 consent of Min. required (*prosp.*).	52, s. 36(1), sch. 4.

Session and Chap. or No. of Measure	Short title or Subject	How affected	Chapter of 1978 Act or number of Measure or Statutory Instrument
26 Geo. 5 & 1 Edw. 8:—*cont.*			
c. 52	Private Legislation Procedure (Scotland) Act 1936.	Saved (*prosp.*) ... S. 5(7)(8) appl. (mods.) (*prosp.*).	51, s. 31(4). 51, s. 31(3).
c. cxv... ...	Merton and Morden Urban District Council Act 1936.	S. 107(1)(*b*) rep. in pt. (street trading) (Gtr. London). S. 108 subst. (street trading) (Gtr. London).	xiii, s. 10(5), sch. 2. xiii, s. 10(1)(2), sch. 1 Pt. I.
1 Edw. 8 & 1 Geo. 6:			
c. 5	Trunk Roads Act 1936	Transfer of functions (*prosp.*). Ss. 6(7) rep. in pt., 12(7) (8)(11) rep., sch. 2 rep. in pt., sch. 4 para. 8, sch. 5 paras. 3, 5–9 rep.	52, s. 9(1), sch. 2 Pt. XV. 45, S.L. (R.), s. 1(1), sch. 1 Pt. XI.
c. 28	Harbours, Piers and Ferries (Scotland) Act 1937.	Ss. 5(6) devolved in pt. (*prosp.*), 9(*a*)(*d*), 26 not devolved (*prosp.*).	51, s. 63, sch. 10 Pt. III.
c. 33	Diseases of Fish Act 1937	Saved (S.) ... ... Transfer of functions (W.) Ext. s. 10(1) (definition of " infected ") am.	35, s. 1(1). S.I. No. 272. S.I. No. 1022.
c. 40	Public Health (Drainage of Trade Premises) Act 1937	Transfer of functions (*prosp.*).	52, s. 9(1), sch. 2 Pt. VII.
c. 43	Public Records (Scotland) Act 1937.	S. 5(4) added (*prosp.*) ...	51, s. 82(2), sch. 16 para. 1.
c. 46	Physical Training and Recreation Act 1937.	Transfer of functions (*prosp.*).	52, s. 9(1), sch. 2 Pt. III.
c. 70	Agriculture Act 1937 ...	Pt. I (ss. 1–5), s. 29 transfer of functions (W.).	S.I. No. 272.
c. xcviii ...	Coulsdon and Purley Urban District Council Act 1937.	S. 81(1)(*b*) rep. in pt. (street trading) (Gtr. London). S. 82 subst. (street trading) (Gtr. London).	xiii, s. 10(5), sch. 2 xiii, s. 10(1)(2), sch. 1 Pt. I.
c. cii	Aberdeen Corporation (Water, Gas, Electricity and Transport) Order Confirmation Act 1937.	Sch., ss. 8 subst., 11 rep.	S.I. No. 208.
1 & 2 Geo. 6:			
c. 8	Unemployment Insurance Act 1938.	Rep.	45, S.L. (R), s. 1(1), sch. 1 Pt. VIII.
c. 12	Population (Statistics) Act 1938.	S. 2(2) transfer of functions (*prosp.*).	52, s. 1(1), sch. 2 Pt. XVII.
c. 22	Trade Marks Act 1938...	Ss. 18, 32(1), 68(1) (definition of "prescribed") am. (N.I.).	23, s. 122(1), sch. 5 Pt. II(1).
c. 63	Administration of Justice (Miscellaneous Provisions) Act 1938.	S. 13 rep.	33, s. 23(2).
c. xvi ...	Bournemouth Gas and Water Act 1938.	S. 49 rep.	S.I. No. 1194.

Session and Chap. or No. of Measure	Short title or Subject	How affected	Chapter of 1978 Act or number of Measure or Statutory Instrument
2 & 3 Geo. 6:			
c. 21	Limitation Act 1939 ...	Ss. 22(1), 26 am., 27(3)–(7) appl.	47, s. 9(1), sch. 1 para. 6.
c. 49	House of Commons Members' Fund Act 1939.	Sch. 1 paras. 1, 2 subst., 2A am.	S.I. No. 1771.
c. 73	Housing (Emergency Powers) Act 1939.	Transfer of functions (*prosp.*).	52, s. 9(1), sch. 2 Pt. IV.
c. lxxxi ...	Bristol Waterworks Act 1939.	Ss. 103 am., rep. in pt., 103A added.	S.I. No. 1249.
c. xcvii ...	London Building Acts (Amendment) Act 1939.	S. 148(2)(3) am. ...	xvi, s. 7(3)(4), sch. 2 Pts. I, II.
3 & 4 Geo. 6:			
c. 14	Agriculture (Miscellaneous War Provisions) Act 1940.	S. 15(1) transfer of functions (W.).	S.I. No. 272.
		transfer of functions (*prosp.*).	52, s. 9(1), sch. 2 Pt. IX.
c. 42	Law Reform (Miscellaneous Provisions) (Scotland) Act 1940.	S. 7 rep.	33, s. 23(2).
4 & 5 Geo. 6:			
c. 3	Local Elections and Register of Electors (Temporary Provisions) Act 1940.	Rep.	45, S.L. (R.), s. 1(1), sch. 1 Pt. VI.
c. 34	Repair of War Damage Act 1941.	Transfer of functions (*prosp.*).	52, s. 9(1), sch. 2 Pt. IV.
c. 50	Agriculture (Miscellaneous Provisions) Act 1941.	S. 11 transfer of functions (W.).	S.I. No. 272.
c. xiv ...	Portsmouth Water Act 1941.	S. 67 ext.	S.I. No. 1932.
6 & 7 Geo. 6:			
c. 2	Supreme Court (Northern Ireland) Act 1942.	Rep. (*prosp.*)	23, s. 122(2), sch. 7 Pt. I.
c. 16	Agriculture (Miscellaneous Provisions) Act 1943.	S. 17 transfer of functions (W.).	S.I. No. 272.
c. 21	War Damage Act 1943	S. 33(1) am. (N.I.) (*prosp.*)	23, s. 122(1), sch. 5 Pt. II(1).
		S. 71 transfer of functions (*prosp.*).	52, s. 9(1), sch. 2 Pt. XV.
c. 32	Hydro-Electric Development (Scotland) Act 1943.	S. 14(2) rep. in pt. ...	45, S.L. (R.), s. 1(1), sch. 1 Pt. VII.
c. 39	Pensions Appeal Tribunals Act 1943.	Ss. 6(2) am. (N.I.) (*prosp.*), 14 am. (*prosp.*), sch. am. (N.I.) (*prosp.*).	23, s. 122(1), sch. 5 Pt. II(1).
C.A.M.:			
No. 1 ...	New Parishes Measure 1943.	S. 17(1) am.	G.S.M. No. 3 s. 7.
7 & 8 Geo. 6:			
c. 2	Local Elections and Register of Electors (Temporary Provisions) Act 1943.	Rep.	45, S.L. (R.), s. 1(1), sch. 1 Pt. VI.

Session and Chap. or No. of Measure	Short title or Subject	How affected	Chapter of 1978 Act or number of Measure or Statutory Instrument
7 & 8 Geo. 6: *—cont.*			
c. 10	Disabled Persons (Employment) Act 1944.	Not devolved (S.) (*prosp.*)	51, s. 63, sch. 10 Pt. III.
c. 26	Rural Water Supplies and Sewerage Act 1944.	Transfer of functions (*prosp.*).	52, s. 9(1), sch. 2 Pt. IX.
c. 28	Agriculture (Miscellaneous Provisions) Act 1944.	S. 1(1) transfer of certain functions (W.).	S.I. No. 272.
c. 31	Education Act 1944 ...	Transfer of certain functions (*prosp.*).	52, s. 9(1), sch. 2 Pt. III.
		S. 84 transfer of functions (W.).	S.I. No. 274.
		S. 107 rep.	45, S.L. (R.), s. 1(1), sch. 1 Pt. V.
		S. 114(2) (definition of " school ") appl. (S.).	29, s. 108(1).
		S. 120(2) rep., (3) sch. 8 Pt. I rep. in pt., Pt. II rep.	45, S.L. (R.), s. 1(1), sch. 1 Pt. V.
c. xxi ...	Middlesex County Council Act 1944.	S. 326(1)(*b*) rep. in pt. (street trading) (Gtr. London).	xiii, s. 10(5), sch. 2.
		S. 327 subst. (street trading) (Gtr. London).	xiii, s. 10(1)(2), sch. 1 Pt. I.
8 & 9 Geo. 6:			
c. 5	Representation of the People Act 1945.	Rep.	45, S.L. (R.), s. 1(1), sch. 1 Pt. VI.
c. 12	Northern Ireland (Miscellaneous Provisions) Act 1945.	S. 8 rep. (*prosp.*) ...	23, s. 122(2), sch. 7 Pt. I.
c. 16	Limitation (Enemies and War Prisoners) Act 1945.	S. 2(1) am.	47, s. 9(1), sch. 1 para. 6.
c. 27	Welsh Church (Burial Grounds) Act 1945.	Transfer of functions (*prosp.*).	52, s. 9(1), sch. 2 Pt. II.
c. 28	Law Reform (Contributory Negligence) Act 1945	S. 1 (3) rep. (E. & W.) (5) rep. in pt. (E. & W.)	47, s. 9(2), sch. 2.
		S. 5(b) subst.	47, s. 9(1), sch. 1 para. 1.
c. 37	Education (Scotland) Act 1945.	Sch. 4 rep. in pt. ...	45, S.L. (R.), s. 1(1), sch. 1 Pt. V.
c. 42	Water Act 1945 ...	Transfer of certain functions (*prosp.*). ...	52, s. 9(1), sch. 2 Pt. IX.
		Ss. 9, 10, 12(5), 13, 18, 19, 23, 24, 33 sch. 1 pt. sch. 2 power to intervene (*prosp.*).	52, s. 63 sch. 8 Pts. III, IV.
c. 43	Requisitioned Land and War Works Act 1945.	Ss. 15–20 transfer of functions (*prosp.*). ...	52, s. 9(1), sch. 2 Pt. XV.
		S. 52 transfer of functions (*prosp.*).	52, s. 9(1), sch. 2 Pt. XV.
		concurrent powers of Min. (*prosp.*). ...	52, s. 9(2), sch. 3.
		am. (*prosp.*). ...	51, s. 23(3), sch. 5.

Session and Chap. or No. of Measure	Short title or Subject	How affected	Chapter of 1978 Act or number of Measure or Statutory Instrument
9 & 10 Geo. 6:			
c. 15	Public Health (Scotland) Act 1945.	S. 1(1)(b) am. (*prosp.*).	51, s. 23(1)(2) sch. 4.
c. 29	Agriculture Artificial Insemination Act 1946.	S. 1 transfer of functions (W).	S.I. No. 272.
c. 30	Trunk Roads Act 1946	S. 9 rep.	45, S.L. (R.), s. 1(1), sch. 1 Pt. XI.
c. 36	Statutory Instruments Act 1946.	Appl.	34, s. 2(4).
		Appl. (S.)(*prosp.*). ...	28, s. 60(7).
		S. 1 am. (*prosp.*). ...	52, s. 77(1), sch. 11 para. 4.
		Ss. 1(3), 4(4) added (*prosp.*).	51, s. 82(2), sch. 16 paras. 2–4.
		S. 5 appl. ... ... appl. (*prosp.*). ...	23, s. 56(1). 23, s. 119(2).
		Ss. 5A, 6A added (*prosp.*). 7(1)(2) am. (*prosp.*) (4) (5) added (*prosp.*) 8(1) (b) am. (*prosp.*). ...	51, s. 82(2), sch. 16 paras. 5–8.
c. 42	Water (Scotland) Act 1946.	Sch. 4 Pt. III ss. 10(3)(4) appl. (mods.) ...	S.I. No. 208.
c. 49	Acquisition of Land (Authorisation Procedure Act 1946.	Appl.	3, s. 7.
		Ss. 3,5 transfer of certain functions (*prosp.*). ...	52, s. 9(1), sch. 2 Pt. VIII.
		Sch. 1 para. 7B(2)(a), (3)(a) am. (*prosp.*) 6) rep. in pt. (*prosp.*). ...	52, s. 77(1), sch. 11 para. 5.
		Sch. 1 paras. 10–12 transfer of certain functions (*prosp.*).	52, s. 9(1), sch. 2 Pt. VIII.
c. 50	Education Act 1946	Transfer of functions (*prosp.*).	52, s. 9(1), sch. 2 Pt. III.
		Ss. 8(4), 15 rep. sch. 2 Pt. I rep. in pt.	45, S.L. (R.), s. 1(1), sch. 1 Pt. V.
c. 73	Hill Farming Act 1946	Act (except s. 32(2)(4)) transfer of functions (W.)	S.I. No. 272.
		Act (except ss. 23–31) not devolved (S.) (*prosp.*).	51, s. 63 sch. 10 Pt. III.
		S. 38 (definition of "the Ministers") am.	S.I. No. 272.
c. 82	Cable and Wireless Act 1946.	Ss. 1(2)(3), 2, 4(1)(2)(3), 5, 6. 7(b) sch. 1–3 rep.	45, S.L. (R.), s. 1(1) sch 1. Pt. IX.
10 & 11 Geo. 6:			
c. 14	Exchange Control Act 1947.	Sch. 4 para. 8(2) am. ...	23, s. 122(1), sch. 5 Pt. II(1).
c. 19	Polish Resettlement Act 1947.	S. 1 am.	S.I. No. 1526.
		S. 11(3)(b) am. ...	29, s. 109 sch. 16 para 1.
c. 27	National Health Service (Scotland) Act 1947.	Rep. (saving for ss. 27, 37, 53, 74 sch. 11 Pt. I).	29, s. 109 sch. 15 paras. 4, 10, 15 sch. 17.
		Ss. 34, 39, 40, 42 am. (*prosp.*).	51, s. 23(1)(2) sch. 4.
		Sch. 3 para. 6 not devolved (*prosp.*). ...	51, s. 63 sch. 10 Pt. III.

Session and Chap. or No. of Measure	Short title or Subject	How affected	Chapter of 1978 Act or number of Measure or Statutory Instrument
10 & 11 Geo. 6: *—cont.*			
c. 39	Statistics of Trade Act 1947.	Not devolved. (S.) (*prosp.*)	51, s. 63 sch. 10 Pt. III.
		S. 1(1) am. (*prosp.*)	51, s. 82(2) sch. 16 para. 9(1).
		am. (*prosp.*)	52, s. 77(1) sch. 11 para. 6.
		S. 9(1) ext. (*prosp.*)	51, s. 82(2) sch. 16 para. 9(2).
		appl. (*prosp.*)	52, s. 77(1) sch. 11 para. 7.
		S. 19(3) rep.	45, S.L. (R.), s. 1(1), sch. 1 Pt. XVII.
c. 40	Industrial Organisation and Development Act 1947.	Transfer of functions (W.) S. 10 rep.	S.I. No. 272. 45, S.L. (R.), s. 1(1), sch. 1 Pt. IX.
c. 41	Fire Services Act 1947	Transfer of certain functions (*prosp.*). ...	52, s. 9(1) sch. 2 Pt. V.
		S. 26 am. (*prosp.*) ...	51, s. 23(1)(2) sch. 4.
c. 42	Acquisition of Land (Authorisation Procedure) (Scotland) Act 1947.	Appl. (*retrosp.*)	14, s. 10.
		Appl.	3, s. 7.
		Not devolved (*prosp.*)	51, s. 63, sch. 10 Pt. III.
		Transfer of certain functions (*prosp.*) ...	51, s. 63, sch. 11 Group E.
		S. 1(1)(*d*) am.	29, s. 109 sch. 16 para. 2.
c. 44	Crown Proceedings Act 1947.	S. 4(1) saved (E. & W.)	47, s. 5.
		saved (N.I.) ...	47, s. 8.
		(2) rep. (E.W.N.I.) ...	47, s. 9(2), sch. 2.
		Ss. 20(2), 38(2) (definition of "Civil proceedings") mod. (*prosp.*).... ...	23, s. 122(1), sch. 5 Pt. II(1)
c. 48	Agriculture Act 1947 ...	Ss. 58, 78 transfer of functions (W.).	S.I. No. 272.
		S. 78 am. (*prosp.*) ...	51, s. 23(3), sch. 5.
		Ss. 79–95, 97–109 transfer of functions (W.).	S.I. No. 272.
		S. 109(3), sch. 2 para. 3(1)(*b*) am.	S.I. No. 446.
		Sch. 9 paras. 22, 23 transfer of functions (W.).	S.I. No. 272.
c. 54	Electricity Act 1947 ...	S. 54(3)(5) am.	44, s. 130, sch. 10 para. 7.
		S. 68(8) rep.	S.I. No. 1175.
		Sch. 4 Pt. I rep. in pt. ...	45, S.L. (R), s. 1(1), sch. 1 Pt. VII.
c. xlvi ...	London County Council (General Powers) Act 1947.	S. 21(3)(*e*) rep. in pt. (street trading) (Gtr. London).	xiii, s. 10(5), sch. 2.
		S. 23(4) am.	xvi, s. 10(1).
		S. 26 subst. (street trading) (Gtr. London).	xiii, s. 10(1)(2), sch. 1 Pt. II.
C.A.M.:			
No. 2... ...	Church Commissioners Measure 1947.	S. 10(1) am. (*prosp.*) ...	G.S.M. No. 3, s. 3(1).
		Sch. 1 paras. 1, 2 am., 5A added.	G.S.M. No. 3, s. 4.

Session and Chap. or No. of Measure	Short title or Subject	How affected	Chapter of 1978 Act or number of Measure or Statutory Instrument
11 & 12 Geo. 6:			
c. 7	Ceylon Independence Act 1947.	S. 4(2) rep.	30, s. 25(1), sch. 3.
c. 11	Medical Practitioners and Pharmacists Act 1947.	Rep. (*prosp.*)	12, ss. 17(2), 31 (2), sch. 7.
c. 17	Requisitioned Land and War Works Act 1948.	S. 3 transfer of functions (*prosp.*).	52, s. 9(1), sch. 2 Pt. XV.
c. 22	Water Act 1948 ...	Transfer of certain functions (*prosp.*).	52, s. 9(1), sch. 2 Pt. IX.
		S. 8 power to intervene (*prosp.*).	52, s. 63, sch. 8 Pt. III.
c. 26	Local Government Act 1948.	S. 85 excl.	S.I. Nos. 1174, 1175.
		Ss. 86 rep., 87(1) mod....	S.I. No. 1174.
		Ss. 91, 92 rep.	S.I. No. 1175.
		S. 94 excl.	S.I. No. 1174.
		S. 94(2) rep. in pt., (4)(*a*) rep.	45, S.L. (R), s. 1(1), sch. 1 Pt. XII.
		Ss. 96 rep., 97 excl., 98, 99 rep.	S.I. No. 1175.
		S. 100 excl.	S.I. Nos. 1174, 1175.
		S. 100(1) rep. in pt. ...	45, S.L. (R), s. 1(1), sch. 1 Pt. XII.
		Ss. 102, 105 excl. ...	S.I. Nos. 1174, 1175.
		S. 107 rep.	S.I. No. 1175.
		S. 109 excl.	S.I. No. 1174.
		Ss. 109(1), 110 rep. in pt.	45, S.L. (R), s. 1(1), sch. 1 Pt. XII.
		Ss. 110 excl., 124(1) am., (1)(*a*)(i) rep.	S.I. No. 1174.
		S. 143 rep.	45, S.L. (R), s. 1(1), sch. 1 Pt. XII.
c. 29	National Assistance Act 1948.	Transfer of functions (*prosp.*).	52, s. 9(1), sch. 2 Pt. VI.
		S. 43(4) am. (E. & W.) (*prosp.*).	22, s. 89, sch. 2 para. 6.
		S. 43(7) rep. (*prosp.*) ...	22, s. 89, sch. 3.
		S. 44(2) am. (E. & W.) (*prosp.*).	22, s. 89, sch. 2 para. 7.
		S. 47(8)(10) am. ...	29, s. 109, sch. 16 para. 3.
		S. 58 rep.	45, S.L. (R), s. 1(1), sch. 1 Pt. XII.
		S. 64 (definition of " hospital "), sch. 6 para. 9(3)(*c*) am.	29, s. 109, sch. 16 para. 3.
c. 33	Superannuation (Miscellaneous Provisions) Act 1948.	S. 2 am. (*prosp.*) ...	51, s. 23(1)(2), sch. 4.
c. 37	Radioactive Substances Act 1948.	Transfer of certain functions (*prosp.*).	52, s. 9(1), sch. 2 Pt. VII.
		Ss. 5(1)(*b*), 7 devolved in pt. (S.) (*prosp.*).	51, s. 63, sch. 10 Pt. III.
c. 38	Companies Act 1948 ...	S. 150(4) appl.	1, s. 1(4).
		(definition of " wholly owned subsidiary ") appl.	11, s. 2(4).

Session and Chap. or No. of Measure	Short title or Subject	How affected	Chapter of 1978 Act or number of Measure or Statutory Instrument
11 & 12 Geo. 6: c. 38 —*cont.*	Companies Act 1948 —*cont.*	S. 154 appl. ... ... (definition of "subsidiary") appl. appl. appl. (*prosp.*)	1, s. 1(4). 4, s. 2. 11, s. 2(4). 51, s. 82(2), sch. 16 para. 19(1).
		S. 319 am.	44, s. 121.
c. 40	Education (Miscellaneous Provisions) Act 1948.	Transfer of certain functions (*prosp.*).	52, s. 9(1), sch. 2 Pt. III.
		S. 13 rep., sch. 1 Pt. I rep. in pt.	45, S.L. (R), s. 1(1), sch. 1 Pt. V.
c. 41	Law Reform (Personal Injuries) Act 1948.	S. 2(4) am.	29, s. 109, sch. 16 para. 4.
c. 43	Children Act 1948 ...	Transfer of certain functions (*prosp.*).	52, s. 9(1), sch. 2 Pt. VI.
		Pt. II (ss. 11–22) (except s. 17) appl. (E. & W.) (*prosp.*).	22, s. 10(4)(*a*).
		Pt. III (ss. 23–26) appl. (E. & W.) (*prosp.*).	22, s. 10(4)(*b*).
		S. 26(1)(4) am. (*prosp.*)...	22, s. 89, sch. 2 para. 8.
		S. 59(1) (definition of "hospital") am.	29, s. 109, sch. 16 para. 5.
c. 45	Agriculture (Scotland) Act 1948.	Pt. IV (ss. 55–63) devolved in pt. (*prosp.*), Pt. V (ss. 64–67) devolved (*prosp.*).	51, s. 63, sch. 10 Pt. III.
c. 47	Agricultural Wages Act 1948.	Ss. 2, 9, 12 transfer of functions (W.), 13, 14 transfer of certain functions (W.), 16, sch. 1 transfer of functions (W.), sch. 3 transfer of certain functions (W.).	S.I. No. 272.
c. 53	Nurseries and Child-Minders Regulation Act 1948.	S. 13(2) (definition of "hospital") am.	29, s. 109, sch. 16 para. 6.
c. 56	British Nationality Act 1948.	S. 1(2) rep. in pt. ...	30, s. 25(1), sch. 3.
		S. 1(3) am. ... ... am. ... ... am.	15, s. 2(1). 20, s. 2(1). S.I. Nos. 1030, 1899.
		S. 6(2) excl. ... ... excl. ... ... excl.	15, s. 5(3). 20, s. 2(3). S.I. Nos. 1030, 1899.
		Pt. III (ss. 23–34) (except s. 23) appl. appl. ... ... appl.	15, s. 6(2). 20, s. 3(5). S.I. Nos. 1030, 1899.
		S. 26 saved (*prosp.*) ...	23, s. 22(2)(*a*).
		S. 32(1) am. ... ... (definition of "British protected person") appl. appl. (S.) ...	15, s. 4(5). 33, s. 4(5). 29, s. 49, sch. 10 para. 3.

Session and Chap. or No. of Measure	Short title or Subject	How affected	Chapter of 1978 Act or number of Measure or Statutory Instrument
11 & 12 Geo. 6: —*cont.*			
c. 58	Criminal Justice Act 1948	S. 14 mod.	44, s. 135, sch. 11 para. 23.
c. 63	Agricultural Holdings Act 1948.	Transfer of functions (W.) S. 14(1) am. ... ... Ss. 47(1) restr., mod., (2)(a), 56(2)(3) mod. S. 63(1)(b) am. ... ... Ss. 63(2), 64 proviso, 65(2) mod., sch. 4 paras. 3 rep., 5–7 am., 12 added.	S.I. No. 272. S.I. No. 447. S.I. No. 742. S.I. No. 447. S.I. No. 742.
c. 65	Representation of the People Act 1948.	Ss. 55(1) rep., 74(1)(3) rep. in pt., 75(1), 77(1) (definitions of " electoral area ", " local government election ", " parish "), 78(3), 80(2)(5)(6)(7) proviso (c), (8)–(10) sch. 10 Pt. II para. 6 rep.	45, S.L. (R.), s. 1(1), sch. 1 Pt. VI.
c. xi	Shoreham Harbour Act 1948	S. 28 rep.	S.I. No. 647.
12, 13 & 14 Geo. 6:			
c. 11	Railway and Canal Commission (Abolition) Act 1949.	Ss. 6, 7 rep.	45, S.L. (R.), s. 1(1), sch. 1 Pt. XV.
c. 15	Minister of Food (Financial Powers) Act 1949.	Transfer of functions (W.)	S.I. No. 272.
c. 20 ...	Cinematograph Film Production (Special Loans) Act 1949.	S. 9(1) rep., (2) rep. in pt.	45, S.L. (R.), s. 1(1), sch. 1 Pt. IX.
c. 27 ...	Juries Act 1949	Rep. (E., W. & N.I.), ss. 30, 35(3) rep. (S.).	45, S.L. (R.), s. 1(1), sch. 1 Pt. I.
c. 31	Water (Scotland) Act 1949.	S. 2 appl. (mods.) ... S. 5 excl. ... ... S. 17 excl.	S.I. Nos. 1173, 1174, 1175, 1176. S.I. No. 1176. S.I. No. 1175.
c. 37	Agriculture (Miscellaneous Provisions) Act 1949.	S. 10 transfer of functions (W.).	S.I. No. 272.
c. 39	Commonwealth Telegraphs Act 1949.	S. 6(4) am.	44, s. 130, sch. 10 para. 12.
c. 43	Merchant Shipping (Safety Convention) Act 1949.	S. 2 am. ... ... am. ... ... am.	15, s. 7(4), sch. para. 4. 20, s. 4(3), sch. 2 para. 4. S.I. Nos. 1030, 1899.
c. 47	Finance Act 1949 ...	S. 15 rep.	45, S.L. (R.), s. 1(1), sch. 1 Pt. IX.
c. 54	Wireless Telegraphy Act 1949.	S. 19(1) (definition of " wireless telegraphy ") appl. (N.I.).	5, s. 15(5).
c. 55	Prevention of Damage by Pests Act 1949.	Transfer of functions (W.)	S.I. No. 272.

Session and Chap. or No. of Measure	Short title or Subject	How affected	Chapter of 1978 Act or number of Measure or Statutory Instrument
12, 13 & 14 Geo. 6:—*cont.*			
c. 61	Housing (Scotland) Act 1949.	S. 27 rep. (1.4.1979) ...	14, s. 16(2), sch. 3.
c. 66	House of Commons (Redistribution of Seats) Act 1949.	S. 2(4)(5) appl. (mods.)	10, s. 3, sch. 1 para. 1, sch. 2 para. 4.
		appl. (mods.) (*prosp.*).	51, s. 1, sch. 1 para. 2.
		appl. (mods.) (*prosp.*).	52, s. 1, sch. 1 para. 2.
		S. 3 appl. (mods.) ...	10, s. 3, sch. 1 para. 1, sch. 2 para. 4.
		appl. (mods.) (*prosp.*)	51, s. 1, sch. 1 para. 2.
		appl. (mods.) (*prosp.*)	52, s. 1, sch. 1 para. 2.
		Sch. 1 Pt. III paras. 3, 4 appl. (mods.) (*prosp.*).	51, s. 1, sch. 1 para. 2.
		appl. (mods.) (*prosp.*)	52, s. 1, sch. 1 para. 2.
		para. 4 appl. (mods.).	10, s. 3, sch. 1 para. 1, sch. 2 para. 4.
c. 67	Civil Aviation Act 1949	S. 8(2)(c) saved ...	8, s. 9(2).
		S. 9(1)(3) am.	8, s. 14(1), sch. 1 Pt. I para. 1.
		S. 10(1) rep. in pt. ...	8, s. 14(1)(2), sch. 1 Pt. II para. 9(1)(2), sch. 2.
		Pt. III (ss. 16–39) transfer of certain functions (*prosp.*).	52, s. 9(1), sch. 2 Pt. XIV.
		(except s. 37) devolved (S.) (*prosp.*).	51, s. 63, sch. 10 Pt. III.
		S. 18 am. (N.I.) ...	8, s. 14(1), sch. 1 Pt. II para. 9(1)(3).
		S. 18(1)(b)(2) rep. in pt.	8, s. 14(1)(2) sch. 1 Pt. II para. 9(1)(3), sch. 2.
		S. 19(1) am., (2A) added (*retrosp.*).	8, s. 14(1), sch. 1 Pt. II para. 9(1)(4)(7).
		S. 20 am.	8, s. 14(1), sch. 1 Pt. II para. 9(1)(5).
		S. 26 am.	8, s. 14(1), sch. 1 Pt. I para. 2(2)(3)(6)(7).
		S. 29(2)–(5) appl. (mods.)	8, s. 14(1), sch. 1 Pt. I para. 2(4)(5).
		S. 31 excl.	8, s. 14(1), sch. 1 Pt. I para. 2(8).
		S. 56 devolved (S.) (*prosp.*)	51, s. 63, sch. 10 Pt. III.
		transfer of functions (*prosp.*).	52, s. 9(1), sch. 2 Pt. XIV.

Session and Chap. or No. of Measure	Short title or Subject	How affected	Chapter of 1978 Act or number of Measure or Statutory Instrument
12, 13 & 14 Geo. 6: c. 67—*cont.*	Civil Aviation Act 1949 —*cont.*	S. 59 am.	18, s. 14(1), sch. 1 Pt. II para. 9(1)(6).
c. 68	Representation of the People Act 1949.	Appl. (mods.)	S.I. Nos. 1912, 1915.
		S. 48(7) appl.	10, s. 4(2).
		S. 64(2)(*a*) subst. ...	32, s. 1.
		Ss. 66(6), 74(9), 109(8), 110(1) am. (N.I.) (*prosp.*).	23, s. 122(1), sch. 5 Pt. II(1).
		S. 111(1)(4) rep. (N.I.) (*prosp.*).	23, s. 122(2), sch. 7 Pt. I.
		Ss. 123(1), 126(2), 128(6), 145(4), 152(6) am. (N.I.) (*prosp.*).	23, s. 122(1), sch. 5 Pt. II(1).
		S. 155 appl.	10, s. 4(2).
		S. 160 rep. (N.I.) ...	23, s. 122(2), sch. 7 Pt. I.
		S. 163 (definition of " prescribed ") am. (N.I.).	23, s. 122(1), sch. 5 Pt. II(1).
c. 69	New Forest Act 1949 ...	Sch. 1 para. 6 am. ...	S.I. No. 440.
c. 70	Docking and Nicking of Horses Act 1949.	Transfer of functions (W.)	S.I. No. 272.
c. 74	Coast Protection Act 1949.	Transfer of functions (W.)	S.I. No. 272.
		Transfer of certain functions (*prosp.*) (saving for ss. 2, 18, 31) (*prosp.*).	52, ss. 9(1), 75, sch. 2 Pt. VIII sch. 10.
		Pt. I (ss. 1–33) devolved in pt. (S.) (*prosp.*).	51, s. 63, sch. 10 Pt. III.
		S. 5 consent of Min. required (*prosp.*).	52, s. 36(1), sch. 4.
		S. 5(4)(5) am. (*prosp.*), (5A) added (*prosp.*).	51, s. 82(2), sch. 16 para. 10 (1)–(3).
		S. 8 consent of Min. required (*prosp.*).	52, s. 36(1), sch. 4.
		Ss. 8(4)(5) am. (*prosp.*), (5A) added (*prosp.*), 17(4) am. (*prosp.*), (4A) added (*prosp.*).	51, s. 82(2), sch. 16 para. 10.
c. 75	Agricultural Holdings (Scotland) Act 1949.	S. 86 devolved in pt. (*prosp.*).	51, s. 63, sch. 10 Pt. III.
		Sch. 1 Pt. III paras. 25 rep., 28, 31, 32 am.	S.I. No. 798.
c. 76	Marriage Act 1949 ...	S. 3(5) am. (*prosp.*) ...	22, s. 89, sch. 2 para. 9.
		S. 63 appl. (mods.) ...	G.S.M. No. 2, s. 20(3).
		S. 74 transfer of certain functions (*prosp.*).	52, s. 9(1), sch. 2 Pt. XVII.
		am. (*prosp.*) ...	52, s. 77(1), sch. 11.
c. 93	National Health Service (Amendment) Act 1949.	Ss. 8, 10, 11, 14–18, 20(1)(3), 21, 23(1) rep.	29, s. 109, sch. 17.
		S. 23(2) rep. (saving) (S.)	29, s. 109, sch. 15 para. 11, sch. 17.
		Ss. 28 rep., 32(1) rep. in pt. (S.), sch. Pt. II rep.	29, s. 109, sch. 17.

Session and Chap. or No. of Measure	Short title or Subject	How affected	Chapter of 1978 Act or number of Measure or Statutory Instrument
12, 13 & 14 Geo. 6:—*cont.*			
c. 94	Criminal Justice (Scotland) Act 1949.	S. 75(1)(*b*), (3)(*f*) am. (*prosp*).	51, s. 23(3), sch. 5.
c. 97	National Parks and Access to the Countryside Act 1949.	Am. (W.) (*prosp*) ...	52, s. 77(1), sch. 11 para. 10(2).
		S. 1 rep. in pt. (E.) (*prosp*.), rep. (W.) (*prosp*.).	52, s. 77(1), sch. 11 paras. 9, 10(3).
		Ss. 2, 3 rep. (W.) (*prosp*.).	52, s. 77(1), sch. 11 para. 10(3).
		S. 4 mod. (*prosp*.) ...	52, s. 62(2)(*a*).
		S. 4(1)(3) am. (W.) (*prosp*.), (4) subst. (W.) (*prosp*.).	52, s. 77(1), sch. 11 para. 10(4).
		Pt. II (ss. 5–14) transfer of functions (*prosp*.).	52, s. 9(1), sch. 2 Pt. XI.
		mod. (*prosp*.)	52, s. 62(2)(9).
		S. 5 rep. in pt. (E.) (*prosp*.), (W.) (*prosp*.).	52, s. 77(1), sch. 11 paras. 9, 10(5).
		S. 6 rep. in pt. (W.), (3)(*b*)(4)(*e*)(*f*)(*g*) am. (W.).	52, s. 77(1), sch. 11 para. 10(5).
		Pt. IV (ss. 27–58) transfer of certain functions (*prosp*.).	52, s. 9(1), sch. 2 Pt. XI.
		mod. (*prosp*.)	52, s. 62(2)(9).
		S. 51 rep. in pt. (E.), (*prosp*.), (W.) (*prosp*.).	52, s. 77(1), sch. 11 paras. 9, 10(6).
		Pt. V (ss. 59–83) transfer of functions (*prosp*.).	52, s. 9(1), sch. 2 Pt. XI.
		mod. (*prosp*.)	52, s. 62(2)(9).
		S. 69 transfer of functions (W.).	S.I. No. 272.
		Pt. VI (ss. 84–115) devolved in pt. (S.) (*prosp*.).	51, s. 63, sch. 10 Pt. III.
		transfer of certain functions (*prosp*.).	52, s. 9(1), sch. 2 Pt. XI.
		mod. (*prosp*.)	52, s. 62(2)(9).
		S. 87 rep. in pt. (E.) (*prosp*.), (W.) (*prosp*.).	52, s. 77(1), sch. 11 paras. 9, 10(6).
c. 101	Justices of the Peace Act 1949.	S. 13(4) am. (*prosp*). ...	22, s. 89 sch. 2 para. 10.
		S. 15 ext. (*prosp*). ...	22, ss. 84(1), 85 (1).
		Ss. 45(4), 46(2), sch. 7 Pts. I, III rep.	45, S.L. (R), s. 1(1), sch. 1 Pt. I.
c. xxix ...	British Transport Commission Act 1949.	S. 53 am. (E & W) ...	xxi, s. 25(2)
		rep. in pt.	xxi, s. 25(3).
		S. 53(2) rep. (E. & W.)...	xxi, ss. 25(5)(*b*), 30, sch. 4.
c. lix	Shoreham Harbour Act 1949.	S. 36 rep.	S.I. No. 647.
14 Geo. 6:			
c. 27	Arbitration Act 1950 ...	Excl.	44, s. 128(3), sch. 9 para. 4.
		S. 38(3) subst. (N.I.) ...	23, s. 122(1), sch. 5 Pt. II(1).

Session and Chap. or No. of Measure	Short title or Subject	How affected	Chapter of 1978 Act or number of Measure or Statutory Instrument
14 Geo. 6: c. 27—*cont.*	Arbitration Act 1950 —*cont.*	S. 42(4) rep.	23, s. 122(2), sch. 7 Pt. I.
		S. 43 rep.	45, S.L. (R.), s. 1(1), sch. 1 Pt. I.
c. 28	Shops Act 1950 ...	Pt. I (ss. 1–16) s. 43, Pt. IV (ss. 47–67) transfer of functions (*prosp*). ...	52, s. 9(1) sch. 2 Pt. II.
		S. 67 devolved (S) (*prosp*).	51, s. 63 sch. 10 Pt. III.
		S. 69 transfer of ceratin functions (*prosp*).	52, s. 9(1), sch. 2 Pt. II.
c. 29	Medical Act 1950	Rep.	12, s. 31(2), sch. 7
c. 31	Allotments Act 1950	Transfer of functions (*prosp*).	52, s. 9(1), sch. 2 Pt. VIII.
c. 34	Housing (Scotland) Act 1950.	Ss. 89, 105 rep. (1.4.1979)	14, s. 16(2) sch. 3.
c. 36	Diseases of Animals Act 1950.	Transfer of functions (W.), ss. 24(1), 36B(1), 37(4A), 84(1)(*aa*) am.	S.I. No. 272.
c. 37	Maintenance Orders Act 1950.	S. 2(3) rep. (*prosp*). ...	22, s. 89 sch. 3
		S. 3(2) am. (*prosp*.)	22, s. 89, sch. 2 para. 11.
		S. 13(1) am. (*prosp*.) ...	23, s. 122(1), sch. 5 Pt. II(1).
		S. 13(2), rep. (*prosp*). ...	23, s. 122(2) sch. 7 Pt. I.
		Ss. 15(1)(*a*), 16(2)(*a*), 22(1) am. (*prosp*.).	22, s. 89, sch. 2 paras. 12–14.
		Ss. 25(2), 28(1) (definition of " prescribed ") am. (*prosp*.).	23, s. 122(1), sch. 5 Pt. II(1).
c. 39	Public Utilities Street Act 1950.	Transfer of certain functions (*prosp*.) (saving for sch. 6 para. 1) (*prosp*.).	52, ss. 9(1), 75, sch. 2 Pt. XV. sch. 10.
		S. 19(4) am.	47, s. 9(1), sch. 1 para. 2.
		S. 33(2), sch. 5 rep. in pt.	45, S.L. (R), s. 1, sch. 1 Pt. XI.
14 & 15 Geo. 6: c. 11	Administration of Justice (Pensions) Act 1950.	Ss. 2–8 sch. 1 am. ...	44, s. 128(3), sch. 9 para. 11(6).
c. iii	Gun Barrel Proof Act 1950.	Ext. (S., N.I.)	9, s. 6.
		S. 4 am.	9, s. 8(1), sch. 3 para. 20.
c. 25	Supplies and Services (Defence Purposes) Act 1951.	Rep.	45, S.L. (R.), s. 1(1), sch. 1 Pt. XI.
c. 26	Salmon and Freshwater Fisheries (Protection) (Scotland) Act 1951.	S. 15 am. (*prosp*.) ...	51, s. 23(3), sch. 5.
c. 30	Sea Fish Industry Act 1951.	S. 21(1) transfer of functions (W.).	S.I. No. 272.
c. 31	National Health Service Act 1951.	Rep.	29, s. 109, sch. 17.
c. 39	Common Informers Act 1951.	Sch. rep. in pt.	45, S.L. (R.), s. 1(1), sch. 1 Pt. XVII.

Session and Chap. or No. of Measure	Short title or Subject	How affected	Chapter of 1978 Act or number of Measure or Statutory Instrument
14 & 15 Geo. 6:			
—*cont.*			
c. 55	Nurses (Scotland) Act 1951.	S. 22(1), am. ...	29, s. 109, sch. 16 para. 7.
		Pt. III (ss. 27–32) devolved (*prosp.*).	51, s. 63, sch. 10 Pt. III.
c. 64	Rivers (Prevention of Pollution) Act 1951.	Transfer of certain functions (*prosp.*).	52, s. 9(1) sch. 2 Pt. VII.
c. 65	Reserve and Auxiliary Forces (Protection of Civil Interests) Act 1951.	Sch. 2 para. 15 am. ...	29, s. 109, sch. 16 para. 8.
c. 66	Rivers (Prevention of Pollution) (Scotland) Act 1951.	S. 29 not devolved (*prosp.*)	51, s. 63, sch. 10 Pt. III.
15 & 16 Geo. 6 & 1 Eliz. 2:			
c. 12	Judicial Officers (Salaries, &c.) Act 1952.	S. 4(2) rep. (*prosp.*) ...	23, s. 122(2), sch. 7 Pt. I.
c. 15	Agriculture (Fertilisers) Act 1952.	Transfer of functions (W.)	S.I. No. 272.
c. 25	National Health Service Act 1952.	Rep.	29, s. 109, sch. 17.
c. 31	Cremation Act 1952 ...	Transfer of functions (*prosp.*)	52, s. 9(1), sch. 2 Pt. II.
		S. 4 rep.	45, S.L. (R.), s. 1(1), sch. 1 Pt. XVII.
c. 35	Agriculture (Ploughing Grants) Act 1952.	Transfer of functions (W.) s. 5(2)(*c*) am.	S.I. No. 272.
c. 44	Customs and Excise Act 1952.	Ss. 17(1), 22(1) am. ...	42, s. 79, sch. 12 para. 19(7)(*a*).
		S. 25(1) am.	42, s. 79, sch. 12 para. 19(7)(*b*).
		S. 28(1) proviso (*c*) added	S.I. No. 1602.
		S. 34(1)(4) am. ...	42, s. 79, sch. 12 para. 19(4).
		S. 37(1) expld.	42, s. 79, sch. 12 para. 9.
		rep. in pt. ...	42, ss. 79, 80(5) sch. 12 para. 9, sch. 13 Pt. I.
		S. 43 am.	42, s. 79, sch. 12 para. 10.
		S. 47(1) am., rep. in pt.	S.I. No. 1602.
		S. 47(5) am.	S.I. No. 1603.
		S. 49(1) am.	S.I. No. 1602.
		S. 55(3) am.	S.I. No. 1603.
		S. 70 rep. and superseded	42, ss. 5(3), 80(5) sch. 13 Pt. I.
		Ss. 73, 79(1) am. ...	42, s. 79, sch. 12 para. 19(5).
		Ss. 80(1) am. (*a*) subst....	S.I. No. 1603.
		(1)(*c*) am.	42, s. 79, sch. 12 para. 11.
		(1)(*e*) rep., (1A), (1B), (1C) added, (3) am.	S.I. No. 1603.
		S. 85(1) am.	42, s. 79, sch. 12 para. 19(7)(*a*).
		am.	S.I. No. 1603.

Session and Chap. or No. of Measure	Short title or Subject	How affected	Chapter of 1978 Act or number of Measure or Statutory Instrument
15 & 16 Geo. 6 & 1 Eliz. 2: c. 44—*cont.*	Customs and Excise Act 1952—*cont.*	S. 90(1) am., (4) added...	S.I. No. 1603.
		Pt. IV (ss. 93–172 except ss. 167–170) am.	42, s. 79, sch. 12 para. 1(1)–(3).
		S. 96(5) am.	S.I. No. 1603.
		S. 103(1) am.	42, s. 79, sch. 12 para. 1(4).
		am.	S.I. No. 1603.
		(4) am.	42, s. 79, sch. 12 para. 1(4).
		S. 115(2) am. ...	42, s. 79, sch. 12 para. 1(3)(*a*).
		S. 126(1) am.	S.I. No. 1603.
		S. 137(1) am.	42, s. 79, sch. 12 para. 1(4).
		am.	S.I. No. 1603.
		(3) am.	42, s. 79, sch. 12 para. 1(3)(*b*).
		S. 138 am.	42, s. 79, sch. 12 para. 1(4).
		S. 138(1) am.	S.I. No. 1603.
		S. 140(2) am.	42, s. 79, sch. 12 para. 1(5).
		S. 142(1) am.	S.I. No. 1603.
		S. 144(1) am.	42, s. 79, sch. 12 para. 1(3)(*c*).
		am.	S.I. No. 1603.
		Ss. 161(4), 162(1), 164(1), 165(*b*) am.	42, s. 79, sch. 12 para. 1(3)(*d*)–(*f*).
		Ss. 171(1)(3), 172(1)(4) am.	42, s. 79, sch. 12 para. 1(6).
		Ss. 220(1)(*c*)(3), 221(1)(2) am.	42, s. 79, sch. 12 para. 6(1)(2).
		S. 221(2) rep. in pt. ...	42, ss. 79, 80(5), sch. 12 para. 6(2)(*b*), sch. 13 Pt. I.
		S. 221(4) am.	42, s. 79, sch. 12 para. 6(2)(*a*).
		S. 222(1)(*a*)(2) rep. in pt., (3) rep.	42, ss. 79, 80(5), sch. 12 para. 6(3), sch. 13 Pt. I.
		Ss. 244(1), 245(2), 246, 247(1), 248(1) am.	42, s. 79, sch. 12 para. 19(3).
		Ss. 248(2), 249(5) rep. in pt.	42, s. 80(5), sch. 13 Pt. I.
		S. 259(1) am.	42, s. 79, sch. 12 para. 13.
		S. 263(1) am.	42, s. 79, sch. 12 para. 14.
		S. 266(1)(2) am. ...	S.I. No. 1603.
		S. 272(1) am. (*prosp.*) ...	42, s. 79, sch. 12 para. 15.
		S. 283(2)(*a*) rep. in pt. (saving) (N.I.).	42, s. 79, sch. 12 para. 24(4).
		S. 285(2)(*b*) am. ...	42, s. 79, sch. 12 para. 16.

Session and Chap. or No. of Measure	Short title or Subject	How affected	Chapter of 1978 Act or number of Measure or Statutory Instrument
15 & 16 Geo. 6 & 1 Eliz. 2: c. 44—*cont.*	Customs and Excise Act 1952—*cont.*	S. 287 am.	42 s. 79, sch. 12 para. 17.
		S. 294(5) am.	42, s. 79, sch. 12 para. 19(7)(*c*).
		S. 306A added	42, s. 79, sch. 12 para. 18.
		S. 307(1) (definition of " Community transit goods ") added.	S.I. No. 1602.
		(definitions of " customs Acts ", " excise Acts ") subst.	42, s. 79, sch. 12 para 19(1)(*a*).
		(definitions of " excise trade ", " excise trader ") rep.	42, ss. 79, 80(5), sch. 12 para. 19(1)(*b*) sch. 13 Pt. I.
		(definition of " excise licence trade ") added.	42, s. 79, sch. 12 para. 19(1)(*b*).
		(definitions of " excise warehouse ", " customs warehouse") added.	S.I. No. 1603.
		(definition of " holiday ") subst.	42, s. 79, sch. 12 para. 19(1)(*d*).
		(definition of " importer ") rep. in pt.	42, ss 79, 80(5), sch. 12 para. 19(7)(*a*), sch. 13 Pt. I.
			42, s.
		(definition of " prohibited or restricted goods ") added.	42, s. 79, sch. 12 para. 19(1)(*c*).
		(definition of "revenue trader", "the revenue trade provisions of the customs and excise Acts ") added.	42, s. 79, sch. 12 para 19(1)(*b*).
		(definitions of " tobacco ", " tobacco refuse ") rep.	42, s. 80(5), sch. 13 Pt. I.
		(definition of " warehouse ") am.	S.I. No. 1603.
		S. 308(1)(2) rep.... ...	42, s. 80(5), sch. 13 Pt. I.
		S. 309(3) am.	42, s. 79, sch. 12 para. 20.
		rep. in pt. ...	42, ss. 79, 80(5), sch. 12 para. 20, sch. 13 Pt. I.
		S. 309(5) rep. in pt. ...	42, s. 80(5), sch. 13 Pt. I.
		S. 310(1)(*a*) am. ...	42, s. 79, sch. 12 para. 19(7)(*a*).
		S. 311 sch. 8 rep. ...	42, s. 80(5), sch. 13 Pt. I.
c. 54	Town Development Act 1952.	Transfer of functions (*prosp.*).	52, s. 9(1), sch. 2 Pt. VIII.

Session and Chap. or No. of Measure	Short title or Subject	How affected	Chapter of 1978 Act or number of Measure or Statutory Instrument
15 & 16 Geo. 6 & 1 Eliz. 2: —*cont.*			
c. 55	Magistrates' Courts Act 1952.	S. 44 am. (*prosp.*) ...	22, s. 75.
		S. 52 saved (*prosp.*), appl. (mods.) (*prosp.*).	22, s. 32(2).
		S. 52(2) am. (*prosp.*) ...	22, s. 89, sch. 2 para. 15.
		S. 53 excl. (*prosp.*) ...	22, s. 23(2).
		restr. (*prosp.*) ...	22, s. 47(2).
		am. (*prosp.*) ...	22, s. 76.
		S. 53A added (*prosp.*) ...	22, s. 77.
		S. 54(2) excl. (*prosp.*) ...	22, s. 23(2).
		restr. (*prosp.*) ...	22, s. 47(2)
		S. 54(3) am. (*prosp.*) (4) subst. (*prosp.*).	22, s. 78(1)(2).
		S. 55(1) am. (*prosp.*) ...	22, s. 23(1).
		S. 56(1) replaced (*prosp.*)	22, s. 79(1).
		(definition of " domestic proceedings ") appl. (*prosp.*).	22, s. 88(1).
		Ss. 56A, 56B added (*prosp.*).	22, s. 80.
		S. 57(2) subst. (*prosp.*), (2A), (2B) added (*prosp.*).	22, s. 81(1)(2).
		(4) rep. (*prosp.*) ...	2, s. 89, sch. 3.
		S. 58(1) am. (*prosp.*), (1A), (1B) added (*prosp.*), (2) subst. (*prosp.*).	22, s. 82(1)(2)(3).
		S. 59 rep. (*prosp.*) ...	22, s. 89, sch. 3.
		S. 60(1)(2)(*a*) rep. in pt. (*prosp.*).	22, ss. 83(*a*)(*b*), 89, sch. 3.
		(3) replaced (*prosp.*)	22, s. 83(*c*)(*d*).
		(4) am. (*prosp.*).	
		Ss. 61 rep. in pt. (*prosp.*) 62 rep. (*prosp.*).	22, s. 89, sch. 3.
		S. 99 am.	S.I. No. 1910.
		S. 121(2) rep. (*prosp.*) ...	22, s. 89, sch. 3.
		S. 124(1) (definition of " magistrates' court ") appl.	30, s. 5, sch. 1.
		Sch. 4, Pt. III, para. 3 rep. sch. 5 rep. in pt.	45, SL(R), s. 1(1), sch. 1 Pt. I.
		Sch. 5 rep. in pt. ...	30, s. 25(1), sch. 3.
c. 62	Agriculture (Calf Subsidies) Act 1952.	Transfer of certain functions (W.), s. 1(2)(*b*) am.	S.I. No. 272.
c. 66	Defamation Act 1952 ...	S. 10 am. (*prosp.*) ...	51, s. 82(2), sch. 16 para. 11.
		am. (*prosp.*) ...	52, s. 77(1), sch. 11 para. 11.
		Sch. para. 1A added (*prosp.*).	51, s. 82(2), sch. 16 para. 12.
		para. 1B added (*prosp.*).	52, s. 77(1), sch. 11 para. 12.
		para. 13 am. (*prosp.*) (definition of "Scottish Assembly ") added (*prosp.*).	51, s. 82(2), sch. 16 para. 13.
		(definition of " Welsh Assembly ") added (*prosp.*).	52, s. 77(1), sch. 11 para. 13.

Session and Chap. or No. of Measure	Short title or Subject	How affected	Chapter of 1978 Act or number of Measure or Statutory Instrument
15 & 16 Geo. 6 & 1 Eliz. 2: —*cont.*			
c. 67	Visiting Forces Act 1952	S. 1(1)(*a*) am.	15, s. 7(4), sch. para. 3.
		am.	20, s. 4(3), sch. 2, para. 3.
		am.	S.I. Nos. 1030, 1899.
		S. 10(1)(*a*) restr. ...	15, s. 7(4), sch. para. 3.
		restr. ...	20, s. 4(3), sch. 2 para. 3.
		Sch. para. 1(*b*)(ix) added (E. & W.).	37, s. 1(7).
		Sch. paras. 1(*c*), 2(*c*), 3(*i*), added (*prosp.*).	17, s. 2(4).
		Sch. para. 3 am., (N.I.)	S.I. No. 1407.
		Sch. para. 3(*j*) added (E. & W.).	31, s. 5(4).
		Sch. para. 4(*c*) added (*prosp.*).	17, s. 2(4).
c. xxxviii ...	City of London (Guild Churches) Act 1952.	Ss. 23(2), 25 am. ...	G.S.M. No. 2 s. 26(1), sch. 3 paras. 3, 4.
1 & 2 Eliz. 2:			
c. 13	Transport Act 1953 ...	S. 24 rep.	45, S.L.(R.), s. 1(1), sch. 1 Pt. XV.
c. 20	Births and Deaths Registration Act 1953.	S. 39 transfer of certain functions (*prosp.*)	52, s. 9(1), sch. 2 Pt. XVII.
		renumbered (*prosp.*) (2) added (*prosp.*).	52, s. 77(1), sch. 11 para. 14.
c. 26	Local Government (Miscellaneous Provisions) Act 1953.	Transfer of certain functions (*prosp.*).	52, s. 9(1), sch. 2 Pt. I.
c. 28	Dogs (Protection of Livestock) Act 1953.	S. 1(5) transfer of functions (W.).	S.I. No. 272.
c. 33	Education (Miscellaneous Provisions) Act 1953.	Transfer of certain functions (*prosp.*).	52, s. 9(1), sch. 2 Pt. III.
		Ss. 13, 19 rep.	45, S.L.(R.), s. 1(1), sch. 1 Pt. V.
c. 34	Finance Act 1953. ...	S. 3(3) rep. in pt. ...	42, s. 80(5), sch. 13 Pt. I.
c. 37	Registration Service Act 1953.	Ss. 10(3), 14, 19 transfer of functions (*prosp.*).	52, s. 9(1), sch. 2 Pt. XVII.
		Ss. 19, 20 am. (*prosp*).	52, s. 77(1), sch. 11 para. 15
		S. 20(*a*), (*b*), (*d*) transfer of certain functions (*prosp.*).	52, s. 9(1), sch. 2 Pt. XVII.
c. 41	Hospital Endowments (Scotland) Act 1953.	Rep.	29, s. 109, sch. 17.
c. 49	Historic Buildings and Ancient Monuments Act 1953.	Pt. I (ss. 1—9) transfer of certain functions. (*prosp.*).	52, s. 9(1), sch. 2 Pt. XII.
		S. 1(3) mod. (*prosp.*) ...	52, s. 77(1), sch. 11 para. 17(1).

Session and Chap. or No. of Measure	Short title or Subject	How affected	Chapter of 1978 Act or number of Measure or Statutory Instrument
1 & 2 Eliz. 2:			
c. 49—*cont.*	Historic Buildings and Ancient Monuments Act 1953—*cont.*	Ss. 4–6 concurrent powers of Min. (*prosp*). am. (*prosp*).	52, s. 9(2), sch. 3. 51, s. 23(3), sch. 5.
		S. 7 restr. (*prosp*). ...	52, s. 77(1), sch. 11 para. 17(2).
		not devolved (S.) (*prosp*.).	51, s. 63, sch. 10 Pt. III.
c. xli	Berkshire County Council Act 1953.	S. 74(7)(*a*)–(*d*) am. ...	S.I. No. 473.
c. xliii. ...	London County Council (General Powers) Act 1953.	S. 42 rep. (saving) ...	xiii, s. 13(1) (3) sch. 3 Pt. I.
2 & 3 Eliz. 2:			
c. 30	Protection of Birds Act 1954.	S. 10(1)(*d*) transfer of functions (W.).	S.I. No. 272.
		Sch. 1 Pt. I am. (S) ...	S.I. No. 1872
		Sch. 4 am. (E & W) ...	S.I. No. 1212
		(S)	S.I. No. 1071
c. 32	Atomic Energy Authority Act 1954.	S. 6(3)(*bb*) added ...	25, s. 2(3).
c. 36	Law Reform (Limitation of Actions, &c.) Act 1954.	Rep.	45, S.L. (R), s. 1(1), sch. 1 Pt. I.
c. 37	Superannuation (President of Industrial Court) Act 1954.	Rep.	45, S.L. (R), s. 1(1), sch. 1 Pt. I.
c. 38	Supreme Court Officers (Pensions) Act 1954.	Rep. (*prosp*.)	23, s. 122(2), sch. 7 Pt. I.
c. 39	Agriculture (Miscellaneous Provisions) Act 1954.	S. 10 transfer of functions (W.).	S.I. No. 272.
c. 46	Protection of Animals (Anaesthetics) Act 1954.	Transfer of functions (W.), s. 1(3) am.	S.I. No. 272.
c. 48	Summary Jurisdiction (Scotland) Act 1954.	Sch. 2 Pt. II rep. in pt., Pt. III rep., Pt. IV rep. in pt.	S.I. No. 834.
c. 56	Landlord and Tenant Act 1954.	Transfer of certain functions (*prosp*.).	52, s. 9(1), sch. 2 Pt. IV.
c. 60	Electricity Reorganisation (Scotland) Act 1954.	Ss. 10(2) rep. in pt., 13 rep., sch. 1 Pt. II rep. in pt.	45, S.L. (R), s. 1(1), sch. 1 Pt. VII.
c. 64	Transport Charges &c. (Miscellaneous Provisions) Act 1954.	S. 6 transfer of certain functions (*prosp*.).	52, s. 9(1), sch. 2 Pt. XIV.
c. 68	Pests Act 1954	Transfer of functions (W.)	S.I. No. 272.
c. 70	Mines and Quarries Act 1954.	S. 148(1)(2) am. ...	S.I. No. 1951.
c. iv	Dover Harbour Consolidation Act 1954.	Ss. 39, 55, 62, 67(2) rep., 74(1) am., sch. 6 rep.	S.I. No. 1069.
3 & 4 Eliz. 2:			
c. 7	Fisheries Act 1955 ...	S. 2 transfer of functions (W.).	S.I. No. 272.
		Ss. 3(1), 4, 6(1) rep. ...	45, S.L. (R.), s. 1(1), sch. 1 Pt. X.

Session and Chap. or No. of Measure	Short title or Subject	How affected	Chapter of 1978 Act or number of Measure or Statutory Instrument
3 & 4 Eliz. 2: —*cont.*			
c. 8	Northern Ireland Act 1955.	S. 2 rep. (*prosp.*) ...	23, s. 122(2), sch. 7 Pt. I.
c. 13	Rural Water Supplies and Sewerage Act 1955.	Transfer of functions (*prosp.*).	52, s. 9(1), sch. 2 Pt. IX.
c. 18	Army Act 1955	Restr. (Solomon Islands)	15, s. 7(2)(*a*).
		(Tuvalu)	20, s. 4(2)(*a*).
		S. 102(2) saved	19, s. 7(4)(5).
		S. 225(1) (definition of ''Commonwealth force '') am.	15, s. 7(2)(*b*).
		am.	20, s. 4(2)(*b*).
		am.	S.I. Nos. 1030, 1899.
c. 19	Air Force Act 1955 ...	Restr. (Solomon Islands)	15, s. 7(2)(*a*).
		(Tuvalu)	20, s. 4(2)(*a*).
		S. 102(2) saved	19, s. 7(4)(5).
		S. 223(1) (definition of ''Commonwealth force '') am.	15, s. 7(2)(*b*).
		am.	20, s. 4(2)(*b*).
		am.	S.I. Nos. 1030, 1899.
c. 24	Requisitioned Houses and Housing (Amendment) Act 1955.	Rep.	45, S.L. (R.), s. 1(1), sch. 1 Pt. XII.
4 Eliz. 2: c. 16	Food and Drugs Act 1955.	Transfer of certain functions (W.).	S.I. No. 272.
		S. 125(1)(*b*) transfer of certain functions (*prosp.*).	52, s. 9(1), sch. 2 Pt. II.
		S. 135(1) (definition of " food ") appl.	38, s. 94.
		(definition of " the Ministers ") am.	S.I. No. 272.
c. 19	Friendly Societies Act 1955.	S. 5 rep.	45, S.L. (R.), s. 1(1), sch. 1 Pt. XVII.
c. xxix ...	London County Council (General Powers) Act 1955.	S. 37(3) proviso rep. ...	xiii, ss. 11, 13(1), sch. 3 Pt. I.
4 & 5 Eliz. 2: c. 46	Administration of Justice Act 1956.	Sch. 1 Pt. I para. 2 rep. (*prosp.*).	23, ss. 30, 122(2), sch. 7 Pt. I.
		para. 3 rep. in pt. (*prosp.*).	23, s. 122(2), sch. 7 Pt. I.
		para. 4A added (*prosp.*).	23, s. 122(1), sch. 5 Pt. II(1)
c. 48	Sugar Act 1956	S. 17(1) am., s. 18 transfer of certain functions (W.).	S.I. No. 272.
		S. 18(7)(8) rep.	45, S.L. (R.), s. 1(1) sch. 1 Pt. XVII.
		(9)(*a*) am. s. 23(1) transfer of certain functions (W.).	S.I. No. 272

Session and Chap. or No. of Measure	Short title or Subject	How affected	Chapter of 1978 Act or number of Measure or Statutory Instrument
4 & 5 Eliz. 2: c. 48—*cont.*	Sugar Act 1956—*cont.*		
		Ss. 34, 35(1), (2) (definition of " the Government ") rep.	45, S.L. (R.), s⁻ 1(1), sch. 1 Pt. XVII.
c. 52	Clean Air Act 1956 ...	Transfer of certain functions (*prosp.*).	52, s. 9(1), sch. 2 Pt. VII.
		S. 1(2) transfer of certain functions (S.) (*prosp.*).	51, s. 63, sch. 11 Group F.
		S. 22 devolved in pt. (S.) (*prosp.*).	51, s. 63, sch. 10 Pt. III.
c. 60	Valuation and Rating (Scotland) Act 1956.	S. 8(1) rep. (1.4.1979) ...	40, s. 9(3), sch. 2.
		S. 12 rep.	S.I. No. 252.
		S. 24, sch. 4 rep. ...	S.I. No. 1176.
c. 68	Restrictive Trade Practices Act 1956.	Excl. (*retrosp.*)	1, s. 1(2).
c. 69	Sexual Offences Act 1956	Sch. 3 rep. in pt. ...	26, s. 9, sch. 2.
c. 76	Medical Act 1956 ...	S. 1–6 rep. (*prosp.*) ...	12, s. 31(2), sch. 7.
		S. 7(1) (a) am. (3) am. (*prosp*).	12, s. 31(1), sch. 6 paras. 29, 30.
		S. 7A(1) rep.	12, s. 31(1) (2) sch. 6 para. 31
		s. 8(1) am. (*prosp*). ...	12, s. 31(1), sch. 6 para. 1.
		(2) replaced. ...	12, s. 31(1), sch. 6 para. 32.
		(4) subst. (*prosp.*)	12, s. 31(1), sch. 6 para. 13.
		S. 9(1) am. (*prosp.*) ...	12, s. 15(8).
		rep. in pt. (*prosp.*)	12, s. 31(1)(2), sch. 6 para. 2 sch. 7.
		(1)–(4) am. (*prosp.*)...	12, s. 31(1), sch. 6 para. 1.
		(5) rep. (*prosp.*) ...	12, s. 31(2), sch. 7.
		S. 10(1) rep. (*prosp.*) ...	12, s. 31(1)(2), sch. 6 para. 3(2) sch. 7.
		(2) am.	12, s. 31(1), sch. 6 para. 33.
		am. (*prosp.*) ...	12, s. 31(1), sch. 6 para. 1.
		(3) am. (*prosp.*) ...	12, ss. 15(8), 31(1), sch. 6 paras. 1, 3(3).
		(4) am.	12, s. 31(1), sch. 6 para. 33.
		am. (*prosp*). ...	12, s. 31(1), sch. 6 para. 3(4).
		(5)(6) am. (*prosp.*)	12, s. 31(1), sch. 6 para. 1.
		(7) rep. (*prosp*).	12, s. 31(2), sch. 7.
		S. 11(1)(2) subst., (3) am.	12, s. 31(1), sch. 6 para. 34.
		(3) am. (*prosp.*) ...	12, s. 31(1), sch. 6 para. 1.

Session and Chap. or No. of Measure	Short title or Subject	How affected	Chapter of 1978 Act or number of Measure or Statutory Instrument
4 & 5 Eliz. 2: c. 76—*cont.*	Medical Act 1956—*cont.*	S. 11(3) rep. in pt. (*prosp.*)	12, s. 31(1)(2), sch. 6 para. 4, sch. 7.
		(4) rep.	12, s. 31(1)(2), sch. 6 para. 34, sch. 7.
		S. 12(1) am.	12, s. 31(1), sch. 6 para. 35.
		am. (*prosp.*) ...	12, s. 31(1), sch. 6 para. 1.
		(2) rep.	12, s. 31(2), sch. 7.
		S. 13(1) am.	12, s. 31(1), sch. 6 para. 36.
		(1)(2) am. (*prosp.*)	12, s. 31(1), sch. 6 paras. 1, 5.
		(3) rep. in pt. ...	12, s. 31(1)(2), sch. 6 para. 36, sch. 7.
		(4) am. (*prosp.*) ...	12, s. 31(1), sch. 6 para. 1.
		S. 14 rep.	12, s. 31(2), sch. 7
		S. 15(3) subst. (saving) (*prosp.*)	12, s. 16(1)(2)
		(3A) added (saving) (*prosp.*)	12, s. 16(1)(3)
		am. (*prosp.*)	12, s. 15(8).
		(3B)(3C) added ... (saving) (*prosp.*) ...	12, s. 16(1)(3)
		(4)(5) rep. (saving) (*prosp.*).	12, ss. 16(1)(4), 31(2), sch. 7.
		(6) am. (saving) (*prosp.*)	12, s. 16(1)(5)
		appl. (*prosp.*) ...	12, s. 20(3)
		S. 15(7)(*a*) am. (*prosp.*).	12, s. 31(1), sch. 6 para. 37.
		(8) am. (*prosp.*) ...	12, s. 31(1), sch. 6 paras. 1, 38
		am. (saving) ... (*prosp.*)	12, s. 16(1)(6)
		(9) am. (*prosp.*)	12, s. 31(1), sch. 6 para. 1
		S. 16(1)(2)(*a*) am. ...	29, s. 109, sch. 16 para. 9.
		S. 16(3) am. (*prosp.*) ...	12, s. 31(1), sch. 6 para. 1.
		(4) am. (*prosp.*) ...	12, s. 31(1), sch. 6 para. 39.
		S. 16A(*b*) subst. (*prosp.*)	12, s. 31(1), sch. 6 para. 6.
		am. (*prosp.*)...	12, s. 31(1), sch. 6 para. 14.
		S. 17(3) rep. in pt. ...	12, s. 31(2), sch. 7.
		(4) am. (*prosp.*) ...	12, s. 31(1), sch. 6 para. 40.
		S. 18 mod.	12, s. 29(1)
		Ss. 18–21 rep. (*prosp.*)	12, ss. 17(2), 31 (2), sch. 7

Session and Chap. or No. of Measure	Short title or Subject	How affected	Chapter of 1978 Act or number of Measure or Statutory Instrument
4 & 5 Eliz. 2: c. 76—*cont.*	Medical Act 1956—*cont.*	Ss. 22, 23 rep. (saving) (*prosp.*)	12, ss. 1(15) 17, 22(15), 31(2), sch. 5 para. 10 sch. 7.
		S. 23 mod.	12, s. 29(1)
		S. 24 restr.	12, s. 29(2)
		rep. (saving) (*prosp.*)	12, ss. 1(15), 17, 22(15), 31(2), sch. 5 para. 11 sch. 7.
		S. 25 rep.	12, ss. 17(1), 31(2), sch. 7.
		S. 26 rep. in pt. ...	12, ss. 17(1), 31(2), sch. 7.
		rep. (saving) (*prosp.*)	12, ss. 1(15), 17, 22(15), 31(2), Sch. 5 paras. 7, 12 sch. 7.
		S. 27(1) am. (*prosp.*) ...	12, s. 31(1), sch. 6 para. 7.
		S. 28(1)(*b*) rep. (*prosp.*)	12, s. 31(2), sch. 7.
		(2) am.	12, s. 31(1) sch. 6 para. 41.
		Ss. 28(3), 30 rep. (*prosp*).	12, s. 31(2), sch. 7.
		Pt. V. (Ss. 32–39) ext.	12, s. 31(1), sch 6 para. 15.
		Ss. 32–38 rep. (saving) (*prosp.*).	12, ss. 6(4)(5), 31(2), sch. 7.
		S. 39(2) am. (*prosp.*), (3) added (*prosp.*).	12, s. 31(1), sch. 6 para. 42.
		Ss. 40 rep. (*prosp.*), 48 rep.	12, s. 31(2), sch. 7.
		S. 49(1) am.	12, s. 31(1), sch. 6 para 44.
		am. (*prosp.*) ...	12, s. 31(1), sch. 6 para. 8(1)(2) (*d*).
		rep. in pt. (*prosp.*)	12, s. 31(1)(2), sch. 6 para. 8 (1)(2)(*a*), sch. 7.
		(*a*) rep. (*prosp.*)	12, s. 31(2), sch. 7.
		(*b*) am. (*prosp.*)	12, s. 31(1), sch. 6 para. 8(1)(2) (b).
		(*c*) am.	12, s. 31(1), sch. 6 para. 43.
		am. (*prosp.*) ...	12, s. 31(1), sch. 6 para. 8(1)(2) (*c*).
		S. 49(2) am.	12, s. 31(1), sch. 6 para. 45.
		(3) added (*prosp.*)	12, s. 31(1), sch. 6 para. 8(1)(3)
		S. 50(1)(2) am.	12, s. 31(1), sch. 6 para. 46.

Session and Chap. or No. of Measure	Short title or Subject	How affected	Chapter of 1978 Act or number of Measure or Statutory Instrument
4 & 5 Eliz. : c. 76—*cont.*	Medical Act 1956—*cont.*	S. 51 ext (*prosp.*) ...	12, s. 31(1), sch. 6 para. 47.
		rep. in pt. (*prosp.*)	12, s. 31(2), sch. 7.
		S. 52(1)(2) am. (*prosp.*)	12, s. 31(1), sch. 6 para. 48.
		S, 54(1) (definition of " additional qualification") appl. (*prosp.*).	12, s. 19.
		(definitions of "appointed member," "elected member," "General Council") subst. (*prosp*). ...	12, s. 31(1), sch. 6 para. 49.
		(definition of "fully registered person ") subst.	
		appl. ...	12, s. 30
		appl. ...	30, s. 5 sch. 1.
		appl. (S) ...	29, s. 108(1).
		mod. ...	12, ss. 1(15), 17, 22(15), sch. 5 para. 15.
		(definitions of " the Education Committee ", " the prescribed knowledge and skill ", " the prescribed pattern of experience ", " the prescribed standard of proficiency ") added (*prosp.*).	12, s. 31(1), sch. 6 para. 9.
		(definitions of " nominated member", " party ") rep. (*prosp.*).	12, s. 31(2), sch. 7.
		(definition of ''primary qualification ") replaced (*pt. prosp.*).	12, s. 31(1), sch. 6 para. 49.
		S. 54(3) rep. (*prosp.*) ...	12, s. 31(2), sch. 7.
		S. 56(3) rep.	12, s. 31(1)(2), sch. 6 para. 50 sch. 7.
		S. 57(2) rep.	12, s. 31(1)(2), sch. 6 para. 16. sch. 7.
		S. 57(5)(6)(11)(12), sch. 1 rep. (*prosp.*). sch. 3 Pt. I rep. in pt.	12, s. 31(2), sch. 7.
		Sch. 3 Pt. II am. (*prosp.*)	12, s. 31(1), sch. 6 para. 10.
		Sch. 4 rep. (saving) (*prosp.*).	12, ss. 6(4)(5), 31(2), sch. 7.
c lxxxiv ...	Walthamstow Corporation Act 1956.	S. 33 subst. (street trading) (Gtr. London).	xiii, s. 10(1)(2), sch. 1 Pt. II.
		S. 34(*e*) rep. (street trading) (Gtr. London).	xiii, s. 10(5), sch. 2.

Session and Chap. or No. of Measure	Short title or Subject	How affected	Chapter of 1978 Act or number of Measure or Statutory Instrument
4 & 5 Eliz. 2: —_cont._			
c. xc	Middlesex County Council Act 1956.	S. 58(3)(_e_) rep. in pt. (street trading) (Gtr. London).	xiii, s. 10(5), sch. 2.
		S. 63 subst. (street trading) (Gtr. London).	xiii, s. 10(1)(2), sch. 1 Pt. II.
		S. 64(1)(_e_) rep. in pt. (street trading) (Gtr. London).	xiii, s. 10(5), sch. 2.
		(1)(_f_) rep. (street trading) (Gtr. London).	xvi, s. 10(4), sch. 1 Pt. II.
C.A.M. No. 3... ...	Parochial Church Councils (Powers) Measure 1956.	S. 1 (definition of " Diocesan Authority") appl.	G.S.M. No. 1 s. 3, sch. para. 15(3).
5 & 6 Eliz. 2: c. 6	Ghana Independence Act 1957.	S. 4(1) rep.	30, s. 25(1), sch. 3.
c. 16	Nurses Agencies Act 1957	Transfer of functions (_prosp._).	52, s. 9(1), sch. 2 Pt. VI.
c. 28	Dentists Act 1957 ...	S. 42(4) am.	29, s. 109, sch. 16 para. 10.
c. 42	Parish Councils Act 1957	S. 5 transfer of functions (_prosp._).	52, s. 9(1), sch. 2 Pt. XV.
c. 48	Electricity Act 1957 ...	S. 39 rep.	45, S.L. (R.), s. 1(1), sch. 1 Pt. VII.
c. 49	Finance Act 1957 ...	S. 5, sch. 2 para. 1(1) am.	42, s. 79, sch. 12 para. 13.
		para. 1(2) rep. in pt., (3), 2 rep.	42, ss. 79, 80(5), sch. 12 para. 13, sch. 13 Pt. I.
		para. 3 am.	42, s. 79, sch. 12 para. 13.
		para. 4(2)(_b_) rep.	42, ss. 79, 80(5), sch. 12 para. 13, sch. 13 Pt. I.
c. 52	Geneva Conventions Act 1957.	S. 4(1) am. (_prosp._) ...	23, s. 122(1), sch. 5 Pt. II(1).
c. 53	Naval Discipline Act 1957	Restr. (Solomon Islands) (Tuvalu)	15, s. 7(2)(_a_). 20, s. 4(2)(_a_).
		S. 60(6) saved	19, s. 7(4)(5).
		S. 135(1) (definition of ''Commonwealth country ") am.	15, s. 7(2)(_b_).
		am. ...	20, s. 4(2)(_b_).
		am. ...	S.I. Nos. 1030, 1899.
c. 55	Affiliation Proceedings Act 1957.	S. 3(1)(3) am. (_prosp._) ...	22, s. 49.
		S. 4(2) am. (_prosp._), (3) replaced (_prosp._).	22, s. 50.
		S. 5(1)(3)(4) am. (_prosp._)	22, s. 51(1)(2)(3).
		S. 6 subst. (_prosp._) ...	22, s. 52(1).
		S. 6A added (_prosp._) ...	22, s. 53.
		S. 7(1)–(3) rep. (_prosp._)	22, ss. 52(2), 89, sch. 3.
		S. 7(4) am. (_prosp._) ...	22, s. 52(2).
		S. 9(2) am. (_prosp._) ...	22, s. 89, sch. 2 para. 16.

Session and Chap. or No. of Measure	Short title or Subject	How affected	Chapter of 1978 Act or number of Measure or Statutory Instrument
5 & 6 Eliz. 2: *—cont.*			
c. 56	Housing Act 1957 ...	Transfer of certain functions (*prosp.*).	52, s. 9(1), sch. 2 Pt. IV.
		Sch. 10 rep. in pt. ...	45, S.L. (R.), s. 1(1), sch. 1 Pt. XII.
c. 57	Agriculture Act 1957 ...	Pt. I (ss. 1–11) transfer of functions (W.).	S.I. No. 272.
c. 59	Coal Mining (Subsidence) Act 1957.	S. 9 transfer of functions (*prosp.*).	52, s. 9(1), sch. 2 Pt. XII.
c. xxxv ...	London County Council (General Powers) Act 1957.	S. 72(1)(*f*) rep. (street trading) (Gtr. London).	xvi, s. 10(4), sch. 1 Pt. II.
		(1)(*g*) rep. (street trading) (Gtr. London).	xiii, s. 10(5), sch. 2.
		(2) rep. (street trading) (Gtr. London).	xvi, s. 10(4), sch. 1 Pt. II.
6 & 7 Eliz. 2:			
c. 6	Import Duties Act 1958	S. 5(1) rep. in pt. ...	42, s. 80(5), sch. 13 Pt. I.
		S. 5(4) rep. in pt. ...	S.I. No. 1148.
		S. 6(4) am.	42, s. 79, sch. 12 para. 19(7)(*d*).
		Sch. 4 para. 3 rep. (1.4.1979).	S.I. No. 1704.
c. 11	Isle of Man Act 1958 ...	S. 1(4) rep.	45, S.L. (R.), s. 1(1), sch. 1 Pt. IX.
		S. 2 am.	S.I. No. 273.
c. 16	Commonwealth Institute Act 1958.	Sch. 2 am.	15, s. 7(4), sch. para. 8.
		am.	20, s. 4(3), sch. 2 para. 8.
		am.	S.I. Nos. 1030, 1899.
c. 24	Land Drainage (Scotland) Act 1958.	Sch. 1 para. 6(*b*)(ii) am.	S.I. No. 1154.
c. 26	House of Commons (Redistribution of Seats) Act 1958.	S. 4 appl. (mods.) ...	10, s. 3, sch. 1 para. 1, sch. 2 para. 4.
		appl. (mods.) (*prosp.*)	51, s. 1, sch. 1 para. 2.
		appl. (mods.) (*prosp.*)	52, s. 1, sch. 1 para. 2.
c. 30	Land Powers (Defence) Act 1958.	S. 1(3) rep.	45, S.L. (R.), s. 1(1), sch. 1 Pt. XI.
		Ss. 9(1)–(3), 21 transfer of certain functions (*prosp.*).	52, s. 9(1), sch. 2 Pt. XV.
c. 32	Opticians Act 1958 ...	Ss. 21(2)(*b*) am., 30(1) (definition of "health service ophthalmic lists", "health service tribunal") am. (S.).	29, s. 109, sch. 16 para. 11.
c. 33	Disabled Persons (Employment) Act 1958.	Not devolved (S.) (*prosp.*)	51, s. 63, sch. 10 Pt. III.
		Sch. para. 1(1)(*d*) rep. in pt.	45, SL(R), s. 1(1), sch. 1 Pt. XII.

Session and Chap. or No. of Measure	Short title or Subject	How affected	Chapter of 1978 Act or number of Measure or Statutory Instrument
6 & 7 Eliz. 2: *—cont.*			
c. 42	Housing (Financial Provisions) Act 1958.	Transfer of functions (*prosp.*).	52, s. 9(1), sch. 2 Pt. IV.
c. 43	Horse Breeding Act 1958	Transfer of functions (W.)	S.I. No. 272.
c. 45	Prevention of Fraud (Investments) Act 1958.	Not devolved (S.) (*prosp.*)	51, s. 63, sch. 10 Pt. III.
c. 47	Agricultural Marketing Act 1958.	Act (except s. 22) transfer of functions (W.).	S.I. No. 272.
c. 55	Local Government Act 1958.	Ss. 56(1) rep. in pt. 61 rep. 63(1), 64, 66(1), (2) rep. in pt. (3), 67 proviso (*f*) sch. 8 paras. 27, 28 rep., 35 rep. in pt.	45, S.L.(R.), s. 1(1), sch. 1 Pt. XII.
c. 65	Children Act 1958 ...	Transfer of functions (*prosp.*).	52, s. 9(1), sch. 2 Pt. VI.
		S. 2 (definition of "foster child ") appl. (S.) (*prosp.*).	28, s. 2(*c*).
		(4A) subst. (S.) (*prosp.*).	28, s. 66(2), sch. 3 para. 1.
		Ss. 6(1)(*f*), 17 am. (S.) (*prosp.*).	28, s. 66(2), sch. 3 paras. 2, 3.
c. 69	Opencast Coal Act 1958	S. 2 not devolved (S.) (*prosp.*).	51, s. 63, sch. 10 Pt. III.
		S. 2(1A) added (*prosp.*)	51, s. 82(2), sch. 16 para. 17.
		S. 2(1A) added (*prosp.*) ...	52, s. 77(1) sch. 11 para. 21.
		S. 39 transfer of functions (W.).	S.I. No. 272.
		S. 39(6) transfer of functions (*prosp.*).	52, s. 9(1), sch. 2 Pt. VIII.
c. 70	Slaughterhouses Act 1958	Rep.	45, S.L. (R.), s. 1(1), sch. 1 Pt. XVII.
c. xxi	London County Council (General Powers) Act 1958.	S. 27(5), subst. (1.4.1979)	xvi, s. 4.
C.A.M.: No. 1	Church Funds Investment Measure 1958.	S. 5(1)(2)(3) rep. in pt. ...	45, S.L. (R.), s. 1(1), sch. 1 Pt. II.
7 Eliz. 2: c. 5	Adoption Act 1958 ...	Rep (S.) (*prosp.*) ...	28, s. 66(3), sch. 4.
		Ss. 30, 32 transfer of functions (*prosp.*).	52, s. 9(1), sch. 2 Pt. VI.
		S. 32(2), am.	22, s. 89, sch. 2 para. 17.
		S. 34A transfer of functions (*prosp.*).	52, s. 9(1), sch. 2 Pt. VI.
		S. 34A(3) am.	22, s. 89, sch. 2, para. 18.
		S. 50 transfer of functions (*prosp.*).	52, s. 9(1), sch. 2 Pt. VI.

Session and Chap. or No. of Measure	Short title or Subject	How affected	Chapter of 1978 Act or number of Measure or Instrument
7 & 8 Eliz. 2:			
c. 12	Agriculture (Small Farmers) Act 1959.	Transfer of functions (W.).	S.I. No. 272.
c. 22	County Courts Act 1959	S. 89 am.	S.I. No. 1910.
		S. 89(3), rep. in pt. ...	45, S.L. (R.), s. 1(1), sch. 1 Pt. I.
		S. 109(2)(g) am. (*prosp.*), (h)(i) am.	22, s. 89, sch. 2 para. 19 (a)–(c).
		S. 147(2) rep. in pt. ...	45, S.L. (R.), s. 1(1), sch. 1 Pt. I.
		S. 205(5)(e) rep. ...	45, S.L. (R.), s. 1(1), sch. 1 Pt. VI.
c. 23	Overseas Resources Development Act 1959.	Rep.	2, s. 18(1), sch. 2.
c. 24	Building (Scotland) Act 1959.	S. 26 devolved in pt. (*prosp.*).	51, s. 63, sch. 10 Pt. III.
c. 25	Highways Act 1959 ...	Transfer of certain functions (*prosp.*) (saving for ss. 7, 9, 11, 13, 20, 28, 110, 111) (*prosp.*).	52, ss. 9(1), 75, sch. 2 Pt. XV, sch. 10.
		S. 295(1) (definition of " carriageway ") appl.	3, s. 3(3).
c. 33	House Purchase and Housing Act 1959.	Transfer of certain functions (*prosp.*).	52, s. 9(1), sch. 2 Pt. IV.
c. 44	Fire Services Act 1959 ...	Transfer of functions (*prosp.*).	52, s. 9(1), sch. 2 Pt. V.
c. 53	Town and Country Planning Act 1959.	Ss. 23, 24, 26, 27 transfer of certain functions (*prosp.*).	52, s. 9(1), sch. 2 Pt. VIII.
c. 54	Weeds Act 1959 ...	Transfer of functions (W.)	S.I. No. 272.
		Devolved (S.) (*prosp.*) ...	51, s. 63, sch. 10 Pt. III.
c. 55	Dog Licences Act 1959	Transfer of functions (W.)	S.I. No. 272.
c. 60	Education Act 1959 ...	Transfer of functions (*prosp.*).	52, s. 9(1), sch. 2 Pt. III.
c. 65	Fatal Accidents Act 1959	S. 1(4) rep.	47, s. 9(2), sch. 2.
c. 72	Mental Health Act 1959	S. 3(4) Pt. IV (ss. 25–59) transfer of certain functions (*prosp.*).	52, s. 9(1), sch. 2 Pt. VI.
		S. 28(2) am. (*prosp.*) ...	52, s. 77(1), sch. 11 para. 22.
		Ss. 64, 81, 85, 99, 133, 142, 143, sch. 1 transfer of certain functions (*prosp.*).	52, s. 9(1), sch. 2 Pt. VI.
8 & 9 Eliz. 2:			
c. 16	Road Traffic Act 1960 ...	Pts. I, II (ss. 1–116) not devolved (S.) (*prosp.*), Pt. III (ss. 117–163, except s. 137(1)) devolved in pt. (S.) (*prosp.*).	51, s. 63, sch. 10 Pt. III.
		Ss. 120, 121, 123, 125(2) transfer of certain functions (*prosp.*).	52, s. 9(1), sch. 2 Pt. XIV.
		S. 127 excl.	55, s. 5(5).

Session and Chap. or No. of Measure	Short title or Subject	How affected	Chapter of 1978 Act or number of Measure or Instrument
8 & 9 Eliz. 2: c. 16—*cont.*	Road Traffic Act 1960 —*cont.*	S. 135(2) replaced (saving)	55, s. 8(1)(2), sch. 2 para. 1.
		(4)(*b*) am. (saving), (*e*) added.	55, s. 8(1)(2), sch. 2 para. 2.
		S. 137(1) not devolved (S.) (*prosp.*).	51, s. 63, sch. 10 Pt. III.
		S. 139A added	55, s. 8(1), sch. 2 para. 3.
		Ss. 143, 149 transfer of certain functions (*prosp.*).	52, s. 9(1), sch. 2 Pt. XIV.
		S. 153(2) am., (*b*) added	55, s. 8(1), sch. 2 para. 4.
		Ss. 155, 159, 160 transfer of certain functions (*prosp.*).	52, s. 9(1), sch. 2 Pt. XIV.
		S. 160(1)(*cc*) added ...	55, s. 8(1), sch. 2 para. 5.
		Pts. IV–VII (ss. 164–271) not devolved (S.) (*prosp.*).	51, s. 63, sch. 10 Pt. III.
		Sch. 12 Pt. II subst. ... Pt. V para. 13(*c*) (*d*) added.	55, s. 7(1), sch. 1. 55, s. 7(2).
c. 18	Local Employment Act 1960.	Rep.	45, S.L. (R.), s. 1(1), sch. 1 Pt. VIII.
c. 20	Requisitioned Houses Act 1960.	Rep.	45, S.L. (R.), s. 1(1), sch. 1 Pt. XII.
c. 34	Radioactive Substances Act 1960.	Transfer of certain functions (*prosp.*).	52, s. 9(1), sch. 2 Pt. VII.
		Devolved in pt. (S.) (*prosp.*).	51, s. 63, sch. 10 Pt. III.
		Ss. 6–9, 11, 12(7) transfer of functions (W.).	S.I. No. 272.
		Sch. 1 paras. 18 rep. (N.I.) (*prosp.*), 21 rep. in pt. (N.I.) (*prosp.*), 23, 25 rep. (N.I.) (*prosp.*).	S.I. No. 1049.
c. 48	Matrimonial Proceedings (Magistrates' Courts) Act 1960.	Rep. (*prosp.*)	22, s. 89, sch. 3.
c. 54	Clean Rivers (Estuaries and Tidal Waters) Act 1960.	Transfer of functions (*prosp.*).	52, s. 9(1), sch. 2 Pt. VII.
c. 55	Nigeria Independence Act 1960.	S. 3(1) rep.	30, s. 25(1), sch. 3.
c. 58	Charities Act 1960 ...	S. 45(1) (definition of " exempt charity ") appl.	G.S.M. No. 1 s. 19(4).
		S. 49(2)(*a*)(*b*) rep. ...	45, S.L. (R.), s. 1(1), sch. 1 Pt. II.
c. 59	Adoption Act 1960 ...	Rep. (S.) (*prosp.*) ...	28, s. 66(3), sch. 4.
c. 61	Mental Health (Scotland) Act 1960.	S. 2(4) devolved in pt. (*prosp.*).	51, s. 63, sch. 10 Pt. III.
		S. 6 (definition of "mental disorder ") appl.	29, s. 108(1).

Session and Chap. or No. of Measure	Short title or Subject	How affected	Chapter of 1978 Act or number of Measure or Instrument
8 & 9 Eliz. 2: c. 61—*cont.*	Mental Health (Scotland) Act 1960—*cont.*	S. 27(*c*) am.	29, s. 109, sch. 16 para. 12.
		S. 89 appl.	29, s. 108(1).
		S. 89(3) (definition of " State hospitals ") appl. (*prosp.*).	51, s. 43(1), sch. 8.
		S. 90(3) am. (*prosp.*) ...	51, s. 23(1)(2), sch. 4.
		Ss. 101(2), 111 (definition of " hospital ") am.	29, s. 109, sch. 16 para. 13.
c. 62	Caravan Sites and Control of Development Act 1960.	Transfer of certain functions (*prosp.*).	52, s. 9(1), sch. 2 Pt. VIII.
c. 63	Road Traffic and Roads Improvement Act 1960.	S. 22(1) rep.	45, S.L. (R.), s. 1(1), sch. 1 Pt. XI.
c. 65	Administration of Justice Act 1960.	Ss. 1–6, 9(1) rep. (N.I.) (*prosp.*), 9(2) rep. (N.I.) 9(3)(4), 13 rep. (N.I.) (*prosp.*).	23, s. 122(2), sch. 7 Pt. I.
		S. 13 saved	44, s. 136(4).
		Ss. 15, 16, 17(1)(3)(4), 18(3) rep. (N.I.) (*prosp.*).	23, s. 122(2), sch. 7 Pt. I.
		S. 18(4) rep. in pt. ...	45, S.L. (R.), s. 1(1), sch. 1 Pt. I.
		Sch. 2 Pt. I para. 1 rep. (*prosp.*).	23, s. 122(2), sch. 7 Pt. I.
		para. 2 am. (*prosp.*).	23, s. 122(1), sch. 5 Pt. II(1).
		para. 3 rep. (*prosp.*), Pt. II rep. in pt. (*prosp.*).	23, s. 122(2), sch. 7 Pt. I.
		Sch. 3 rep. in pt. ...	45, S.L. (R.), s. 1(1), sch. 1 Pt. I.
c. 66	Professions Supplementary to Medicine Act 1960.	Sch. 2 para. 2(2) am. (*prosp.*).	23, s. 122(1), sch. 5 Pt. II(1).
c. 67	Public Bodies (Admission to Meetings) Act 1960.	Transfer of functions (*prosp.*).	52, s. 9(1), sch. 2 Pt. I.
		Sch. para. 2(*d*) am. ...	29, s. 109, sch. 16 para. 14.
c. iii	Glasgow Corporation Consolidation (General Powers) Order Confirmation Act 1960.	S. 96(1) am.	S.I. No. 124.
c. xl	Croydon Corporation Act 1960.	S. 145(1)(*c*), proviso rep. (street trading) (Gtr. London).	xiii, s. 10(5), sch. 2.
		S. 146(1) subst. (street trading) (Gtr. London).	xiii, s. 10(1)(2), sch. 1 Pt. II.
9 Eliz. 2: c. 6	Ministers of the Crown (Parliamentary Secretaries) Act 1960.	Ss. 4(1) rep. in pt., 5 rep., sch. 1 rep. in pt.	45, S.L. (R.), s. 1(1), sch. 1 Pt. III.

Session and Chap. or No. of Measure	Short title or Subject	How affected	Chapter of 1978 Act or number of Measure or Instrument
9 & 10 Eliz. 2:			
c. 11	Diplomatic Immunities (Conferences with Commonwealth Countries and Republic of Ireland) Act 1961.	S. 1(5) am. ... ... am.	20, s. 4(3), sch. 2 para. 1. S.I. Nos. 1030, 1899.
c. 16	Sierra Leone Independence Act 1961.	S. 3(1) rep.	30, s. 25(1), sch. 3.
c. 19	National Health Service Act 1961.	Rep.	29, s. 109, sch. 17.
c. 21	Oaths Act 1961 ...	Rep.	19, s. 7(1), sch. Pt. I.
c. 27	Carriage by Air Act 1961	S. 4(1)(*a*) rep. (E., W., N.I.). S. 5(2) am.	47, s. 9(1)(2), sch. 1 para. 5(1), sch. 2. 47, s. 9(1), sch. 1 para. 5(2).
c. 33	Land Compensation Act 1961.	Ss. 18, 37, sch. 2 para. 2 transfer of certain functions (*prosp.*).	52, s. 9(1), sch. 2 Pt. VIII.
c. 36	Finance Act 1961 ...	S. 9 cont. (until 31.8.1979) excl. ... ... S. 11(1) rep. in pt. ...	42, s. 10. 42, s. 6(4). 45, S.L. (R.), s. 1(1), sch. 1 Pt. IX.
c. 39	Criminal Justice Act 1961	Sch. 4 rep. in pt. (*prosp.*)	22, s. 89, sch. 3.
c. 40	Consumer Protection Act 1961.	Rep. (*prosp.*) ... ... S. 3(2), sch. para. 5 am. (*transitional*).	38, s. 10(1), sch. 3. 38, s. 10(3).
c. 41	Flood Prevention (Scotland) Act 1961.	S. 14(2) not devolved (*prosp.*).	51, s. 63, sch. 10 Pt. III.
c. 50	Rivers (Prevention of Pollution) Act 1961.	Transfer of certain functions (*prosp.*).	52, s. 9(1), sch. 2 Pt. VII.
c. 54	Human Tissue Act 1961	Devolved (S.) (*prosp.*) ...	51, s. 63, sch. 10 Pt. III.
c. 63	Highways (Miscellaneous Provisions) Act 1961.	Transfer of functions (*prosp.*) (saving for s. 3) (*prosp.*).	52, ss. 9(1), 75, sch. 2 Pt. XV, sch. 10.
c. 64	Public Health Act 1961	Transfer of certain functions (*prosp.*).	52, s. 9(1), sch. 2 Pt. VIII.
c. 65	Housing Act 1961 ...	Transfer of functions (*prosp.*).	52, s. 9(1), sch. 2 Pt. IV.
C.A.M.: No. 2 ...	Baptismal Registers Measure 1961.	Ss. 1(1), 3 am.	G.S.M. No. 2 s. 26(1), sch. 3 paras. 5, 6.
10 Eliz. 2: c. 1	Tanganyika Independence Act 1961.	S. 3(1) rep.	30, s. 25(1), sch. 3.
10 & 11 Eliz. 2: c. 9	Local Government (Financial Provisions etc.) (Scotland) Act 1962.	S. 2(1) rep. ... ... S. 2(2) rep. ... ... S. 3 rep. ... ... S. 4 mod. (1.4.1979) ... Sch. 2 paras. 2, 3 rep. ...	S.I. No. 1174. S.I. No. 1175. S.I. No. 1176. 40, s. 5(6). S.I. No. 1175.

Session and Chap. or No. of Measure	Short title or Subject	How affected	Chapter of 1978 Act or number of Measure or Instrument
10 & 11 Eliz. 2:			
—*cont.*			
c. 12	Education Act 1962 ...	Transfer of certain functions (*prosp.*).	52, s. 9(1), sch. 2 Pt. III.
		S. 3(*a*)(*c*)(*d*) transfer of functions (W.).	S.I. No. 274.
		Ss. 11 rep., 12(1) rep. in pt., 14(3) rep., (5) rep. in pt.	45, S.L. (R.), s. 1(1), sch. 1 Pt. V.
c. 15	Criminal Justice Administration Act 1962.	S. 19, sch. 1 rep., sch. 4 rep. in pt.	45, S.L. (R.), s. 1(1), sch. 1 Pt. I.
c. 30	Northern Ireland Act 1962.	Ss. 1–5 rep. (*prosp.*), 7–9 rep. 10, 11 rep.(*prosp.*).	23, s. 122(2), sch. 7 Pt. I.
		S. 25(1)(*b*) rep.	45, S.L. (R.), s. 1(1), sch. 1 Pt. III.
		S. 27 rep.	30, s. 25(1), sch. 3.
		S. 29(2) rep. in pt. ...	45, S.L. (R.), s. 1(1), sch. 1 Pt. III.
		Sch. 1 rep.	23, s. 122(2), sch. 7 Pt. I.
c. 33	Health Visiting and Social Work (Training) Act 1962.	S. 5 transfer of functions (*prosp.*).	52, s. 9(1), sch. 2 Pt. VI.
c. 35	Shops (Airports) Act 1962.	Transfer of functions (*prosp.*).	52, s. 9(1), sch. 2 Pt. II.
c. 37	Building Societies Act 1962.	S. 28 mod.	27, s. 3(3).
		S. 41 excl.	27, s. 3(4).
		S. 134(1)(2) appl. ...	27, s. 6(3).
c. 40	Jamaica Independence Act 1962.	S. 3(1) rep.	30, s. 25(1), sch. 3.
c. 43	Carriage by Air (Supplementary Provisions) Act 1962.	S. 3(1) rep. in pt. (E., W., N.I.).	47, s. 9(2), sch. 2.
c. 46	Transport Act 1962 ...	Am. (*prosp.*)	51, ss. 60, 61, sch. 9.
		Devolved in pt. (S.) (*prosp.*).	51, s. 63, sch. 10 Pt. III.
		S. 57(3)(*b*) rep. in pt. ...	45, S.L. (R.), s. 1(1), sch. 1 Pt. XV.
		S. 66 excl.	S.I. No. 1174.
		S. 70(1)–(4) rep. (E. & W.).	xxi, ss. 25(6), 30, sch. 4.
		S. 74(6) am.	44, s. 130, sch. 10 para. 21.
		S. 92(1) (definitions of " pension ", " pension scheme ") appl.	55, s. 20(1).
		(definition of " subsidiary ") appl.	55, s. 24(2).
c. 47	Education (Scotland) Act 1962.	Devolved in pt. (*prosp.*)	51, s. 63, sch. 10 Pt. III.
		S. 5 (definition of "special education ") appl.	29, s. 15(1)(*f*).
		Ss. 57, 58(2), 58A(2) am.	29, s. 109, sch. 16 paras. 15–17.

Session and Chap. or No. of Measure	Short title or Subject	How affected	Chapter of 1978 Act or number of Measure or Statutory Instrument
10 & 11 Eliz. 2: c. 47—*cont.*	Education (Scotland) Act 1962—*cont.*	Ss. 75(*b*), 76 transfer of certain functions (*prosp.*).	51, s. 63, sch. 11 Group B.
		S. 142(1) rep. in pt. ...	45, S.L. (R.), s. 1(1), sch. 1 Pt. V.
		S. 144(5) transfer of certain functions (*prosp.*).	51, s. 63, sch. 11 Group B.
		S. 145(10) (definition of " central institution "), (14) (definition of " college of education ") appl.	44, s. 29(2)(*c*).
		S. 145(16) (definition of "education authority") appl.	29, s. 108(1).
		(22A) (definition of " Health Board ") am.	29, s. 109, sch. 16 para. 18.
		(42) (definition of " school ") appl.	29, s. 108(1).
c. 50	Landlord and Tenant Act 1962.	Transfer of functions (*prosp.*).	52, s. 9(1), sch. 2 Pt. IV.
		S. 2(2) rep.	45, S.L. (R.), s. 1(1), sch. 1 Pt. XII.
c. 54	Trinidad and Tobago Independence Act 1962.	S. 3(1) rep.	30, s. 25(1), sch. 3.
c. 56	Local Government (Records) Act 1962.	Transfer of functions (*prosp.*).	52, s. 9(1), sch. 2 Pt. I.
		S. 7(2) rep.	45, S.L. (R.), s. 1(1), sch. 1 Pt. XII.
c. 57	Uganda Independence Act 1962.	S. 3(1) rep.	30, s. 25(1), sch. 3.
c. 58	Pipe-lines Act 1962 ...	S. 5 not devolved (S.) (*prosp.*).	51, s. 63, sch. 10 Pt. III.
		S. 5(1A) added (*prosp.*)	51, s. 82(2), sch. 16 para. 18.
		S. 5(1A) added (*prosp.*)	52, s. 77(1), sch. 11 para. 23.
		S. 13(7), sch. 2 para. 8 transfer of functions (*prosp.*).	52, s. 9(1), sch. 2 Pt. VIII.
c. xxx ...	Manchester Corporation Act 1962.	S. 26(1)(*a*)(*b*), (2) rep. ...	S.I. No. 739.
			...
C.A.M.: No. 1... ...	Ecclesiastical Fees Measure 1962.	S. 2(6) saved	G.S.M. No. 2 s. 20(5).
1963: c. 11	Agriculture (Miscellaneous Provisions) Act 1963.	Ss. 5, 10, 12, 13(1)(3)(7), 16 transfer of functions (W.).ss. 16(1), 26(*b*) am.	S.I. No. 272.
c. 12	Local Government (Financial Provisions) (Scotland) Act 1963.	S. 11 rep.	S.I. No. 1174.
		S. 12 rep.	S.I. No. 1176.

Session and Chap. or No. of Measure	Short title or Subject	How affected	Chapter of 1978 Act or number of Measure or Statutory Instrument
1963:—*cont.*			
c. 16	Protection of Depositors Act 1963.	Not devolved (S.) (*prosp.*)	51, s. 63, sch. 10 Pt. III.
		S. 27(1) (definition of " banking or discount company ") appl.	8, s. 1(4).
c. 19	Local Employment Act 1963.	Rep.	45, S.L. (R.), s. 1(1), sch. 1 Pt. VIII.
c. 24	Museum Act 1963 ...	S. 13(3) rep.	45, S.L. (R.), s. 1(1), sch. 1 Pt. XIII.
c. 25	Finance Act 1963 ...	S. 7(2)(4) am.	42, s. 79, sch. 12 para. 7(1).
c. 29	Local Authorities (Land) Act 1963.	Transfer of certain functions (*prosp.*).	52, s. 9(1), sch. 2 Pt. I.
c. 31	Weights and Measures Act 1963.	S. 22(2) mod. (1.7.1979)	S.I. No. 1081.
		Sch. 4 Pt. VII restr. ...	S.I. No. 741.
		Sch. 4 Pts. VIII, XI excl. (1.7.1979).	S.I. No. 1081.
c. 33	London Government Act 1963.	S. 1(1)(6) rep. in pt. ...	30, s. 25(1), sch. 3.
		Ss. 1(6) rep. in pt., 8(2), 62(3), sch. 2 para. 31(i)(ii) rep.	45, S.L. (R.), s. 1(1), sch. 1 Pt. XII.
		Sch. 12 paras. 6A, 6B added.	xiii, s. 4.
c. 37	Children and Young Persons Act 1963.	S. 27(4) am.	37, s. 2(2).
		S. 28(1) am.	19, s. 2.
		Ss. 37, 39, 45 transfer of functions (*prosp.*).	52, s. 9(1), sch. 2 Pt. VI.
		Ss. 47, 58 am. (E. & W.) (*prosp.*).	22, s. 89, sch. 2 para. 20.
c. 38	Water Resources Act 1963.	Transfer of certain functions (*prosp.*).	52, s. 9(1), sch. 2 Pt. IX.
		Am. (*prosp.*)	52, ss. 55(2), 56, sch. 6.
		Ss. 21, 25, 38–40, 44, 47 power to intervene (*prosp.*).	52, s. 63, sch. 8 Pts. III, IV.
		S. 65 transfer of certain functions (W.).	S.I. No. 272.
		Ss. 65–67 power to intervene (*prosp.*).	52, s. 63, sch. 8 Pt. IV.
		S. 70 transfer of certain functions (W.).	S.I. No. 272.
		Ss. 72, 74, 78, 82 power to intervene (*prosp.*).	52, s. 63, sch. 8 Pt. IV.
		Ss. 82(1) transfer of certain functions (W.), 105 transfer of functions (W.), 106, 108 transfer of certain functions (W.).	S.I. No. 272.
		S. 108 power to intervene (*prosp.*).	52, s. 63, sch. 8 Pts. III, IV.
		S. 109 transfer of functions (W.).	S.I. No. 272.

Session and Chap. or No. of Measure	Short title or Subject	How affected	Chapter of 1978 Act or number of Measure or Instrument
1963: c. 38—*cont.*	Water Resources Act 1963—*cont.*	Sch. 7 pt. power to intervene (*prosp.*). paras. 16(*b*)(ii) am., 17 transfer of certain functions (W.). Sch. 8 pt. power to intervene (*prosp.*).	52, s. 63, sch. 8 Pts. III, IV. S.I. No. 272. 52, s. 63, sch. 8 Pt. III.
c. 40	Commonwealth Development Act 1963.	Rep.	2, s. 18(1), sch. 2.
c. 47	Limitation Act 1963 ...	S. 4 subst.	47, s. 9(1), sch. 1 para. 6.
c. 51	Land Compensation (Scotland) Act 1963.	Pts. I, III, V, VI not devolved (*prosp.*).	51, s. 63, sch. 10 Pt. III.
c. 54	Kenya Independence Act 1963.	S. 4(1) rep.	30, s. 25(1), sch. 3.
C.A.M.: No. 2... ...	Cathedrals Measure 1963	Appl. (mods.) ... ... Ss. 16, 17, 27 appl. (mods.). S. 43(1) rep. in pt., (2) renumbered, am., (2)–(4) added. S. 52(1) (definitions of " cathedral church ", " dean and chapter cathedral ", " parish church cathedral ") appl.	G.S.M. No. 1, s. 22(1). G.S.M. No. 1, s. 22(2). G.S.M. No. 3, s. 10. G.S.M. No. 1, s. 22(1).
1964: c. 14	Plant Varieties and Seeds Act 1964.	Transfer of functions (W.) Apptd. day for s. 31(1) (1.7.1979). Ss. 25 mod., 26 excl. ... S. 38(1) am.	S.I. No. 272. S.I. No. 1002. S.I. No. 215. S.I. No. 272.
c. 16	Industrial Training Act 1964.	Ss. 4B(7),am., 12(1) subst. S. 12(2B)(3)(4) rep. ...	44, s. 159(2), sch. 16 para. 4. 44, s. 159(3), sch. 17.
c. 24	Trade Union (Amalgamations, etc.) Act 1964.	S. 4(8) am.	44, s. 159(2), sch. 16 para. 5.
c. 26	Licensing Act 1964 ...	Transfer of functions (*prosp.*). Sch. 14 paras. 5, 7 rep....	52, s. 9(1), sch. 2 Pt. II. 45, S.L. (R), s. 1(1), sch. 1 Pt. XVII.
c. 28	Agriculture and Horticulture Act 1964.	Pt. III (ss. 11–24 except ss. 13(1), 23(1)) transfer of functions (W.), s. 26(2) am.	S.I. No. 272.
c. 29	Continental Shelf Act 1964.	S. 1(7) (definition of " designated area ") appl.	1, s. 1(3).
c. 40	Harbours Act 1964 ...	Ss. 14–16, 30 transfer of functions (W.), 30(4) am., 31, 33 transfer of functions (W.).	S.I. No. 272.

Session and Chap. or No. of Measure	Short title or Subject	How affected	Chapter of 1978 Act or number of Measure or Statutory Instrument
1964: c. 40—*cont.*	Harbours Act 1964 —*cont.*	S. 57(1) (definition of " harbour ") appl.	4, s. 2.
		(definition of " marine work ") subst. (*prosp.*).	51, s. 82(2), sch. 16 para. 19(1).
		S. 60, sch. 3 transfer of functions (W.).	S.I. No. 272.
		Sch. 3 para. 6 transfer of certain functions (*prosp.*).	52, s. 9(1), sch. 2 Pt. VIII.
		Sch. 5 transfer of functions (W.).	S.I. No. 272.
		para. 6 transfer of certain functions (*prosp.*).	52, s. 9(1), sch. 2 Pt. VIII.
c. 41	Succession (Scotland) Act 1964.	S. 23(3)(5) am. (*prosp.*)...	28, s. 66(2), sch. 3 para. 4.
		S. 24(4) rep. (*prosp.*) ...	28, s. 66(3), sch. 4.
		S. 37(1) am. (*prosp.*) ...	28, s. 66(2), sch. 3 para. 5.
c. 42	Administration of Justice Act 1964.	S. 2(3) am. (1.4.1974) ...	22, s. 86(1).
		S. 2(3A) rep.	22, ss. 86(2), 89, sch. 3.
		S. 11(1) am. (*prosp.*) ...	22, s. 89, sch. 2 para. 21.
		Ss. 31 rep., 37(4), 41(6) rep. in pt., sch. 3 paras. 8, 12(3) rep.	45, S.L. (R), s. 1(1), sch. 1 Pt. I.
		Sch. 3 para. 27 rep. (*prosp.*).	22, s. 89, sch. 3.
c. 46	Malawi Independence Act 1964.	S. 4(1) rep.	30, s. 25(1), sch. 3.
c. 48	Police Act 1964 ...	S. 62 (definitions) appl....	30, s. 5, sch. 1.
		rep. in pt. ...	30, s. 25(1), sch. 3.
c. 49	Finance Act 1964 ...	S. 1(5) am.	42, s. 79, sch. 12 para. 2.
c. 56	Housing Act 1964 ...	Transfer of functions (*prosp.*).	52, s. 9(1), sch. 2 Pt. IV.
		S. 8 not devolved (S.) (*prosp.*).	51, s. 63, sch. 10 Pt. III.
c. 57	Adoption Act 1964 ...	Rep. (S.) (*prosp.*) ...	28, s. 66(3), sch. 4.
c. 60	Emergency Laws (Re-enactments and Repeals) Act 1964.	S. 4 transfer of functions (*prosp.*).	52, s. 9(1), sch. 2 Pt. VI.
		Ss. 5 rep., 15 rep. in pt.	29, s. 109, sch. 17.
		Sch. 1 pt. transfer of functions (*prosp.*).	52, s. 9(1), sch. 2 Pt. VI.
c. 67	Local Government (Development and Finance) (Scotland) Act 1964.	S. 7 devolved in pt. (*prosp.*).	51, s. 63, sch. 10 Pt. III.
c. 72	Fishery Limits Act 1964	S. 3(2) rep.	45, S.L. (R.), s. 1(1), sch. 1 Pt. X.
c. 75	Public Libraries and Museums Act 1964.	Transfer of functions (*prosp.*).	52, s. 9(1), sch. 2 Pt. III.

Session and Chap. or No. of Measure	Short title or Subject	How affected	Chapter of 1978 Act or number of Measure or Statutory Instrument
1964:—*cont.*			
c. 81	Diplomatic Privileges Act 1964.	Appl. (mods.)	33, s. 20.
		Saved	33, s. 16(1).
		Sch. 1, Art. 1(*b*) (definition of " members of the mission ") appl.	33, s. 16(1)(*a*).
c. 82	Education Act 1964 ...	Transfer of functions (*prosp.*).	52, s. 9(1), sch. 2 Pt. III.
		Ss. 3, 4 rep., 5(2) rep. in pt., (3) rep., (4)(6) rep. in pt.	45, S.L. (R.), s. 1(1), sch. 1 Pt. V.
c. 86	Malta Independence Act 1964.	S. 4(1) rep.	30, s. 25(1), sch. 3.
c. 92	Finance (No. 2) Act 1964	Ss. 3–6, schs. 1, 2 rep. ...	42, s. 80(5), sch. 13 Pt. I.
c. 93	Gambia Independence Act 1964.	S. 4(1) rep.	30, s. 25(1), sch. 3.
1965:			
c. 2	Administration of Justice Act 1965.	S. 1 appl. (mods.) (N.I.) (*prosp.*).	23, s. 83(1)(2).
		S. 2(3) added (N.I.) (*prosp.*).	23, s. 83(1)(3).
		Ss. 12, 13, 15 appl. (mods.) (N.I.) (*prosp.*).	23, s. 83(1)(2).
		S. 15(1) rep. in pt. (N.I.) (*prosp.*) (3) rep. (N.I.) (*prosp.*).	23, s. 83(1)(4).
		Ss. 30, 32, 33 rep. (*prosp.*)	23, s. 122(2), sch. 7 Pt. I.
c. 3	Remuneration of Teachers Act 1965.	Ss. 6 rep., 9(4) rep. in pt.	45, S.L. (R.), s. 1(1), sch. 1 Pt. V.
c. 4	Science and Technology Act 1965.	Devolved in pt. (S.) (*prosp.*).	51, s. 63, sch. 10 Pt. III.
c. 11	Ministerial Salaries and Members' Pensions Act 1965.	S. 7(4) rep.	56, s. 22(5), sch. 2.
c. 12	Industrial and Provident Societies Act 1965.	S. 7(3) am.	34, s. 1(1).
c. 13	Rivers (Prevention of Pollution) (Scotland) Act 1965.	S. 8 not devolved (*prosp.*)	51, s. 63, sch. 10 Pt. III.
c. 14	Cereals Marketing Act 1965.	Act (except ss. 1, 12) transfer of functions (W.).	S.I. No. 272.
c. 22	Law Commissions Act 1965.	Devolved in pt. (S.) (*prosp.*).	51, s. 63, sch. 10 Pt. III.
c. 25	Finance Act 1965 ...	Pt. III (ss. 19–45) mod.	42, s. 49(3)–(5).
		S. 20(3) rep. in pt. ...	42, s. 80(5), sch. 13 Pt. IV.
		S. 21 rep.	42, ss. 44(7), 80(5), sch. 13 Pt. IV.
		S. 24(11) replaced ...	42, s. 52(1).
		S. 29(4A) added ...	42, s. 50(1).

Session and Chap. or No. of Measure	Short title or Subject	How affected	Chapter of 1978 Act or number of Measure or Statutory Instrument
1965: c. 25—*cont.*	Finance Act 1965—*cont.*	S. 30(1) am.	42, s. 45(1).
		(2) subst. (mod. 1977–1978).	42, s. 45(2)(4)(6).
		(3) am.	42, s. 45(1).
		(4) am.	42, s. 45(3).
		(5)(*b*) am.	42, s. 45(1)(4)(6).
		(*c*) am.	42, s. 45(1).
		S. 33(9) subst.	42, s. 47(1).
		(9A) added ...	42, s. 47(2).
		S. 34(1) replaced ...	42, s. 48(1).
		(3) am.	42, s. 48(2).
		S. 34(4) am., rep. in pt.	42, s. 48(3).
		(6) (definition of " family company ") am.	42, s. 48(4).
		appl. (definition of " trading company ") appl.	42, s. 46(7).
		(definition of " chargeable business asset ") appl.	42, s. 46(8), sch. 8 para. 7(2).
		S. 45(3) appl.	42, s. 49(10).
		Sch. 7 para. 3(4) (definition of " capital distribution ") appl.	42, s. 61(3).
		para. 4(1)(*b*) (definition of " new holding ") appl.	42, ss. 54(2)(*a*), 57(1).
		Sch. 7 para. 5(3)(*b*) (definition of " security ") appl.	42, s. 49(1)(*c*).
		Sch. 10 para. 13 rep. in pt.	42, s. 80(5), sch. 13 Pt. IV.
c. 36	Gas Act 1965	Ss. 28(4) proviso, 31(2) rep.	45, S.L. (R.), s. 1(1), sch. 1 Pt. XVII.
		Sch. 3 paras. 2, 5–7 transfer of functions (S.) (*prosp.*).	51, s. 63, sch. 11 Group E para. 3.
		transfer of functions (*prosp.*).	52, s. 9(1), sch. 2 Pt. VIII.
c. 37	Carriage of Goods by Road Act 1965.	S. 5(1) am. (E., W., N.I.)	47, s. 9(1), sch. 1 para. 7.
c. 45	Backing of Warrants (Republic of Ireland) Act 1965.	S. 2(2) mod.	26, s. 2(2).
		S. 9(2) rep.	45, S.L. (R.), s. 1(1), sch. 1 Pt. I.
c. 46	Highlands and Islands Development (Scotland) Act 1965.	Not devolved (*prosp.*) ...	51, s. 63, sch. 10 Pt. III.
		Transfer of certain functions (*prosp.*).	51, s. 63, sch. 11 Group E para. 2.
		Am. (*prosp.*)	51, s. 42(1)(*b*).
		Ss. 2, 3 am. (*prosp.*) ...	51, s. 42(1)(*c*), sch. 7.
		S. 3(1)(*b*)(*d*) am. (*prosp.*), (*e*) subst. (*prosp.*), (2) am. (*prosp.*), (3A) added (*prosp.*).	51, s. 82(2), sch. 16 para. 20.
		S. 4 am. (*prosp.*) ...	51, s. 42(1)(*c*), sch. 7.

Session and Chap. or No. of Measure	Short title or Subject	How affected	Chapter of 1978 Act or number of Measure or Statutory Instrument
1965:—*cont.*			
c. 49	Registration of Births, Deaths and Marriages (Scotland) Act 1965.	S. 1(1) devolved (*prosp.*)	51, s. 63, sch. 10 Pt. III.
		Ss. 42, 44, 45 ext. (*prosp.*)	28, s. 45(8).
		Sch. 1 paras. 7–10 rep. (*prosp.*).	28, s. 66(3), sch. 4.
c. 51	National Insurance Act 1965.	Ss. 36, 37 cont. am. ...	S.I. Nos. 393, 912.
		S. 118(1) cont.	S.I. No. 393.
c. 56	Compulsory Purchase Act 1965.	Sch. 6 rep. in pt. ...	45, S.L. (R.), s. 1(1), sch. 1 Pt. XVII.
c. 57	Nuclear Installations Act 1965.	Not devolved (S.) (*prosp.*)	51, s. 63, sch. 10 Pt. III.
		Sch. 1 para. 3(2)(*bb*) added.	25, s. 2(3).
c. 59	New Towns Act 1965 ...	Transfer of certain functions (*prosp.*) (savings for ss. 7, 8, 10(5), 26, 28) (*prosp.*).	52, ss. 9(1), 75, sch. 2 Pt. VII, sch. 10.
		Am. (*prosp.*)	52, ss. 55(2), 56, sch. 6.
		Ss. 10(5), 26(5)(6), 28(4) consent of Min. required (*prosp.*).	52, s. 36(1), sch. 4.
		S. 43 restr. (*prosp.*) ...	51, s. 82(2), sch. 16 para. 21.
		restr. (*prosp.*) ...	52, s. 77(1), sch. 11 para. 24.
		S. 54(4) am. (*prosp.*) ...	52, s. 77(1), sch. 11 para. 25.
		Sch. 3 para. 13 transfer of functions (W.).	S.I. No. 272.
c. 62	Redundancy Payments Act 1965.	S. 1 rep. (saving) ...	44, s. 159, sch. 15 para. 11, sch. 17.
		S. 1(2) appl.	42, s. 54(4).
		Ss. 2–26, 30–44, 46–58, 59(2) rep. (saving), (3) rep. in pt. (saving), schs. 1–3 rep. (saving).	44, s. 159, sch. 15 para. 11, sch. 17.
		Sch. 3 para. 7 am. ...	29, s. 109, sch. 16 para. 20.
		Schs. 4–9 rep. (saving)	44, s. 159, sch. 15 para. 11, sch. 17.
c. 64	Commons Registration Act 1965.	S. 19 transfer of certain functions (*prosp.*).	52, s. 9(1), sch. 2 Pt. VIII.
c. 66	Hire-Purchase Act 1965	S. 2(2)(3)(*b*)(4) am. ...	S.I. No. 461.
c. 67	Hire-Purchase (Scotland) Act 1965.	S. 2(2)(3)(*b*)(4) am. ...	S.I. No. 461.
c. 72	Matrimonial Causes Act 1965.	S. 42 rep. (*prosp.*) ...	22, s. 89, sch. 3.
c. 76	Southern Rhodesia Act 1965.	S. 2 cont.	S.I. No. 1625.
c. 81	Housing (Slum Clearance Compensation) Act 1965.	Transfer of functions (*prosp.*).	52, s. 9(1), sch. 2 Pt. IV.
c. xlii	Manchester Corporation Act 1965.	S. 18(6) am.	S.I. No. 844.

Session and Chap. or No. of Measure	Short title or Subject	How affected	Chapter of 1978 Act or number of Measure or Statutory Instrument
1966:			
c. 8	National Health Service Act 1966.	Ss. 2(1), 10(1) am., (3) subst. (S.), 11 am.	29, s. 109, sch. 16 paras. 21–23.
		S. 12(2) rep. (S.) ...	29, s. 109, sch. 17
c. 13	Universities (Scotland) Act 1966.	Sch. 6 paras. 18 rep. (*prosp.*), 19 rep. in pt. (*prosp.*).	12, s. 31(2), sch. 7.
c. 14	Guyana Independence Act 1966.	S. 5(1) rep.	30, s. 25(1), sch. 3.
c. 18	Finance Act 1966 ...	S. 7 rep.	42, s. 80(5), sch. 13 Pt. I.
		S. 11(10) am.	42, s. 79, sch. 12 para. 7(*a*).
		Ss. 29, 53(6) rep. ...	45, S.L. (R), s. 1(1), sch. 1 Pt. IX.
		Sch. 10 para. 2(3) rep. ...	42, s. 80(5), sch. 13 Pt. IV.
c. 19	Law Reform (Miscellaneous Provisions) (Scotland) Act 1966.	S. 8 restr. (*prosp.*) ...	22, s. 60(1).
c. 21	Overseas Aid Act 1966...	S. 4 rep.	2, s. 18(1), sch. 2.
c. 28	Docks and Harbours Act 1966.	S. 58(2) transfer of functions (W.).	S.I. No. 272.
c. 34	Industrial Development Act 1966.	Ss. 16(1)(2) rep., (3) rep. in pt., 20, 21 rep.	45, S.L. (R), s. 1(1), sch. 1 Pt. VIII.
c. 36	Veterinary Surgeons Act 1966.	Transfer of functions (W.) S. 27(1) (definition of " the Ministers ") am.	S.I. No. 272.
		Sch. 2 para. 4(2) am. (*prosp.*).	23, s. 122(1), sch. 5 Pt. II(1).
c. 37	Barbados Independence Act 1966.	S. 4(1) rep.	30, s. 25(1), sch. 3.
c. 38	Sea Fisheries Regulation Act 1966.	Transfer of functions (W.)	S.I. No. 272.
c. 41	Arbitration (International Investment Disputes) Act 1966.	S. 8(*b*) am.	23, s. 122(1), sch. 5 Pt. II(1).
c. 42	Local Government Act 1966.	Transfer of certain functions (*prosp.*).	52, s. 9(1), sch. 2 Pt. I.
		Ss. 35, 36 transfer of functions (W.).	S.I. No. 272.
		Ss. 37 rep., 39, 41(1) rep. in pt.	45, S.L. (R), s. 1(1), sch. 1 Pt. XII.
		Sch. 3 transfer of functions (W.).	S.I. No. 272.
c. 49	Housing (Scotland) Act 1966.	S. 15(7)(*a*)(*c*) appl. ...	14, s. 10.
		S. 25 not devolved (*prosp.*).	51, s. 63, sch. 10 Pt. III.
		S. 26 ext.	14, s. 10.
		S. 138(3) am., (*b*), (4) added.	14, s. 16(1), sch. 2 para. 1(*a*)(*b*).
		S. 138(4) (definition of " hostel ") appl.	14, s. 4(2)(*e*).
		appl. (1.4. 1979)	14, s. 11(1)(*a*).
		S. 145(1)(*d*)(6) am. ...	14, s. 16(1), sch. 2 para. 2.

Session and Chap. or No. of Measure	Short title or Subject	How affected	Chapter of 1978 Act or number of Measure or Statutory Instrument
1966: c. 49—*cont.*	Housing (Scotland) Act 1966—*cont.*	S. 208(1) (definition of "housing association") appl.	29, s. 100(1).
		Sch. 7 para. 6 am. (*prosp.*).	51, s. 23(1)(2, sch. 4.
c. 51	Local Government (Scotland) Act 1966.	Ss. 2–6 am. (*prosp.*) ...	51, s. 68.
		S. 11 transfer of functions (*prosp.*).	51, s. 63, sch. 11 Group D.
		S. 11 not devolved (*prosp.*).	51, s. 63, sch. 10. Pt. III.
		S. 17(1)–(3) rep., (4) am., (4A) added.	S.I. No. 1175.
		(4B) added ...	S.I. No. 1176.
		(4C) added... ...	S.I. No. 1174.
		(4D) added ...	S.I. No. 1173.
		S. 18(1)(2) excl.	S.I. Nos. 1174, 1175, 1176.
		(3) devolved in pt. (*prosp.*).	51, s. 63, sch. 10 Pt. III.
		(3)(4) appl.... ...	4, s. 2.
		(5)(6) s. 19 excl. ...	S.I. Nos. 1174, 1175, 1176.
c. xxv ...	Tees and Hartlepool Port Authority Act 1966.	Ss. 6, 7 rep., 8(3) am., 9, sch. 3 paras. 1, 2, 9, 13 rep.	S.I. No. 941.
1967: c. 3	Education Act 1967 ...	Transfer of functions (*prosp.*).	52, s. 9(1), sch. 2 Pt. III.
c. 4	West Indies Act 1967 ...	S. 3(5) rep.	30, s. 25(1), sch. 3.
c. 8	Plant Health Act 1967...	Transfer of functions (W.)	S.I. No. 272.
c. 9	General Rate Act 1967...	S. 26(3)(*a*) am.	S.I. No. 318.
		S. 40 mod. (1.4.1979) ...	40, s. 2(6).
		S. 45 rep. (1.4.1979) ...	40, s. 9(3), sch. 2.
		S. 68(1) am.	S.I. No. 993.
		S. 76(2) transfer of certain functions (W.).	S.I. No. 272.
		Ss. 76(2)(4), 77 appl. (mods.) (1.4.1979).	40, s. 1(5), sch. 1 para. 11(3).
		Sch. 5 para. 6 excl. ...	S.I. No. 1174.
		Sch. 8 para. 6 am. (*retrosp.*).	S.I. No. 218.
c. 10	Forestry Act 1967 ...	S. 15 devolved (S.) (*prosp.*).	51, s. 63, sch. 10 Pt. III.
c. 13	Parliamentary Commissioner Act 1967.	Devolved (S.) (*prosp.*) ...	51, ss. 63, 76 sch. 10 Pt. III.
		Saved (*prosp.*)	51, s. 76(2).
		S. 6(1)(*b*) am. (*prosp.*) ...	51, s. 82(2), sch. 16 para. 22.
		am. (*prosp.*) ...	52, s. 77(1), sch. 11 para. 26.
		Ss. 7, 8 appl. (mods.) (S.)	29, s. 95.
		S. 8(4) am. (*prosp.*) ...	51, s. 82(2), sch. 16 para. 23.
		Ss. 9, 11 appl. (mods.) (S.)	29, s. 95.
		S. 11(4) am. (*prosp.*) ...	51, s. 82(2), sch. 16 para. 24.
		am (*prosp.*) ...	52, s. 77(1), sch. 11 para. 27.

Session and Chap. or No. of Measure	Short title or Subject	How affected	Chapter of 1978 Act or number of Measure or Statutory Instrument
1967: c. 13—*cont.*	Parliamentary Commissioner Act 1967—*cont.*	S. 12(1) (definition of " enactment ") subst. (*prosp.*).	51, s. 82(2), sch. 16 para. 25.
		Sch. 1 appl. (S.)... ...	29, s. 91(2).
		Sch. 2 am.	S.I. No. 616.
c. 17	Iron and Steel Act 1967...	S. 31(3) rep. in pt. (4)(*b*), (6) rep.	44, s. 159(3), sch. 17.
c. 22	Agriculture Act 1967 ...	Act (except ss. 1(5), 64, 65) transfer of functions (W.).	S.I. No. 272.
		Pt. III (ss. 41–57 except ss. 43, 44) devolved (S.) (*prosp.*).	51, s. 63, sch. 10 Pt. III.
		Ss. 51(7)(*a*), 52(2)(*d*) am.	S.I. No. 244.
		S. 66(3) am.	S.I. No. 272.
c. 24	Slaughter of Poultry Act 1967.	Ext.	S.I. No. 201.
		Act (except s. 4(1)) transfer of functions (W.)	S.I. No. 272.
		S. 8 (definition of " the Ministers ") am.	
c. 28	Superannuation (Miscellaneous Provisions) Act 1967.	S. 7 am. (*prosp.*) ...	51, s. 23(1)(2), sch. 4.
		S. 7(5) am.	29, s. 109, sch. 16 para. 24.
		S. 9 rep.	44, s. 159(3), sch. 17.
c. 29	Housing Subsidies Act 1967.	Transfer of certain functions (*prosp.*).	52, s. 9(1), sch. 2 Pt. IV.
		Pt. II (ss. 24–32) not devolved (S.) (*prosp.*).	51, s. 63, sch. 10 Pt. III.
		S. 27(1)(*g*) added (S.) ...	14, s. 16(1), sch. 2 para. 3.
c. 32	Development of Inventions Act 1967.	S. 4(2)(*b*) am.	S.I. No. 382.
c. 33	Air Corporations Act 1967.	Rep.	85, s. 14(2), sch. 2.
c. 43	Legal Aid (Scotland) Act 1967.	Am.	S.I. No. 1910.
		S. 2(1) am.	S.I. No. 1817.
		Ss. 2(1),(6)(*c*), 3 excl. ...	22, s. 61.
		S. 3(1) am.	S.I. No. 1817.
		S. 4 excl.	22, s. 61.
		S. 4(6) am. (*prosp.*) ...	51, s. 82(2), sch. 10 para. 26.
c. 50	Farm and Garden Chemicals Act 1967.	Transfer of functions (W.)	S.I. No. 272.
		S. 5(1) (definition of "the Ministers ") am.	
c. 52	Tokyo Convention Act 1967.	S. 6(1)(*b*) am.	8, s. 14(1), sch. 1 Pt. I para. 3.
		S. 7(2) appl.	26, s. 4(2).
c. 66	Welsh Language Act 1967.	S. 2(1) appl.	10, s. 3, sch. 1 para. 2(5).
		S. 2(1)(3) am. (*prosp.*) (*aa*) added (*prosp.*).	52, s. 77(1), sch. 11 para. 28.
		S. 4 rep.	30, s. 25(1) sch. 3.
c. 68	Fugitive Offenders Act 1967.	S. 2(1) (definition of " designated Commonwealth country "), (2) (definition of " United Kingdom dependency ") appl.	26, s. 5(1).

Session and Chap. or No. of Measure	Short title or Subject	How affected	Chapter of 1978 Act or number of Measure or Statutory Instrument
1967: c. 68—*cont.*	Fugitive Offenders Act 1967—*cont.*	Ss. 16, 17 ext. (*prosp.*) ... Sch. 1 am. ... ... am. ... ... am. ... ... am. (*prosp.*) ...	17, s. 4(1). 26, s. 3(2). 31, s. 5(3). 37, s. 1(6). 17, s. 3(1).
c. 69	Civic Amenities Act 1967	S. 4(2) transfer of certain functions (*prosp.*). Ss. 18–24, 27, 28 30(1) (definitions of " the Common Council ", " local authority ", "local planning authority" and " owner ") rep.	52, s. 9(1), sch. 2 Pt. XII. 3, s. 12(2), sch. 2.
c. 76	Road Traffic Regulation Act 1967.	Transfer of certain functions (*prosp.*). Transfer of certain functions (S.) (*prosp.*). Ext. ... ... Ss. 20, 52, 53 mod. ... Sch. 6 rep. in pt. ...	52, s. 9(1), sch. 2 Pt. XVI. 51, s. 63, sch. 11 Group G paras. 1–5. 55, s. 12. S.I. No. 889. 55, s. 24(4), sch. 4.
c. 77	Police (Scotland) Act 1967.	S. 47(1) transfer of functions (*prosp.*). am. (*prosp.*). S. 50 (definitions) appl ... rep. in pt. ... S. 51(4) appl. ... ... rep. in pt. ...	51, s. 63, sch. 11 Group K. 51, s. 23(1)(2), sch. 4. 30, s. 5, sch. 1. 30, s. 25(1), sch. 3. 30, s. 5, sch. 1. 30, s. 25(1), sch. 3.
c. 78	Water (Scotland) Act 1967.	S. 34 (definition of " water development board ") appl.	4, s. 2.
c. 80	Criminal Justice Act 1967	S. 47 mod. ... ... S. 106(3)(*d*), sch. 4 paras. 25 rep. (*prosp.*), 26 rep. in pt. (*prosp.*), 27 rep. (*prosp.*). Sch. 3 rep. in pt. (*prosp.*)	44, s. 135(6), sch. 11 para. 23(1). 23, s. 122(2), sch. 7 Pt. I. 22, s. 89, sch. 3.
c. 83	Sea Fisheries (Shellfish) Act 1967.	Transfer of functions (W.), s. 17(3) am.	S.I. No. 272.
c. 84	Sea Fish (Conservation) Act 1967.	Transfer of functions (W.) S. 22(1) (definition of " shellfish ") appl. (S.).	S.I. No. 272. 35, s. 1(6).
c. 86	Countryside (Scotland) Act 1967.	S. 57(1) am. ... ... Ss. 58 not devolved (*prosp.*), 73 devolved in pt. (*prosp.*).	4, s. 6, sch. 51, s. 63, sch. 10 Pt. III.
c. 87	Abortion Act 1967 ...	Not devolved (S.) (*prosp.*), transfer of functions (S.) (*prosp.*). Transfer of functions (*prosp.*). S. 6 am.	51, s. 63, sch. 10 Pt. III, sch. 11 Group A. 52, s. 9(1), sch. 2 Pt. VI. 29, s. 109, sch. 16 para. 25.

Session and Chap. or No. of Measure	Short title or Subject	How affected	Chapter of 1978 Act or number of Measure or Statutory Instrument
1967:—*cont.*			
c. 88	Leasehold Reform Act 1967.	Transfer of certain functions (*prosp.*).	52, s. 9(1), sch. 2 Pt. IV.
c. xx	Greater London Council (General Powers) Act 1967.	S. 14 rep.	S.I. No. 440.
c. xl	Manchester Corporation Act 1967.	Sch. 1 rep. in pt. ...	S.I. No. 739.
1968:			
c. 3	Capital Allowances Act 1968.	Pt. I Ch. I (ss. 1–17) am., ext. (mod.).	42, s. 38(1), sch. 6 para. 8.
		appl. (mod.).	42, ss. 37(1), 38 (1), sch. 6 para. 4.
		S. 1(2) am.	42, s. 38(1), sch. 6 para. 1.
		Ss. 2(3), 3(1)(4) appl. ...	42, s. 38(1), sch. 6 paras. 2, 3, 5.
		S. 7(1)–(3), (5)–(8) excl....	42, s. 38(1), sch. 6 para. 9.
		S. 11(3) appl. (mod.) ...	42, s. 37(5).
		S. 68(1) am.	42, s. 39(1).
		(3A) added ...	42, s. 39(2).
		(4) am.	42, s. 39(3).
		S. 74(6) added	42, s. 39(4).
c. 5	Administration of Justice Act 1968.	S. 1(1)(*b*)(i) am. ...	S.I. No. 1057.
		(*d*)(6) rep. (*prosp.*)	23, s. 122(2), sch. 7 Pt. I.
c. 8	Mauritius Independence Act 1968.	S. 4(1) rep.	30, s. 25(1), sch. 3.
c. 13	National Loans Act 1968	S. 1(6) rep.	30, s. 25(1), sch. 3.
		S. 10(3) rep.	2, s. 18(1), sch. 2.
		Sch. 1 rep. in pt. ...	44, s. 159(3), sch. 17.
c. 16	New Towns (Scotland) Act 1968.	Am. (*prosp.*)	51, ss. 60, 61, sch. 9.
		S. 2 (definition of " development corporation ") appl.	14, s. 18(1).
		S. 4 devolved in pt. (*prosp.*), transfer of certain functions (*prosp.*).	51, s. 63, sch. 10 Pt. III, sch. 11 Group E para. 4.
		am. (*prosp.*) ...	51, s. 42(1)(*c*)(2), sch. 7.
		S. 10(3) devolved in pt. (*prosp.*).	51, s. 63, sch. 10 Pt. III.
		(5) am. (*prosp.*) ...	51, s. 23(1)(2), sch. 4.
		S. 14(2) not devolved (*prosp.*).	51, s. 63, sch. 10 Pt. III.
		S. 18 devolved in pt. (*prosp.*), transfer of certain functions (*prosp.*).	51, s. 63, sch. 10 Pt. III, sch. 11 Group E para. 4.
		am. (*prosp.*) ...	51, s. 42(1)(*c*)(2), sch. 7.
		Ss. 19(1) (proviso), 24 not devolved (*prosp.*).	51, s. 63, sch. 10 Pt. III.

Session and Chap. or No. of Measure	Short title or Subject	How affected	Chapter of 1978 Act or number of Measure or Statutory Instrument
1968: c. 16—*cont.*	New Towns (Scotland) Act 1968—*cont.*	S. 26(5)(6) am. (*prosp.*)...	51, s. 23(1)(2), sch. 4.
		S. 28 devolved in pt. (*prosp.*).	51, s. 63, sch. 10 Pt. III.
		S. 28(4) am. (*prosp.*) ...	51, s. 23(1)(2), sch. 4.
		S. 30(1)(3)(5) devolved in pt. (*prosp.*).	51, s. 63, sch. 10 Pt. III.
		S. 36 am. (*prosp.*) ...	51, s. 23(1)(2), sch. 4.
		Ss. 38A not devolved (*prosp.*), 47(4) devolved in pt. (*prosp.*).	51, s. 63, sch. 10 Pt. III.
		S. 47(4) am. (*prosp.*) ...	51, s. 82(2), sch. 16 para. 27.
		Schs. 3, 4 not devolved (*prosp.*), transfer of functions (*prosp.*).	51, s. 63, sch. 10 Pt. III, sch. 11 Group E para. 5.
		Sch. 8 devolved in pt. (*prosp.*).	51, s. 63, sch. 10 Pt. III.
c. 17	Education Act 1968 ...	Transfer of functions (*prosp.*).	52, s. 9(1), sch. 2 Pt. III.
c. 18	Consular Relations Act 1968.	Saved	33, s. 16(1).
		Sch. 1 Art. 1(*a*) (definition of " consular post ") appl.	
		Art. 1(*d*)(definition of " consular officer ") appl.	30, s. 5, sch. 1.
c. 19	Criminal Appeal Act 1968	Sch. 5 Pt. I am. (*prosp.*)...	23, s. 122(1), sch. 5 Pt. II(1).
c. 21	Criminal Appeal (Northern Ireland) Act 1968.	Am. (*prosp.*)	23, s. 122(1), sch. 5 Pt. II(1).
		Pt. I (ss. 1–7) rep. (*prosp.*)	23, s. 122(2), sch. 7 Pt. I.
		Pt. II (ss. 8–35) am. (*prosp.*).	23, s. 37(1).
		S. 8 excl.	5, s. 7(6).
		S. 14(1) am. (*prosp.*) ...	23, s. 122(1), sch. 5 Pt. II(1).
		(2) am. (*prosp.*) ...	23, s. 37(1).
		rep. in pt. (*prosp.*)	23, s. 122(2), sch. 7 Pt. I.
		S. 20(1) mod.	5, s. 7(7).
		S. 20(3) am. (*prosp.*) ...	23, s. 122(1), sch. 5 Pt. II(1).
		S. 23(2) am. (*prosp.*) ...	23, s. 37(1).
		Ss. 23(4), 24(1)(2), 25(1)(*b*), (3)(*b*), 27 am. (*prosp.*).	23, s. 122(1), sch. 5 Pt. II(1).
		S. 30(2) rep. in pt. (*prosp.*)	23, s. 122(2), sch. 7 Pt. I.
		S. 32(2) am. (*prosp.*) ...	23, s. 122(1), sch. 5 Pt. II(1).
		S. 33(2) am. (*prosp.*) ...	23, s. 37(1).
		S. 34 am. (*prosp.*) ...	23, s. 122(1), sch. 5 Pt. II(1).
		S. 35 (definition of " sentence ") appl. (*prosp.*).	23, s. 120(1).

Session and Chap. or No. of Measure	Short title or Subject	How affected	Chapter of 1978 Act or number of Measure or Instrument
1968:			
c. 21—*cont.*	Criminal Appeal (Northern Ireland) Act 1968 —*cont.*	Ss. 36(1), 46(2)(*b*) am. (*prosp.*).	23, s. 122(1), sch. 5 Pt. II(1).
		S. 46(2)(*b*) rep. in pt. (*prosp.*).	23, s. 122(2), sch. 7 Pt. I.
		Ss. 48(*e*) added (*prosp.*), 48A(5) am. (*prosp.*).	23, s. 122(1), sch. 5 Pt. II(1).
		S. 49(1) rep.	23, s. 122(2), sch. 7 Pt. I.
		(2)(3) am.	23, s. 122(1), sch. 5 Pt. II(1).
		(3) rep. in pt. ...	23, s. 122(2), sch. 7 Pt. I.
		S. 50(1) (definition of " the Court of Appeal ") replaced (*prosp.*) (definition of " rules of court ") am.	23, s. 122(1), sch. 5 Pt. II(1).
		(definitions of " county court ", " the Lord Chief Justice ", " the Supreme Court ") rep. (*prosp.*), 53(1) rep. in pt. (*prosp.*), (2), 54, sch. 3 Pt. I, schs. 4, 5 rep. (*prosp.*).	23, s. 122(2), sch. 7 Pt. I.
c. 22	Legitimation (Scotland) Act 1968.	S. 6(2)(3) am. (*prosp.*) ...	28, s. 66(2), sch. 3 paras. 6, 7.
c. 27	Firearms Act 1968 ...	Ss. 32(1) subst., (3A) cont., 35(1)(3) subst.	S.I. Nos. 267, 360.
c. 29	Trade Descriptions Act 1968.	Not devolved (S.) (*prosp.*)	51, s. 63, sch. 10 Pt. III.
		S. 2(4)(*g*) added, (5)(*a*) am.	38, s. 7(8).
c. 31	Housing (Financial Provisions) (Scotland) Act 1968.	Am. (*prosp.*)	51, ss. 60, 61, sch. 9.
		Ss. 13–15, 18, 21 rep. (1.4.1979).	14, s. 16(2), sch. 3.
		S. 25(1)(*f*)(*g*) added ...	14, s. 16(1), sch. 2 para. 4.
		S. 49(5) added	14, s. 16(1), sch. 2 para. 5.
		S. 50 not devolved (*prosp.*), transfer of certain functions (*prosp.*).	51, s. 63, sch. 10 Pt. III, sch. 11 Group C.
c. 34	Agriculture (Miscellaneous Provisions) Act 1968	Pt. I (Ss. 1–8), Ss. 38, 40, 45, 46 transfer of functions (W).	S.I. No. 272.
c. 35	Water Resources Act 1968.	Transfer of functions (*prosp.*).	52, s. 9(1), sch. 2 Pt. IX.
c. 36	Maintenance Orders Act 1968.	Sch. rep. in pt. (*prosp.*).	22, s. 89, sch. 3.
c. 41	Countryside Act 1968	Transfer of certain functions (*prosp.*).	52, s. 9(1), sch. 2 Pt. XI.
		Mod. (*prosp.*)	52, s. 62(2)(9).
		Am. (W.) (*prosp.*), ss. 1(1) (2) rep. (W.) (*prosp.*), 2(4)(5) am. (W.) (*prosp.*).	52, s. 77(1), sch. 11 para. 29.
		S. 3 rep. (*prosp.*) ...	52, s. 62(12).
		S. 29(4) transfer of functions (W.).	S.I. No. 272.

Session and Chap. or No. of Measure	Short title or Subject	How affected	Chapter of 1978 Act or number of Measure or Instrument
1968:—*cont.*			
c. 46	Health Services and Public Health Act 1968.	Transfer of functions (*prosp.*).	52, s. 9(1), sch. 2 Pt. VI.
		Pt. I (ss. 1–43) rep. ...	29, s. 109, sch. 17.
		S. 45(5)(*b*) rep. in pt. ...	45, S.L. (R.), s. 1(1), sch. 1 Pt. XII.
		Ss. 59(2), 63(2)(*d*)(8) (definition of " the relevant enactments ") (*b*) am.	29, s. 109, sch. 16 para. 26.
		S. 63(8)(definition of "the relevant enactments ") (*b*) rep. in pt.	29, s. 109, sch. 17.
		S. 64(3)(*a*)(ix) subst. (*prosp.*).	22, s. 89, sch. 2 para. 22.
		S. 64(4)(*a*) rep. in pt. ...	29, s. 109, sch. 17.
		S. 64(4)(*a*)(*b*) am. ...	29, s. 109, sch. 16 para. 27.
		S. 65(3)(*b*)(x) subst. (*prosp.*).	22, s. 89, sch. 2 para. 23.
		S. 65(6) am.	29, s. 109, sch. 16 para. 28.
		S. 79(1), rep. in pt., Sch. 2 Pt. II rep., Sch. 3 Pt. I rep. (S.).	29, s. 109, sch. 17.
c. 47	Sewerage (Scotland) Act 1968.	S. 55(4) not devolved (*prosp.*).	51, s. 63, sch. 10 Pt. III.
c. 49	Social Work (Scotland) Act 1968	S. 2(2)(*j*) added (*prosp.*).	28, s. 66(2), sch. 3 para. 8.
		Ss. 5(2)(*c*), 6(1)(*b*), 10(1) (3A) am. (*prosp.*).	28, s. 66(2), sch. 3 paras. 9–11.
		S. 15 ext. (*prosp.*) ...	28, s. 34(3).
		Ss. 16(3)(11)(*a*)(*b*), 18(4A) am. (*prosp.*).	28, s. 66(2), sch. 3 paras. 13–15.
		S. 27 am. (*prosp.*). (1)(*b*) (iii) added (*prosp.*).	49, s. 14, sch. 2 para. 1.
		S. 27A added (*prosp.*) ...	49, s. 9.
		Ss. 60(1)(*f*), 86(3), 94(1) (definition of " hospital ") am.	29, s. 109, s. 16 para. 29.
		Sch. 8 para. 36 rep. (1.4.1979).	40, s. 9(3), sch. 2.
		Sch. 8 paras. 37–41 rep. (S.)(*prosp.*).	28, s. 66(3), sch. 4.
c. 51	Highlands and Islands Development (Scotland) Act 1968.	Am. (*prosp.*)	51, s. 42(1)(*b*).
		Not devolved (*prosp.*), transfer of functions (*prosp.*).	51, s. 63, sch. 10 Pt. III, sch. 11 Group E para. 2.
c. 52	Caravan Sites Act 1968	Transfer of functions (*prosp.*).	52, s. 9(1), sch. 2 Pt. VIII.
c. 53	Adoption Act 1968 ...	Apptd. day for ss. 5–7, 8(1), 9(23.10.1978).	S.I. No. 1430.
		Rep. (S.) (*prosp.*) ...	28, s. 66(3), sch. 4.
c. 54	Theatres Act 1968 ...	19(3), sch. 1 para. 3 ransfer of functions *prosp.*).	52, s. 9(1), sch. 2 Pt. II.

Session and Chap. or No. of Measure	Short title or Subject	How affected	Chapter of 1978 Act or number of Measure or Instrument
1968:—*cont.*			
c. 59	Hovercraft Act 1968 ...	S. 1(1)(*h*) am.	8, s. 14(1), sch. 1 Pt. I para. 4.
c. 60	Theft Act 1968	S. 16(2)(*a*) rep.	31, s. 5(5).
		Ss. 18, 30(1), 31(1) appl.	31, s. 5(1)(2).
c. 61	Civil Aviation Act 1968	S. 1 transfer of functions (*prosp.*).	52, s. 9(1), sch. 2 Pt. XIV.
		devolved (S.) (*prosp.*)	51, s. 63, sch. 10 Pt. III.
		S. 1(3)(4) am.	8, s. 14(1), sch. 1 Pt. I.
		S. 2 transfer of certain functions (*prosp.*).	52, s. 9(1), sch. 2 Pt. XIV.
		devolved (S.) (*prosp.*)	51, s. 63, sch. 10 Pt. III.
		am.	8, s. 8.
		S. 3 devolved (S.) (*prosp.*)	51, s. 63, sch. 10 Pt. III.
		am.	8, s. 8.
		Ss. 3(2)(4), 4 transfer of certain functions (*prosp.*).	52, s. 9(1), sch. 2 Pt. XIV.
		S. 4 devolved (S.) (*prosp.*)	51, s. 63, sch. 10 Pt. III.
		am.	8, s. 8.
		Ss. 5, 6 devolved (S.) (*prosp.*).	5, s. 63, sch. 10 Pt. III.
		S. 6(2) rep. in pt. ...	8, s. 14(1)(2) sch. 1 Pt. II para. 10(1)(4), sch. 2.
		S. 6(3)(4) am.	8, s. 14(1), sch. 1 Pt. II para. 10(1)(4).
		S. 6(5) transfer of functions (*prosp.*).	52, s. 9(1), sch. 2 Pt. XIV.
		S. 8 devolved (S.) (*prosp.*)	51, s. 63, sch. 10 Pt. III.
		S. 8(1) transfer of functions (*prosp.*).	52, s. 9(1), sch. 2 Pt. XIV.
		S. 12 devolved (S.) (*prosp.*)	51, s. 63, sch. 10 Pt. III.
		S. 12(1)(3) transfer of functions (*prosp.*).	52, s. 9(1), sch. 2 Pt. XIV.
		S. 20 rep. in pt. ...	8, s. 14(2), sch. 2.
		Ss. 21, 22 devolved (S.) (*prosp.*).	51, s. 63, sch. 10 Pt. III.
		S. 23(4) am.	8, s. 14(1), sch. 1 Pt. I para. 5.
		S. 27 devolved (S.) (*prosp.*)	51, s. 63, sch. 10 Pt. III.
c. 62	Clean Air Act 1968 ...	Transfer of functions (*prosp.*).	52, s. 9(1), sch. 2 Pt. VII.
c. 63	Domestic and Appellate Proceedings (Restriction of Publicity) Act 1968.	S. 4(2) rep. in pt. (*prosp.*)	23, s. 122(2), sch. 7 Pt. I.
c. 65	Gaming Act 1968 ...	S. 48(3)(4) am. (E. & W.)	S.I. No. 1847.
c. 67	Medicines Act 1968 ...	Transfer of functions (W.)	S.I. No. 272.
		S. 130 appl.	38, s. 9(4).
		Ss. 131(5), 132(1) (definition of "health centre") am.	29, s. 109, sch. 16 paras. 30, 31.
		Sch. 5 para. 12 rep.	29, s. 109, sch. 17.

Session and Chap. or No. of Measure	Short title or Subject	How affected	Chapter of 1978 Act or number of Measure or Statutory Instrument
1968:—*cont.* c. 73	Transport Act 1968 ...	Devolved in pt. (S.) (*prosp.*).	51, s. 63, sch. 10 Pt. III.
		Am. (*prosp.*)	51, ss. 60, 61, sch. 9.
		Am. (*prosp.*)	52, ss. 55(2), 56, sch. 6.
		S. 7 am. (*prosp.*) ...	51, s. 23(1)(2), sch. 4.
		S. 7(2) rep. in pt. (*prosp.*)	51, s. 82(2), sch. 16 para. 28(*a*).
		(4)(*b*) am.	55, s. 15(5)(*a*).
		(7) rep. in pt. (*prosp.*)	51, s. 82(2), sch. 16 para. 28(*a*).
		S. 8 am. (*prosp.*) ...	51, s. 23(1)(2), sch. 4.
		S. 8(2)(5) rep. in pt. (*prosp.*).	51, s. 82(2), sch. 16 para. 28(*a*) (*b*).
		Pt. II (ss. 9–23) transfer of certain functions (*prosp.*).	52, s. 9(1), sch. 2 Pt. XIV.
		S. 21(1) am.	55, s. 8(1), sch. 2 para. 7.
		S. 29 am. (*prosp.*) ...	51, s. 23(1)(2), sch. 4.
		S. 29(5)(*b*) rep. in pt. (*prosp.*).	51, s. 82(2), sch. 16 para. 28(*b*).
		S. 30(1)(*a*) rep. in pt. ...	55, s. 8(1), 24(4), sch. 2 para. 6.
		S. 36 am. (*prosp.*) ...	51, s. 23(1)(2), sch. 4.
		S. 42(3) am.	55, s. 15(5)(*b*).
		Ss. 56, 57 transfer of functions (*prosp.*).	52, s. 9(1), sch. 2 Pt. XIV.
		S. 57 concurrent powers of Min. (*prosp.*).	52, s. 9(2), sch. 3.
		am. (*prosp.*) ...	51, s. 23(3), sch. 5.
		S. 96(11B) added ...	55, s. 10.
		Ss. 112, 113 transfer of certain functions (*prosp.*).	52, s. 9(1), sch. 2 Pt. XIV.
		S. 135(1) appl.	55, s. 15(3).
		(1)(*d*) transfer of functions (*prosp.*).	52, s. 9(1), sch. 2 Pt. XIV.
		(4)(*b*) am. ...	44, s. 159(2), sch. 16 para. 6.
		(7) rep. (*prosp.*) ...	51, s. 82(2), sch. 16 para. 28(*c*).
		S. 136(2)(4) appl. ...	55, s. 15(4).
		S. 158 transfer of certain functions (*prosp.*).	52, s. 9(1), sch. 2 Pt. XIV.
		S. 159(1) (definition of " excursion or tour ") appl.	55, ss. 1(2), 5(3).
		(definition of " subsidiary ") appl. (*prosp.*).	51, s. 63, sch. 10 Pt. II para. 10.
		S. 162 mod.	S.I. No. 1174.
		Sch. 2 para. 3 am. ...	55, s. 15(5)(*c*).
		rep. in pt.	55, s. 24(4), sch. 4.
		Sch. 4 appl.	55, s. 15(3).

Session and Chap. or No. of Measure	Short title or Subject	How affected	Chapter of 1978 Act or number of Measure or Statutory Instrument
1968—*cont.*			
c. 77	Sea Fisheries Act 1968	Ss. 5, 7, 15 transfer of functions (W.).	S.I. No. 272.
c. xxviii ...	Hounslow Corporation Act 1968.	S. 64 rep. (saving) ...	xiii, s. 13(1)(3) sch. 3 Pt. I.
c. xxix ...	Lancashire County Council (General Powers) Act 1968.	S. 5(2) am.	S.I. No. 1453.
c. xxxix ...	Greater London Council (General Powers) Act 1968.	Ss. 15 (definition of "flammable material") am. (1.1.1980) 21(1)(*b*) rep. in pt. (1.1.1980) 22(2)–(4) rep.(1.1.1980)	xvi, s. 3.
		S. 23(2)(3) rep.	xvi, s. 3(4) sch. 1 Pt. I.
C.A.M.			
No. 1. ...	Pastoral Measure 1968	S. 27(6) rep. in pt. (7) added.	G.S.M. No. 2 s. 19(4).
		S. 40 appl.	G.S.M. No. 1 s. 23(2).
		S. 67(1) (definition of "suspension period") appl.	G.S.M. No. 2 s. 6(3).
		S. 90(1) (definition of "church") appl.	G.S.M. No. 2 s. 19(2).
		(definitions of "pastoral order", "pastoral scheme") appl.	G.S.M. No. 3 s. 2(4).
1969:			
c. 2	Local Government Grants (Social Need) Act 1969.	Transfer of functions (*prosp.*).	52, s. 9(1), sch. 2 Pt. VI.
c. 8	Redundancy Rebates Act 1969.	Rep.	44, s. 159(3), sch. 17.
c. 10	Mines and Quarries (Tips) Act 1969.	Pt. II (ss. 11–36) transfer of functions (*prosp.*).	52, s. 9(1), sch. 2 Pt. II.
c. 12	Genocide Act 1969 ...	S. 1(5) rep. (*prosp.*) ...	23, s. 122(2), sch. 7 Pt. I.
		S. 2(1) rep. in pt.	26, s. 9 sch. 2.
c. 14	Horserace Betting Levy Act 1969.	S. 1(2) am.	S.I. No. 496.
c. 15	Representation of the People Act 1969	Appl. (mods.)	S.I. Nos. 1912, 1915.
c. 16	Customs Duties (Dumping and Subsidies) Act 1969.	Am.	42, s. 6(5).
		S. 1(5) am. ...	42, s. 6 sch. 1 para. 1.
		S. 2(4) am.	42, s. 6 sch. 1 para. 2.
		S. 3(1) am.	42, s. 6 sch. 1 para. 3.
		S. 4(1)(3)(4) am. ...	42, s. 6 sch. 1 para. 4.
		S. 5(1) am.	42, s. 6 sch. 1 para. 5(1).
		(2) rep. (saving) ...	42, ss. 6, 80(5), sch. 1 para. 5(2) sch. 13 Pt. I.
		(3) am.	42, s. 6 sch. 1 para. 5(3).
		rep. in pt. (saving)	42, ss. 6, 80(5), sch. 1 para. 5 (3), sch. 13 Pt. I.

Session and Chap. or No. of Measure	Short title or Subject	How affected	Chapter of 1978 Act or number of Measure or Statutory Instrument
1969: c. 16—*cont.*	Customs Duties (Dumping and Subsidies) Act 1969—*cont.*	S. 6 am....	42, s. 6 sch. 1 para. 6.
		S. 10(2)(5), rep. (saving).	42, ss. 6, 80(5), sch. 1 para. 7, sch. 13 Pt. I.
		Ss. 11, 12 rep. (saving).	42, ss. 6, 80(5), sch. 1 para. 8, sch. 13 Pt. I.
		S. 13(1) rep. in pt. (saving).	42, ss. 6, 80(5), sch. 1 para. 9, sch. 13 Pt. I.
		S. 14(1)(3) rep. (saving)	42, ss. 6, 80(5), sch. 1 para. 10 sch. 13 Pt. I.
		S. 15(2) am.	42, s. 79, sch. 12 para. 26.
c. 27	Vehicle and Driving Licences Act 1969.	S. 29(3) rep.	3, s. 12(2), sch. 2.
c. 28	Ponies Act 1969 ...	S. 2 transfer of functions (W.), s. 2(1) am.	S.I. No. 272.
c. 32	Finance Act 1969 ...	Sch. 19 para. 10(3)(*a*)(*b*) am.	42, s. 51(1).
c. 33	Housing Act 1969 ...	Transfer of functions (*prosp.*).	52, s. 9(1), sch. 2 Pt. IV.
c. 34	Housing (Scotland) Act 1969.	Ss. 18(1), 19 am., 20(1)(*e*) added.	14, s. 16(1), sch. 2 paras. 30–32.
		S. 21 not devolved (*prosp.*).	51, s. 63, sch. 10 Pt. III.
		S. 24(1)(*a*), (*b*), (2)(*a*) am., (6) added.	14, s. 16(1), sch. 2 para. 6.
		S. 24A added	14, s. 9.
		S. 25(1A) added ...	14, s. 16(1), sch. 2 para. 7.
		Ss. 31, 32 rep. (1.4.1979), 59, 59A rep. in pt. (1.4.1979).	14, s. 16(2), sch. 3.
c. 35	Transport (London) Act 1969.	S. 24(4)(*a*) rep.	55, s. 24(4), sch. 4.
		S. 37(4)(*b*), sch. 2 para. 6 am.	44, s. 159(2), sch. 16 para. 7.
c. 36	Overseas Resources Development Act 1969.	Rep.	2, s. 18(1), sch. 2.
c. 40	Medical Act 1969 ...	S. 1(2)(*b*) rep. in pt. ...	12, s. 31(1)(2), sch. 6 para. 17, sch. 7.
		S. 3(2) subst.	12, s. 31(1), sch. 6 para. 18(1)(2).
		mod.	12, ss. 1(15), 17, 22(15), sch. 5 para. 16.
		(3) rep. (*prosp.*) ...	12, s. 31(1)(2), sch. 6 para. 18(1)(3), sch. 7.
		(4) am.	12, s. 31(1), sch. 6 para. 51.
		(4)–(6) appl.... ...	12, s. 24(2).
		(7) rep. (*prosp.*) ...	12, s. 31(1)(2), sch. 6 para. 18(1)(3), sch. 7.

Session and Chap. or No. of Measure	Short title or Subject	How affected	Chapter of 1978 Act or number of Measure or Statutory Instrument
1969: c. 40—*cont.*	Medical Act 1969—*cont.*	S. 4(1)(2) appl.	12, s. 24(2).
		(3) am. (*prosp.*) ...	12, s. 31(1), sch. 6 para. 19.
		(6) appl.	12, s. 24(2).
		(6)(*a*) am.	12, s. 31(1), sch. 6 para. 52.
		(7) rep. (*prosp.*) ...	12, s. 31(1)(2), sch. 6 para. 19.
		Ss. 5(1)(*c*) am., 6(2) am. (*prosp.*).	12, s. 31(1), sch. 6 paras. 53, 54.
		S. 6(3) subst.	12, s. 31(1), sch. 6 para. 20.
		S. 7(1) am.	12, s. 31(1), sch. 6 para. 21(1)(2).
		mod.	12, ss. 1(15), 17, 22(15), sch. 5 para. 17(*a*).
		(2) subst., (3) am. ...	12, s. 31(1), sch. 6 para. 21(1)(3) (4).
		(3) mod.	12, ss. 1(15), 17, 22(15), sch. 5 para. 17.
		(4) am.	12, s. 31(1), sch. 6 para. 21(1)(5).
		(5) am.	12, s. 31(1), sch. 6 para. 21(1)(6).
		(*a*) am., (*b*) am. (*prosp.*).	12, s. 31(1), sch. 6 paras. 55, 56.
		(7) am. (*prosp.*) ...	12, s. 31(1), sch. 6 para. 57.
		rep. in pt. ...	12, s. 31(1)(2), sch. 6 para. 21(1)(7), sch. 7.
		S. 8(1)(*a*)–(*c*) replaced ...	12, s. 31(1), sch. 6 para. 22.
		mod. ...	12, ss. 1(15), 17, 22(15), sch. 5 para. 18.
		(2) am.	12, s. 31(1), sch. 6 para. 58.
		(3)(*a*) am. (*prosp.*) ...	12, s. 31(1), sch. 6 para. 59.
		(*b*) rep. (*prosp.*) ...	12, s. 31(1)(2), sch. 6 para. 59, sch. 7.
		(5) am. (*prosp.*) ...	12, s. 31(1), sch. 6 para. 60.
		S. 9(1)(2) am. (*prosp.*) ...	12, s. 31(1), sch. 6 para. 61.
		(3)(4)(*a*) am. (*prosp.*)	12, s. 31(1), sch. 6 para. 23(1)–(3).
		(4)(*a*)(*b*) rep. in pt. (*prosp.*).	12, s. 31(1)(2), sch. 6 para. 23(1)(3)(4).
		(*b*) am. (*prosp.*) ...	12, s. 31(1), sch. 6 para. 23(1)(4).
		S. 10(3) am.	12, s. 31(1), sch. 6 para. 62.
		(7) rep. (*prosp.*) ...	12, s. 31(2), sch. 7.

Session and Chap. or No. of Measure	Short title or Subject	How affected	Chapter of 1978 Act or number of Measure or Statutory Instrument
1969: c. 40—*cont.*	Medical Act 1969—*cont.*	S. 11(2) rep.	12, s. 31(1)(2), sch. 6, para. 24, sch. 7.
		(3) rep. in pt. ...	12, s. 31(1)(2), sch. 6 para. 63, sch. 7.
		(4) am.	12, s. 31(1), sch. 6 para. 64.
		am. (*prosp.*) ...	12, s. 31(1), sch. 6 para. 11.
		S. 12 rep.	12, s. 31(1)(2), sch. 6 para. 24, sch. 7.
		Ss. 13(1), (2)(a)(c), (3), (4), 14 rep. (*prosp.*).	12, s. 31(2), sch. 7.
		Ss. 15, 16 rep (saving) (*prosp.*).	12, ss. 6(4)(5), 31(2), sch. 7.
		S. 17 rep. (*prosp.*) ...	12, s. 31(2), sch. 7.
		S. 18(1) am. (*prosp.*) ...	12, s. 31(1), sch. 6 para. 12.
		rep. in pt. (*prosp.*)	12, s. 31(1)(2). sch. 6 para. 12, sch. 7.
		(3) rep. (*prosp.*) ...	12, s. 31(2), sch. 7.
		S. 19 am.	12, s. 31(1), sch. 6 para. 26(a).
		rep. in pt. ...	12, s. 31(1)(2), sch. 6 para. 26(b), sch. 7.
		S. 21(1) (definition of " the Act of 1978 ") added.	12, s. 31(1), sch. 6 para. 65.
		Sch. 1 paras. 1 rep. (*prosp.*).	12, s. 31(2), sch. 7.
		3, 4 rep. (*prosp.*).	12, s. 31(1)(2), sch. 6 para. 27, sch. 7.
		5, 9–12 rep. (*prosp.*).	12, s. 31(2), sch. 7.
		Sch. 3 paras. 1 rep. (*prosp.*).	12, s. 31(2), sch. 7.
		2, 3 rep.	12, s. 31(1)(2), sch. 6 para. 28, sch. 7.
		4 rep. (*prosp.*).	12, s. 31(2), sch. 7.
		6, 7 rep.	12, s. 31(1)(2), sch. 6 para. 28, sch. 7.
		9 rep. (*prosp.*).	12, s. 31(2), sch. 7.
		10 rep.	12, s. 31(1)(2), sch. 6 para. 28, sch. 7.
		11 rep. (*prosp.*).	12, s. 31(2), sch. 7.
c. 44	National Insurance Act 1969.	Rep.	45, S.L. (R.), s. 1(1), sch. 1 Pt. VIII.

Session and Chap. or No. of Measure	Short title or Subject	How affected	Chapter of 1978 Act or number of Measure or Statutory Instrument
1969—*cont.*			
c. 46	Family Law Reform Act 1969.	S. 5(2) rep. (*prosp.*) ...	22, s. 89, sch. 3.
		S. 6(7) am. (*prosp.*) ...	23, s. 122(1), sch. 5 Pt. II(1).
c. 48	Post Office Act 1969	S. 53 rep.	S.I. No. 1173.
		S. 86(1) (definition of "national health service authority"(*b*)) am.	29, s. 109, sch. 16 para. 32.
		Sch. 4 para. 93(4) not devolved (S.) (*prosp.*).	51, s. 63, sch. 10 Pt. III.
		Sch. 9 para. 33(1)–(4) am. (6) added.	44, s. 159(2), sch. 16 para. 8.
		para. 34 rep.	44, s. 159(3), sch. 17.
c. 50	Trustee Savings Banks Act 1969.	S. 12(1A) added (21.11. 1976).	16, s. 2(1)(6).
		rep. (*prosp.*)	16, s. 2(6).
		Ss. 14(1), 28(1) am. (21. 11.1976).	16, s. 2(3)(6).
		rep. in pt. (*prosp.*).	16, s. 2(6).
		S. 95(1) (definition of "land") appl.	16, s. 1(5).
c. 51	Development of Tourism Act 1969.	Devolved in pt. (S.) (*prosp.*).	51, s. 63, sch. 10 Pt. III.
		Transfer of certain functions (*prosp.*).	52, s. 9(1), sch. 2 Pt. XIII.
		S. 1(2)(*a*) am. (*prosp.*), rep. in pt. (*prosp.*) (*c*)– (*e*) added (*prosp.*).	51, s. 82(2), sch. 16 para. 29.
		S. 2(1)(*a*) restr. (*prosp.*)	51, s. 70(1).
		S. 2(2) am.(*prosp.*) ...	51, s. 82(2), sch. 16 para. 30.
			52, s. 77(1), sch. 11 para. 30.
		(3) am. (*prosp.*) ...	51, s. 82(2), sch. 16 para. 30.
			52, s. 77(1), sch. 11 para. 30.
		S. 3(1) am. (*prosp.*), rep. in pt. (*prosp.*).	51, s. 82(2), sch. 16 para. 31(*a*).
			52, s. 77(1), sch. 11 para. 31(*a*).
		(1A) added (*prosp.*) ...	51, s. 82(2), sch. 16 para. 31(*b*).
		(1B) added (*prosp.*) ...	52, s. 77(1), sch. 11 para. 31(*b*).
		(2) am. (*prosp.*) ...	51, s. 82(2), sch. 16 para. 31(*c*).
			52, s. 77(1), sch. 11 para. 31(*c*).
		(6) am. (*prosp.*) rep. in pt. (*prosp.*).	51, s. 82(2), sch. 16 para. 31(*d*).
			52, s. 77(1), sch. 11 para. 31(*d*).
		(7) added (*prosp.*) ...	52, s. 77(1), sch. 11 para. 31(*e*).
		S. 17 mod. (*prosp.*) ...	52, s. 77(1), Sch. 11 para. 32.

Session and Chap. or No. of Measure	Short title or Subject	How affected	Chapter of 1978 Act or number of Measure or Instrument
1969: c. 51—*cont.*	Development of Tourism Act 1969—*cont.*	S. 17(1) rep. in pt. (*prosp.*)	52, s. 82(2), sch. 16 para. 32.
		S. 18 mod. (*prosp.*) ...	52, s. 77(1), sch. 11 para. 32.
		S. 18(1) rep. in pt. (*prosp.*)	51, s. 82(2), sch. 16 para. 32.
c. 54	Children and Young Persons Act 1969.	Ss. 1, 11A, 19 transfer of functions (*prosp.*).	52, s. 9(1), sch. 2 Pt. VI.
		S. 20 (definition of " care order ") appl. (*prosp.*).	22, s. 53.
		Ss. 24–26, 27(3)(5), 31, 35–37, 39, 40, 43, 45, 47, 48, 58, 63(1)(2)(4)(5) transfer of functions (*prosp.*).	52, s. 9(1), sch. 2 Pt. VI.
		S. 63(6)(*g*) am. (*prosp.*)...	22, s. 89, sch. 2 para. 24.
		Ss. 64, 64A, 65(1)(2) transfer of functions (*prosp.*).	52, s. 9(1), sch. 2 Pt. VI.
		Sch. 5 paras. 33, 35 rep. (S.) (*prosp.*).	28, s. 66(3), sch. 4.
c. 58	Administration of Justice Act 1969.	S. 7(2) rep. in pt. ...	45, S.L. (R), s. 1(1), sch. 1 Pt. I.
		Pt. II (ss. 12–16) saved (*prosp.*).	23, s. 43.
		S. 12(2)(*b*) rep. (N.I.) (*prosp.*), (8) rep. in pt. (N.I.) (*prosp.*).	23, s. 122(2), sch. 7 Pt. I.
		S. 16(1) am. (*prosp.*) ...	23, s. 122(1), sch. 5 Pt. II(1).
		(2) rep. (*prosp.*) ...	23, s. 122(2), sch. 7 Pt. I.
		Ss. 20(5), 21(4) am.	23, s. 122(1), sch. 5 Pt. II(1).
		Ss. 25(2), 26(2)(3), 27(2), (4)–(7), 28, 35(2) rep.	45, S.L. (R), s. 1(1), sch. 1 Pt. I.
		Sch. 1 rep. in pt. (*prosp.*)	23, s. 122(2), sch. 7 Pt. I.
		Sch. 2 rep.	45, S.L. (R), s. 1(1), sch. 1 Pt. I.
c. xxv ...	Lands Improvement Company's Amendment Act 1969.	Transfer of functions (W.)	S.I. No. 272.
C.A.M.: No. 2 ...	Synodical Government Measure 1969.	S. 4(4) excl.	G.S.M. No. 1 s. 4(4).
		Sch. 2 art. 8(1C) added...	G.S.M. No. 3, s. 1.
1970: c. 9	Taxes Management Act 1970.	Ss. 12(2)(*b*), 25(7) am. ...	42, s. 45(5).
		Ss. 58(2), 59(5) am. (*prosp.*).	23, s. 122(1), sch. 5 Pt. II(1).
		S. 98(3) Table am. ...	42, s. 53(8).
		Sch. 4 para. 13 rep. (*prosp.*).	23, s. 122(2), sch. 7 Pt. I.

Session and Chap. or No. of Measure	Short title or Subject	How affected	Chapter of 1978 Act or number of Measure or Instrument
1970—*cont.* c. 10	Income and Corporation Taxes Act 1970.	S. 8(1)(*a*)(*b*), (1A), (1B), (2) am.	42, s. 19(1).
		S. 10 mod.	42, s. 20(1)(2).
		S. 10(5) am.	42, s. 20(3).
		S. 12 rep. in pt. ...	42, ss. 19(2), 80 (5), sch. 3 Pt. III.
		S. 12(1)(ii) am. ...	42, s. 19(2).
		S. 13(*a*) rep. in pt. ...	42, ss. 19(3), 80 (5), sch. 13 Pt. III.
		am.	42, s. 19(3).
		S. 14(2)(3) am. ...	42, s. 19(4).
		S. 17 am.	42, s. 19(5).
		S. 18(1)(*a*)(*b*), (2)(*b*) am.	42, s. 19(6).
		(3)(4) rep. ...	42, ss. 19(6)(*c*), 80(5), sch. 13 Pt. III.
		(5) am.	42, s. 19(5).
		S. 30(3) am.	42, s. 14(3), sch. 2 para. 1.
		S. 34(1)(iii) am.	42, s. 14(3), sch. 2 para. 2.
		S. 36(1) am.	42, s. 14(3), sch. 2 para. 3.
		S. 39(1)(*d*) am.	42, s. 19(5).
		S. 83(1)(*a*) am.	42, s. 32(1)(2)(4).
		(1) (2) (3) rep. in pt. (4)(*b*)(iii), (6) rep.	42, ss. 32(1)(2)(4), 80(5), sch. 13 Pt. III.
		S. 134(1) am.	42, s. 32(1), (3) (*a*)(*d*).
		(1)(ii) rep. in pt., (iii) rep., (2) rep. in pt.	42, ss. 32(1)(3)(*b*) (*c*), (4), 80(5) sch. 13 Pt. III.
		(2) am.	42, s. 32(1)(3)(*d*).
		(7) rep.	42, ss. 32(1) (3)(*d*) (4), 80(5), sch. 13 Pt. III.
		S. 168 restr.	42, s. 31.
		Ss. 168(3)–(5) (7), 169(1)– (9) am.	42, s. 30.
		S. 169(3)(6)(8) mod. ...	42, s. 30(8).
		S. 177(2) restr.	42, s. 31.
		S. 188(3) am.	42, s. 24(1).
		S. 230(7)(*b*) am. ...	42, s. 26(4).
		S. 265(3)(*b*) rep. ...	42, s. 80(5), sch. 13 Pt. IV.
		S. 272(1) (definition of " group ") appl.	42, s. 49(10).
		S. 282 (definition of " close company ") appl., s. 285(6) appl. (mods.).	42, s. 53, sch. 9 para. 11(3).
		S. 287(1)(*c*) am. ...	42, s. 14(3), sch. 2 para. 4.
		Ss. 302(1) excl. appl. (mods.), 303(3)(*a*)(*b*) (*c*) mod.	42, s. 36(2), sch. 5 para. 2.

Session and Chap. or No. of Measure	Short title or Subject	How affected	Chapter of 1978 Act or number of Measure or Instrument
1970: c. 10—_cont._	Income and Corporation Taxes Act 1970—_cont._	S. 304(5) (definition of "investment company") appl.	42, s. 60(1)(_b_).
		S. 323(4)(_a_) am. ...	42, s. 26(5).
		S. 340 transfer of functions (W.).	S.I. No. 272.
		S. 343(3)(_c_), proviso para. (i) am.	42, s. 14(3), sch. 2 para. 5.
		S. 399(4)(_c_) am. ...	42, s. 14(3), sch. 2 para. 6.
		S. 400(3) am.	42, s. 14(3), sch. 2 para. 7.
		S. 403(1) am.	42, s. 14(3), sch. 2 para. 8.
		S. 412(6)(7) am. ...	44, s. 159(2), sch. 16 para. 9.
		S. 413(6) am. (_prosp._) ...	23, s. 122(1), sch. 5 Pt. II(1).
		S. 422(2) am.	42, s. 14(3), sch. 2 para. 9.
		S. 424(_c_) am.	42, s. 14(3), sch. 2 para. 10.
		S. 430(1) am.	42, s. 14(3), sch. 2 para. 11.
		S. 457(1) am.	42, s. 14(3), sch. 2 para. 12.
		S. 458(1) am.	42, s. 14(3), sch. 2 para. 13.
		S. 474(1) am.	42, s. 30.
		S. 526(1)(2) rep. in pt. ...	30, s. 25(1), sch. 3.
		S. 534 appl.	42, s. 53, sch. 9 para. 16.
		Sch. 1 para. 11(1) rep. in pt. (6.4.1979).	42, ss. 25, 80(5), sch. 3 para. 13, sch. 13 Pt. III.
		para. 11(1)(2) am. (6.4.1979).	42, s. 25, sch. 3 para. 13.
		para. 11(3) rep. in pt. (6.4.1979).	42, ss. 25, 80(5), sch. 3 para. 13 sch. 13 Pt. III.
		Sch. 8 para. 3 am., 4 renumbered, 4(2) added.	42, s. 24.
		Sch. 15 para. 11 Table Pt. II rep. in pt.	42, s. 80(5), sch. 13 Pt. IV.
c. 11	Sea Fish Industry Act 1970.	Pt. I (ss. 1–28 except s. 24 (4)) transfer of functions (W.).	S.I. No. 272.
		S. 23 am.	S.I. No. 1821.
		Pt. II (ss. 29–43), ss. 49, 51, 55 schs. 3, 5 transfer of functions (W.)	S.I. No. 272.
c. 20	Roads (Scotland) Act 1970.	S. 28(2) am. (_prosp._) ...	51, s. 23(1)(2), sch. 4.
		S. 44 devolved in pt. (_prosp._).	51, s. 63, sch. 10 Pt. III.
c. 31	Administration of Justice Act 1970.	S. 34(2) am.	23, s. 122(1), sch. 5 Pt. II(1).
		Sch. 1, sch. 8 para. 3 am. (_prosp._).	22, s. 89, sch. 2 paras. 25, 26.

Session and Chap. or No. of Measure	Short title or Subject	How affected	Chapter of 1978 Act or number of Measure or Statutory Instrument
1970—*cont.*			
c. 34	Marriage (Registrar General's Licence) Act 1970.	S. 18 transfer of certain functions (*prosp.*).	52, s. 9(1), sch. 2 Pt. XVII.
		S. 18(2) am. (*prosp.*) ...	52, s. 77(1), sch. 11 para. 33.
c. 35	Conveyancing and Feudal Reform (Scotland) Act 1970.	S. 9(8) (definition of " heritable security ") appl.	16, s. 1(5).
c. 36	Merchant Shipping Act 1970.	Apptd. day for certain specified provisions (1.7.1979).	S.I. No. 797.
c. 38	Building (Scotland) Act 1970.	Devolved in pt. (*prosp.*).	51, s. 63, sch. 10 Pt. III.
c. 39	Local Authorities (Goods and Services) Act 1970.	Transfer of functions (*prosp.*).	52, s. 9(1), sch. 2 Pt. I.
		S. 1(5) concurrent powers of Min. (*prosp.*) ...	52, s. 9(2), sch. 3.
		am (*prosp.*) ...	51, s. 23(3), sch. 5.
c. 40	Agriculture Act 1970 ...	S. 25 Pts. II, III (ss. 28–65), Pt. IV (ss. 66–87) transfer of functions (W.).	S.I. No. 272.
		S. 66(1) (definitions of "feeding stuff", "fertiliser ") appl.	38, s. 9(4).
		(definition of " the Ministers ") am.	S.I. No. 272.
		Ss. 66(1), 76(5) mod.	S.I. No. 1108.
		Ss. 106, 108 transfer of functions (W.).	S.I. No. 272.
c. 41	Equal Pay Act 1970 ...	S.2. appl. (mods.)(*prosp.*)	51, s. 33(3)(4).
		S. 2(7) rep.	44, s. 159(3), sch. 17.
c. 42	Local Authority Social Services Act 1970.	Transfer of certain functions (*prosp.*).	52, s. 9(1), sch. 2 Pt. VI.
		Sch. 1 rep. in pt. ...	45, S.L. (R.), s. 1(1), sch. 1 Pt. XII.
		rep. in pt. (*prosp.*)	22, s. 89, sch. 2 para. 27, sch. 3.
		am. (*prosp.*) ...	22, s. 89, sch. 2 para. 27.
c. 44	Chronically Sick and Disabled Persons Act 1970.	S. 9 not devolved (S.) (*prosp.*).	51, s. 63, sch. 10 Pt. III.
		S. 17 transfer of functions (*prosp.*).	52, s. 9(1), sch. 2 Pt. VI.
		S. 17(1) am.	29, s. 109, sch. 16 para. 33.
		S. 18(1)(3) transfer of functions (*prosp.*). ...	52, s. 9(1), sch. 2 Pt. VI.
		Ss. 21, 23 not devolved (S.) (*prosp.*).	51, s. 63, sch. 10 Pt. III.
		Ss. 25–27 transfer of functions (*prosp.*).	52, s. 9(1), sch. 2 Pt. VI.
c. 45	Matrimonial Proceedings and Property Act 1970.	Ss. 30(1), 31–33 rep. (*prosp.*).	22, s. 89, sch. 3.
c. 46	Radiological Protection Act 1970.	Not devolved (S.) (*prosp.*)	51, s. 63, sch. 10 Pt. III.

Session and Chap. or No. of Measure	Short title or Subject	How affected	Chapter of 1978 Act or number of Measure or Statutory Instrument
1970—*cont.*			
c. 50	Fiji Independence Act 1970.	S. 4(1) rep.	30, s. 25(1), sch. 3.
c. li	Manchester Corporation Act 1970.	Ss. 4 (definitions of "hackney carriage by-laws," private hire vehicles") rep. 6, 7 rep. (saving) 8–15, 17, 18 rep.	S.I. No. 739.
c. lxxvi ...	Greater London Council (General Powers) Act 1970.	S. 14(4)(iii) added ...	xvi, s. 8
1971:			
c. 3	Guardianship of Minors Act 1971.	S. 1 appl. (*prosp.*) ...	22, s. 15.
		Ss. 1, 4(4), 9(1)(2) am. (*prosp.*).	22, s. 36(1)(*a*).
		S. 9(2) subst. (*prosp.*) ...	22, s. 41(2).
		(3) rep. (*prosp.*) ...	22, s. 89, sch. 3
		(4) am. (*prosp.*) ...	22, s. 41(2).
		S. 10 am. (*prosp.*) ...	22, s. 36(1)(*a*).
		(1)(*b*) subst. (*prosp.*), (2) am. (*prosp.*).	22, s. 41(3).
		S. 11 am. (*prosp.*) ...	22, s. 36(1)(*a*).
		(*b*) subst. (*prosp.*), (*c*) am. (*prosp.*).	22, s. 41(4).
		S. 11A added (*prosp.*) ...	22, s. 37.
		S. 12 subst. (*prosp.*) ...	22, s. 42.
		Ss. 12A–C, added (*prosp.*)	22, s. 43.
		S. 13(1) am. (*prosp.*) ...	22, s. 36(1)(*b*).
		(2) am. (*prosp.*) ...	22, s. 89, sch. 2 para. 29.
		S. 13A added (*prosp.*) ...	22, s. 39.
		S. 14(3) am. (*prosp.*) ...	22, ss. 36 (1)(*a*), 89, sch. 2 para. 30.
		(4) rep. (*prosp.*) ...	22, s. 89, sch. 3.
		S. 14A added (*prosp.*) ...	22, s. 40.
		S. 15(1) am. (*prosp.*) ...	22, s. 47(1).
		(2)(*a*) rep. (*prosp.*) ...	22, s. 38(1).
		(4) am. (*prosp.*) ...	22, ss. 36(1)(*a*), 47(1).
		(6) am. (*prosp.*) ...	22, s. 36(1)(*a*).
		S. 16(5) am. (*prosp.*) ...	22, s. 89, sch. 2 para. 31.
		(6)–(8) added (*prosp.*).	22, s. 48.
		S. 20(2) am. (*prosp.*) ...	22, s. 36(1)(*c*).
c. 8	Hospital Endowments (Scotland) Act 1971.	Rep.	29, s. 109, sch. 17.
c. 10	Vehicles (Excise) Act 1971.	S. 7(2) subst.	42, s. 8(1).
		S. 26(1)(*c*), (2)(*a*) ext. ...	42, s. 8(4).
c. 11	Atomic Energy Authority Act 1971.	S. 10(1)–(4) am. ...	44, s. 159(2), sch. 16 para. 10.
c. 12	Hydrocarbon Oil (Customs & Excise) Act 1971.	Ss. 1(1), 2(3), 3(1) am. ...	42, s. 79, sch. 12 para. 8.
		Ss. 13(1), 14 am. ...	S.I. No. 1603.
		S. 21(3) am.	42, s. 79, sch. 12 para. 8.
		Sch. 1 para. 4 rep. in pt.	42, s. 80(5), sch. 13 Pt. I.
		Sch. 5 para. 2(1) am. ...	42, s. 79, sch. 12 para. 8.

Session and Chap. or No. of Measure	Short title or Subject	How affected	Chapter of 1978 Act or number of Measure or Statutory Instrument
1971—*cont.*			
c. 15	Consumer Protection Act 1971.	Rep. (*prosp.*)	38, s. 10(1), sch. 3.
c. 17	Industry Act 1971 ...	Ss. 1 rep., 3(2) rep. in pt., sch. 1, sch. 2 Pt. I rep., Pt. II rep. in pt.	45, S.L. (R.), s. 1(1), sch. 1 Pt. XVII.
c. 32	Attachment of Earnings Act 1971.	Sch. 1 am. (*prosp.*) ...	22, s. 89, sch. 2 para. 32.
c. 34	Water Resources Act 1971.	Transfer of functions (*prosp.*).	52, s. 9(1), sch. 2 Pt. IX.
		S. 1 power to intervene (*prosp.*).	52, s. 63, sch. 8 Pts. III, IV.
c. 38	Misuse of Drugs Act 1971	S. 2 (definition of " controlled drug ") appl.	38, s. 9(4).
		S. 34 rep. (*prosp.*) ...	22, s. 89, sch. 3.
		Sch. 3 para. 5(2) am. (*prosp.*).	23, s. 122(1), sch. 5 Pt. II(1).
c. 39	Rating Act 1971 ...	S. 2(4) am.	S.I. No. 318.
c. 40	Fire Precautions Act 1971	Transfer of certain functions (*prosp.*).	52, s. 9(1), sch. 2 Pt. V.
		S. 28(5) proviso rep. ...	45, S.L. (R.), s. 1(1), sch. 1 Pt. XVII.
		Ss. 36(4)–(6), 41 not devolved (S.) (*prosp.*).	51, s. 63, sch. 10 Pt. III.
c. 41	Highways Act 1971 ...	Transfer of certain functions (*prosp.*), saving for s. 1 (*prosp.*).	52, ss. 9(1), 75, sch. 2 Pt. XV, sch. 10.
c. 56	Pensions (Increase) Act 1971.	Ext.	S.I. No. 211.
		S. 13(2)–(5) am. (*prosp.*)	51, s. 23(1)(2), sch. 4.
c. 58	Sheriff Courts (Scotland) Act 1971.	S. 4(3) rep. in pt. ...	30, s. 25(1), sch. 3.
c. 60	Prevention of Oil Pollution Act 1971.	Act (except s. 23(*b*)) not devolved (S.) (*prosp.*), s. 23(*b*) devolved in pt. (S.) (*prosp.*).	51, s. 63, sch. 10 Pt. III.
c. 61	Mineral Workings (Offshore Installations) Act 1971.	S. 8(4) rep. in pt. ...	8, s. 14(2), sch. 2.
c. 62	Tribunals and Inquiries Act 1971.	Devolved in pt. (S.) (*prosp.*). ss. 1–4(1) not devolved(S.) (*prosp.*).	51, s. 63, sch. 10 Pt. III.
		Ss. 5(1), 12 transfer of certain functions (*prosp.*).	52, s. 9(1), sch. 2 Pt. XVIII.
		S. 13(1A) added ...	44, s. 159(2), sch. 16 para. 11.
		S. 13(7)(*a*)–(*c*) am. (*prosp.*)	23, s. 122(1), sch. 5 Pt. II(1).
		S. 15(1)(5) not devolved (S.) (*prosp.*).	51, s. 63, sch. 10 Pt. III.
		Sch. 1 Pt. II para. 41(*a*)(*b*)(*c*) am.	29, s. 109, sch. 16 para. 35.
c. 66	Friendly Societies Act 1971.	S. 11(6) rep.	45, S.L. (R), s. 1(1), sch. 1 Pt. XVII.
c. 68	Finance Act 1971 ...	S. 7(*d*) added	42, s. 8(3).
		S. 32(1)(*a*) am., (*aa*) added.	42, s. 14(1).
		(1A)–(1D) added ...	42, s. 14(2).

Session and Chap. or No. of Measure	Short title or Subject	How affected	Chapter of 1978 Act or number of Measure or Statutory Instrument
1971 :			
c. 68—*cont.*	Finance Act 1971—*cont.*	S. 57 rep. (*retrosp.*) ...	42, ss. 44(7), 80 (5), sch. 13 Pt. IV.
		Sch. 1 para. 1(2)(7) am.	S.I. No. 1602.
		Sch. 7 para. 2(2) am. ...	42, s. 14(3), sch. 2 para. 14.
		Sch. 11 rep. (*retrosp.*) ...	42, s. 80(5), sch. 13 Pt. IV.
		Sch. 13 para. 1(1) am. ...	29, s. 109, sch. 16 para. 36.
c. 69	Medicines Act 1971 ...	Transfer of functions (W.)	S.I. No. 272.
c. 70	Hijacking Act 1971 ...	S. 3(1) rep. in pt. ...	26, s. 9, sch. 2.
c. 74	Education (Milk) Act 1971.	Transfer of functions (*prosp.*).	52, s. 9(1), sch. 2 Pt. III.
c. 75	Civil Aviation Act 1971	Devolved in pt. (*prosp.*)	51, s. 63, sch. 10 Pt. III.
		S. 4(2A) added	8, s. 10.
		S. 4(3) am.	8, s. 14(1), sch. 1 Pt. II para. 11(1)(2).
		S. 6(2) replaced ...	8, s. 6.
		S. 8(1)(3) am.	8, s. 5(2).
		S. 8(5) am.	8, s. 5(1).
		S. 9(5) rep. in pt. ...	8, s. 14(1)(2), sch. 1 Pt. II para. 11(1)(3), sch. 2.
		S. 9(7) rep. in pt. (*retrosp.*)	8, ss. 7, 14(2), sch. 2.
		S. 10(2) am.	8, s. 14(1), sch. 1 Pt. I para. 6(1)(2).
		S. 21(2) restr.	15, s. 7(4), sch. para. 6. 20, s. 4(3), sch. 2 para. 6.
		S. 21(5)(*a*)(*b*) am. ...	8, s. 11.
		S. 22(3) restr.	15, s. 7(4), sch. para. 6. 20, s. 4(3), sch. 2 para. 6.
		Ss. 23(5) am., (6) added, 29(3) replaced, (4) am., (*a*)(*c*) am., (*cc*) added, (*e*), (5) am.	8, s. 14(1), sch. 1 Pt. I para. 6(1)(3)–(6).
		S. 29(7)(8) transfer of functions (*prosp.*), concurrent powers of Min. (*prosp.*).	52, s. 9(1)(2), sch. 2 Pt. XIV, sch. 3.
		S. 29(8A) added, (9) am.	8, s. 14(1), sch. 1 Pt. II para. 11(1)(4).
		S. 29(10) rep. in pt. ...	8, s. 14(2), sch. 2.
		Ss. 29(11) am., 29A(6A) added.	8, s. 14(1), sch. 1 Pt. I para. 6(1)(7)(8).
		S. 29A transfer of functions (*prosp.*).	52, s. 9(1), sch. 2 Pt. XIV.
		S. 31 am.	8, s. 8.
		S. 32(3) rep. in pt. ...	8, s. 14(1)(2), sch. 1 Pt. II para. 11(1)(5), sch. 2.

Session and Chap. or No. of Measure	Short title or Subject	How affected	Chapter of 1978 Act or number of Measure or Statutory Instrument
1971: c. 75—*cont.*	Civil Aviation Act 1971—*cont.*	S. 36(1)(*bb*) added, (*c*) am., (1A) added, (2) am., (*dd*) added.	8, s. 14(1), sch. 1 Pt. I para. 6(1)(9).
		S. 60(1) (definitions of "subsidiary" and "joint subsidiary") appl.	8, s. 12(6).
		S. 63(4) am.	8, s. 14(1), sch. 1 Pt. I para. 6(1)(10).
		Sch. 9 para. 1(1)–(4) am., (6) added.	44, s. 159(2), sch. 16 para. 12(1).
		para. 2 rep. ...	44, s. 159(3), sch. 17.
		para. 4(1)(2) am.	44, s. 159(2), sch. 16 para. 12(2).
c. 76	Housing Act 1971 ...	Transfer of functions (*prosp.*).	52, s. 9(1), sch. 2 Pt. IV.
c. 77	Immigration Act 1971 ...	Sch. 1 Appendix saved	S.I. No. 1030.
c. 78	Town and Country Planning Act 1971.	Apptd. day for specified provisions (23.5.1978)	S.I. No. 557.
		(28.6.1978)	S.I. Nos. 725, 727.
		Transfer of certain functions (*prosp.*) (saving for s. 233, sch. 20 para. 3) (*prosp.*) ...	52, ss. 9(1), 75, sch. 2 Pt. VIII. sch. 10.
		Ss. 35–37 power to intervene (*prosp.*). ...	52, s. 64, sch. 9 Pt. I.
		S. 40(1A) added (*prosp.*)	52, s. 77(1), sch. 11 para. 34.
		Ss. 45, 51, 88, 95 power to intervene (*prosp.*).	52, s. 64, sch. 9 Pt. I.
		S. 113 concurrent powers of Min. (*prosp.*).	52, s. 9(2), sch. 3.
		S. 230(4)(5) consent of Min. required (*prosp.*).	52, s. 36(1), sch. 4.
		Ss. 232, 233 transfer of certain functions (W.)	S.I. No. 272.
		S. 233(4) consent of Min. required (*prosp.*).	52, s. 36(1), sch. 4.
		Ss. 234–237 transfer of certain functions (W.).	S.I. No. 272.
		S. 237(4) consent of Min. required (*prosp.*).	52, s. 36(1), sch. 4.
		S. 238 transfer of certain functions (W.)	S.I. No. 272.
		S. 254A added (*prosp.*) ...	52, s. 77(1), sch. 11 para. 35.
		S. 273 consent of Min. required (*prosp.*).	52, s. 36(1), sch. 4.
		S. 276(pt.) power to intervene (*prosp.*). ...	52, s. 64, sch. 9 Pt. I.
		S. 276(5) am. (*prosp.*) ...	52, s. 64, sch. 9 Pt. II para. 6(2).
		S. 281(1)–(5) mod. ...	3, s. 8(2).
		Ss. 282, 283 mod. ...	3, s. 8(3).

Session and Chap. or No. of Measure	Short title or Subject	How affected	Chapter of 1978 Act or number of Measure or Statutory Instrument
1971: c. 78—*cont.*	Town and Country Planning Act 1971—*cont.*	S. 283 appl. (*prosp.*) ...	52, s. 64, sch. 9 Pt. II para. 7(2).
		S. 284 mod. ... ... Sch. 5 Pt. I, sch. 6 excl.	3, s. 8(3). S.I. Nos. 724, 726.
		Sch. 23 Pt. II rep. in pt.	3, s. 12(2), sch. 2.
c. 80	Banking and Financial Dealings Act 1971.	S. 1(2A) added (*prosp.*)	51, s. 82(2), sch. 16 para. 33.
		(2B) added (*prosp.*)	52, s. 77(1), sch. 11 para. 36.
		(3A) added (*prosp.*)	51, s. 82(2), sch. 16 para. 34.
		(3B) added (*prosp.*)	52, s. 77(1), sch. 11 para. 37.
c. lxv ...	Exeter Corporation Act 1971.	Ss. 9, 10 rep. (saving) 11, 13–20 rep. 23 rep. in pt.	S.I. No. 651.
c. lxvii ...	Manchester Corporation (General Powers) Act 1971.	S. 23(1) am.	S.I. No. 844.
1972: c. 5	Local Employment Act 1972.	S. 7(1) am. (S.)(*prosp.*) rep. in pt. (S.) (*prosp.*). am. (W.)(*prosp.*) rep. in pt. (W.)(*prosp.*)(1A) added (*prosp.*).	51, s. 82(2), sch. 16 para. 35(1). 52, s. 77(1), sch. 11 para. 38.
		(1B) added (*prosp.*)	51, s. 82(2), sch. 16 para. 35(2).
		(3) am. (*prosp.*) ...	51, s. 82(2), sch. 16 para. 35(3). 52, s. 77(1), sch. 11 para. 38.
		S. 8(4) am. ... ... S. 22(2) rep. sch. 3 rep. in pt. sch. 4 rep. ...	50, s. 14. 45, S L. (R.), s. 1(1), sch. 1 Pt. VIII.
c. 6	Summer Time Act 1972	Ss. 2(1)(*b*) am. (*prosp.*) 2A added (*prosp.*) 4(1), 5(1)(2) am. (*prosp.*).	51, s. 82(2), sch. 16 para. 36.
c. 11	Superannuation Act 1972	Ss. 7, 8, 10, 24 am. (*prosp.*)	51, s. 23(1)(2), sch. 4.
		Sch. 6 paras. 54, 55 rep.	44, s. 159(3), sch. 17.
c. 14	Transport Holding Company Act 1972.	S. 2(3)(*c*)(7) am. ...	44, s. 159(2), sch. 16 para. 13.
c. 17	Electricity Act 1972 ...	Ss. 3, 4(3), sch. rep. ...	45, S.L. (R.), s. 1(1), sch. 1 Pt. VII.
c. 18	Maintenance Orders (Reciprocal Enforcement) Act 1972.	S. 5(7)(8) am. (*prosp.*) ... S. 8(3) am. (*prosp.*) ...	22, s. 54(*a*)(*b*). 22, s. 89, sch. 2 para. 33.
		Ss. 8(7)(8), 9(8)(9) am. (*prosp.*).	22, s. 54.
		S. 17(1)–(3) rep. (*prosp.*)	22, s. 89, sch. 3.

Session and Chap. or No. of Measure	Short title or Subject	How affected	Chapter of 1978 Act or number of Measure or Statutory Instrument
1972: c. 18—*cont.*	Maintenance Orders (Reciprocal Enforcement) Act 1972—*cont.*	S. 21(1) (definition of " maintenance ") rep., (definition of " maintenance order ") am., (2) am. (S.), am. (E. & W.) (*prosp.*).	22, s. 55.
		S. 27(1) am. (*prosp.*) ...	22, s. 89, sch. 2 para. 34(*a*).
		(2) am. (E. & W.) (*prosp.*), rep. in pt. (E. & W.) (*prosp.*).	22, s. 56.
		(3) rep. (*prosp.*) ...	22, s. 89, sch. 3.
		(9) am. (E. & W.) (*prosp.*).	22, s. 89, sch. 2 para. 34(*b*).
		S. 28 subst. (E. & W.) (*prosp.*).	22, s. 57.
		S. 28A added (E. & W.) (*prosp.*).	22, s. 58.
		S. 29A added (E. & W., N.I.) (*prosp.*).	22, s. 59.
		S. 31(1A) added (G.B.) (*prosp.*), (2) am. (G.B.) (*prosp.*), (2A), (4)–(6) added (G.B.) (*prosp.*).	22, s. 60(1).
		S. 34(5) am. (*prosp.*) ...	22, s. 60(2).
		S. 35(1) am. (E. & W.) (*prosp.*).	22, s. 89, sch. 2 para. 35.
		Ss. 36(1) am. (G.B.) (*prosp.*), 39 (definition of " maintenance ") am. (*prosp.*).	22, s. 60(3)(4).
		S. 41(1) am. (E. & W.) (*prosp.*), (2) replaced (E. & W.) (*prosp.*).	22, s. 89, sch. 2 para. 36.
		S. 42(1) am. (E. & W.) (*prosp.*).	22, s. 89, sch. 2 para. 37.
		S. 43A added (S.), added (E. & W.) (*prosp.*).	22, s. 61.
		Sch. para. 1 rep. (*prosp.*)	22, s. 89, sch. 3.
c. 19	Sunday Cinema Act 1972	Ss. 1, 3, 4, sch. rep. ...	45, S.L. (R.), s. 1(1), sch. 1 Pt. IX.
c. 20	Road Traffic Act 1972	S. 15 transfer of functions (S.) (*prosp.*).	51, s. 63, sch. 11 Group C para. 6.
		transfer of functions (*prosp.*).	52, s. 9(1), sch. 2 Pt. XVI.
		S. 20 transfer of functions (S.) (*prosp.*).	51, s. 63, sch. 11 Group C para. 6.
		transfer of functions (*prosp.*).	52, s. 9(1), sch. 2 Pt. XVI.
		S. 26 transfer of functions (S.) (*prosp.*).	51, s. 63, sch. 11 Group C para. 6.
		transfer of functions (*prosp.*).	52, s. 9(1), sch. 2 Pt. XVI.

Session and Chap. or No. of Measure	Short title or Subject	How affected	Chapter of 1978 Act or number of Measure or Statutory Instrument
1972: c. 20—*cont.*	Road Traffic Act 1972—*cont.*	S. 31(5) transfer of functions (S.) (*prosp.*).	51, s. 63, sch. 11 Group C para. 6.
		transfer of functions (*prosp.*).	52, s. 9(1), sch. 2 Pt. XVI.
		S. 36A(3A) transfer of functions (S.) (*prosp.*).	51, s. 63, sch. 11 Group C para. 6.
		transfer of functions (*prosp.*).	52, s. 9(1), sch. 2 Pt. XVI.
		S. 36B(4) transfer of functions (S.) (*prosp.*).	51, s. 63, sch. 11 Group C para. 6.
		transfer of functions (*prosp.*).	52, s. 9(1), sch. 2 Pt. XVI.
		S. 38 transfer of functions (S.) (*prosp.*).	51, s. 63, sch. 11 Group C para. 6.
		transfer of functions (*prosp.*).	52, s. 9(1), sch. 2 Pt. XVI.
		S. 39 transfer of functions (S.) (*prosp.*).	51, s. 63, sch. 11 Group C para. 6.
		transfer of functions (*prosp.*).	52, s. 9(1), sch. 2 Pt. XVI.
		S. 44 am.	55, s. 5(10).
		S. 45(6)(*a*)(iii) added	55, s. 9(2).
		S. 56(4) am.	55, s. 9(1), sch. 3 para. 1.
		S. 57(4A) added	55, s. 9(1), sch. 3 para. 2(1).
		(7) rep. in pt.	55, ss. 9(1), 24(4), sch. 3 para. 2(2)(*a*), sch. 4.
		am.	55, s. 9(1), sch. 3 para. 2(2)(*b*).
		(7A) subst.	55, s. 9(1), sch. 3 para. 2(2)(*c*).
		S. 58(2A), (5A) added, (6) am.	55, s. 9(1), sch. 3 para. 3.
		S. 82 (definition of "official testing station") added.	55, s. 9(1), sch. 3 para. 4.
		S. 83(5) am.	55, s. 9(1), sch. 3 para. 5.
		Ss. 154–156 devolved (S.) (*prosp.*).	51, s. 63, sch. 10 Pt. III.
		S. 160(2) am., (2A) added	55, s. 9(1), sch. 3 para. 6.
		Sch. 4 Pt. I am.	55, s. 9(1), sch. 3 para. 7.
c. 21	Deposit of Poisonous Waste Act 1972.	Transfer of functions (*prosp.*).	52, s. 9(1), sch. 2 Pt. VII.
c. 25	Betting and Gaming Duties Act 1972.	Sch. 4 para. 2(2)(*b*)(3)(*a*)(*b*)(4) am.	S.I. No. 44.
c. 27	Road Traffic (Foreign Vehicles) Act 1972.	Ss. 1(6)(7), 2(3A)(3B) added, 7(1) (definition of "official testing station") added.	55, s. 9(1), sch. 3 paras. 8–10.

Session and Chap. or No. of Measure	Short title or Subject	How affected	Chapter of 1978 Act or number of Measure or Statutory Instrument
1972—*cont.*			
c. 33	Carriage by Railway Act 1972.	S. 6(2) am.	47, s. 9(1), sch. 1 para. 8.
		S. 6(6)(*a*) rep.	47, s. 9(2), sch. 2.
c. 35	Defective Premises Act 1972.	S. 2 transfer of functions (*prosp.*).	52, s. 9(1), sch. 2 Pt. IV.
c. 40	Overseas Investment and Export Guarantees Act 1972.	Ss. 1, 2 rep.	18, s. 16(2), sch.
c. 41	Finance Act 1972 ...	Ss. 2(1)(2), 5(1)(2)(3)(*a*), 8B(1), 11(2)(*a*), 12(5)(6)(8), 16(2) am., (3) expld.	S.I. No. 273.
		S. 17(1) am.	42, s. 79, sch. 12 para. 21.
		S. 19(4) am. (*prosp.*) ...	51, s. 82(2), sch. 16 para. 37.
			52, s. 77(1), sch. 11 para. 39.
		S. 20(1) am.	42, s. 11(1).
		Ss. 21(3), 24(1)(2A) am.	S.I. No. 273.
		S. 40(1)(*gg*) added ...	42, s. 11(4).
		(*l*) added ...	42, s. 12(5).
		Ss. 46(4), 49 am. ...	S.I. No. 273.
		S. 70 am. (S.) ...	29, s. 109, sch. 16 para. 37.
		S. 87(5)(*c*)(6) am. ...	42, s. 14(3), sch. 2 para. 15.
		Ss. 93(2), 95(2)(3) ...	42, s. 17.
		S. 112(3)(*b*)(*c*) am. ...	42, s. 44(8).
		(3)(*c*) rep. in pt. ...	42, s. 80(5), sch. 13 Pt. IV.
		S. 113 am. (6.4.1979) ...	42, s. 44(8).
		S. 119(2)(*a*) rep. in pt. (*retrosp.*).	42, s. 80(5), sch. 13 Pt. IV.
		S. 128(1) rep.	42, s. 80(5), sch. 13 Pt. I.
		Sch. 1 paras. 1, 2 am., 10A added, 11 renumbered, 11(2) added.	42, s. 11.
		Sch. 6 paras. 1, 2, 7 am....	S.I. No. 273.
		Sch. 16 para. 5(2)(*d*)(6A) am.	42, s. 14(3), sch. 2 para. 16.
		para. 8(3)–(5) added.	42, s. 36(2), sch. 5 para. 1.
		paras. 9(3)(4), 10(3)(*b*) am.	42, s. 35.
		para. 11 (definition of " trading company ") appl.	42, s. 49(10).
		para. 12A added	42, s. 36(2), sch. 5 para. 2.
c. 42	Town and Country Planning (Amendment) Act 1972.	S. 10 transfer of functions (*prosp.*).	52, s. 9(1), sch. 2 Pt. VIII.
c. 43	Field Monuments Act 1972.	Transfer of functions (*prosp.*).	52, s. 9(1), sch. 2 Pt. XII.

Session and Chap. or No. of Measure	Short title or Subject	How affected	Chapter of 1978 Act or number of Measure or Statutory Instrument
1972—*cont.*			
c. 46	Housing (Financial Provisions) (Scotland) Act 1972.	S. 1(2) subst. (1.4.1979)	14, s. 16(1), sch. 2 para. 33(*a*).
		(3) am. (1.4.1979) ...	14, s. 16(1), sch. 2 para. 33(*b*).
		rep. in pt. (1.4. 1979).	14, s. 16(1)(2), sch. 2 para. 33(*b*), sch. 3.
		S. 2–4 rep. (1.4.1979) ...	14, s. 16(2), sch. 3.
		Ss. 5(2), 6(2) am., (5) added.	14, s. 16(1), sch. 2 paras. 34, 35.
		Ss. 8–10, 12 rep. (1.4. 1979).	14, s. 16(2), sch. 3.
		Ss. 15(1)(3)(4), 16(3) am., (*b*) added, (4)(5)(5A) am.	14, s. 16(1), sch. 2 paras. 8–10.
		S. 16A added	14, s. 13.
		S. 22(1) (definition of " supplementary benefit ") subst.	14, s. 16(1), sch. 2 para. 36.
		S. 23(1)(*f*) added (1.4. 1979), (3) subst. (1.4. 1979).	14, s. 11(1).
		S. 63(7)(8) added ...	14, s. 14.
		S. 78(1) (definitions of " development corporation house ", "Scottish Special Housing Association house ", " standard rent "), (3) am.	14, s. 11.
		Sch. 2 para. 8(1)(2) subst.	S.I. No. 1392.
		Sch. 2 para. 9 am. ...	S.I. No. 1526.
		para. 12(1)(1A) subst.	S.I. No. 1392.
		Sch. 2 Pt. II rep. ...	14, s. 16(2), sch. 3.
		Sch. 3 paras. 3(1), 4(1) am., (1A) added, (2)(*b*) am.	S.I. No. 1392.
		Pt. II rep. ...	14, s. 16(2), sch. 3.
		Sch. 4 para. 1(*c*) subst. (1.4.1979), (*e*)(*f*) replaced (1.4.1979).	14, s. 16(1), sch. 2 para. 37.
		para. 2(*a*)(vi) added (1.4.1979).	14, s. 11(2).
		para. 2(*a*) am. (1.4. 1979), (*cc*) added (1.4. 1979).	14, s. 16(1), sch. 2 para. 38.
		para. 3 am. ...	S.I. No. 1333.
c. 47	Housing Finance Act 1972.	Transfer of certain functions (*prosp.*).	52, s. 9(1), sch. 2 Pt. IV.
		S. 8(3) Table am. (1978–1979).	S.I. No. 34.
		Sch. 3 paras. 1(3) am., 8 subst.	S.I. No. 1302.
		para. 9 am. ...	S.I. No. 1526.
		para. 12(1)(1A) subst.	S.I. No. 1302.

Session and Chap. or No. of Measure	Short title or Subject	How affected	Chapter of 1978 Act or number of Measure or Statutory Instrument
1972: c. 47—*cont.*	Housing Finance Act 1972—*cont.*	Sch. 4 paras. 3(1), 4(1) am., (1A) added.	S.I. No. 1302.
		para. 4(2) subst.	S.I. No. 217.
		para. 10(4B) am.	S.I. No. 1302.
c. 48	Parliamentary and other Pensions Act 1972.	S. 2(2)(3) am., (4) replaced	56, s. 13.
		S. 3(2) am. (saving) ...	56, s. 14.
		(6) (definition of " a Member's ordinary salary ") appl.	56, ss. 7(10), 8(10).
		(7) subst.	56, s. 15(1).
		S. 4(1) am.	56, s. 22(4), sch. 1 para. 1(*a*).
		S. 6(1)(2)(*b*) am. (saving)	56, s. 12(1)(2)(3) (7)(8).
		(2A) added (saving)	56, s. 12(1)(4)(7) (8).
		(3) am. (saving) ...	56, ss. 12(1)(5)(7) (8), 22(4), sch. 1 para. 1(*a*).
		(3A) added (saving)	56, s. 12(1)(6)– (8).
		S. 7 ext. (mods.) ...	56, ss. 2, 4.
		S. 7(1)(*c*) restr. ...	56, s. 18(3).
		(4A) added ...	56, s. 1.
		(6) added ...	56, s. 22(4), sch. 1 para. 2.
		S. 9 ext. (mods.) ...	56, ss. 3, 4.
		(1) am. (saving) ...	56, ss. 16, 22(4), sch. 1 para. 1(*a*).
		S. 10(7) added ...	56, s. 22(4), sch. 1 para. 3.
		S. 12 appl.	56, s. 17(1).
		(2) am.	56, s. 17(2).
		(2A) added ...	56, s. 17(3).
		S. 13(1)(*b*) am. (saving)	56, s. 22(4), sch. 1 paras. 4, 10.
		(3) saved	56, s. 7(8).
		(4) appl. (mods.) ...	56, s. 8(8).
		saved	56, s. 7(8).
		(5) appl. (mods.) ...	56, s. 8(8).
		saved	56, s. 7(8).
		S. 14(1)(*b*) am. (saving)	56, s. 22(4), sch. 1 paras. 4, 10.
		(1A) added ...	56, s. 6(1).
		(3)(4) mod. ...	56, s. 6(2).
		S. 15(2) rep. in pt. (saving)	56, ss. 9(1)(2)(5), 22(5), sch. 2.
		am. (saving) ...	56, s. 9(1)(2)(5).
		(3) rep. (saving) (4) rep. in pt. (saving).	56, ss. 9(1)(3)(5), 22(5) sch. 2.
		(4)(5) appl. (mods.)	56, s. 8(9).
		(6) (definition of "relevant child") appl.	56 ss. 7(10), 8 (10).
		(*a*) am. (saving)...	56, s. 9(1)(4)(5).

Session and Chap. or No. of Measure	Short title or Subject	How affected	Chapter of 1978 Act or number of Measure or Statutory Instrument
1972: c. 48—*cont.*	Parliamentary and other Pensions Act 1972—*cont.*	S. 16(1) rep. in pt. (saving)	56, ss. 10(1)(2)(5), 22(5), sch. 2.
		am. (saving) ...	56, ss. 10(1)(2)(5).
		(*b*) am.	56, s. 22(4), sch. 1 para. 1(*b*).
		(1A)(1B) added ... (saving).	56, s. 10(1)(3)(5).
		(2) rep. (saving). ...	56, ss. 10(1)(4)(5), 22(5), sch. 2.
		S. 18(2) am. (saving) ...	56, s. 22(4), sch. 1 paras. 5(*a*), 10.
		(3)(*a*)(*b*) am. ...	56, s. 22(4), sch. 1 para. 1(*a*)(*c*).
		(*c*) am. (saving) ...	56, s. 22(4), sch. 1 paras. 5(*b*), 10.
		S. 19(*a*) am.	56, s. 22(4), sch. 1 para. 1(*b*).
		S. 21(1)(*b*) subst. ...	56, s. 22(4), sch. 1 para. 1(*d*).
		(2)(*a*)(*b*) am. (*c*) and definition of "overseas fund or scheme" added.	56, s. 18(1).
		(4)(*a*) restr.	56, s. 18(3).
		S. 22(1)(*b*), (2), (*a*) am.	56, s. 22(4), sch. 1 paras. 1(*a*)(*c*), 6.
		S. 23(*b*) am.	56, s. 22(4), sch. 1 para. 1(*a*).
		S. 25(2) am.	56, s. 22(4), sch. 1 para. 7(2).
		rep. in pt. (saving)	56, s. 22(4)(5), sch. 1 para. 7(1)(2) 10. sch. 2.
		(*b*) am. (saving)	56, s. 22(4), sch. 1 para. 1(*b*), 7(1)(2)(*c*) 10.
		(2A) added. ...	56, s. 22(4), sch. 1 para 7(3).
		S. 30(3) am.	56, s. 19.
		S. 31(4) am.	56, s. 22(4), sch. 1 para. 8.
		S. 35(1), (definition of "the Act of 1978") added.	56, s. 22(4), sch. 1 para. 9.
		(definition of "effective resolution") added.	56, s. 15(2).
		(definition of "interest") am.	56, s. 20.
c. 49	Affiliation Proceedings (Amendment) Act 1972.	S. 3(1)(2) rep. (*prosp.*) ...	22, s. 89, sch. 3.

Session and Chap. or No. of Measure	Short title or Subject	How affected	Chapter of 1978 Act or number of Measure or Statutory Instrument
1972:—*cont.*			
c. 50	Legal Advice and Assistance Act 1972.	Am. ... ... S.1 am. ... ... S. 4(2), sch. 1 am. ...	S.I. No. 1910. S.I. No. 1818. S.I. No. 1564.
c. 52	Town and Country Planning (Scotland) Act 1972.	Ss. 32–34 power to intervene (*prosp.*).	51, s. 71, sch. 14 paras. 1, 2.
		S. 37 not devolved (*prosp.*) transfer of certain functions (*prosp.*).	51, s. 63, sch. 10 Pt. III sch. 11 Group E para. 6.
		S. 37(1A) added (*prosp.*)	51, s. 82(2), sch. 16 para. 38.
		S. 42 power to intervene (*prosp.*).	51, s. 71, sch. 14 para. 1.
		Ss. 44, 45, 46(4) devolved in pt. (*prosp.*) 47 not devolved (*prosp.*).	51, s. 63, sch. 10 Pt. III.
		S. 49 power to intervene (*prosp.*).	51, s. 71, sch. 14 para. 1.
		Ss. 64–70 not devolved (*prosp.*).	51, s. 63, sch. 10 Pt. III.
		S. 91 power to intervene (*prosp.*).	51, s. 71, sch. 14 paras. 1, 2.
		S. 103 not devolved (*prosp.*).	51, s. 63, sch. 10 Pt. III.
		S. 103 mod. (*prosp.*) ...	51, s. 73.
		S. 108(2) not devolved (*prosp.*).	51, s. 63, sch. 10 Pt. III.
		S. 113 am. (*prosp.*) ...	51, s. 42(1)(*c*)(2), sch. 7.
		S. 117(1) (proviso) 121(1) not devolved (*prosp.*).	51, s. 63, sch. 10 Pt. III.
		S. 121(1) transfer of certain functions (*prosp.*).	51, s. 63, sch. 11 Group E para. 7.
		Ss. 195(6) devolved in pt. (*prosp.*), 209 not devolved (*prosp.*).	51, s. 63, sch. 10 Pt. III.
		S. 219 am. (*prosp.*) ...	51, s. 23(1)(2), sch. 4.
		S. 221, 222 devolved in pt. (*prosp.*).	51, s. 63, sch. 10 Pt. III.
		S. 222 am. (*prosp.*) ...	51, s. 23(1)(2), sch. 4.
		Ss. 224, 225 devolved in pt. (*prosp.*).	51, s. 63, sch. 10 Pt. III.
		S. 226(4) am. (*prosp.*) ...	51, s. 23(1)(2), sch. 4.
		Ss. 227–229, 240 not devolved (*prosp.*).	51, s. 63, sch. 10 Pt. III.
		S. 240 transfer of functions (*prosp.*).	51, s. 63, sch. 11 Group E para. 8.
		S. 241 not devolved (*prosp.*).	51, s. 63, sch. 10 Pt. III.
		S. 241A added (*prosp.*) ...	51, s. 82(2), sch. 16 para. 39.
		Ss. 253, 254 devolved in pt. (*prosp.*).	51, s. 63, sch. 10 Pt. III.
		S. 259 am. (*prosp.*) ...	51, s. 23(1)(2), sch. 4.

Session and Chap. or No. of Measure	Short title or Subject	How affected	Chapter of 1978 Act or number of Measure or Statutory Instrument
1972: c. 52—*cont.*	Town and Country Planning (Scotland) Act 1972—*cont.*	S. 260 power to intervene (*prosp.*).	51, s. 71, sch. 14 para. 1.
		S. 260(5) am.	51, s. 71 sch. 14. para. 8(2).
		S. 266(1)–(5) mod. ...	3, s. 8(4).
		S. 266(6) devolved in pt. (*prosp.*).	51, s. 63, sch. 10 Pt. III.
		S. 267–269 mod. ...	3, s. 8(4).
		S. 269 appl. (*prosp.*) ...	51, s. 71, sch. 14 para. 9(2).
		S. 270 mod.	3, s. 8(4).
		S. 275(1) (definition of "statutory undertakings") appl.	4, s. 2.
		S. 275(2), sch. 18 para. 4(2) devolved in pt. (*prosp.*).	51, s. 63, sch. 10 Pt. III.
		Sch. 21 Pt. II rep. in pt.	3, s. 12(2), sch. 2.
		Sch. 22 para. 70 not devolved (*prosp.*).	51, s. 63, sch. 10 Pt. III.
c. 53	Contracts of Employment Act 1972.	Rep.	44, s. 159(3), sch. 17.
c. 54	British Library Act 1972	Not devolved (S.) (*prosp.*)	51, s. 63, sch. 10 Pt. III.
		Sch. para. 13(2) rep. in pt.	44, s. 159(3), sch. 17.
		para. 13(3)(*a*) am. ...	44, s. 159(2), sch. 16 para. 15.
∩. 58	National Health Service (Scotland) Act 1972.	Ss. 1–24(1)(3), 25, 29–31 rep.	29, s. 109, sch. 17.
		S. 34A am. (*prosp.*) ...	51, s. 23(1)(2), sch. 4.
		Ss. 37–46 rep., 47, 48 rep. (S.), 49 rep., 50(1) rep. (S.), 50(2), 51, 54–60, 61(4)(5), 62, 63 rep.	29, s. 109, sch. 17.
		S. 64(1) rep. (saving) ...	29, s. 109, sch. 15 para. 10, sch. 17.
		Ss. 64(2) rep., 65(1) rep. (S.), (2) rep., (3)(4) rep. (S.), schs. 1, 2 rep., 3 rep. (S.), 5 rep.	29, s. 109, sch. 17.
		Sch. 6 rep. (saving) (S.)...	29, s. 109, sch. 15 para. 10, sch. 17.
		Sch. 7 rep. (S.)	29, s. 109, sch. 17.
c. 60	Gas Act 1972	S. 34(1) rep. in pt., (3)(*b*) rep.	S.I. No. 1176.
		S. 36(5) am.	44, s. 159(2), sch. 16 para. 16.
		Sch. 6 paras. 6(1)(3), 10, 11 rep.	S.I. No. 1176.
c. 62	Agriculture (Miscellaneous Provisions) Act 1972.	S. 1(1)–(4) transfer of functions (W.), (8) (definition of "the Ministers") am.	S.I. No. 272.
		Ss. 17(2), 19 transfer of functions (W.).	S.I. No. 272.

Session and Chap. or No. of Measure	Short title or Subject	How affected	Chapter of 1978 Act or number of Measure or Statutory Instrument
1972:—*cont.*			
c. 66	Poisons Act 1972 ...	S. 11(2) rep. in pt. ...	45, S.L. (R), s. 1(1), sch. 1 Pt. XII.
c. 68	European Communities Act 1972.	Apptd. day for specified provisions in Sch. 3 Pt. III (1.9.1978).	S.I. No. 1003.
		S. 1 appl.	30 s. 5, sch. 1.
		S. 1(2) rep. in pt. ...	30, s. 25(1), sch. 3.
		S. 2(2) am. (*prosp.*) ...	51, s. 82(2), sch. 16 para. 41. 52, s. 77(1), sch. 11 para. 40(1).
		(4) am. (*prosp.*) ...	51, s. 82(2), sch. 16 para. 41.
		S. 5(6A) added	42, s. 6(8).
		S. 6 transfer of functions (W.).	S.I. No. 272.
		S. 6(5) am.	42, s. 79, sch. 12 para. 22.
		S. 7(3) transfer of functions (W.), (4) am.	S.I. No. 272.
		Sch. 1 appl.	30, s. 5, sch. 1.
		Sch. 2 para. 2(2) mod. (*prosp.*).	51, s. 82(2), sch. 16 para. 42.
		restr. (*prosp.*).	52, s. 77(1), sch. 11 para. 40(3).
		Sch. 3 Pt. I rep. in pt., sch. 4 para. 2(4) rep.	42, s. 80(5), sch. 13 Pt. I.
		Sch. 4 para. 2(5) rep. ...	S.I. No. 1603.
c. 70	Local Government Act 1972.	Ss. 55, 68(1)–(7), 74, Pt. V (ss. 79–100) transfer of functions (*prosp.*).	52, s. 9(1), sch. 2 Pt. I.
		S. 88(2) rep. in pt. ...	45, S.L. (R), s. 1(1), sch. 1 Pt. XII.
		Pts. VI, VII (ss. 101–146) transfer of certain functions (*prosp.*).	52, s. 9(1), sch. 2 Pt. I.
		S. 137(1) saved	50, s. 13.
		Pt. VIII (ss. 147–178) transfer of certain functions (*prosp.*).	52, s. 9(1), sch. 2 Pt. I.
		S. 177(1)(*f*), (2)(*c*) concurrent powers of Min. (*prosp.*).	52, s. 9(2), sch. 3.
		Pt. IX (ss. 179–215) transfer of certain functions (*prosp.*).	52, s. 9(1), sch. 2 Pt. I.
		S. 186(2) rep.	3, s. 12(2), sch. 2.
		S. 203 rep.	55, s. 24(4), sch. 4.
		S. 214(1) appl.	G.S.M. No. 2, s. 3(4).
		Pts. XI, XII (ss. 222–274) transfer of certain functions (*prosp.*).	52, s. 9(1), sch. 2 Pt. I.
		S. 250(2)(3) appl. ...	10, s. 3, sch. 1 para. 1, sch. 2 para. 6.

Session and Chap. or No. of Measure	Short title or Subject	How affected	Chapter of 1978 Act or number of Measure or Statutory Instrument
1972:			
c. 70—*cont.*	Local Government Act 1972—*cont.*	S. 250(2)(3) appl. (*prosp.*)	52, ss. 1, 25(2), sch. 1 para. 3.
		appl. (mods.) (*prosp.*).	52, s. 63, sch. 8 Pt. II para. 12.
		S. 250(4)(5) appl. (*prosp.*)	52, s. 25(2).
		appl. (mods.) (*prosp.*).	52, s. 63, sch. 8 Pt. II para. 12.
		S. 254(2)(c) appl. ...	3, s. 12(6).
		S. 269 rep. in pt. ...	30, s. 25(1), sch. 3.
		S. 270(1) (definition of "local authority") appl.	43, s. 2(2). 44, s. 29(2)(*a*).
		Sch. 2 paras. 6(4), 7(3), 8, Pt. II (paras. 9–14) rep.	45, S.L. (R), s. 1(1), sch. 1 Pt. XII.
		Sch. 13 am. (*prosp.*) ...	52, s. 48(1).
		Sch. 14 para. 45 rep. ...	3, s. 12(2), sch. 2.
		Sch. 17 paras. 9–13, 15, 17, 19 mod. (*prosp.*).	52, s. 62(2)(9).
		am. (W.)(*prosp.*)	52, s. 77(1), sch. 11 para. 41.
		Sch. 19 Pt. III rep. ...	3, s. 12(2), sch. 2.
		Sch. 23 para. 10 rep. (*prosp.*).	22, s. 89, sch. 3.
		Sch. 29 para. 18(2) rep. (*prosp.*).	38, s. 10(1), sch. 3.
c. xx	Stromness (Vehicle Ferry Terminal) Pier &c. Order Confirmation Act 1972.	Rep.	iv, s. 1, sch., s. 9, sch. 2.
1973:			
c. 5	Housing (Amendment) Act 1973.	Transfer of functions (*prosp.*).	52, s. 9(1), sch. 2 Pt. IV.
c. 9	Counter-Inflation Act 1973.	Not devolved (S.)(*prosp.*)	51, s. 63, sch. 10 Pt. III.
		S. 10 cont.	54, s. 1(1).
c. 11	Fire Precautions (Loans) Act 1973.	Transfer of certain functions (*prosp.*).	52, s. 9(1), sch. 2 Pt. V.
		S. 1(3)(4) not devolved (S.) (*prosp.*).	51, s. 63, sch. 10 Pt. III.
c. 14	Costs in Criminal Cases Act 1973.	S. 13(1) rep. in pt. ...	30, s. 25(1), sch. 3.
c. 15	Administration of Justice Act 1973.	S.I. (definition of "commission area") appl. (*prosp.*).	22, ss. 75, 88(1).
		S. 12 saved (*prosp.*) ...	23, s. 14(3).
		S. 18(2)(*a*) am. (*prosp.*)	23, s. 122(1), sch. 5 Pt. II (1).
		(*b*) rep. in pt. (*prosp.*).	23, s. 122(2), sch. 7 Pt. I.
c. 16	Education Act 1973 ...	Transfer of certain functions (*prosp.*).	52, s. 9(1), sch. 2 Pt. III.
c. 18	Matrimonial Causes Act 1973.	S. 4(1) am. (*prosp.*) ...	22, s. 89, sch. 2 para. 38.
		S. 4(3) am. (*prosp.*)(4)(5) added (*prosp.*).	22, s. 62.
		S. 27(1) subst. (*prosp.*)(3)(4) replaced (*prosp.*), (6) am. (*prosp.*), (6A) added (*prosp.*).	22, s. 63(1)–(4).

Session and Chap. or No. of Measure	Short title or Subject	How affected	Chapter of 1978 Act or number of Measure or Statutory Instrument
1973:			
c. 18—*cont.*	Matrimonial Causes Act 1973—*cont.*	S. 27(8) rep. (*prosp.*) ...	22, ss. 63(5), 89 sch. 3.
		Ss. 47(2)(*e*), 50(2)(*b*) am. (*prosp.*).	22, s. 89, sch. 2 paras. 39, 40.
		S. 52(1) (definition of "child of the family") appl. (*prosp.*).	22, ss. 64, 65, 67.
c. 19	Independent Broadcasting Authority Act 1973.	S. 2(1) am.	43, s. 1.
		S. 4(2)(5) restr.	43, s. 2(1).
c. 24	Employment of Children Act 1973.	Transfer of functions (*prosp.*).	52, s. 9(1), sch. 2 Pt. VI.
c. 26	Land Compensation Act 1973.	Ss. 15(2), 20, 22(5), 41(2), 42(5), 51, 72 transfer of functions (*prosp.*).	52, s. 9(1), sch. 2 Pt. VIII.
c. 27	Bahamas Independence Act 1973.	S. 4(1) rep.	30, s. 25(1), sch. 3.
c. 29	Guardianship Act 1973	Ss. 1 am. (*prosp.*), 1(1) (definition of "legal custody") added (*prosp.*), 2 am. (*prosp.*).	22, s. 36(2).
		S. 2(2) am. (*prosp.*) ...	22, s. 38(2).
		appl. (mods.) (*prosp.*).	22, s. 64.
		(3) replaced (*prosp.*)	22, s. 44(1).
		(3)(3A)(3B) appl. (mods.) (*prosp.*).	22, s. 64.
		(4) subst. (*prosp.*) ...	22, s. 45(2).
		appl. (mods.) (*prosp.*).	22, s. 64.
		(5) rep. in pt. (*prosp.*).	22, ss. 45(3), 89, sch. 3.
		(5A)–(5E) added (*prosp.*).	22, s. 45(4).
		(5A)–(5E)(6) appl. (mods.) (*prosp.*).	22, s. 64.
		S. 3 am. (*prosp.*) ...	22, s. 36(2).
		appl. (mods.) (*prosp.*)	22, s. 64.
		S. 3(2) am. (*prosp.*) ...	22, s. 38(3).
		rep. in pt. (*prosp.*)	22, s. 89, sch. 3.
		S. 4 am. (*prosp.*) ...	22, s. 36(2).
		appl. (mods.) (*prosp.*)	22, s. 64.
		(2) am. (*prosp.*) ...	22, s. 89, sch. 2 para. 41.
		(2A) added (*prosp.*)	22, s. 38(4).
		(3) am. (*prosp.*) ...	22, s. 89, sch. 2 para. 42.
		(3A) am. (*prosp.*), (3B)–(3D) added (*prosp.*).	22, s. 44(2).
		(6) am. (*prosp.*) ...	22, s. 89, sch. 2 para. 43.
		S. 5 am. (*prosp.*) ...	22, s. 36(2).
		(2) am. (*prosp.*) ...	22, s. 89, sch. 2 para. 44.
		S. 5A added (*prosp.*) ...	22, s. 46.
		S. 8 rep. (*prosp.*) ...	22, s. 89, sch. 3.
		S. 11(2)(4)(5) appl. (*prosp.*).	28, s. 26(3).
		Sch. 2 para. 1(2) rep. (*prosp.*).	22, s. 89, sch. 3.

Session and Chap. or No. of Measure	Short title or Subject	How affected	Chapter of 1978 Act or number of Measure or Statutory Instrument
1973:—*cont.*			
c. 32	National Health Service Reorganisation Act 1973.	Transfer of certain functions (*prosp.*).	52, s. 9(1), sch. 2 Pt. VI.
		Rep. (S.) (saving for s. 57(1), sch. 4).	29, s. 109, sch. 15 para. 10, sch. 17.
		S. 55(2) rep. in pt. ...	30, s. 25(1), sch. 3.
		Sch. 4 para. 106 rep. ...	44, s. 159(3), sch. 17.
		Sch. 4 para. 108 rep. (1.4.1979).	40, s. 9(3), sch. 2.
c. 35	Employment Agencies Act 1973.	Not devolved (S.) (*prosp.*)	51, s. 63, sch. 10 Pt. III.
c. 36	Northern Ireland Constitution Act 1973.	Sch. 3 para. 2 rep. in pt. (*prosp.*).	23, s. 122(2), sch. 7 Pt. I.
c. 37	Water Act 1973 ...	Am. (*prosp.*)	52, ss. 55(2), 56, sch. 6.
		Transfer of certain functions (*prosp.*).	52, s. 9(1), sch. 2 Pt. IX.
		S. 1(1) transfer of functions (W.).	S.I. No. 272.
		subst. (*prosp.*), (2) am. (*prosp.*).	52, s. 77(1), sch. 11 paras. 42, 43.
		(3) transfer of functions (W.).	S.I. No. 272.
		subst. (*prosp.*), (7) am. (*prosp.*).	52, s. 77(1), sch. 11 paras. 44, 45.
		S. 2(3) rep. in pt. ...	30, s. 25(1), sch. 3.
		(4) transfer of certain functions (W.).	S.I. No. 272.
		division of powers (*prosp.*).	52, s. 63, sch. 8 Pt. I.
		(5) transfer of certain functions (W.).	S.I. No. 272.
		S. 3(1)–(3)(9) division of powers (*prosp.*).	52, s. 63, sch. 8 Pt. I.
		(10) replaced (*prosp.*)	52, s. 77(1), sch. 11 para. 46.
		S. 5(1) transfer of certain functions (W.).	S.I. No. 272.
		(4) added (*prosp.*) ...	52, s. 77(1), sch. 11 para. 47.
		Ss. 8(3), 24(5)(6)(11)(12), 29 transfer of certain functions (W.).	S.I. No. 272.
		S. 29 division of powers (*prosp.*).	52, s. 63, sch. 8 Pt. I.
		S. 30 transfer of certain functions (W.).	S.I. No. 272.
		division of powers (*prosp.*).	52, s. 63, sch. 8 Pt. I.
		S. 31 transfer of certain functions (W.).	S.I. No. 272.
		division of powers (*prosp.*).	52, s. 63, sch. 8 Pt. I.
		S. 38(2) rep.	30, s. 25(1), sch. 3.

Session and Chap. or No. of Measure	Short title or Subject	How affected	Chapter of 1978 Act or number of Measure or Statutory Instrument
1973:			
c. 37—*cont.*	Water Act 1973—*cont.*	Sch. 2 para. 4. sch. 3 para. 11 transfer of certain functions (W.).	S.I. No. 272.
		Sch. 3 para. 11 division of powers (*prosp.*).	52, s. 63, sch. 8 Pt. I.
		paras. 32, 38, 40, 41 transfer of certain functions (W.).	S.I. No. 272.
		Sch. 4 Pt. II power to intervene (*prosp.*).	52, s. 63, sch. 8 Pt. III.
		Sch. 6 para. 15, sch. 7 transfer of certain functions (W.).	S.I. No. 272.
c. 38	Social Security Act 1973	Not devolved (S.) (*prosp.*)	51, s. 63, sch. 10 Pt. III.
		Sch. 27 paras. 54–59 rep.	44, s. 159(3), sch. 17.
c. 41	Fair Trading Act 1973 ...	Not devolved (S.) (*prosp.*)	51, s. 63, sch. 10 Pt. III.
c. 47	Protection of Aircraft Act 1973.	S. 5(1) rep. in pt. ...	26, s. 9, sch. 2.
		S. 23 am.	8, s. 1(2).
		restored (*prosp.*) ...	8, s. 4(2).
		S. 26(1) (definition of " aerodrome ") appl.	8, s. 2(10).
c. 50	Employment and Training Act 1973.	Not devolved (S.) (*prosp.*)	51, s. 63, sch. 10 Pt. III.
		S. 5(1)(*b*)(*c*) rep. ...	6, s. 3(7)(*a*).
		Sch. 2 Pt. I para. 15 rep.	44, s. 159(3), sch. 17.
c. 51	Finance Act 1973 ...	S. 16 excl.	42, s. 53(6)(*a*).
		Sch. 15 para. 2(*b*) am. ...	42, s. 29(3).
c. 53	Northern Ireland (Emergency Provisions) Act 1973.	Ss. 2–4, 6–8, 10–18, 19(1)–(7), 20, 21, 23–27 rep., 28(1) rep. in pt., 29, 30(1)–(3) rep., (4)(5) rep. in pt., (6)(7), 31(2) (3)(5) rep., (7) rep. in pt. schs. 2–5.	5, s. 35(3), sch. 6 Pt. I.
c. 54	Nature Conservancy Council Act 1973.	Not devolved (S.) (*prosp.*)	51, s. 63, sch. 10 Pt. III.
		S. 1(1)(*a*)(iia) added (*prosp.*).	52, s. 77(1), sch. 11 para. 48.
		(v) added (*prosp.*).	51, s. 82(2), sch. 16 para. 43.
c. 56	Land Compensation (Scotland) Act 1973.	Pt. I (ss. 1–17 except s. 14) not devolved (*prosp.*), s. 14 Pt. II (ss. 18–26) devolved in pt. (*prosp.*), Pt. III (ss. 27–40 except ss. 36–40) not devolved (*prosp.*).	51, s. 63, sch. 10 Pt. III.
		S. 27(1)(*e*)(v) added (3A) am.	14, s. 16(1), sch. 2 para. 12(*a*)(*b*).
		(7)(*a*) am.	14, s. 16(1), sch. 2 para. 39.
		(9) am.	14, s. 16(1), sch. 2 para. 12(*c*).
		S. 28(1) am.	S.I. No. 323.
		S. 34(1)(*e*)(v) added (3) (3A)(9) am.	14, s. 16(1), sch. 2 para. 13.

Session and Chap. or No. of Measure	Short title or Subject	How affected	Chapter of 1978 Act or number of Measure or Statutory Instrument
1973: c. 56—*cont.*	Land Compensation (Scotland) Act 1973—*cont.*	S. 36 devolved in pt. (*prosp.*).	51, s. 63, sch. 10 Pt. III.
		S. 36(1)(*d*) added, (6) am.	14, s. 16(1), sch. 2 para. 14.
		Ss. 37–40 devolved in pt. (*prosp.*), Pt. IV (ss. 41–63) not devolved (*prosp.*), Pt. V (ss. 64–77) devolved in pt. (*prosp.*), Pt. VI (ss. 78–83) not devolved (*prosp.*).	51, s. 63, sch. 10 Pt. III.
c. 57	Badgers Act 1973 ...	Transfer of functions (W.).	S.I. No. 272.
c. 62	Powers of Criminal Courts Act 1973.	S. 2(1) am.	S.I. No. 474.
		Ss. 14(4), 15 appl. (*prosp.*)	49, s. 6(3), sch. 1 para. 2.
		S. 16 appl. (mods.) (*prosp.*).	49, s. 6(3), sch. 1 paras. 2, 3.
		S. 17 appl. (mods.) (*prosp.*).	49, s. 6(3), sch. 1 paras. 2, 5.
c. 65	Local Government (Scotland) Act 1973.	Ss. 4–8 not devolved (*prosp.*).	51, s. 63, sch. 10 Pt. III.
		S. 8 am.	4, s. 6, sch. para. 2.
		Ss. 9–11, 20, 29–37, 59 not devolved (*prosp.*), 71, 73, 74 devolved in pt. (*prosp.*).	51, s. 63, sch. 10 Pt. III.
		S. 74, 74A am. (*prosp.*)...	51, s. 42(1)(*c*)(2), sch. 7.
		S. 74A devolved in pt. (*prosp.*).	51, s. 63, sch. 10 Pt. III.
		S. 83(1) saved	50, s. 13.
		Ss. 87, 94 devolved in pt. (*prosp.*).	51, s. 63, sch. 10 Pt. III.
		S. 94 am. (*prosp.*) ...	51, s. 52(1).
		Ss. 125(1), 126 am. ...	4, s. 6, sch. paras. 3, 4.
		S. 148 (definition of " water authority ") appl.	4, s. 2.
		S. 171(3) rep.	45, S.L. (R.), s. 1(1), sch. 1 Pt. XII.
		S. 197(1) am.	29, s. 109, sch. 16 para. 38.
		Ss. 197(2)–(5) not devolved (*prosp.*), 199, 202(9)(10), 209(2)(3), 210 devolved in pt. (*prosp.*).	51, s. 63, sch. 10 Pt. III.
		S. 210(4)(5) appl. ...	10, s. 3, sch. 1 para. 1, sch. 2 para. 6.
		appl. (*prosp.*)	51, s. 1, sch. 1 Pt. I para. 3.
		Ss. 211, 215 devolved in pt. (*prosp.*).	51, s. 63, sch. 10 Pt. III.
		Ss. 219, 220 am. (*prosp.*)	51, s. 23(1)(2), sch. 4.

Session and Chap. or No. of Measure	Short title or Subject	How affected	Chapter of 1978 Act or number of Measure or Statutory Instrument
1973:			
c. 65—*cont.*	Local Government (Scotland) Act 1973—*cont.*	S. 225 devolved in pt. (*prosp.*).	51, s. 63, sch. 10 Pt. III.
		S. 225(6) am.	4, s. 5.
		S. 225 devolved in pt. (*prosp.*).	51, s. 63, sch. 10 Pt. III.
		S. 229(1) am.	4, s. 5.
		S. 233 devolved in pt. (*prosp.*).	51, s. 63, sch. 10 Pt. III.
		S. 235 (definition of "local authority") appl.	43, s. 2(2). 44, s. 29(2)(*a*). 29, s. 2, sch. 1 para. 1.
		Sch. 9 para. 74 rep. ...	S.I. No. 1173.
		Sch. 18 para. 31 rep. ...	55, s. 24(4), sch. 4.
		Sch. 27 para. 142 rep. (*prosp.*).	28, s. 66(3), sch. 4.
		paras. 149, 150 rep. (*prosp.*).	38, s. 10(1), sch. 3.
		paras. 169, 170 rep.	3, s. 12(2), sch. 2.
c. xxxvi ...	North Wales Hydro Electric Power Act 1973.	S. 49 mod. (*prosp.*) ...	52, s. 62(2)(9).
1974:			
c. 3	Slaughterhouses Act 1974.	Pt. I (ss. 1–35), Pt. II (ss. 36–45) transfer of functions (W.).	S.I. No. 272.
c. 4	Legal Aid Act 1974 ...	Am. (1.3.1979)	S.I. No. 1910.
		S. 1(1) am.	S.I. No. 1568.
		S. 4(2)(3) am.	S.I. No. 1567.
		Ss. 6(1), 9(1)(*a*)(*b*) am. ...	S.I. No. 1571.
		Sch. 1 para. 3(*a*) rep. (*prosp.*).	22, s. 89, sch. 2 para.45(*a*),sch. 3.
		paras. 3(*d*) am., (*h*) added (*prosp.*).	22, s. 89, sch. 2 paras. 45(*b*)(*c*), 52.
c. 5	Horticulture (Special Payments) Act 1974.	Transfer of functions (W.)	S.I. No. 272.
c. 6	Biological Weapons Act 1974.	S. 2(2) rep. (*prosp.*) ...	23, s. 122(2), sch. 7 Pt. I.
c. 7	Local Government Act 1974.	Apptd. day for specified provisions of sch. 8 (1.4.1979).	S.I. No. 1583.
		Pt. I (ss. 1–10) am. (W.) (*prosp.*).	52, s. 77(1), sch. 11 paras. 50, 52, 53.
		(except s. 8(2)) mod. (*prosp.*).	52, s. 58.
		S. 1(1) rep. in pt. (E.) (*prosp.*).	52, s. 77(1), sch. 11 para. 49.
		rep. in pt. (W.) (*prosp.*).	52, s. 77(1), sch. 11 paras. 50, 51.
		S. 1(2) am. (W.) (*prosp.*)	52, s. 77(1), sch. 11 paras. 50, 54.

Session and Chap. or No. of Measure	Short title or Subject	How affected	Chapter of 1978 Act or number of Measure or Statutory Instrument
1974: c. 7—*cont.*	Local Government Act 1974—*cont.*	S. 1(3)(*b*) rep. in pt. (E.) (*prosp.*).	52, s. 77(1), sch. 11 para. 49.
		rep. in pt. (W.) (*prosp.*).	52, s. 77(1), sch. 11 paras. 50, 51.
		S. 1(6)(7) rep. in pt. (W.) (*prosp.*).	52, s. 77(1), sch. 11 paras. 50, 55, 56.
		S. 3 restr. (W.) (*prosp.*)...	52, s. 77(1), sch. 11 paras. 50, 67.
		(2) rep. (W.) (*prosp.*), (3) am. (W.) (*prosp.*).	52, s. 77(1), sch. 11 paras. 50, 57.
		S. 4(1) restr. (W.) (*prosp.*)	52, s. 77(1), sch. 11 paras. 50, 67.
		S. 5(1) rep. in pt. (W.) (*prosp.*), am. (W.) (*prosp.*), (2) mod. (W.) (*prosp.*).	52, s. 77(1), sch. 11 paras. 50, 58, 59.
		S. 5(2) restr. (W.) (*prosp.*)	52, s. 77(1), sch. 11 paras. 50, 67.
		S. 6(1) am.	55, s. 22(*c*).
		(1)(*c*) rep. in pt. ...	55, ss. 22(*a*), 24 (4), sch. 4.
		(*e*) added ...	55, s. 22(*b*).
		S. 7(3) am. (W.) (*prosp.*)	52, s. 77(1), sch. 11 paras. 50, 60.
		S. 8(3) am. (W.) (*prosp.*)	52, s. 77(1), sch. 11 paras. 50, 61.
		S. 9 am. (W.) (*prosp.*) ...	52, s. 77(1), sch. 11 paras. 50, 62.
		S. 10(3) restr. (W.) (*prosp.*)	52, s. 77(1), sch. 11 paras. 50, 67.
		S. 10(4) restr. (W.) (*prosp.*)	52, s. 77(1), sch. 11 paras. 50, 63.
		Ss. 11–13 transfer of functions (*prosp.*).	52, s. 9(1), sch. 2 Pt. I.
		S. 20 rep. (1.4.1979) ...	40, s. 9(3), sch. 2.
		S. 23(7) transfer of functions (*prosp.*).	52, s. 9(1), sch. 2 Pt. I.
		S. 23(12) am. (*prosp.*) ...	52, s. 77(1), sch. 11 para. 68.
		S. 24 transfer of functions (*prosp.*).	52, s. 9(1), sch. 2 Pt. I.
		S. 26(6)(*b*) am. (*prosp.*)...	52, s. 77(1), sch. 11 para. 69.
		S. 27(1)(*b*) subst. (*prosp.*)	52, s. 77(1), sch. 11 para. 70.
		S. 29(3) am. (*prosp.*) ...	52, s. 77(1), sch. 11 para. 71.
		S. 31(3) added	39, s. 1.
		S. 32(3)(5) am. (*prosp.*)...	52, s. 77(1), sch. 11 paras. 72, 73.

Session and Chap. or No. of Measure	Short title or Subject	How affected	Chapter of 1978 Act or number of Measure or Statutory Instrument
1974: c. 7—*cont.*	Local Government Act 1974—*cont.*	Ss. 35(3), 40(1) transfer of certain functions (*prosp.*).	52, s. 9(1), sch. 2 Pt. I.
		Sch. 1 paras. 6, 8(1), 11 am. (W.) (*prosp.*).	52, s. 77(1), sch. 11 paras. 50, 64–66.
		Sch. 1 para. 11 restr. (W.) (*prosp.*).	52, s. 77(1), sch. 11 paras. 50, 67.
		Sch. 4 para. 9 transfer of functions (*prosp.*).	52, s. 9(1), sch. 2 Pt. I.
c. 10	Representation of the People Act 1974.	Rep.	32, s. 3(2).
c. 20	Dumping at Sea Act 1974	Act (except s. 1(7)) transfer of functions (W.), ss. 6(1), 12(3) am.	S.I. No. 272.
c. 23	Juries Act 1974	Sch. 1 Pt. III am. ... am. (*prosp.*)	10, s. 5(1). 51, s. 75(1). 52, s. 33(1).
c. 24	Prices Act 1974	Not devolved (S.) (*prosp.*)	51, s. 63, sch. 10 Pt. III.
c. 28	Northern Ireland Act 1974.	Sch. 1 para. 1(4)(5) mod.	48, s. 3.
c. 29	Parks Regulation (Amendment) Act 1974.	Transfer of functions (S.) (*prosp.*).	51, s. 63, sch. 11 Group J.
c. 30	Finance Act 1974 ...	S. 15(1) rep. in pt. ...	42, ss. 21, 80(5), sch. 13 Pt. III.
		S. 23(2) am.	42, s. 30.
		S. 34 rep.	42, s. 80(5), sch. 13 Pt. IV.
		Sch. 1 para. 5(1) am. ...	42, s. 18.
c. 32	Town and Country Amenities Act 1974.	Transfer of certain functions (*prosp.*).	52, s. 9(1), sch. 2 Pt. XII.
c. 33	Northern Ireland (Young Persons) Act 1974.	Rep.	5, s. 35(3), sch. 6 Pt. I.
c. 37	Health and Safety at Work etc. Act 1974.	Act (except s. 75) not devolved (S.) (*prosp.*).	51, s. 63, sch. 10 Pt. III.
		S. 1(1)(*d*) transfer of functions (*prosp.*).	52, s. 9(1), sch. 2 Pt. VII.
		transfer of certain functions (S) (*prosp.*).	51, s. 63, sch. 11 Group F para. 2.
		S. 3(3) transfer of functions (*prosp.*).	52, s. 9(1), sch. 2 Pt. VII.
		transfer of certain functions (S.) (*prosp.*).	51, s. 63, sch. 11 Group F para. 3.
		S. 5 transfer of functions (*prosp.*).	52, s. 9(1), sch. 2 Pt. VII.
		transfer of certain functions (S.) (*prosp.*).	51, s. 63, sch. 11 Group F para. 3.
		S. 11 transfer of functions (*prosp.*).	52, s. 9(1), sch. 2 Pt. VII.
		transfer of certain functions (S.) (*prosp.*).	51, s. 63, sch. 11 Group F para. 3.
		Ss. 12, 14 transfer of functions (*prosp.*).	52, s. 9(1), sch. 2 Pt. VII.

Session and Chap. or No. of Measure	Short title or Subject	How affected	Chapter of 1978 Act or number of Measure or Statutory Instrument
1974: c. 37—*cont.*	Health and Safety at Work etc. Act 1974 —*cont.*	S. 14(1)(2)(3) transfer of certain functions (S.) (*prosp.*).	51, s. 63, sch. 11 Group F para. 3.
		S. 14(3)(4) mod. (*prosp.*)	52, s. 77(1), sch. 11 para. 74.
		S. 14(4)(*c*) mod. (*prosp.*)	51, s. 82(2), sch. 16 para. 44.
		Ss. 14(5)(6), 15 transfer of certain functions (S.) (*prosp.*).	51, s. 63, sch. 11 Group F para. 3.
		Ss. 15, 16 transfer of functions (*prosp.*).	52, s. 9(1), sch. 2 Pt. VII.
		S. 16 transfer of certain functions (S.) (*prosp.*).	51, s. 63, sch. 11 Group F para. 3.
		S. 18(2) transfer of functions (*prosp.*).	52, s. 9(1), sch. 2 Pt. VII.
		transfer of certain functions (S.) (*prosp.*).	51, s. 63, sch. 11 Group F para. 3.
		S. 20(3) transfer of functions (*prosp.*).	52, s. 9(1), sch. 2 Pt. VII.
		transfer of certain functions (S.) (*prosp.*).	51, s. 63, sch. 11 Group F para. 3.
		S. 27(1) transfer of functions (*prosp.*).	52, s. 9(1), sch. 2 Pt. VII.
		transfer of certain functions (S) (*prosp.*).	51, s. 63, sch. 11 Group F para. 3.
		S. 44 transfer of functions (*prosp.*).	52, s. 9(1), sch. 2 Pt. VII.
		transfer of certain functions (S.) (*prosp.*).	51, s. 63, sch. 11 Group F para. 3.
		S. 44(1) am. (*prosp.*) ...	51, s. 82(2), sch. 16 para. 45. 52, s. 77(1), sch. 11 para. 75.
		S. 45 transfer of functions (*prosp.*).	52, s. 9(1 , sch. 2 Pt. VII.
		transfer of certain functions (S.) (*prosp.*).	51, s. 63, sch. 11 Group F para. 3.
		S. 48(4) am. (*prosp.*) ...	51, s. 82(2), sch. 16 para. 46. 52, s. 77(1), sch. 11 para. 76.
		S. 50 transfer of functions (*prosp.*).	52, s. 9(1), sch. 2 Pt. VII.
		transfer of certain functions (S.) (*prosp.*).	51, s. 63, sch. 11 Group F para. 3.
		S. 80 transfer of functions (*prosp.*).	52, s. 9(1), sch. 2 Pt. VII.
		transfer of certain functions (S.) (*prosp.*).	51, s. 63, sch. 11 Group F para. 3.
		S. 80(2A) added ...	44, s. 159(2), sch. 16 para. 17.
		S. 84(3) ext. (*prosp.*) ...	51, s. 82(2), sch. 16 para. 47.

Session and Chap. or No. of Measure	Short title or Subject	How affected	Chapter of 1978 Act or number of Measure or Statutory Instrument
1974:—*cont.* c. 39	Consumer Credit Act 1974.	Not devolved (S.) (*prosp.*)	51, s. 63, sch. 10 Pt. III.
		S. 189(1) (definitions of " conditional sale agreement ", " credit sale agreement ", " hire purchase agreement ") appl.	38, s. 9(4).
		Sch. 4 paras. 20, 21, 46, 47 rep. (*prosp.*).	38, s. 10(1), sch. 3.
c. 40	Control of Pollution Act 1974.	Apptd. day for s. 2 (S.) (1.9.1978).	S.I. No. 816.
		for s. 13 pt. (E. & W.) (1.8.1978).	S.I. No. 954.
		Transfer of certain functions (*prosp.*).	52, s. 9(1), sch. 2 Pt. VII.
		Act (except ss. 30(5), 75–77, 100–103) transfer of certain functions (S.) (*prosp.*).	51, s. 63, sch. 11 Group F para. 4(*d*).
		Ss. 21, 30(5) devolved in pt. (S.) (*prosp.*).	51, s. 63, sch. 10 Pt. III.
		Pt. II (ss. 31–56) transfer of functions (W.).	S.I. No. 272.
		Ss. 35, 37, 39 power to intervene (*prosp.*).	52, s. 63, sch. 8 Pt. IV.
		S. 39(2) am.	S.I. No. 272.
		S. 39(2) consent of Min. required (*prosp.*).	52, s. 36(1), sch. 4.
		Ss. 42, 49, 51 power to intervene (*prosp.*).	52, s. 63, sch. 8 Pt. IV.
		S. 51(2) am.	S.I. No. 272.
		S. 52 division of powers (*prosp.*).	52, s. 63, sch. 8 Pt. I.
		Ss. 56(1) devolved in pt. (S.) (*prosp.*), 75–77 not devolved (S.) (*prosp.*).	51, s. 63, sch. 10 Pt. III.
		S. 97 power to intervene (*prosp.*).	52, s. 63, sch. 8 Pt. IV.
		Ss. 100–103 not devolved (S.) (*prosp.*).	51, s. 63, sch. 10 Pt. III.
		Sch. 3 para. 25 rep. ...	3, s. 12(2), sch. 2.
c. 41	Policing of Airports Act 1974.	Not devolved (S.) (*prosp.*)	51, s. 63, sch. 10 Pt. III.
		S. 7 am.	8, s. 1(2).
		restored (*prosp.*) ...	8, s. 4(2).
c. 43	Merchant Shipping Act 1974.	Apptd. day for ss. 1, 2, 4–8 (16.10.1978).	S.I. No. 1466.
c. 44	Housing Act 1974 ...	Transfer of certain functions (*prosp.*).	52, s. 9(1), sch. 2 Pt. IV.
		Am. (*prosp.*)	51, ss. 60, 61, sch. 9. 52, ss. 55(2), 56, sch. 6.
		S. 10(2) am.	27, s. 5(1).
		S. 29 restr. (S.)	14, s. 7(7).
		S. 33 restr. (S.)	14, s. 7(8)(*b*).
		S. 107 rep. (1.4.1979) ...	14, s. 16(2),sch. 3.
		S. 128(4) am.	27, s. 5(2).
		Sch. 10A para. 4(7) added	14, s. 16(1), sch. 2 para. 15.

H 3

Session and Chap. or No. of Measure	Short title or Subject	How affected	Chapter of 1978 Act or number of Measure or Statutory Instrument
1974:—*cont.*			
c. 45	Housing (Scotland) Act 1974.	S. 1(3) am., (4) added ...	14, s. 16(1), sch. 2 para. 16.
		Ss. 3(2)(3) replaced, 5(1A) added, (5) am.	14, s. 16(1), sch. 2 paras. 17, 18.
		S. 6(1)(*b*) am.	14, s. 16(1), sch. 2 para. 40.
		Ss. 7(1A) added, 9(9) am.	14, s. 16(1), sch. 2 paras. 19, 20.
		S. 10A added	14, s. 8.
		S. 11(1) am.	14, s. 16(1), sch. 2 para. 41(*a*).
		(6) am.	14, s. 16(1), sch. 2 para. 21.
		(7)–(10) replaced ...	14, s. 16(1), sch. 2 para. 41(*b*).
		S. 14A added	14, s. 10.
		S. 15(2) am., (*b*) added, (3) am.	14, s. 16(1), sch. 2 para. 22.
		Ss. 16(4) am., (*c*) added, 17(4) am., (*b*) added, (5) am., (*c*) added.	14, s. 16(1), sch. 2 paras. 23, 24.
		S. 29(2) am.	14, s. 16(1), sch. 2 para. 42.
		S. 30 not devolved (*prosp.*).	51, s. 63, sch. 10 Pt. III.
		S. 30(1) am., (3)(4) added	14, s. 16(1), sch. 2 para. 25.
		S. 43(1) am.	14, s. 16(1), sch. 2 para. 43.
		Ss. 44(1) am., 44A added, 49(3) (definitions of "owner", "prescribed") sch. 2 para. 7 am.	14, s. 16(1), sch. 2 paras. 26–29.
		Sch. 3 para. 44 rep. (1.4.1979).	14, s. 16(2), sch. 3.
c. 46	Friendly Societies Act 1974.	Not devolved (S.) (*prosp.*)	51, s. 63, sch. 10 Pt. III.
		S. 64(1)(*c*)(*d*) am.	S.I. No. 920.
c. 47	Solicitors Act 1974 ...	Ss. 20, 22, 25(1), 39(1) am.	S.I. No. 1910.
c. 48	Railways Act 1974 ...	S. 3(1)(4) am.	55, s. 14(1)(2).
		S. 4 am.	55, s. 15(7).
		S. 8 devolved (*prosp.*) ...	51, s. 63, sch. 10 Pt. III.
		transfer of functions (*prosp.*).	52, s. 9(1), sch. 2 Pt. XIV.
		S. 8(1)(2) am.	55, s. 16.
		S. 10(2) (definition of "the relevant transport regulations") appl.	55, s. 14(4).
c. 49	Insurance Companies Act 1974.	Ss. 2, 3 mod., 5 restr., 7(1)(2) mod., 8, 17, 18 restr., 18(3)(*a*) mod., 28(1)(*b*)(i) ext., 28(1)(*e*) mod., 38 restr., mod., 39, 52–54 mod., 78 ext.	S.I. No. 720.
c. 50	Road Traffic Act 1974	S. 17 transfer of functions (*prosp.*).	52, s. 9(1), sch. 2 Pt. XVI.
		transfer of functions (S.) (*prosp.*).	51, s. 63, sch. 11 Group G para. 7.

Session and Chap. or No. of Measure	Short title or Subject	How affected	Chapter of 1978 Act or number of Measure or Statutory Instrument
1974:—*cont.*			
c. 52	Trade Union and Labour Relations Act 1974.	S. 1(2)(*b*)(*c*) rep., (*d*) rep. in pt.	44, s. 159(3), sch. 17.
		S. 8(7) am.	44, s. 159(2) sch. 16 para. 18.
		S. 28(1) (definition of " trade union ") appl.	36, s. 1(5), sch. 1 para. 5(6).
		Ss. 28(2) (definition of " employers association "), 29 (definition of " trade dispute "), 30(1) (definition of "collective agreement") appl.	44, s. 153(1).
		S. 30(1) (definitions of " dismissal procedures agreement ", "job position ") rep.	44, s. 159(3), sch. 17.
		(definition of " official union membership agreement ") appl.	44, s. 153(1).
		(definition of " workers ") appl.	44, s. 135(3).
		S. 30(2) am.	29, s. 109, sch. 16 para. 39.
		S. 30(3)(4) (definition of " successor "), (5A) (definition of " employees ") appl.	44, s. 153(1).
		Sch. 1 paras. 4–16, 17(1) rep. (saving).	44, s. 159, sch. 15 para. 9(1), sch. 17.
		para. 17(2)(3) saved.	44, s. 159, sch. 15 para. 9(2).
		para. 18 rep. (saving).	44, s. 159, sch. 15 para. 9(1), sch. 17.
		para. 19 saved ...	44, s. 159, sch. 15 para. 9(2).
		paras. 20–27, 30, 32(1)(*b*), (2)(*b*)–(*e*), 33(3)(*c*)(*d*)(4A) rep. (saving).	44, s. 159, sch. 15 para. 9(1), sch. 17.
		Sch. 3 para. 16, sch. 4 paras. 1, 3, 6(4) rep.	44, s. 159(3), sch. 17.
c. xxx ...	Orkney County Council Act 1974.	S. 3(1) (definition of " dangerous goods ") subst.	iv, s. 1, sch., s. 6.
		(definition of " harbour work ") am.	iv, s. 1, sch., s. 3.
		(definition of " tidal work ") am.	iv, s. 1, sch., s. 5.
		S. 46(3) am.	iv, s. 1, sch., s. 7.
		S. 64(1)(*e*) added ...	iv, s. 1, sch., s. 8.
		S. 80(*b*) rep.	iv, s. 1, sch., s. 9, sch. 2.
		Sch. am.	iv, s. 1, sch., s. 3(2), sch. 1.

Session and Chap. or No. of Measure	Short title or Subject	How affected	Chapter of 1978 Act or number of Measure or Statutory Instrument
1975:			
c. 2	Education Act 1975 ...	Transfer of functions (*prosp.*).	52, s. 9(1), sch. 2 Pt. III.
c. 6	Housing Rents and Subsidies Act 1975.	Transfer of certain functions (*prosp.*).	52, s. 9(1), sch. 2 Pt. IV.
c. 7	Finance Act 1975 ...	Pt. III (ss. 19–52) appl.	42, s. 68.
		S. 20(7) am.	42, s. 74(1).
		S. 22(2) am.	42, s. 69(1).
		(2)(3) expld. ...	42, s. 69(6).
		S. 37(3) Tables subst. ...	42, s. 62 sch. 10.
		S. 47(1) rep. (saving) ...	42, s. 80(5), sch. 13 Pt. V.
		(1A) am.	42, s. 70(5).
		(2)(5) rep. (saving)	42, s. 80(5.), sch. 13 Pt. V.
		Sch. 2 para. 19(1A), am.	42, s. 14(3), sch. 2 para. 18.
		Sch. 4 para. 13(7) rep. in pt.	42, ss. 66, 80(5), sch. 13 Pt. V.
		para. 13(7)(c) added.	42, s. 66.
		para. 25(4) am. ...	42, s. 68(6).
		Sch. 5 para. 4(5) am. ...	42, s. 69(1).
		(5)(6) expld.	42, s. 69(6).
		para. 6(2A) added	42, s. 70(1).
		(5) am. ...	42, s. 70(2).
		(6B) added	42, s. 69(2).
		expld.	42, s. 69(6).
		para. 7(2) mod. ...	42, s. 62(4).
		para. 11(8) am. ...	42, s. 70(3).
		para. 14(5) am. ...	42, s. 69(3).
		expld.	42, s. 69(6).
		para. 17(4) am. (*b*) subst.	42, s. 67(7), sch. 11 para. 1.
		para. 18(2)(3) replaced.	42, s. 71(1).
		Sch. 6 para. 1(2)(3) ...	42, s. 63.
		paras. 10(2), 11 (1A), am.	42, s. 70(4).
		para. 12(1) am. (*prosp.*).	51, s. 82(2), sch. 16 para. 48. 52, s. 77(1), sch. 11 para. 78.
		paras. 12(2), 13 (1A) am.	42, s. 70(4).
		para. 15(4A) am.	42, s. 69(4).
		rep. in pt.	42, ss. 69(4), 80 (5) sch. 13 Pt. V.
		para. 15(4A) expld.	42, s. 69(6).
		(4B) added	42, s. 69(5).
		expld.	42, s. 69(6).
		Sch. 7 para. 3(2A)(2B) added.	42, s. 72.
		Sch. 9 para. 3 mod. ...	42, s. 62(5).
		renumbered para. 3(2) added	42, s. 65.
		Sch. 10 para. 11(2) subst.	42, s. 73(1).

Session and Chap. or No. of Measure	Short title or Subject	How affected	Chapter of 1978 Act or number of Measure or Statutory Instrument
1975—*cont.*			
c. 14	Social Security Act 1975	Ss. 7(1)(5), 8(1), 9(2), 10 (1) am.	S.I. No. 1840.
		S. 30(1) am.	S.I. No. 912.
		S. 32 saved (S.) (*prosp.*)	28, s. 41(3).
		S. 37A(6) am. (S.) ...	29, s. 109, sch. 16 para. 40.
		Ss. 45(3), 66(4) am. ...	S.I. No. 912.
		Ss. 70(3)(*b*), 72, 73(2) saved (S.) (*prosp.*).	28, s. 41(4)(5).
		S. 114 (2A) added. ...	44. s. 159(2), sch. 16 para. 19(1).
		S. 119(1)(2) excl. ...	44, s. 132(4).
		Ss. 124–126 appl. ...	S.I. No. 393.
		S. 139(2A) added. ...	44, s. 159(2), sch. 16 para. 19(2).
		Sch. 2 para. 3(1) am. ...	42, s. 30.
		para. 3(2)(*a*) added.	42, s. 27, sch. 4 para. 8.
		Sch. 4 am.	S.I. No. 912.
		Sch. 4 Pt. III para. 3A col. 2 am.	S.I. No. 475.
		Sch. 20 appl.	42, s. 54(4)(*b*).
c. 15	Social Security (Northern Ireland) Act 1975.	S. 94(5) am.	23, s. 122(1), sch. 5 Pt. II(1).
		Sch. 2 para. 3(2)(*cc*) added.	42, s. 27, sch. 4 para. 8.
c. 16	Industrial Injuries and Diseases (Old Cases) Act 1975.	Ss. 2(6)(*c*), 7(2)(*b*) am. ...	S.I. No. 912.
c. 18	Social Security (Consequential Provisions) Act 1975.	Sch. 2 paras. 19–23 rep....	44, s. 159(3), sch. 17.
c. 21	Criminal Procedure (Scotland) Act 1975.	Ss. 5, 10, 11 not devolved (*prosp.*).	51, s. 63, sch. 10 Pt. III.
		S. 14 am. (*prosp.*) ...	28, s. 37(1).
		Ss. 21 not devolved (*prosp.*), 35 devolved in pt. (*prosp.*), 41, 76, 113 (4), 114 not devolved (*prosp.*).	51, s. 63, sch. 10 Pt. III.
		S. 183(4) am. (*prosp.*), (5A) added (*prosp.*), (6) am. (*prosp.*).	49, s. 7.
		S. 186(2)(*d*) added (*prosp.*)	49, s. 8.
		S. 188(1) am. (*prosp.*) ...	49, s. 14, sch. 2 para. 2.
		Ss. 245(1), 263 not devolved (*prosp.*).	51, s. 63, sch. 10 Pt. III.
		S. 289B appl.	8, s. 2(7)(*b*). 44, ss. 104(10)(*b*), 107(5)(*b*). 38, s. 9(4).
		S. 323 am. (*prosp.*) ...	28, s. 37(1).
		S. 384(4) am. (*prosp.*), (5A) added, (6) am. (*prosp.*).	49, s. 7.
		S. 387(2)(*d*) added (*prosp.*)	49, s. 8.
		S. 389(1) am. (*prosp.*) ...	49, s. 14, sch. 2 para. 3.

Session and Chap. or No. of Measure	Short title or Subject	How affected	Chapter of 1978 Act or number of Measure or Statutory Instrument
1975; c. 21—*cont.*	Criminal Procedure (Scotland) Act 1975.—*cont.*	S. 462(1) (definition of " court of summary jurisdiction ") appl.	3, s. 2(3).
		(definition of " hospital ") am.	29, s. 109, sch. 16 para. 41.
		Sch. 9 para. 6 rep. ...	30, s. 25(1), sch. 3.
c. 22	Oil Taxation Act 1975 ...	S. 13(2) am.	42, s. 30.
c. 23	Reservoirs Act 1975 ...	Transfer of functions (*prosp.*).	52, s. 9(1), sch. 2 Pt. IX.
c. 24	House of Commons Disqualification Act 1975.	S. 1(3) (definition of " civil service of the Crown ", sch. 1 Pt. I am. (*prosp.*).	23, s. 122(2), sch. 5 Pt. II (1).
		Sch. 1 Pt. II am. ...	21, s. 1(6), sch. 1 para. 11.
		am. ...	29, s. 109, sch. 16 para. 42.
		rep. in pt....	45, S.L. (R), s. 1(1), sch. 1 Pt. III.
		Pt. III rep. in pt.	45, S.L. (R), s. 1(1), sch. 1 Pt. III.
		am. (*prosp.*)	23, s. 122(2), sch, 5 Pt. II(1).
			51, s. 82(2), sch. 16 para. 49.
			52, s. 77(1), sch. 11 para. 79.
		rep. in pt. (*prosp.*).	23, s. 122(1)(2), sch. 5 Pt. II(1), sch. 7 Pt. I.
c. 25	Northern Ireland Assembly Disqualification Act 1975.	S. 1(2) (definition of " civil service of the Crown "), sch. 1 Pt. I am. (*prosp.*).	23, s. 122(1), sch. 5 Pt. II(1).
		Sch. 1 Pt. II am. ...	21, s. 1(6), sch. 1 para. 11.
		Pt. III am. (*prosp.*)	23, s. 122(1), sch. 5 Pt. II(1).
			51, s. 82(2), sch. 16 para. 50.
			52, s. 77(1), sch. 11 para. 80.
		rep. in pt. (*prosp.*).	23, s. 122(1)(2), sch. 5 Pt. II(1), sch. 7 Pt. I.
c. 26	Ministers of the Crown Act 1975.	Sch. 2 Pt. I rep. in pt. ...	2, s. 18(1), sch. 2.
c. 27	Ministerial and other Salaries Act 1975.	S. 1(2)(3), sch. 1 Pts. I, II, III, IV, sch. 2 Pt. I am.	S.I. No. 1102.
c. 28	Housing Rents and Subsidies (Scotland) Act 1975.	S. 2 subst.	14, s. 15.
c. 30	Local Government (Scotland) Act 1975.	S. 3 appl. (1.4.1979) ...	40, s. 7(1).
		S. 5 expld., s. 5(4) excl....	S.I. Nos. 1173, 1174, 1175, 1176.
		S. 6 subst.	4, s. 1.

Session and Chap. or No. of Measure	Short title or Subject	How affected	Chapter of 1978 Act or number of Measure or Statutory Instrument
1975: c. 30—*cont.*	Local Government (Scotland) Act 1975.—*cont.*	S. 29(3) added	39, s. 1.
		S. 37(1) (definition of " material change of circumstances ") appl.	42, s. 7(6).
		Sch. 1 paras. 1–4 replaced	4, s. 2.
		Sch. 3 paras. 2–9, 26 not devolved (*prosp.*).	51, s. 63 sch. 10 Pt. III.
		Sch. 4 para. 3(1) subst....	4, s. 4.
		Sch. 6 para. 22 rep.	S.I. No. 1176.
		para. 43 rep. ...	S.I. No. 1173.
c. 32	Prices Act 1975	Not devolved (S.) (*prosp.*)	51, s. 63 sch. 10 Pt. III.
c. 34	Evidence (Proceedings in Other Jurisdictions) Act 1975.	S. 4 rep. in pt. (*prosp.*)	23, s. 122, sch. 7 Pt. I.
c. 35	Farriers (Registration) Act 1975.	Apptd. day for s. 16 (E. & W.) (1.6.1979).	S.I. No. 1928.
c. 36	Air Travel Reserve Fund Act 1975.	Not devolved (S.) (*prosp.*)	51, s. 63, sch. 10 Pt. III.
c. 37	Nursing Homes Act 1975	Transfer of certain functions (*prosp.*).	52, s. 9(1), sch. 2 Pt. VI.
c. 38	Export Guarantees Act 1975.	Rep.	18, s. 16(2), sch.
c. 45	Finance (No. 2) Act 1975	S. 8(3) am.	42, s. 79, sch. 12 para. 23.
		Ss. 14(5), 15(6) am. ...	42, s. 79, sch. 12 paras. 3, 4.
		S. 16(2)(*d*) am.	S.I. No. 1603.
		(*e*) added ...	42, s. 3.
		(*f*) added ...	S.I. No. 1603.
		S. 18(2) am.	S.I. No. 273.
		S. 19(2) rep.	42, s. 80(5), sch. 13 Pt. II.
		S. 34(4)(*c*) am.	42, s. 14(3), sch. 2 para. 19.
		S. 49(1) ext.	42, s. 40(1).
		S. 55 rep.	42, s. 80(5), sch. 13 Pt. IV.
		S. 69(4) am.	42, s. 33.
c. 48	Conservation of Wild Creatures and Wild Plants Act 1975.	S. 8(1)(*e*) transfer of functions (W.).	S.I. No. 272.
c. 49	Mobile Homes Act 1975	Transfer of functions (*prosp.*).	52, s. 9(1), sch. 2 Pt. VIII.
c. 51	Salmon and Freshwater Fisheries Act 1975.	Transfer of certain functions (W.).	S.I. No. 272.
		Transfer of certain functions (*prosp.*).	52, s. 9(1), sch. 2 Pt. X.
		Ss. 26, 28 sch. 3 power to intervene (*prosp.*).	52, s. 63, sch. 8 Pt. IV.
c. 52	Safety of Sports Grounds Act 1975.	Transfer of functions (*prosp.*).	52, s. 9(1), sch. 2 Pt. VIII.
		Devolved (S.) (*prosp.*) ...	51, s. 63, sch. 10 Pt. III.
		S. 17(1) (definitions of " local authority ", " safety certificate ", " sports stadium ") appl.	42, s. 40(5).

Session and Chap. or No. of Measure	Short title or Subject	How affected	Chapter of 1978 Act or number of Measure or Statutory Instrument
1975:—_cont._			
c. 57	Remuneration, Charges and Grants Act 1975.	Not devolved (S.) (_prosp._)	51, s. 63, sch. 10 Pt. III.
c. 59	Criminal Jurisdiction Act 1975.	S. 4(1) am.	5, s. 34(3).
		rep. in pt., sch. 2 paras. 1, 2(1), 3 rep.	5, s. 35(3), sch. 6 Pt. I.
		Sch. 3 para. 2(2) subst. (N.I.).	26, s. 6(1).
c. 60	Social Security Pensions Act 1975.	Apptd. days for certain specified provisions (7.6.1978), (20.9.1978), (6.9.1978), (20.12.1978).	S.I. No. 367.
		Not devolved (S.) (_prosp._)	51, s. 63, sch. 10 Pt. III.
		S. 6(1)(_a_) am.	S.I. No. 912.
		S. 15(3) mod. (6.4.1979)	S.I. No. 529.
		S. 30(5) rep.	44, s. 159(3), sch. 17.
c. 62	Northern Ireland (Emergency Provisions) (Amendment) Act 1975.	Ss. 2–5, 6(1)(2)(_a_), 8, 9(1)(3), 10–13 rep., 14 rep. in pt., 15–19, 21, 22, 23(2) sch. 1 Pt. I, schs. 2, 3 rep.	5, s. 35(3), sch. 6 Pt. I.
c. 64	Iron and Steel Act 1975	S. 19(2) am.	41, s. 1.
c. 65	Sex Discrimination Act 1975.	Appl.	44, s. 71(3)(_b_).
		Not devolved (S.) (_prosp._)	51, s. 63, sch. 10 Pt. III.
		Pt. II (ss. 6–21) appl. (mods.) (_prosp._).	51, s. 33(3)(4).
		S. 10(5) ext.	46, s. 1(2).
		Ss. 24, 25(2) transfer of functions (_prosp._).	52, s. 9(1), sch. 2 Pt. III.
		Ss. 25(3)(5), 27 transfer of certain functions (S.) (_prosp._).	51, s. 63, sch. 11 Group I.
		S. 27 transfer of certain functions (_prosp._).	52, s. 9(1), sch. 2 Pt. III.
		Pt. IV (ss. 37–42) appl. (mods.) (_prosp._).	51, s. 33(3)(4).
		S. 65(2) am.	44, s. 159(2), sch. 16 para. 20.
		S. 66(5) transfer of functions (_prosp._).	52, s. 9(1), sch. 2 Pt. III.
		transfer of certain functions (S.) (_prosp._).	51, s. 63, sch. 11 Group I.
		S. 75(5)(_c_) am.	44, s. 159(2), sch. 16 para. 20.
		S. 78 transfer of certain functions (_prosp._).	52, s. 9(1), sch. 2 Pt. III.
		S. 79, sch. 2 transfer of certain functions (S.) (_prosp._).	51, s. 63, sch. 11 Group I.
c 67	Housing Finance (Special Provisions) Act 1975.	Transfer of functions (_prosp._).	52, s. 9(1), sch. 2 Pt. I.
c. 69	Scottish Development Agency Act 1975.	Am. (_prosp._)	51, ss. 42(1), 60, 61, sch. 9.
		S. 1 transfer of functions (_prosp._).	51, s. 63, sch. 11 Group E para 9(i).

Session and Chap. or No. of Measure	Short title or Subject	How affected	Chapter of 1978 Act or number of Measure or Statutory Instrument
1975: c. 69—*cont.*	Scottish Development Agency Act 1975—*cont.*	S. 2(1)(*d*), (2)(*d*)(*e*)(*g*)(*h*) devolved (*prosp*), (*i*)(3) (4)(*a*)–(*f*) devolved in pt. (*prosp*), (*g*)–(*m*) devolved (*prosp*.).	51, s. 63, sch. 10 Pt. III.
		S. 2(6)(7) transfer of certain functions (*prosp*.).	51, s. 63, sch. 11 Group E para 9(ii)(iii).
		Ss. 2(7) devolved in pt. (*prosp*.), (8)(9) devolved (*prosp*.), (10), 3, 4 devolved in pt. (*prosp*.).	51, s. 63, sch. 10 Pt. III.
		S. 4 transfer of certain functions (*prosp*.).	51, s. 63, sch. 11 Group E para. 9(iv)–(vi).
		am. (*prosp*.) ...	51, s. 42(1)(*c*), (2) sch. 7.
		S. 6 devolved (*prosp*.) ...	51, s. 63, sch. 10 Pt. III.
		am. (*prosp*.) ...	51, s. 42(1)(*e*)(2) sch. 7.
		Ss. 7, 8(1)–(5), 9 devolved (*prosp*.).	51, s. 63, sch. 10 Pt. III.
		S. 9 am. (*prosp*.) ...	51, s. 42(1)(*c*)(2), sch. 7.
		Ss. 10 devolved in pt. (*prosp*.), 11(1)–(5) devolved (*prosp*.).	51, s. 63, sch. 10 Pt. III.
		S. 12 transfer of certain functions (*prosp*.).	51, s. 63, sch. 11 Group E para. 9(vii).
		Ss. 12, 13(1) devolved in pt. (*prosp*.), (2)–(5) devolved (*prosp*.).	51, s. 63, sch. 10 Pt. III.
		S. 14 transfer of functions (*prosp*.).	51, s. 63, sch. 11 Group E para. 9(viii).
		Ss. 16 devolved in pt. (*prosp*.), 18 devolved (*prosp*.).	51, s. 63, sch. 10 Pt. III.
		S. 18 am. (*prosp*.) ...	51, s. 82(2), sch. 16 para. 51(1).
		S. 19 devolved in pt. (*prosp*.), transfer of certain functions (*prosp*.).	51, s. 63, sch. 10 Pt. III, sch. 11 Group E para. 9(ix).
		Ss. 21, 22, 24 devolved (*prosp*.), 25–28 devolved in pt. (*prosp*.).	51, s. 63, sch. 10 Pt. III.
		Schs. 1 transfer of functions (*prosp*.), 2 (except para. 6) transfer of certain functions (*prosp*.).	51, s. 63, sch. 11 Group E para. 9(x)(xi).
		Sch. 2 paras. 2–5, 7–9 devolved in pt. (*prosp*.).	51, s. 63, sch. 10 Pt. III.
		Sch. 2 para. 9(1) subst. (*prosp*.), (2A) added (*prosp*.), (3) am. (*prosp*.).	51, s. 82(2), sch. 16 para. 51(2).
		Sch. 3 para. 6 am. ...	44, s. 159(2), sch. 16 para. 21.

Session and Chap. or No. of Measure	Short title or Subject	How affected	Chapter of 1978 Act or number of Measure or Statutory Instrument
1975:—*cont.*			
c. 70	Welsh Development Agency Act 1975.	Transfer of certain functions (*prosp.*).	52, s. 9(1), sch. 2 Pt. VIII.
		Am. (*prosp.*)	52, ss. 55(2), 56, sch. 6.
		Sch. 2 para. 7 am. ...	44, s. 159(2), sch. 16 para. 22.
		Sch. 3 para. 9 subst. (*prosp.*).	52, s. 77(1), sch. 11 para. 81.
c. 71	Employment Protection Act 1975.	Appl. (mods.) (*prosp.*) ...	51, s. 33(1)(2)(4).
		S. 6(2) rep. in pt., am. ...	44, s. 159(2), sch. 16 para. 23(1)(2).
		S. 8(2) am.	S.I. No. 1329.
		S. 8(9) am.	44, s. 159(2), sch. 16 para. 23(1)(3).
		S. 15 appl.	44, ss. 23(5), 32(1), 58(4).
		Pt. II (ss. 22–88) (except s. 40) rep. (saving).	44, s. 159, sch. 15 para. 9(1), sch. 17.
		Ss. 102(4), 104(1)(*a*) am.	44, s. 159(2), sch. 16 para. 23(1)(4)(5).
		S. 106(1) appl.	36, s. 1(5), sch. 1 para. 5(6).
		Ss. 106(3), 108(1) am. ...	44, s. 159(2), sch. 16 para. 23(1)(6)(7).
		Ss. 108(2)–(8), 109, 112 rep. (saving), 18(2)(*a*) rep. in pt. (saving), (*b*)(*c*) rep. (saving).	44, s. 159, sch. 15 para. 9(1), sch. 17.
		S. 119(1) am.	44, s. 159(2), sch. 16 para. 23(1)(8).
		S. 119(2) rep. (saving), (3)(4)(5)(7) rep. in pt. (saving), (8)–(11) rep. (saving), (12) rep. in pt. (saving).	44, s. 159, sch. 15 para. 9(1), sch. 17.
		(17) added ...	44, s. 159(2), sch. 16 para. 23(1)(9).
		Ss. 120 rep. (saving), 121(1)(5) rep. in pt. (saving).	44, s. 159, sch. 15 para. 9(1), sch. 17.
		S. 121(5)(6)(7) am. ...	44, s. 159(2), sch. 16 para. 23(1)(10)(11).
		S. 121(8) rep. (saving) ...	44, s. 159, sch. 15 para. 9(1), sch. 17.
		S. 122(1) rep. in pt. (saving).	44, s. 159, sch. 15 para. 9(1), sch. 17.
		(1)(*b*)(*c*) am., (3)–(7) replaced.	36, s. 5(3), sch. 2 para. 5.

Session and Chap. or No. of Measure	Short title or Subject	How affected	Chapter of 1978 Act or number of Measure or Statutory Instrument
1975: c. 71—*cont.*	Employment Protection Act 1975—*cont.*	S. 122(3)(4) (definition of " civil employment claim ") rep. (saving), (5) rep. in pt. (saving).	44, s. 159, sch. 15 para. 9(1), sch. 17.
		(8) am.	36, s. 5(3), sch. 2 para. 5.
		(9) rep.	36, s. 5(4), sch. 3.
		Ss. 123(2)(*b*) rep. in pt. (saving), 124(2)–(4) rep. (saving).	44, s. 159, sch. 15 para. 9(1), sch. 17.
		Ss. 125(1), 126(1) am. ...	44, s. 159(2), sch. 16 para. 23(1) (12)(13).
		Ss. 126(1) (definitions of " guarantee payment ", " maternity pay "), (3) (5), 127(1)(*c*)(*d*) rep. (saving).	44, s. 159, sch. 15 para. 9(1), sch. 17.
		S. 127(2) ext.	46, s. 1(1).
		Ss. 127(3)(*g*), 128(1) rep. in pt. (saving), (2) rep. (saving), (3) rep. in pt. (saving), 129(2), schs. 2–6 rep. (saving), sch. 12 para. 1 rep. in pt. (saving), paras. 8–12 rep. (saving).	44, s. 159, sch. 15 para. 9(1), sch. 17.
		Sch. 14 para. 2(2)–(5) rep.	6, s. 3(7)(*b*).
		Sch. 16 Pts. I, II, Pt. III paras. 8–30, 34 rep. (saving).	44, s. 159, sch. 15 para. 9(1), sch. 17.
		Pt. IV para. 1 rep. para. 14 sch.	36, s. 5(4), sch. 3. 44, s. 159, sch. 15, para. 9(1), sch. 17.
		17 paras. 7–10, 16, 17 rep. (saving).	
c. 72	Children Act 1975 ...	Apptd. day for s. 24 (E. & W.) (23.10.1978)	S.I. No. 1433.
		for s. 24 (S.) (23.10.1978).	S.I. No. 1440.
		Transfer of certain functions (*prosp.*).	52, s. 9(1), sch. 2 Pt. VI.
		Pt. I (ss. 1–32) rep. (S.) (*prosp.*).	28, s. 66(3), sch. 4.
		S. 17(1) rep. in pt. (E. & W.) (*prosp.*).	22, ss. 72(1), 89 sch. 3.
		S. 21(1)(2) am. (E. & W.) rep. in pt. (E. & W.) (2A) added (E. & W.).	22, s. 73.
		(3) rep. (*prosp.*). ...	22, s. 89, sch. 3.
		S. 24(8A) added. ...	22, s. 74(1).
		Pt. II (ss. 33–55) appl. (E. & W.) (*prosp.*).	22, s. 8(3).
		S. 34 subst. (*prosp.*) ...	22, s. 64.
		Ss. 34A, 34B added (*prosp.*).	22, s. 65.
		S. 35(3)(4) am. (*prosp.*), (4A) added (*prosp.*), (5) (6) am. (*prosp.*), (7)–(11) added (*prosp.*).	22, s. 66.

Session and Chap. or No. of Measure	Short title or Subject	How affected	Chapter of 1978 Act or number of Measure or Statutory Instrument
1975: c. 72—*cont.*	Children Act 1975—*cont.*	S. 35A added (*prosp.*) ...	22, s. 67.
		S. 36(5) replaced (*prosp.*)	22, s. 68.
		(6) am. (*prosp.*), s. 37 (4A) added (*prosp.*).	22, s. 89, sch. 2 para. 46.
		S. 43(2) am. (*prosp.*) ...	22, s. 89, sch. 2 para. 47.
		S. 43A added (*prosp.*) ...	22, s. 70,
		S. 46(3) am. (*prosp.*) ...	22, s. 89, sch. 2 para. 48.
		S. 47(5) am. (*prosp.*) ...	28, s. 66(2), sch. 3 para. 16.
		Pt. IV (ss. 85–94) appl.	30, s. 5, sch. 1.
		S. 89 rep.	30, s. 25(1), sch. 3.
		S. 91 rep. (*prosp.*) ...	22, s. 89, sch. 3.
		S. 100(4)(5)(9) rep. (S.) (*prosp.*).	28, s. 66(3), sch. 4.
		S. 101(1) am. (E. & W.)	22, s. 89, sch. 2 para. 49.
		(4) added (E. & W.) (*prosp.*).	22, s. 71.
		S. 102(1) rep. in pt. (S.) (*prosp.*).	28, s. 66(3), sch. 4.
		S. 103(1)(*a*)(*i*) subst. (S.) (*prosp.*).	28, s. 66(2), sch. 3 para. 17.
		S. 105 am. (S.) (*prosp.*)	28, s. 66(2), sch. 3 para. 18.
		S. 107(1) (definition of "adoption society") am. (S.) (*prosp.*).	28, s. 66(2), sch. 3 para. 19.
		(definition of "child") appl.	30, s. 5, sch. 1.
		Ss. 107(1) (definitions of "approved adoption society," "British adoption order," "British territory," "the Convention," "Convention adoption order," "Convention country", "United Kingdom national", "guardian" para(*b*) rep. (S.) (*prosp.*), (2A) rep. (*prosp.*), 108(5)(6), sch. 2 paras 1–4, 5(1)(2)(4), 6(1)(3), (7) rep. (S.) (*prosp.*).	28, s. 66(3), sch. 4.
		Sch. 3 para. 12 rep. (*prosp.*).	22, s. 89, sch. 3.
		paras. 17, 21–26 rep. (S.) (*prosp.*).	28, s. 66(3), sch. 4.
		para. 26 rep. ...	22, ss. 74(3), 89, sch. 3.
		paras. 27–40, 44, 45, 61–65 rep. (S.) (*prosp.*).	28, s. 66(3), sch. 4.
c. 74	Petroleum and Submarine Pipe-lines Act 1975.	S. 16(1) (definition of "petroleum") appl.	1, s. 1(6).

Session and Chap. or No. of Measure	Short title or Subject	How affected	Chapter of 1978 Act or number of Measure or Statutory Instrument
1975—*cont.* c. 76	Local Land Charges Act 1975.	S. 4 (definition of "the appropriate local land charges register") appl.	30, s. 5, sch. 1.
		rep. in pt. ...	30, s. 25(1), sch. 3.
c. 77	Community Land Act 1975.	Transfer of certain functions (*prosp.*).	52, s. 9(1), sch. 2 Pt. VIII.
		Not devolved (S.) (*prosp.*) transfer of certain functions (S.) (*prosp.*).	51, s. 63, sch. 10 Pt. III sch. 11 Group E para. 10.
		S. 1(1) (definition of "authority") appl.	42, s. 34(1).
		Pt. II (ss. 8–14) am. (*prosp.*).	52, s. 55(2), 56, sch. 6.
		S. 18 am. (*prosp.*) ...	51, s. 23(3), sch. 5.
		Ss. 18, 37 concurrent powers of Min. (*prosp.*).	52, s. 9(2), sch. 3.
		S. 37(1)(2)(4)–(8) mod. (*prosp.*).	51, s. 73.
		S. 45 am. (*prosp.*) ...	51, s. 42(1)(*c*)(2) sch. 7.
		Sch. 4 para. 17 consent of Min. required (*prosp.*).	52, s. 36(1), sch. 4.
c. 78	Airports Authority Act 1975.	S. 2(3) am.	8, s. 14(1), sch. 1 Pt. I para. 7(1)(2).
		S. 7 not devolved (S.) (*prosp.*).	51, s. 63, sch. 10 Pt. III.
		S. 9 am.	8, s. 8.
		S. 14(1)(*a*)(3)(*a*) subst. ...	3, s. 12(1), sch. 1.
		S. 17(4)(*c*) rep.	8, s. 14(2), sch. 2.
		Sch. 2 para. 2(*a*) rep. ...	8, s. 14(1)(2), sch. 1 Pt. I para. 7(1)(3)(*a*), sch. 2.
		paras. 4, 6 am. ...	8, s. 14(1), sch. 1 Pt. I para. 7(1)(3)(*b*)(*c*).
		Sch. 3 para. 7 rep. 9(1) rep. in pt. (2) sch. 5 Pt. II para. 4(*b*) rep.	8, s. 14(2), sch. 2.
c. i	British Railways Act 1975	S. 9(6) rep.	xxi, s. 30, sch. 4.
G.S.M. No. 2... ...	Ecclesiastical Offices (Age Limit) Measure 1975.	Excl.	G.S.M. No. 3 s. 2(3).
		S. 1(1) expld. (4)(*d*) mod.	G.S.M. No. 3 s. 2(1)(2).
1976: c. 2	Consolidated Fund Act 1976.	Rep.	57, s. 3, sch. (C).
c. 3	Road Traffic (Drivers' Ages and Hours of Work) Act 1976.	Apptd. day for s. 2 (26.1.1978)	S.I. No. 6.

Session and Chap. or No. of Measure	Short title or Subject	How affected	Chapter of 1978 Act or number of Measure or Statutory Instrument
1976—*cont.*			
c. 4	Trustee Savings Banks Act 1976.	Apptd. day for specified provisions (28.4.1978) (18.8.1978)	S.I. No. 533. S.I. No. 1079.
		S. 12(1) expld.	16, s. 2(2).
		rep. in pt., (2) rep.	16, s. 5, sch.
		(3) am.	16, s. 2(4).
		S. 16(3) rep.	16, s. 5, sch.
		(4) rep. in pt. ...	16, ss. 2(5), 5, sch.
		S. 35(1) (definitions of "current account deposit", "savings account deposit") rep., sch. 3 para. 22 rep. in pt.	16, s. 5, sch.
c. 5	Education (School-leaving Dates) Act 1976.	Transfer of functions (*prosp.*).	52, s. 9(1), sch. 2 Pt. III.
c. 7	Trade Union and Labour Relations (Amendment) Act 1976.	Ss. 1(*e*), 3(5)(6) rep. (saving).	44, s. 159, sch. 15 para. 9(1), sch. 17.
c. 8	Prevention of Terrorism (Temporary Provisions) Act 1976.	Sch. 3 para. 8 am. ... rep. in pt.	5, s. 34(2). 5, s. 35(3), sch. 6 Pt. I.
c. 15	Rating (Caravan Sites) Act 1976.	S. 3(5)(*b*) rep. (1.4.1979)	40, s. 9(3), sch. 2.
c. 16	Statute Law (Repeals) Act 1976.	Sch. 2 Pt. I rep. in pt. ...	45, S.L. (R.), s. 1(1), sch. 1 Pt. XVII.
c. 20	Education (Scotland) Act 1976.	Apptd. day for ss. 3, 6(2) in pt., sch. 2 in pt. (16.8.1978).	S.I. No. 970.
c. 24	Development Land Tax Act 1976.	S. 13(1) am. (*retrosp.*) ...	42, s. 76.
c. 27	Theatres Trust Act 1976	Ext.	24, s. 1(1).
		S. 2(3) added	24, s. 1(2).
		S. 6(4) rep. in pt. ...	24, s. 1(3).
c. 30	Fatal Accidents Act 1976	S. 1(3) (definition of " dependent ") appl.	47, s. 6(3).
c. 32	Lotteries and Amusements Act 1976.	Pt. I (ss. 1–6 except ss. 5(3)(*d*)(ii), 6(2)(*c*)), Pt. II (ss. 7–13 except ss. 9, 12(5)(*a*)) devolved (S.) (*prosp.*), s. 18(1)(*e*) (2) not devolved (S.) (*prosp.*).	51, s. 63, sch. 10 Pt. III.
c. 34	Restrictive Trade Practices Act 1976.	Excl. (*retrosp.*)	1, s. 1(2).
		S. 16(3)(5) excl. ...	27, s. 2(5).
		S. 33 transfer of functions (W.).	S.I. No. 272.
		S. 43(1) (definition of " agreement ") appl.	1, s. 1(6).
c. 36	Adoption Act 1976	Ss. 3–5, 8, 9, transfer of functions (*prosp.*).	52, s. 9(1), sch. 2 Pt. VI.
		Ss. 22, 23 rep. (S.) (*prosp.*)	28, s. 66(3), sch. 4.
		S. 26(1) rep. in pt. (*prosp.*)	22, ss. 72(2), 89, sch. 3.

Session and Chap. or No. of Measure	Short title or Subject	How affected	Chapter of 1978 Act or number of Measure or Statutory Instrument
1976: c. 36—*cont.*	Adoption Act 1976—*cont.*	S. 28(3) am.	22, s. 89, sch. 2 para. 50.
		(10) transfer of functions (*prosp.*).	52, s. 9(1), sch. 2 Pt. VI.
		S. 32 appl. (S.) (*prosp.*)	28, s. 32(2).
		S. 51(3) rep. (S.) (*prosp.*)	28, s. 66(3), sch 4.
		S. 53(1) am.	22, s. 74(2).
		S. 57 transfer of functions (*prosp.*).	52, s. 9(1), sch. 2 Pt. VI.
		S. 63(4) rep. in pt. ...	22, s. 89, sch. 2 para. 51.
		S. 64 am.	22, s. 73(2).
		S. 64(c) rep. (*prosp.*) ...	22, s. 89, sch. 3.
		Ss. 73(2) rep. (S.) (*prosp.*), 74(3) rep. in pt. (S.) (*prosp.*).	28, s. 66(3), sch. 4.
		Sch. 1 para. 6 rep. in pt.	22, ss. 74(4), 89, sch. 3.
		Sch. 3 para. 4 rep. (*prosp.*)	22, s. 89, sch. 3.
		para. 18 am. ...	22, s. 89, sch. 2 para. 52.
		Pt. II (paras. 25–44) rep. (*prosp.*).	28, s. 66(3), sch. 4.
c. 39	Divorce (Scotland) Act 1976.	S. 5(4)(5) ext. (GB) (*prosp.*).	22, s. 60(1).
c. 40	Finance Act 1976 ...	S. 2(6) am.	42, s. 79, sch. 12 para. 5.
		S. 4(1) mod.	42, s. 1(1).
		(2) saved	42, s. 1(2).
		S. 6(4) am.	42, s. 79, sch. 12 para. 7(2).
		S. 13 rep.	42, ss. 8(2), 9(2), 80(5), sch. 13 Pt. I.
		Ss. 36(9), 41 am. ...	42, s. 30.
		Ss. 51, rep. (*retrosp.*), 52(2) rep. (4) rep. (*retrosp.*).	42, s. 80(5), sch. 13 Pt. IV.
		S. 56(1) subst.	42, s. 67, sch. 11 para. 2(1).
		(2)(a) rep. in pt. (*retrosp.*).	42, s. 80(5), sch. 13 Pt. IV.
		(6) am.	42, s. 67, sch. 11 para. 2(2).
		S. 64(2)(a) am.	S.I. No. 434.
		S. 69(1)(b)(3)(a) am. ...	42, s. 23.
		S. 73(b) rep. in pt. (*retrosp.*).	42, ss. 64(6)(7), 80(5), sch. 13 Pt. V.
		Ss. 79(1)(b)(ii), 81(4)(b) mod.	42, s. 62(6).
		S. 87(1)(a) mod. ...	42, s. 62(7).
		S. 90(2) rep.	42, ss. 67, 80(5). sch. 11 para. 3(1) sch. 13 Pt. V.
		(3) am.	42, s. 67, sch. 11 para. 3(1).

Session and Chap. or No. of Measure	Short title or Subject	How affected	Chapter of 1978 Act or number of Measure or Statutory Instrument
1976: c. 40—*cont.*	Finance Act 1976—*cont.*	S. 90 (3)(*a*)(*c*) rep. in pt.	42, s. 80(5), sch. 13 Pt. V.
		(4) am.	42, s. 67, sch. 11 para. 3(2).
		(5) appl.	42, s. 67(6).
		Sch. 4 am.	42, s. 25, sch. 3 para. 2.
		restr.	42, s. 25, sch. 3 para. 11.
		Sch. 4 para. 1 am. ...	42, s. 25, sch. 3 para. 3.
		para. 2A added ...	42, s. 25, sch. 3 para. 4.
		para. 5A added ...	42, s. 25, sch. 3 para. 5.
		para. 6 rep. ...	42, ss. 25, 80(5), sch. 3 para. 6 sch. 13 Pt. III.
		para. 13(1)(4) am.	42, s. 25, sch. 3 para. 7.
		para. 14 am, re-numbered 14(2) added	42, s. 25, sch. 3 para. 8.
		para. 14A added	42, s. 25, sch. 3 para. 9.
		para. 16(2)(*a*) re-numbered, 16(2) am.	42, s. 25, sch. 3 para. 10.
		Sch. 5 para. 6 am. ...	42, s. 30.
		para. 6(4)(7) mod.	42, s. 30(9).
		para. 31(2)(*d*) added.	42, s. 27, sch. 4 para. 7.
		Sch. 7 Tables A, B, C subst.	S.I. No. 434.
		Sch. 10 para. 1 am. (*retrosp.*).	42, s. 64(6)(7).
		rep. in pt.	42, s. 80(5), sch. 13 Pt. V.
		para. 2(1) am., (1A) added.	42, s. 64(2).
		para. 3(1)(*b*) rep. in pt.	42, s. 80(5), sch. 13 Pt. V.
		para. 3(1)(*bb*) added.	42, s. 64(3).
		para. 3(1A) added	42, s. 64(4).
		para. 4(5) added	42, s. 64(5).
		para. 9, sch. 14 para. 19 rep.	42, s. 80(5), sch. 13 Pt. V.
c. 41	Iron and Steel (Amendment) Act 1976.	Sch. am.	41, s. 1.
c. 43	Appropriation Act 1976	Rep.	57, s. 3, sch. (C).
c. 44	Drought Act 1976 ...	Transfer of functions (*prosp.*).	52, s. 9(1), sch. 2 Pt. IX.
		Power to intervene (*prosp.*).	52, s. 63, sch. 8 Pts. III, IV.
c. 48	Parliamentary and other Pensions and Salaries Act 1976.	S. 7 rep.	29, s. 109, sch. 17.
c. 50	Domestic Violence and Matrimonial Proceedings Act 1976.	S. 2(4) am.	22, s. 89, sch. 2 para. 53.

Session and Chap. or No. of Measure	Short title or Subject	How affected	Chapter of 1978 Act or number of Measure or Statutory Instrument
1976—*cont.*			
c. 55	Agriculture (Miscellaneous Provisions) Act 1976.	Apptd. day for ss. 13, 14 (7.4.1978).	S.I. No. 402.
		Ss. 2(2), 9, 18(6) transfer of functions (W.).	S.I. No. 272.
c. 57	Local Government (Miscellaneous Provisions) Act 1976.	Pts. I (ss. 1–44), III (ss. 81–83) transfer of functions (*prosp.*).	52, s. 9(1), sch. 2 Pt. I.
c. 59	National Health Service (Vocational Training) Act 1976.	Rep.	29, s. 109, sch. 17.
c. 60	Insolvency Act 1976 ...	Apptd. day for ss. 12, 14 residue, sch. 3 residue (1.3.1978).	S.I. No. 139.
c. 63	Bail Act 1976	Apptd. day for remaining provisions (17.4.1978).	S.I. No. 132.
		Sch. 2 para. 5 rep. ...	30, s. 25(1), sch. 3.
c. 64	Valuation and Rating (Exempted Classes) (Scotland) Act 1976.	Not devolved (S.) (*prosp.*)	51, s. 63, sch. 10 Pt. III.
c. 66	Licensing (Scotland) Act 1976.	S. 50(2) rep. in pt. ...	45, S.L. (R.), s. 1(1), sch. 1 Pt. XVII.
		Ss. 54(3)(*j*), 87(3), 138(1)(*a*) not devolved (*prosp.*).	51, s. 63, sch. 10 Pt. III.
		S. 138(1)(*aa*) added (*prosp.*).	51, s. 82(2), sch. 16 para. 52.
c. 68	New Towns (Amendment) Act.	Transfer of certain functions (*prosp.*).	52, s. 9(1), sch. 2, Pt. VIII.
		S. 13(5) rep. in pt. ...	44, s. 159(3), sch. 17.
		(5)(6) am.	44, s. 159(2), sch. 16 para. 24.
c. 70	Land Drainage Act 1976	Transfer of certain functions (*prosp.*), (saving for s. 62) (*prosp.*).	52, ss. 9(1), 75, sch. 2 Pt. IX, sch. 10.
		S. 2 transfer of certain functions (W.).	S.I. No. 272.
		division of powers (*prosp.*).	52, s. 63, sch. 8 Pt. I.
		S. 3 transfer of certain functions (W.).	S.I. No. 272.
		S. 3(1)–(8) division of powers (*prosp.*).	52, s. 63, sch. 8 Pt. I.
		S. 4 transfer of certain functions (W.).	S.I. No. 272.
		division of powers (*prosp.*).	52, s. 63, sch. 8 Pt. I.
		S. 7(3) transfer of certain functions (W.).	S.I. No. 272.
		mod. (*prosp.*) ...	52, s. 63(4).
		S. 20 transfer of functions (W.).	S.I. No. 272.
		S. 23 mod (*prosp.*) ...	52, s. 63(4).
		consent of Min. required (*prosp.*).	52, s. 36(1), sch. 4.
		division of powers (*prosp.*).	52, s. 63, sch. 8 Pt. I.

Session and Chap. or No. of Measure	Short title or Subject	How affected	Chapter of 1978 Act or number of Measure or Statutory Instrument
1976: c. 70—*cont.*	Land Drainage Act 1976 —*cont.*	Ss. 23(2)(4)(5) transfer of certain functions (W.), 25 transfer of functions (W.), 26, 27 transfer of certain functions (W.), 29 transfer of functions (W.).	S.I. No. 272.
		S. 30(2)(*c*) am.	S.I. No. 319.
		Ss. 31 transfer of certain functions (W.), 36 transfer of functions (W.), 37, 38 transfer of certain functions (W.), 43 transfer of functions (W.), 46 transfer of certain functions (W.).	S.I. No. 272.
		S. 48(1) am.	S.I. No. 319.
		S. 49 transfer of certain functions (W.).	S.I. No. 272.
		S. 49(1) am.	S.I. No. 319.
		(1)(*b*) division of powers (*prosp.*).	52, s. 63, sch. 8 Pt. I.
		Ss. 50, 51 transfer of certain functions (W.).	S.I. No. 272.
		Ss. 51(2), 52(1) am. ...	S.I. No. 319.
		Ss. 53, 60 transfer of certain functions (W.).	S.I. No. 272.
		Ss. 60(5), 62 division of powers (*prosp.*).	52, s. 63, sch. 8 Pt. I.
		Ss. 62(1)(4)(5), 68 transfer of certain functions (W.).	S.I. No. 272.
		S. 68 mod. (*prosp.*) ...	52, s. 63(4).
		S. 69 transfer of certain functions (W.).	S.I. No. 272.
		Ss. 69–74 mod. (*prosp.*) ...	52, s. 63(4).
		S. 75 transfer of certain functions (W.).	S.I. No. 272..
		Ss. 75, 76 mod. (*prosp.*) ...	52, s. 63(4).
		S. 77 transfer of certain functions (W.).	S.I. No. 272.
		mod. (*prosp.*) ...	52, s. 63(4).
		S. 78 transfer of functions (W.).	S.I. No. 272.
		mod. (*prosp.*). ...	52, s. 63(4).
		Ss. 81(4), 84 transfer of certain functions (W.).	S.I. No. 272.
		S. 84 mod. (*prosp.*) ...	52, s. 63(4).
		Ss. 85–87 transfer of certain functions (W.).	S.I. No. 272.
		mod. (*prosp.*)	52, s. 63(4).
		Ss. 90–93 transfer of functions (W.), 94 transfer of certain functions (W.).	S.I. No. 272.
		S. 94 mod. (*prosp.*) ...	52, s. 63(4).
		division of powers (*prosp.*).	52, s. 62, sch. 8 Pt. I.

Session and Chap. or No. of Measure	Short title or Subject	How affected	Chapter of 1978 Act or number of Measure or Statutory Instrument
1976: c. 70—*cont.*	Land Drainage Act 1976 —*cont.*	Ss. 95, 96 transfer of certain functions (W.), 98(1)(2)(12) transfer of functions (W.).	S.I. No. 272.
		S. 116(1) am.	S.I. No. 319.
		Sch. 1 division of powers (*prosp.*).	52, s. 63, sch. 8 Pt. I.
		Sch. 1 paras. 4, 10 transfer of certain functions (W.).	S.I. No. 272.
		Sch. 2 mod. (*prosp.*) ...	52, s. 63(4).
		Sch. 2 Pt. I transfer of certain functions (W.).	S.I. No. 272.
		Sch. 2 para. 1(1)(*a*)(*b*)(*d*) am.	S.I. No. 319.
		Sch. 3 para. 1 transfer of functions (W.), sch. 4 transfer of certain functions (W.).	S.I. No. 272.
¬. 71	Supplementary Benefits Act 1976.	S. 18 excl.	44, s. 132(4).
		S. 18(7) rep. in pt. (*prosp.*)	22, s. 89, sch. 3.
		S. 19(2) am. (*prosp.*) ...	22, s. 89, sch. 2 para. 54.
		S. 20 excl.	44, s. 132(4).
		S. 34(1) (definition of " supplementary benefit ") appl.	44, s. 132(6).
		Sch. 1 paras. 7, 8 subst., 10(1)(*a*)(*b*) am.	S.I. No. 913.
		para. 23 am. ...	S.I. No. 1526.
		Sch. 7 para. 4 rep. in pt. (*prosp.*).	22, s. 89, sch. 3.
		para. 40 rep. ...	44, s. 159(3), sch. 17.
c. 72	Endangered Species (Import and Export) Act 1976.	Sch. 1 Pt. I rep. in pt., Pt. II, sch. 2 am., sch. 3 paras. 5–22 replaced.	S.I. No. 1939.
c. 74	Race Relations Act 1976	Appl.	44, s. 71(3)(*c*).
		Not devolved (S.) (*prosp.*)	51, s. 63, sch. 10 Pt. III.
		Pt. II (ss. 4–16) appl. (mods.) (*prosp.*).	51, s. 33(3)(4).
		S. 8(5) ext.	46, s. 1(2).
		S. 19(2) transfer of functions (*prosp.*).	52, s. 9(1), sch. 2 Pt. III.
		(3), (5) transfer of certain functions (S.) (*prosp.*).	51, s. 63, sch. 11 Group H.
		Pt. IV (ss. 28–33) appl. (mods.) (*prosp.*).	51, s. 33(3)(4).
		S. 56(2) am.	44, s. 159(2), sch. 16 para. 25.
		S. 57(5) transfer of functions (*prosp.*).	52, s. 9(1), sch. 2 Pt. III.
		transfer of certain functions (S.) (*prosp.*).	51, s. 63, sch. 11 Group H.
		S. 66(7), sch. 2 para. 11(3) am., (4)(*a*)(*b*) replaced.	44, s. 159(2), sch. 16 para. 25.
		Sch. 3 para. 1(2)–(4) rep.	44, s. 159(3), sch. 17.

Session and Chap. or No. of Measure	Short title or Subject	How affected	Chapter of 1978 Act or number of Measure or Statutory Instrument
1976—*cont.*			
c. 75	Development of Rural Wales Act 1976.	Transfer of certain functions (*prosp.*) (saving for s. 6(2)(*a*), sch. 3 paras. 2, 16, 44, 46) (*prosp.*).	52, ss. 9(1), 75, sch. 2 Pt. VIII, sch. 10.
		Am. (*prosp.*)	52, ss. 55(2), 56, sch. 6.
		S. 3(1)(*e*) rep. in pt. (*prosp.*), am. (*prosp.*), (8) am. (*prosp.*).	52, s. 77(1), sch. 11 para. 82.
		Sch. 1 para. 17 subst. (*prosp.*).	52, s. 77(1), sch. 11 para. 83.
		Sch. 2 para. 6 am. ...	44, s. 159(2), sch. 16 para. 26.
		Sch. 3 paras. 44(6)(7), 46(4) consent of Min. required (*prosp.*).	52, s. 36(1), sch. 4.
		Sch. 6 para. 6 am. ...	44, s. 159(2), sch. 16 para. 26.
c. 76	Energy Act 1976 ...	S. 21 (definition of "petroleum products") appl.	1, s. 1(6).
c. 79	Dock Work Regulation Act 1976.	Not devolved (S.) (*prosp.*)	51, s. 63, sch. 10 Pt. III.
		S. 14(1)–(5), (6)(*a*) rep., (*b*) rep. in pt.	44, s. 159(3), sch. 17.
		S. 14(7), sch. 1 para. 17(1) am.	44, s. 159(2), sch. 16 para. 27.
		para. 17(2) rep.	44, s. 159(3), sch. 17.
c. 80	Rent (Agriculture) Act 1976.	Transfer of certain functions (*prosp.*).	52, s. 9(1), sch. 2 Pt. IV.
		Ss. 29–31, sch. 3 para. 12 transfer of functions (W.).	S.I. No. 272.
c. 81	Education Act 1976 ...	Transfer of functions (*prosp.*).	52, s. 9(1), sch. 2 Pt. III.
c. 82	Sexual Offences (Amendment) Act 1976.	Apptd. day for ss. 5(1)(*b*), 6(4)(*b*) (22.4.1978).	S.I. No. 485.
c. 83	Health Services Act 1976	Ss. 2, 4, 5, 7–11 rep. ...	29, s. 109, sch. 17.
		S. 14(5) mod. (*prosp.*) ...	52, s. 77(1), sch. 11 para. 84.
		S. 23(1) rep. in pt., (3)(4) sch. 1 Pt. VI, sch. 3 rep.	29, s. 109, sch. 17.
c. 84	Consolidated Fund (No. 2) Act 1976.	Rep.	57, s. 3, sch. (C).
c. 85	National Insurance Surcharge Act 1976.	S. 1(1) am.	42, s. 75.
c. 86	Fishery Limits Act 1976	Transfer of functions (W.)	S.I. No. 272.
G.S.M.:			
No. 1 ...	Cathedrals Measure 1976	Appl. (mods.)	G.S.M. No. 1 s. 22(1).
No. 3 ...	Church of England (Miscellaneous Provisions) Measure 1976.	S. 3 appl.	G.S.M. No. 2 s. 23.
No. 4 ...	Endowments and Glebe Measure 1976.	S. 3(3) am.	G.S.M. No. 3 s. 11(1).
		S. 43 am.	G.S.M. No. 3 s. 11(2).

Session and Chap. or No. of Measure	Short title or Subject	How affected	Chapter of 1978 Act or number of Measure or Statutory Instrument
1977:			
c. 3	Aircraft and Shipbuilding Industries Act 1977.	Ss. 49(10), 50(3)(*b*) am.	44, s. 159(3), sch. 16 para. 28.
c. 5	Social Security (Miscellaneous Provisions) Act 1977.	S. 13(3)(*a*) am. (S.) ...	29, s. 109, sch. 16 para. 44.
		S. 16 rep.	44, s. 159(3) sch. 17.
		S. 18(1)(*c*)(2)(*a*)(*b*)(*e*) am.	44 s. 159(2), sch. 16 para. 29.
c. 6	International Finance, Trade and Aid Act 1977.	S. 4 rep.	18, s. 16(2), sch.
		Ss. 5, 6 rep.	2, s. 18(1), sch. 2.
		Sch. 1 rep.	18, s. 16(2), sch.
c. 12	Agricultural Holdings (Notices to Quit) Act 1977.	Apptd. day for whole Act (7.4.1978).	S.I. No. 256.
		Transfer of functions (W.)	S.I. No. 272.
c. 13	British Airways Board Act 1977.	S. 9(1) am.	8, s. 5(3)(*a*).
		S. 18 rep. and superseded	8, ss. 12, 14(2), sch. 2.
		S. 21(2) am.	8, s. 5(3)(*b*).
		S. 21(3) rep. in pt. ...	8, s. 14(1)(2), sch. 1 Pt. I para. 8, sch. 2.
c. 14	Returning Officers (Scotland) Act 1977.	Appl. (mods.)	S.I. No. 1912.
c. 16	New Towns (Scotland) Act 1977.	S. 3(6) am.	44, s. 159(2), sch. 16 para. 30.
c. 21	Passenger Vehicles (Experimental Areas) Act 1977.	Transfer of functions (*prosp.*).	52, s. 9(1), sch. 2 Pt. XIV.
		Act (except s. 2(3)(8)) devolved (S.) (*prosp.*), s. 2(8) devolved in pt. (S.) (*prosp.*).	51, s. 63, sch. 10 Pt. III.
c. 22	Redundancy Rebates Act 1977.	Rep.	44, s. 159(3), sch. 17.
c. 25	Minibus Act 1977 ...	Transfer of certain functions (*prosp.*).	52, s. 9(1), sch. 2 Pt. XIV.
		Act (except ss. 1, 3(1)(*a*)) not devolved (S.) (*prosp.*).	51, s. 63, sch. 10 Pt. III.
		S. 1(5) rep.	55, s. 24(4), sch. 4.
c. 27	Presumption of Death (Scotland) Act 1977.	Apptd. day for whole Act (1.3.1978).	S.I. No. 159.
c. 28	Control of Food Premises (Scotland) Act 1977.	Apptd. day for whole Act (16.3.1978).	S.I. No. 172.
c. 30	Rentcharges Act 1977 ...	Apptd. day for remaining provisions (1.2.1978).	S.I. No. 15.
		Transfer of certain functions (*prosp.*).	52, s. 9(1), sch. 2 Pt. IV.
c. 32	Torts (Interference with Goods) Act 1977.	Apptd. day for remaining provisions (E. & W.) (1.6.1978).	S.I. No. 627.
c. 33	Price Commission Act 1977.	Not devolved (S.) (*prosp.*)	51, s. 63, sch. 10 Pt. III.
		Sch. 2 para. 2 rep. in pt.	54, s. 1(2).
c. 34	Northern Ireland (Emergency Provisions) (Amendment) Act 1977.	Rep.	5, s. 35(3), sch. 6 Pt. I.

Session and Chap. or No. of Measure	Short title or Subject	How affected	Chapter of 1978 Act or number of Measure or Statutory Instrument
1977—*cont.*			
c. 36	Finance Act 1977 ...	S. 2(2) am.	42, s. 1(3).
		S. 13 rep.	42, s. 80(5), sch. 13 Pt. I.
		S. 15 rep.	42, s. 80(5), sch. 13 Pt. II.
		Ss. 21, 22(1)(*a*)(*b*) rep., (*c*) rep. in pt., (*d*) rep., (3) rep. in pt.	42, s. 80(5), sch. 13 Pt. III.
		S. 23(3) cont., am. ...	42, s. 20(4).
		S. 24 rep.	42, s. 80(5), sch. 13 Pt. III.
		S. 25 cont.	42, s. 20(5).
		Ss. 26(5), 28 rep., 35(3) rep. in pt.	42, s. 80(5), sch. 13 Pt. III.
		S. 44(1) rep. (6.4.1979), (2) rep. (*retrosp.*), (3)–(5) rep.	42, s. 80(5), sch. 13 Pt. IV.
c. 37	Patents Act 1977 ...	Apptd. day for specified provisions (1.6.1978).	S.I. No. 586.
		S. 55 am. (*prosp.*) ...	51, s. 82(2), sch. 16 para. 53.
		mod. (*prosp.*) ...	52, s. 77(1), sch. 11 para. 85.
		Ss. 55(4) mod. (*prosp.*), 56 am. (*prosp.*).	51, s. 82(2), sch. 16 para. 53.
		S. 56 mod. (*prosp.*) ...	52, s. 77(1), sch. 11 para. 85.
		S. 56(4)(*a*) am.	29, s. 109, sch. 16 para. 45.
		Ss. 57–59 am. (*prosp.*) ...	51, s. 82(2), sch. 16 para. 53.
		mod. (*prosp.*)...	52, s. 77(1), sch. 11 para. 85.
c. 38	Administration of Justice Act 1977.	Apptd. day for s. 19(2), (3), (5) (3.7.1978).	S.I. No. 810.
		S. 6 rep.	44, s. 159(3), sch. 17.
		Ss. 8, 32(2) rep. ...	19, s. 7(1), sch. Pt. I.
		S. 32(11) rep.	44, s. 159(3), sch. 17.
		Sch. 2 Pt. III para. 12 rep. (*prosp.*).	23, s. 122(2), sch. 7 Pt. I.
c. 42	Rent Act 1977 ...	Transfer of certain functions (*prosp.*).	52, s. 9(1), sch. 2 Pt. IV.
		Sch. 23 para. 21 rep. ...	45, S.L. (R.), s. 1(1), sch. 1 Pt. XII.
c. 43	Protection from Eviction Act 1977.	S. 5 transfer of functions (*prosp.*).	52, s. 9(1), sch. 2 Pt. IV.
c. 45	Criminal Law Act 1977	Apptd. day for s. 62 (19.6.1978) other specified provisions (E., W., N.I.) (17.7.1978)	S.I. No. 712.
		for specified provisions (S.) (17.7.1978)	S.I. No. 900.
		S. 27 ext.	42, s. 79, sch. 12 para. 24.
		mod. (N.I.) ...	42, s. 79, sch. 12 para. 24(2).

Session and Chap. or No. of Measure	Short title or Subject	How affected	Chapter of 1978 Act or number of Measure or Statutory Instrument
1977:			
c. 45—*cont.*	Criminal Law Act 1977 —*cont.*	S. 28 ext.	25, s. 2(6).
		ext. appl.	38, ss. 9(4), 11(*g*).
		appl.	8, s. 7(*a*).
		S. 28(2)(7) ext. ...	42, s. 79, sch. 12 para. 24.
		S. 28(7) appl.	44, ss. 104(10)(*a*), 107(5)(*a*).
		Ss. 28(8), 31(5)(6)(8)(9) (11), 32(1), 61 ext.	42, s. 79, sch. 12 para. 24.
		S. 64(1) rep. in pt. ...	30, s. 25(1), sch. 3.
		Sch. 12 rep. in pt. (S.) (*prosp.*).	28, s. 66(3), sch. 4.
c. 46	Insurance Brokers (Registration) Act 1977.	Apptd day for ss. 2–5, 9, 13–18, 19(1)–(3), 20 (20.10.1978).	S.I. No. 1393.
c. 48	Housing (Homeless Persons) Act 1977.	Transfer of functions (*prosp.*).	52, s. 9(1), sch. 2 Pt. IV.
		S. 14(4)(*a*)(*b*) am. ...	44, s. 159(2), sch. 16 para. 31.
		S. 14(4)(*b*) rep. in pt. ...	44, s. 159(2)(3), sch. 16 para. 31(*b*), sch. 17.
c. 49	National Health Service Act 1977.	Transfer of certain functions (*prosp.*).	52, s. 9(1), sch. 2 Pt. VI.
		S. 8(1) appl.	44, s. 29(2)(*b*).
		Ss. 29, 34–43 mod. (*prosp.*).	52, ss. 9(1), 77(1), sch. 2 Pt. VI sch. 11 para. 86.
		S. 111(1)(*b*) subst. (*prosp.*)	52, s. 77(1), sch. 11 para. 87.
		S. 119(1)(*d*) am. (*prosp.*) (3)(4) mod. (*prosp.*).	52, s. 77(1), sch. 11 para. 88.
		S. 128(1) (definition of "illness") appl. (1.4. 1979)	40, s. 2(3).
		Sch. 4 para. 1(1) subst., (2)(*a*) am.	S.I. No. 489.
		Sch. 5 para. 10(1) mod. (*prosp.*).	52, ss. 9(1), 77(1), sch. 2 Pt. VI sch. 11 para. 86.
		Sch. 13 para. 17 am. (*prosp.*).	52, s. 77(1), sch. 11 para. 89.
		Sch. 14 para. 13(1)(*b*) am.	44, s. 159(2), sch. 16 para. 32.
		rep.	45, S.L. (R.), s. 1(1), sch. 1 Pt. XVII.
		in pt. sch. 15 para. 11 rep.	
		Sch. 15 para. 39 rep. (1.4.1979).	40, s. 9(3), sch. 2.
		para. 68 rep.	45, S.L. (R.), s. 1(1), sch. 1 Pt. XVII.
c. 50	Unfair Contract Terms Act 1977.	S. 30 rep. (*prosp.*) ...	38, s. 10(1), sch. 3.
c. 51	Pensioners Payments Act 1977.	Am. (saving)	58, s. 1.

Session and Chap. or No. of Measure	Short title or Subject	How affected	Chapter of 1978 Act or number of Measure or Statutory Instrument
1977:—*cont.*			
c. 53	Finance (Income Tax Relief) Act 1977.	S. 1 rep.	42, s. 80(5), sch. 13 Pt. III.
1978:			
c. 3	Refuse Disposal (Amenity) Act 1978.	Transfer of certain functions (*prosp.*).	52, s. 9(1), sch. 2 Pt. VII.
		S. 4(2) not devolved (S.) (*prosp.*).	51, s. 63, sch. 10 Pt. III.
c. 5	Northern Ireland (Emergency Provisions) Act 1978.	Ss. 2(1)(*a*), 3(1) am. (*prosp.*), 6 subst. (*prosp.*), 7(6), 33(5)(7) am. (*prosp.*).	23, s. 122(1), sch. 5 Pt. II(1).
		S. 34(1) rep. (*prosp.*) ...	23, s. 122(2), sch. 7 Pt. I.
c. 8	Civil Aviation Act 1978	Apptd. days for ss. 1(1), (3)–(5), 2, 3, 13, 16 (23.3.1978), 1(2) (1.4. 1978), remaining provisions (1.5.1978).	S.I. No. 486.
		Ss. 8, 9 not devolved (S.) (*prosp.*).	51, s. 63, sch. 10 Pt. III.
c. 9	Gun Barrel Proof Act 1978.	Apptd. day for specified provisions (1.12.1978).	S.I. No. 1587.
c. 12	Medical Act 1978 ...	Apptd. days for specified provisions (23.8.1978) (1.12.1978) (15.2.1979).	S.I. No. 1035.
		Sch. 6 para. 48 rep. in pt.	30, s. 25(1), sch. 3.
c. 15	Solomon Islands Act 1978	S. 7(1) rep.	30, s. 25(1), sch. 3.
c. 20	Tuvalu Act 1978 ...	S. 4(1) rep.	30, s. 25(1), sch. 3.
c. 22	Domestic Proceedings and Magistrates' Courts Act 1978.	Apptd. day for specified provisions (18.7.1978).	S.I. No. 997.
		for (E., W., N.I.) (20.11. 1978).	S.I. No. 1489.
		for (S.) (23.10.1978) ...	S.I. No. 1490.
		Pt. I (ss. 1–35) appl. (mods.) (*prosp.*).	22, s. 58.
		Ss. 74(1)(3) rep. (S.) (*prosp.*), 90(2) rep. in pt. (*prosp.*), sch. 2 paras. 17, 18 rep. (S.) (*prosp.*).	28, s. 66(3), sch. 4.
c. 23	Judicature (Northern Ireland) Act 1978.	Apptd. day for specified provisions (21.8.1978).	S.I. No. 1101.
		(2.1.1979)...	S.I. No. 1829.
		S. 53(1)(*e*) subst. (*temp.*)	S.I. No. 1101.
c. 26	Suppression of Terrorism Act 1978.	Apptd. day for whole Act (21.8.1978).	S.I. No. 1063.
		S. 4(2) rep. (*prosp.*), (4) (5) am. (*prosp.*), (6) rep. (*prosp.*).	17, s. 5(4).
c. 27	Home Purchase Assistance and Housing Corporation Guarantee Act 1978.	Apptd. day for ss. 1–3 (1.12.1978).	S.I. No. 1412.
		Ss. 1, 2(2)–(4) transfer of certain functions (*prosp.*).	52, s. 9(1), sch. 2 Pt. IV.
		Sch. Pt. II am.	S.I. No. 1785.

Session and Chap. or No. of Measure	Short title or Subject	How affected	Chapter of 1978 Act or number of Measure or Statutory Instrument
1978:—*cont.*			
c. 29	National Health Service (Scotland) Act 1978.	S. 108(1) (definition of " illness ") appl. (1.4. 1979).	40, s. 5(3).
c. 33	State Immunity Act 1978	Apptd. day for whole Act (22.11.1978).	S.I. No. 1572.
c. 36	House of Commons (Administration) Act 1978.	Sch. 2 para. 1 am. ...	44, s. 159(2), sch. 16 para. 34.
c. 38	Consumer Safety Act 1978.	Apptd. day for whole Act except s. 10 pt., sch. 3 (1.11.1978).	S.I. No. 1445.
c. 44	Employment Protection (Consolidation) Act 1978.	Pts. I (ss. 1–7), II (ss. 12–32) appl. (mods.) (*prosp.*).	51, s. 33(1)(2)(4).
		S. 15(1) am.	S.I. No. 1777.
		Pts. III (ss. 33–48 except s. 44), V (ss. 54–80) appl. (mods.) (*prosp.*).	51, s. 33(1)(2)(4).
		S. 75(1) am.	S.I. No. 1778.
		S. 122(5) am.	S.I. No. 1777.
		Pts. VIII (ss. 128–136), IX (ss. 137–160) appl. (mods.) (*prosp.*).	51, s. 33(1)(2)(4).
		Sch. 9 para. 1(5)(*c*) appl. (mods.) (*prosp.*).	51, s. 33(3)(4).
		Sch. 14 para. 8(1)(*a*)(*b*)(*c*) am.	S.I. No. 1777.
c. 50	Inner Urban Areas Act 1978.	Not devolved (S.) (*prosp.*)	51, s. 63, sch. 10 Pt. III.
		S. 1 transfer of functions (*prosp.*).	52, s. 9(1), sch. 2 Pt. VIII.
		transfer of functions (S.) (*prosp.*).	51, s. 63, sch. 11 Group E para. 11(*a*).
		S. 2(4)(*b*) mod. (*prosp.*)	51, s. 82(2), sch. 16 para. 54(1). 52, s. 77(1), sch. 11 para. 90(1).
		S. 2(4)(*b*) pt. transfer of functions (*prosp.*).	52, s. 9(1), sch. 2 Pt. VIII.
		S. 3(2) transfer of certain functions (S.) (*prosp.*).	51, s. 63, sch. 11 Group E para. 11(*b*).
		Ss. 3(2) pt., 7 transfer of functions (*prosp.*).	52, s. 9(1), sch. 2 Pt. VIII.
		S. 7(1) transfer of functions (S.) (*prosp.*).	51, s. 63, sch. 11 Group E para. 11(*a*).
		S. 8 transfer of functions (*prosp.*).	52, s. 9(1), sch. 2 Pt. VIII.
		consent of Min. required (*prosp.*).	52, s. 36(1), sch. 4.
		S. 8(1) am. (*prosp.*) ...	51, s. 23(1)(2), sch. 4.
		transfer of functions (S.) (*prosp.*).	51, s. 63, sch. 11 Group E para. 11(*a*).
		S. 9(6) transfer of functions (*prosp.*).	52, s. 9(1), sch. 2 Pt. VIII.
		transfer of functions (S.) (*prosp.*).	51, s. 63, sch. 11 Group E para. 11(*a*).

Session and Chap. or No. of Measure	Short title or Subject	How affected	Chapter of 1978 Act or number of Measure or Statutory Instrument
1978: c. 50—*cont.*	Inner Urban Areas Act 1978—*cont.*	S. 12 transfer of functions (*prosp.*).	52, s. 9(1), sch. 2 Pt. VIII.
		Sch. para. 1(3)(*b*) mod. (*prosp.*).	51, s. 82(2), sch. 16 para. 54(2). 52, s. 77(1), sch. 11 para. 90(2).
		Sch. para. 2 am. (*prosp.*)	51, s. 23(3), sch. 5.
		transfer of functions (*prosp.*).	52, s. 9(1), sch. 2 Pt. VIII.
		concurrent powers of Min. (*prosp.*).	52, s. 9(2), sch. 3.
		transfer of functions (S.) (*prosp.*).	51, s. 63, sch. 11 Group E para. 11(*a*).
		Sch. para. 3(3)(*b*) mod. (*prosp.*).	51, s. 82(2), sch. 16 para. 54(2). 52, s. 77(1), sch. 11 para. 90(2).
c. 51	Scotland Act 1978 ...	S. 33(1)(*a*) replaced (1)(2) am.	44, s. 159(2), sch. 16 para. 33.
c. 55	Transport Act 1978 ...	Apptd. days for specified provisions (4.8.1978) (1.9.1978) (1.11.1978).	S.I. No. 1150. S.I. No. 1187.
		for ss. 19, 20 (1.10.1978).	S.I. No. 1289.
		Devolved in pt. (S.) (*prosp.*).	51, s. 63, sch. 10 Pt. III.
		S. 3(5)(*b*) transfer of functions (*prosp.*).	52, s. 9(1), sch. 2 Pt. XIV.
G.S.M.: No. 2... ...	Parochial Registers and Records Measure 1978.	S. 20(2)(*b*) subst. (5) am.	G.S.M. No. 3 s. 6.

TABLE VII

Table of Textual Amendments of Acts and Measures (in chronological order), showing those provisions which were amended or partially repealed by Statutory Instruments made during 1978

(*Note: Total repeals of sections, subsections or paragraphs are noted in the Table of Effect of Legislation (Table VI) above. Reference should also be made to the relevant statutory instrument for any transitional provisions and savings relating to the amendments listed below.*)

Number of Statutory Instrument of 1978	Act or Measure and how amended
No. 639 (local). *Art. 16, Sch. 2.*	PLATE ASSAY (SHEFFIELD AND BIRMINGHAM) ACT 1772 (c. 52) In s. 2 omit the words following " The Guardians of the Standard of Wrought Plate ". In s. 8 omit the words following " in pursuance of this Act ".
No. 844 (local). *Art. 3, Sch.*	MANCHESTER POLICE REGULATION ACT 1844 (c. xl) In s. 187 for the sum of 25p substitute " £8 ".
No. 1050 (N.I.). *Art. 77(3), Sch. 10 (prosp.— see Art. 1).*	DEFENCE ACT 1859 (c. 12) In s. 6 omit from " or as provided " onwards.
No. 1823 (local). *Art. 3(1).*	HARTLEPOOL GAS AND WATER ACT 1867 (c. xxxii) In s. 45 for the word " six " substitute " seven ".
Art. 3(2).	After s. 50 insert:— " Change of financial year. 50A. If by resolution passed before 31st December in any year the directors so determine, the accounts of the Company shall be made up in respect of the period of 15 months from 1st January in that year to 31st March in the next succeeding year; and thereafter the accounts of the Company shall be made up in respect of the period from 1st April in any year to 31st March in the next succeeding year; and, as from the end of the said period of 15 months, the following provisions of this section shall have effect:— (*a*) for the purposes of section 14 of the Companies Clauses Act 1863(a) as incorporated in this Act or in any other Act relating to the Company the prescribed day shall be 31st March; (*b*) the expression " year " where used in any local enactment relating to the Company shall mean a year ending on 31st March.

Number of Statutory Instrument of 1978	Act or Measure and how amended
	Dividend on ordinary stock. 50B. If the accounts of the Company are made up under section 50A (Change of financial year) of this Act then, notwithstanding anything contained in section 50 (Directors may declare dividends half yearly) of this Act the directors may declare and pay a dividend on the ordinary stock of the Company in respect of the three months concluding the account period of 15 months referred to in the said section 50A."
No. 270.	EXPLOSIVES ACT 1875 (c. 17)
Reg. 2(1).	In s. 15 (as amended by S.I. 1968/170, 248 and 1969 c. 19) for " £2·25 " substitute " £17·50 ".
Reg. 2(2).	In s. 18 (as amended by S.I. 1970/1954 (E., W.) and S.I. 1968/248 (S.)) for " 63p " (E., W.) and " s.12.6d " (S.) substitute " £17·50 " in each case.
No. 440.	NEW FOREST ACT 1877 (c. cxxi)
Art. 6.	In s. 38, second paragraph, for the words following " appointed by " substitute " the County Council of Hampshire, and there shall be paid to such auditor in respect of his services by the verderers such sum as may be fixed by the said council ". In the third paragraph of s. 38 for " the county of Southampton " substitute " the county of Hampshire ". In sch. 3, the third paragraph, for " The sheriff of the county of Southampton " substitute " The high sheriff of Hampshire ".
No. 252 (S.).	VALUATION OF LANDS (SCOTLAND) AMENDMENT ACT 1879 (c. 42)
Reg. 16.	In s. 9 for the words " copy of any evidence taken as aforesaid " substitute " transcript of any evidence recorded at the hearing of such appeal or complaint ".
No. 1030	MERCHANT SHIPPING ACT 1894 (c. 60)
Art. 6, Sch., para. 6.	In s. 427(2) (as set out in 1949 c. 43, s. 2) before the words " or in any " insert " , Dominica or St. Lucia ".
No. 1899 *Art. 4, Sch., para. 6.*	
No. 639 (local).	SHEFFIELD ASSAY ACT 1906 (c. ix)
Art. 15(1) (a)(c).	In s. 3(1) omit the words following " the said fund ". In subs. (3) of s. 3 for the words following " invested " substitute:— " in the purchase of any investments or property of any description either real or personal and wheresoever situate, and whether or not being investments or property authorised by law for the investment of trust funds, or upon loan upon the security of any property of any description or without security."
Art. 15(2).	In s. 4 omit the words " not exceeding in quantity two acres ".
Art. 15(3).	In s. 5 for the words " necessary to make it up o en thousand pounds " substitute " thought fit ".

Number of Statutory Instrument of 1978	Act or Measure and how amended
	In the same section, for the first head beginning " To the payment of gratuities " substitute:— " To payments for the purposes mentioned in article 12 (Pensions, employees' clubs, etc.) of the Sheffield Assay Office Order 1978 ". After the last head beginning " To the payment of donations " insert:— " In this section any reference to gold or silver plate or to gold and silver plate shall include reference to precious metal as defined in section 22 of the Hallmarking Act 1973 ".
No. 1387 (E., W.). *Art 3.*	CINEMATOGRAPH ACT 1909 (c. 30) In s. 2(5) (as amended by S.I. 1968/170, 248 and 1969 c. 19 s. 10) for the sum of £5 in both places where it occurs, and for " £1·25 " in both places where it occurs, substitute " £15 " and " £3·75 " respectively.
No. 1545 (S.). *Art 3.*	
No. 1540 (local). *Art. 2(1).*	PILOTAGE ORDER (LONDON) CONFIRMATION ACT 1913 (c. clxv) For paragraph 4(1) and (3) of the Schedule substitute:— " *4.*—(1) There shall be constituted in accordance with the provisions contained in the Appendix to this Order a Pilotage Committee of the Trinity House for the London Pilotage District (to be known as the Trinity House London Pilotage Committee and in this Order referred to as " the Pilotage Committee ") consisting of persons appointed by the Trinity House and of representatives of shipowners, pilots and port authorities." " (3) The Trinity House shall delegate to the Pilotage Committee all their powers or duties under the Pilotage Act 1913, in respect of the London Pilotage District, except as follows:— (*a*) the provision of all pilot vessels, buildings and equipment necessary to the organisation and maintenance of the pilotage services in the Pilotage District; (*b*) control of the Trinity House Pilot Fund and Trinity House Cutter Fund; (*c*) the sealing of any document relating to the pilotage services in the Pilotage District; (*d*) the employment or dismissal of any employee of the Trinity House and any matter affecting such employee's terms and conditions of employment. The decisions of the Pilotage Committee on matters so delegated shall not require confirmation by the Trinity House but the Pilotage Committee shall report its proceedings to the Trinity House."
Art. 2(2).	For paragraphs 1 to 10 inclusive of the Appendix to the Schedule substitute:— " *1.* The Pilotage Committee shall consist of:— (1) Three persons appointed by the Trinity House from the serving Elder Brethren; (2) One person appointed annually by the Port of London Authority; (3) Two persons appointed by Dover Harbour Board, Harwich Harbour Conservancy Board and Medway Ports Authority on a rota basis, so that in each period of three years from the 10th December following the commencement of this Order the representatives for the first year shall be appointed by the Harwich Harbour Board and the Medway Ports Authority, those for the second year by Harwich Harbour Board and Dover Harbour Board, and those for the third year by Dover Harbour Board and Medway Ports Authority;

Number of Statutory Instrument of 1978	Act or Measure and how amended

(4) Five persons representative of shipowners appointed annually by the London General Shipowners' Society or if at any time such body shall in the opinion of the Secretary of State cease to be representative of the shipowners using the ports within the London Pilotage District, then by the General Council of British Shipping or such other body or bodies representing shipowners as shall be nominated by the Secretary of State;

(5) Five persons elected by pilots in the manner hereinafter appearing;

(6) The Chairman of the Pilotage Committee shall be one of the three persons appointed under sub-paragraph (1) above and he shall be elected annually by the Pilotage Committee. In the case of an equality of votes on a question at a meeting of the Pilotage Committee, the person presiding as Chairman of the meeting shall have a second or casting vote.

2. The Dover Harbour Board, the Harwich Harbour Conservancy Board, the Felixstowe Dock and Railway Company, the British Railways Board and the Medway Port Authority may raise with the Committee any matters that affect their areas, and a representative of the port authority concerned may (at the discretion of the Chairman of the Committee or of the Committee itself) attend any relevant meeting of the Committee and take part in the proceedings when they affect its area; but such a representative shall not have the right to vote.

3. The pilots licensed for the London Pilotage District (hereinafter referred to as " licensed pilots ") shall in each year elect five persons (hereinafter referred to as " pilots' representatives ") being one from each of the Inward (North), Inward (South), Channel, River Thames and River Medway Stations who may attend and vote at meetings of and serve upon the Pilotage Committee as members thereof.

4. Every pilots' representative to be elected as aforesaid shall be a licensed pilot. The meeting for election of pilots' representatives shall take place on or within seven days after the first day of December in each year at a time and place to be fixed by the Town Clerk of the City of London, and advertised by him 10 days at least, or in his default by a person to be appointed for the purpose by the Secretary of State, five days at least, before the day appointed for such meeting in one or more of the newspapers published and circulating in the City of London.

5. With respect to the election of the pilots' representatives the following provisions shall have effect, that is to say:—

(1) The Lord Mayor of London for the time being, or a person nominated by him or if the Lord Mayor is unwilling to act or nominate such a person, a person nominated by the Secretary of State, shall be the Chairman of the meeting and the Returning Officer;

(2) Every licensed pilot shall be entitled to attend the meeting and take part and vote in the election;

(3) Every candidate shall at the meeting be nominated and seconded by licensed pilots, and if the number of persons so nominated does not exceed the number of persons to be elected the persons so nominated shall be deemed to be duly elected, but if the number of persons nominated exceeds the number to be elected the election shall be decided by the majority of votes;

(4) Every licensed pilot present or represented at any election shall be entitled to one vote which shall only be cast for a candidate from his own Station except that a pilot from a Station other than those enumerated in paragraph 3 of this Appendix may vote for any candidate;

Number of Statutory Instrument of 1978	Act or Measure and how amended

	(5) Any licensed pilot not present at any election may by writing under his hand appoint another licensed pilot as proxy to represent him, provided that all instruments in writing appointing such proxy shall be lodged with the Town Clerk of the City of London not less than 48 hours before the time appointed for the meeting;
	 (6) In the event of two or more candidates at any election having the same number of votes the Chairman shall have a casting vote;
	 (7) As soon as may be after the election, the Chairman shall certify in writing to the Secretary of the Trinity House the names of the persons elected, and every person so certified to be elected shall be deemed duly elected.
	    6. A pilots' representative, a port authority's representative and a shipowners' representative shall come into office on the tenth day of December in the year in which they are elected or appointed, and shall remain in office until the following tenth day of December, and shall then go out of office, but may be re-appointed or re-elected as the case may be.
	    7. In case there is a failure in any year to elect any pilots' representatives or in case of any vacancy occurring in the pilots', port authorities' or shipowners' representatives, otherwise than by effluxion of time, the Secretary of State may appoint any duly qualified person to fill the vacancy, and the person so appointed shall hold office as though he had been elected or appointed at the same time as the person in whose place he is appointed.
	    8. No act or proceeding of the Committee shall be questioned on account of any vacancy in their body or on account of the election or appointment of any member having been defective or on account of any member being absent from a meeting of the Committee.
	    9. A pilots' representative, a port authority's representative or a shipowners' representative shall not take any part in any proceedings of the Pilotage Committee relating to any question affecting himself personally.
	    10. The costs, charges and expenses preliminary and incidental to elections of pilots' representatives shall be paid by the Trinity House out of the Trinity House Pilot Fund."

No. 1030.	IMPERIAL INSTITUTE ACT 1925 (c. xvii)
Art. 6, sch., para. 8. No. 1899. *Art.4, Sch., para. 8*	At the end of s. 8(2) (as amended by 1958 c. 16) insert "Dominica and St. Lucia".
No.443	UNIVERSITIES AND COLLEGE ESTATES ACT 1925 (c. 24)
Art. 2, Sch., para. 1.	In s. 10(1) (i) (iii) for the word "acreage" substitute "area".
para. 2.	In s. 15(1) (as amended by 1964 c. 51 Sch. 1) for the words "one acre" and "five acres" substitute "0.40 hectare" and "two hectares" respectively.
No.647 (local) *Art. 29*	SHOREHAM HARBOUR ACT 1926 (c. xlvii) In s. 72(2) for the words "twenty pounds" substitute "one hundred pounds".

Part III   **K**

Number of Statutory Instrument of 1978	Act or Measure and how amended
No. 635 *Reg. 2(1)*	PETROLEUM (CONSOLIDATION) ACT 1928 (c. 32) For Schedule 1 (as amended by S.I. 1968/170, 248 and 1969 c. 19) substitute:—

"FIRST SCHEDULE

RATES OF FEES PAYABLE IN RESPECT OF LICENCES TO KEEP PETROLEUM-SPIRIT

	Rates per annum of fees payable £
In respect of a licence to keep a quantity—	
not exceeding 2,500 litres	10
exceeding 2,500 litres, not exceeding 50,000 litres	15
exceeding 50,000 litres	30

Note:— In the case of a solid substance for which by virtue of an Order in Council made under section nineteen of this Act, a licence is required to be granted under the said section, the fee payable under this Schedule shall be calculated as if one kilogram of the substance were equivalent to one litre".

No. 1482 (local).	MINISTRY OF HEALTH PROVISIONAL ORDER CONFIRMATION ACT 1935 (c. 1xx) (EAST SURREY WATER ORDER)
Art. 10, Sch.	In s. 9 of the Order omit the words "with the approval of the Minister and subject to such conditions as the Minister may think fit to impose" and the words "not exceeding one and a half per centum".
No. 635	PETROLEUM (TRANSFER OF LICENCES) ACT 1936(c ¡ 27)
Reg. 2(2)	In s. 1(4) (as amended by S.I. 1968/170, 248 and 1969 c. 19) for the sum of "50p" substitute "£2".
No. 1022	DISEASES OF FISH ACT 1937 (c. 33)
Art. 4	In s. 10(1) definition of "infected" (as substituted by S.I. 1973/2093), after the word "columnaris," insert "bacterial kidney disease".
No. 208 (S.) (local)	ABERDEEN CORPORATION (WATER, GAS, ELECTRICITY AND TRANSPORT) ORDER CONFIRMATION ACT 1937 (c. cii)
Art. 3	For s. 8 of the Order (as substituted by 1955 c. iii s. 47) substitute:

"**8.**—(1) Subject to the provisions of subsection (2) of this section the Council may for the purposes of their water undertaking take, by means of the works, from the River Dee at Cairnton in the City of Aberdeen District in the Grampian Region

(i) until 31 December 1985 a quantity of water not exceeding 91,000 cubic metres in any one day,

(ii) from 1 January 1986 a quantity of water not exceeding 70,000 cubic metres in any one day.

(2) When the flow in the said River Dee is less than 680,000 cubic metres per day for seven consecutive days the said Council shall prohibit or restrict, within the City of Aberdeen District and surrounding areas supplied with water by means of the works, the use, for the purpose of watering private gardens or washing private motor cars, of any water supplied by them and drawn through a hosepipe or similar apparatus. Such prohibition or restriction may only be lifted by the said Council when the flow in the said River Dee is not less than 770,000 cubic metres per day for seven consecutive days.

(3) If by reason of the operation of this section the Dee District Salmon Fishery Board suffer damage, the Board shall be entitled to payment of compensation; any question arising under this subsection as to the fact

Number of Statutory Instrument of 1978	Act or Measure and how amended

	of damage or as to the amount of compensation shall in case of dispute be determined by arbitration, such arbitration to be by a single arbiter appointed by agreement between the parties or in default of agreement by the Secretary of State.
	
	(4) As from 1 January 1986 the provisions of subsection (2) and (3) of this section and the words "Subject to the provisions of subsection (2) of this section" where they appear in subsection (1) of this section shall cease to have effect.
	
	(5) For the purpose of securing compliance with the provisions of subsections (1) and (2) above:—
	    (*a*) all water taken from the said River Dee by the said Council by means of the works shall be measured through or over the existing meter constructed in pursuance of the repealed Acts, situated at Invercannie Water Works at N.G. Ref NO 661964.
	    (*b*) flows in the said River Dee for any day shall be measured through or over the gauge situated on the said river at Woodend at N.G. Ref NO 632960 owned by the North East River Purification Board.
	
	(6) For the purposes of this section:—
	"day" means any period of 24 hours reckoned from midmight;
	"private motor car" means a mechanically propelled vehicle intended or adapted for use on roads and includes any vehicle drawn by a private motor car, but does not include a public service vehicle within the meaning of section 117(1) of the Road Traffic Act 1960(a) or a motor vehicle constructed or adapted for use for the carriage of goods, or a trailer so constructed or adapted;
	"works" means the waterworks vested in the said Council by by section 6 of this order, and the authorised water works."

No. 1771. *Paras.* (*a*) (*b*)(*c*) (*Resolution of House of Commons 30.11.78*).	House of Commons Members' Fund Act 1939 (c. 49) In Schedule 1 for paragraphs 1 and 2 (as amended by S.I. 1977/2073) substitute:— " 1. The annual amount of any periodical payment made to any person by virtue of his past membership of the House of Commons shall not exceed £1,230 or such sum as, in the opinion of the trustees, will bring his income up to £2,245 per annum, whichever is the less: Provided that if, having regard to length of service and need, the trustees think fit, they may make a larger payment not exceeding £2,370 or such sum as, in their opinion, will bring his income up to £3,385 per annum, whichever is the less; 2. The annual amount of any periodical payment to any person by virtue of her being a widow of a past Member of the House of Commons shall not exceed £615 or such sum as, in the opinion of the trustees, will bring her income up to £1,630 per annum, whichever is the less: Provided that if, having regard to her husband's length of service or to her need, the trustees think fit, they may make a larger payment not exceeding £1,185 or such sum as, in the opinion of the trustees, will bring her income up to £2,200 per annum, whichever is the less; " In para. 2A of Schedule 1 for the words " the annual amount of any periodical payment " to the end of the paragraph, substitute:— " the annual amount of any periodical payment made to any such widower shall not exceed £615 or such sum as, in the opinion of the trustees, will bring his income up to £1,630 per annum, whichever is the less: Provided that if, having regard to his wife's length of service or to his needs, the trustees think fit, they may make a larger payment not exceeding £1,185 or such sum as, in the opinion of the trustees, will bring his income up to £2,200 per annum, whichever is the less ".

K 2

Number of Statutory Instrument of 1978	Act or Measure and how amended
No. 1249 (local). Art. 3(1).	BRISTOL WATERWORKS ACT 1939 (c. lxxxi)

In s. 103 omit the words from the beginning of the section to " once only in each year (a) ", and for the words from " pay in any year " to the end of the section substitute " declare and pay interim dividends out of the profits of the undertaking ". |
| Art. 3(2). | After s. 103 insert:—

" Change of financial year.   **103A.** If by resolution passed before 1st December in any year the directors so determine, the accounts of the Company shall be made up in respect of the period of 15 months from 1st January in that year to 31st March in the next succeeding year, and thereafter the accounts of the Company shall be made up in respect of the period from 1st April in any year to 31st March in the next succeeding year; and, as from the end of the said period of 15 months, the following provisions shall have effect:—

    (a) for the purposes of section 14 of the Companies Clauses Act 1863 as incorporated in the local enactments relating to the Company, the prescribed day shall be 31st March; and

    (b) the expression " year " where used in the said local enactments in relation to the Company shall be taken to mean a year ending on 31st March.". |
No. 272.	HILL FARMING ACT 1946 (c. 73)
Art. 11(2), Sch. 5, para. 1.	In s. 38, definition of " the Ministers ", for the words " the Secretary of State " substitute " the Secretary of State for Scotland and the Secretary of State for Wales ".
No. 446.	AGRICULTURE ACT 1947 (c. 48)
Reg. 2(1).	In s. 109(3), definition of " allotment garden ", for the words " forty poles " substitute " 0·10 hectare ".
Reg. 2(2).	In Schedule 2, paragraph 3(1)(b) for the word " acre " in each place where it occurs substitute " hectare ".
No. 1174.	LOCAL GOVERNMENT ACT 1948 (c. 26)
Art. 8(4)(b).	In s. 124(1) insert at the beginning " Subject to the provisions of any other enactment ".
No. 1030.	BRITISH NATIONALITY ACT 1948 (c. 56)
Art. 2(1).	At the end of s. 1(3) insert " , Dominica and St. Lucia ".
No. 1899. Art 2(1).	
No. 447.	AGRICULTURAL HOLDINGS ACT 1948 (c. 63)
Reg. 2(1).	In s. 14(1) (as amended by 1969 c. 19 s. 10) for the words " five pence per acre " substitute " twelve pence per hectare ".
Reg. 2(2).	In s. 63(1)(b) for the word " acre " in each place where it occurs substitute " hectare ".

Number of Statutory Instrument of 1978	Act or Measure and how amended

Art. 3, Sch., para. 1(2)–(4).
 	
para. 2.
	In Schedule 4, Pt. I, paragraph 5, after the word " Liming " insert " (including chalking) ".
	In paragraph 6 of Pt. I of the Schedule for the words " manure (including artificial manure) " substitute " manure and fertiliser, whether organic or inorganic ".
	In paragraph 7, for the words from " by " to the end substitute " by horses, cattle, sheep, pigs or poultry ".
	At the end of Part II of Schedule 4, insert:—
	    " 12(1) Where a holding is situated in a district in which the growing o a succession of tillage crops on the same arable land is normal farming practice, the residual fertility value of the sod of the excess qualifying leys on the holding, if any:
	    Provided that—
	      (*a*) the qualifying leys comprising the excess qualifying leys shall be those indicated to be such by the tenant; and
	      (*b*) qualifying leys laid down at the expense of the landlord without reimbursement by the tenant or any previous tenant of the holding or laid down by and at the expense of the tenant pursuant to agreement by him with the landlord for the establishment of a specified area of leys on the holding as a condition of the landlord giving consent to the ploughing or other destruction of permanent pasture or pursuant to a direction given by an arbitrator on a reference under section 10(1) of this Act, shall not be included in the excess qualifying leys.
	    (2) In this paragraph—
	    " leys " means land laid down with clover, grass, lucerne, sainfoin or other seeds, but does not include permanent pasture;
	    " qualifying leys " means—
	      (*a*) leys continuously maintained as such for a period of three or more growing seasons since being laid down excluding, if the leys were undersown or autumn-sown, the calendar year in which the sowing took place, and
	      (*b*) arable land which within the three growing seasons immediately preceding the termination of the tenancy was ley continuously maintained as aforesaid before being destroyed by ploughing or some other means for the production of a tillage crop or crops:
	      Provided that for the purpose of paragraph (*a*) above the destruction of a ley (by ploughing or some other means) followed as soon as practicable by re-seeding to a ley without sowing a crop in the interval between such destruction and such re-seeding shall be treated as not constituting a break in the continuity of the maintenance of the ley;
	    " the excess qualifying leys " means the area of qualifying leys on the holding at the termination of the tenancy which is equal to the area (if any) by which one third of the aggregate of the areas of leys on the holding on the following dates, namely,
	      (*a*) at the termination of the tenancy,
	      (*b*) on the date one year prior to such termination, and
	      (*c*) on the date two years prior to such termination,
	exceeds the accepted proportion at the termination of the tenancy;
	    " the accepted proportion " means the area which represents the proportion which the aggregate area of the leys on the holding would be expected to bear to the area of the holding, excluding the permanent pasture thereon, in accordance with normal farming practice in the district or if a greater proportion is provided for by or under the terms of the tenancy, that proportion."

Number of Statutory Instrument of 1978	Act or Measure and how amended
No. 1030.	MERCHANT SHIPPING (SAFETY CONVENTION) ACT 1949 (c. 43)
Art. 6, Sch., para. 6.	In s. 2 before the words " or in any " insert " , Dominica or St. Lucia ".
No. 1899. *Art. 4, Sch., para. 6.*	
No. 440.	NEW FOREST ACT 1949 (c. 69)
Art. 6(2).	In Schedule 1, paragraph 6, for the words " the sheriff of the county of Southampton " substitute " the high sheriff of Hampshire ".
No. 798 (S.).	AGRICULTURAL HOLDINGS (SCOTLAND) ACT 1949 (c. 75)

Art. 3, Sch., para. 1(2)–(4).	In Schedule 1, Part III:
	    in paragraph 28, after the word " liming " insert " (including chalking) ".
	    in paragraph 31, for the words " manure (including artificial manure) " substitute " manure and fertiliser, whether organic or inorganic ".
	    in paragraph 32, for the words from " by " to the end substitute " by horses, cattle, sheep, pigs or poultry ".

No. 272.	DISEASES OF ANIMALS ACT 1950 (c. 36)
Art. 11(2), Sch. 5, para. 1.	In ss. 24(1) and 36B for the words " the Secretary of State " substitute " the Secretary of State for Scotland and the Secretary of State for Wales ".
para. 2.	In s. 37(4A) after the words " in Scotland " insert " or in Wales ". After the words " Secretary of State " in the second place where they occur, insert " for Scotland and the Secretary of State for Wales ".
para. 1.	In s. 84(1)(*aa*) for the words " the Secretary of State " substitute " the Secretary of State for Scotland and the Secretary of State for Wales ".
No. 272.	AGRICULTURE (PLOUGHING GRANTS) ACT 1952 (c. 35)
Art. 11(2), Sch. 5, para. 3.	In s. 5(2)(*c*) for the words " either or both of those countries " substitute " Great Britain or the United Kingdom, that Minister and the Secretary of State for Scotland and the Secretary of State for Wales acting jointly, and in relation to a joint scheme for Northern Ireland ".
No. 1602.	CUSTOMS AND EXCISE ACT 1952 (c. 44)

Reg. 2(2).	In s. 28(1) after paragraph (*b*) of the proviso insert:—
	    " or
	    (*c*) Community transit goods.".

Reg. 2(3).	In s. 47(1) (as amended by 1978 c. 42 s. 79 sch. 12 para. 19(8)) after the word " exporter " insert " shall, unless the goods are Community transit goods ". In s. 47(1)(*a*)(*b*) omit the word " shall ".
No. 1603. *Reg. 2(2).*	In s. 47(5) after the words " goods from warehouse " insert " other than goods which have been kept, without being warehoused, in the warehouse by virtue of section 80(1C) of this Act ".
No. 1602. *Reg. 2(4).*	In s. 49(1) after the word " shall " insert " , unless the goods are Community transit goods ".

Number of Statutory Instrument of 1978	Act or Measure and how amended
No. 1603. *Reg. 2(3).*	In s. 55(3) after the words " goods from warehouse " insert " other than goods which have been kept, without being warehoused, in the warehouse by virtue of section 80(1C) of this Act ".
Reg. 2(4)(a).	In s. 80(1) for subs. (*a*) substitute:— " (*a*) of imported goods chargeable as such with excise duty (whether or not also chargeable with customs duty) without payment of the excise duty; ".
Reg. 2(4)(c).	For the words after " referred to " substitute " as an ' excise warehouse ' ".
Reg. 2(5).	After subs. (1) of s. 80 insert:— " (1A) The Commissioners may approve, for such periods and subject to such conditions as they think fit, places of security for the deposit, keeping and securing— (*a*) of imported goods chargeable with customs duty or otherwise not for the time being in free circulation in Member States (whether or not also chargeable with excise duty) without payment of the customs duty; (*b*) of such other goods as the Commissioners may allow to be warehoused for exportation or for use as stores in cases where relief from or repayment of any customs duty or other payment is conditional on their exportation or use as stores, subject to and in accordance with regulations under section 16(2) of the Finance (No. 2) Act 1975; and any place of security so approved is in this Act referred to as a " customs warehouse ". (1B) The same place may be approved under this section both as a customs and as an excise warehouse. (1C) Notwithstanding subsection (1A) above and the terms of the approval of the warehouse but subject to directions under subsection (2) below, goods of the following descriptions, not being goods chargeable with excise duty which has not been paid, that is to say— (*a*) goods originating in Member States; (*b*) goods which are in free circulation in Member States; (*c*) goods placed on importation under a customs procedure (other than warehousing) involving the suspension of, or the giving of relief from, customs duties, may be kept, without being warehoused, in a customs warehouse.".
Reg. 2(6).	In s. 80(3) after the word " warehouse " insert " as an excise warehouse ".
Reg. 2(7).	In s. 85(1) after the words " the duty " insert " chargeable or deemed under regulations under section 16(2) of the Finance (No. 2) Act 1975 to be chargeable ".
Reg. 2(8)(a).	In s. 90(1) for the words " three months before " substitute " the beginning of the prescribed period ending with ".
Reg. 2(8)(b).	After subs. (3) of s. 90 insert:— " (4) In this section " the prescribed period " means— (*a*) in the case of a warehouse which is a customs warehouse but not also an excise warehouse, such period as may be prescribed by regulations under section 16(2) of the Finance (No. 2) Act 1975; and (*b*) in the case of a warehouse which is or is also an excise warehouse, three months.".
Reg. 2(9).	In s. 96(5) for the words " a warehouse approved under " substitute " an excise warehouse approved under subsection (1) of ".
Reg. 2(10).	In s. 103(1) after the word " warehouse " insert " in an excise warehouse ".
Reg. 2(11).	In s. 126(1) for the words " a warehouse " substitute " an excise warehouse ".
Reg. 2(12).	In s. 137(1) (as amended by 1975 c. 45 sch. 3 Pt. II) for the words " a warehouse " substitute " an excise warehouse ".
Reg. 2(13).	In s. 138(1) after the word " warehouse " where it occurs first, insert " in an excise warehouse ".

Number of Statutory Instrument of 1978	Act or Measure and how amended
Reg. 2(14).	In s. 142(1) (as amended by 1975 c. 45 sch. 3 Pt. II) for the word " warehouse " substitute " an excise warehouse ".
Reg. 2(15).	In s. 144(1) (as amended by 1975 c. 45 sch. 3 Pt. II) for the word " warehouse " substitute " an excise warehouse ".
Reg. 2(16).	In s. 266(1) after the words " the warehousing ", and in subs. (2) after the words " their warehousing ", insert " in an excise warehouse ".

No. 1602 *Reg. 2(5)*	In s. 307(1), after the definition of "Commissioners", insert:—
	" "Community transit goods"—
	    (*a*) in relation to imported goods, means—
	        (i) goods which have been imported under the internal or external Community transit procedure for transit through the United Kingdom with a view to exportation where the importation was and the transit and exportation are to be part of one Community transit operation; or
	        (ii) goods which have, at the port or airport at which they were imported, been placed under the internal or external Community transit procedure for transit through the United Kingdom with a view to exportation where the transit and exportation are to be part of one Community transit operation;
	    (*b*) in relation to goods for exportation, means—
	        (i) goods which have been imported as mentioned in paragraph (*a*) (i) of this definition and are to be exported as part of the Community transit operation in the course of which they were imported; or
	        (ii) goods which have, under the internal or external Community transit procedure, transitted the United Kingdom from the port or airport at which they were imported and are to be exported as part of the Community transit operation which commenced at that port or airport.".

No. 1603 *Reg. 2(17)* (*a*)	In s. 307(1) insert in alphabetical order the following definitions:— " "excise warehouse" means a place of security approved by the Commissioners under subsection (1) (whether or not it is also approved under subsection (1A)) of section 80 of this Act and, except in that section, also includes a distiller's warehouse;" ""customs warehouse" means a place of security approved by the Commissioners under subsection (1A) (whether or not it is also approved under subsection (1)) of section 80 of this Act;" and"
Reg. 2(17) (*b*)	In the definition of "warehouse" in s. 307(1), after the word "under" insert "subsection (1) or (1A) or (1) and (1A) of", and after the word "shall" insert ", subject to subsection (1C) of that section,"
No. 272	Agriculture (Calf Subsidies) Act 1952 (c. 62)
Art. 11(2), *Sch. 5* *para. 4*	In s. 1(2) (b) for the words "any other joint scheme" substitute "a joint scheme for Great Britain or the United Kingdom, that Minister and the Secretary of State for Scotland and the Secretary of State for Wales acting jointly, and in relation to a joint scheme for Northern Ireland and Scotland".

Number of Statutory Instrument of 1978	Act or Measure and how amended
No. 1030	VISITING FORCES ACT 1952 (c. 67)
Art. 6, Sch. para. 4 No. 1899 Art.4 Sch. para. 4	At the end of s. 1(1) (a) insert "Dominica or St. Lucia".
No. 1407 (N.I.) Art. 7(3)	At the end of para. 3(j) of the Schedule insert "and the Theft (Northern Ireland) Order 1978".
No. 473 (local) Art. 3	BERKSHIRE COUNTY COUNCIL ACT 1953 (c. xli) In s. 74(7) (a)-(d) (as amended by S.I. 1975/336) for "£5", "£1.25", "£5", "£1.25" and "25p" substitute "£20", "£5", "£20", "£5" and "£2" respectively.
No. 1069 (local) Art. 3(2)	DOVER HARBOUR CONSOLIDATION ACT 1954 (c. iv) In s. 74(1) for the words in brackets substitute:— "(so far as they are not empowered to make a charge under any other provision of this Act or levy a ship, passenger or goods due under Section 26(2) of the Harbours Act 1964)".
No. 1872 (S.) Art. 2	PROTECTION OF BIRDS 1954 (c. 30) In Sch. 1 pt. I insert in alphabetical order "Lapland bunting".

No. 1071 (S.) *Art. 2,* Sch.

(Only as to **)
No. 1212 (E.,W.) Art. 2

In Schedule 4 insert in alphabetical order the following words:—

"Buzzard, Common	Harrier, Montagu's
Buzzard, Honey	Hobby
Buzzard, Rough-legged	Kestrel
Eagle, Golden	Kestrel, Lesser
Eagle, White-tailed	Kite, Black
Falcon, Gyr	Kite, Red
Falcon, Red-footed	Merlin
Goshawk	Osprey
Harrier, Hen	Owl, Little **
Harrier, Marsh	Peregrine
	Sparrowhawk"

No. 272.	PROTECTION OF ANIMALS (ANAESTHETICS) ACT 1954 (c. 46)
Art. 11(2), Sch. 5, para. 5.	In s. 1 for the words " the Secretary of State " in the first place where they occur substitute " the Secretary of State for Scotland and the Secretary of State for Wales ". For the words " the Minister and the Secretary of State " in the second and third places where those words occur substitute " those Ministers ".
No. 1951.	MINES AND QUARRIES ACT 1954 (c. 70)
Art. 2.	In s. 148(1), after the words " of this Act " insert " or by health and safety regulations ". In subs. (2) of s. 148 for the word " ten " in each place where it occurs substitute " thirteen "; for the words " by regulations having effect by virtue of Part IV of this Act " substitute " by health and safety regulations relating to quarries "; for the word " twelve " substitute " fifteen ".

Number of Statutory Instrument of 1978	Act or Measure and how amended
No. 1030.	ARMY ACT 1955 (c. 18)
Art. 6, *Sch.,* *para. 2.*	At the end of the definition of " Commonwealth Force " in s. 225(1) insert " , Dominica or St. Lucia ".
No. 1899. *Art. 4,* *Sch.,* *para. 2.*	
No. 1908 (N.I.). *Art. 4(5).*	In Schedule 5A, paragraph 5(2)(*d*), add at the end " or of the Rehabilitation of Offenders (Northern Ireland) Order 1978 ".
No. 1030.	AIR FORCE ACT 1955 (c. 19)
Art. 6, *Sch.,* *para. 2.*	At the end of the definition of " Commonwealth Force " in s. 223(1) insert " , Dominica or St. Lucia ".
No. 1899. *Art. 4,* *Sch.,* *para. 2.*	
No. 1908 (N.I.). *Art. 4(5).*	In Schedule 5A, paragraph 5(2)(*d*), add at the end " or of the Rehabilitation of Offenders (Northern Ireland) Order 1978 ".
No. 272.	FOOD AND DRUGS ACT 1955 (c. 16 4 & 5 Eliz. 2)
Art. 11(2), *Sch. 5,* *para. 6.*	In s. 135(1) at the end of the definition of " the Ministers " add " or, in relation to any function under this Act to which the Transfer of Functions (Wales) (No. 1) Order 1978 applies, the Minister, the Secretary of State for Social Services and the Secretary of State for Wales acting jointly; ".
No. 272.	SUGAR ACT 1956 (c. 48)
Art. 11(2), *Sch. 5,* *para. 1.*	In s. 17(1) for the words " the Secretary of State " substitute " the Secretary of State for Scotland and the Secretary of State for Wales ".
para. 7.	In s. 18(9)(*a*) for the words " the Ministers " substitute " the Minister, the Secretary of State for Scotland and the Secretary of State for Wales ".
No. 1030.	NAVAL DISCIPLINE ACT 1957 (c. 53)
Art. 6, *Sch.,* *para. 2.*	At the end of the definition of " Commonwealth country " in s. 135(1) insert " , Dominica or St. Lucia ".
No. 1899. *Art. 4,* *Sch.,* *para. 2.* No. 1908 (N.I.). *Art. 4(5).*	At the end of para. 5(2)(*d*) of Schedule 4A insert " or of the Rehabilitation of Offenders (Northern Ireland) Order 1978 ".

Number of Statutory Instrument of 1978	Act or Measure and how amended
No. 1148.	IMPORT DUTIES ACT 1958 (c. 6)
Reg. 2.	In s. 5(4) omit the words " or section 5(6) of the European Communities Act 1972 ".
No. 1030.	COMMONWEALTH INSTITUTE ACT 1958 (c. 16)
Art. 6, Sch., para. 8.	In Schedule 2, at the end of the entry relating to 1925 c. xvii s. 8, insert " , Dominica and St. Lucia ".
No. 1899. *Art. 4, Sch., para. 8.*	
No. 1154 (S.).	LAND DRAINAGE (SCOTLAND) ACT 1958 (c. 24)
Art. 3.	In Schedule 1, paragraph 6(*b*)(ii) (as amended by S.I. 1977/2007) for the figure of " £100 " substitute " three hundred and twenty-five pounds ".
No. 124 (S.) (local).	GLASGOW CORPORATION CONSOLIDATION (GENERAL POWERS) ORDER CONFIRMATION ACT 1960 (c. iii)
Art. 2.	In s. 96(1)(*a*)(i) (as amended by S.I. 1976/1055) for the words " seventy-five pence (75p) " substitute " ninety-five pence (95p) ".
No. 1030.	DIPLOMATIC IMMUNITIES (CONFERENCES WITH COMMONWEALTH COUNTRIES AND REPUBLIC OF IRELAND) ACT 1961 (c. 11)
Art. 6, Sch., para. 1.	In s. 1(5) before " and " in the last place where it occurs insert " , Dominica St. Lucia ".
No. 1899. *Art. 4, Sch., para. 1.*	
No. 272.	AGRICULTURE (MISCELLANEOUS PROVISIONS) ACT 1963 (c. 11)
Art. 11(2), Sch. 5, para. 8(a). para. 8(b).	In s. 16(1) for the words "the Ministers " substitute "the Minister of Agriculture, Fisheries and Food, the Secretary of State for Scotland and the Secretary of State for Wales acting jointly ". In s. 26(*b*) for the words " any other joint scheme " substitute " any joint scheme for Great Britain or the United Kingdom, the Minister of Agriculture, Fisheries and Food and the Secretary of State for Scotland and the Secretary of State for Wales acting jointly, and in relation to a joint scheme for Northern Ireland and Scotland ".
No. 272.	WATER RESOURCES ACT 1963 (c. 38)
Art. 11(2), Sch. 5, para. 9.	In Schedule 7, paragraph 16(*b*), insert at the end of sub-para. (ii): " or, if the draft statement or proposals were prepared by the Welsh National Water Development Authority, the Secretary of State is satisfied that the association or person represents such an interest."

Number of Statutory Instrument of 1978	Act or Measure and how amended
No. 272.	PLANT VARIETIES AND SEEDS ACT 1964 (c. 14)
Art. 11(2), *Sch. 5*, *para. 10.*	In s. 38(1) for the words " the said two Ministers " substitute " the Minister, the Secretary of State for Scotland and the Secretary of State for Wales ".
No. 272.	AGRICULTURE AND HORTICULTURE ACT 1964 (c. 28)
Art. 11(2),,, *Sch. 5*, *para. 1.*	In s. 26(2) for the words " the Secretary of State " substitute " the Secretary of State for Scotland and the Secretary of State for Wales ".
No. 272.	HARBOURS ACT 1964 (c. 40)
Art. 11(2), *Sch. 5*, *para. 11.*	In s. 30(4), after the words " and Food " insert " or, if the fishery harbour is in Wales, to the Secretary of State ".
No. 844 (local).	MANCHESTER CORPORATION ACT 1965 (c. xlii)
Art. 3, *Sch.*	In s. 18(6) for the sum of " £1 " substitute " £15 ".
No. 912	NATIONAL INSURANCE ACT 1965 (c. 51)
Art. 5.	In s. 36(1) for " 2½ pence " substitute " 2·59 pence ". (Although 1965 c. 51 repealed by 1975 c. 18, ss. 36, 37 continued (as modified) by S.I. 1975/557).
No. 461.	HIRE-PURCHASE ACT 1965 (c. 66)
Art. 2.	In s. 2(2)(3)(*b*)(4) for the sum of " £2,000 " substitute " £5,000 ".
No. 461.	HIRE-PURCHASE (SCOTLAND) ACT 1965 (c. 67)
Art. 2.	In s. 2(2)(3)(*b*)(4) for the sum of " £2,000 " substitute " £5,000 ".
No. 941 (local). *Art. 6.*	TEES AND HARTLEPOOL PORT AUTHORITY ACT 1966 (c. xxv) In s. 8(3) for the words "on the 31st December" substitute "on the last day of February".
No. 272.	VETERINARY SURGEONS ACT 1966 (c. 36)
Art. 11(2), *Sch. 5*, *para. 1.*	In s. 27(1) for the words "the Secretary of State" substitute "the Secretary of State for Scotland and the Secretary of State for Wales".
No. 1175 (S.). *Art. 8(3)* *(a)*	LOCAL GOVERNMENT (SCOTLAND) ACT 1966 (c. 51) In s. 17(4) after the words "subsequent years" insert "up to and including the year 1977–78".
Art. 8(3) *(b).*	After subsection (4) of s. 17 insert:— "(4A) As respects the year 1978–79 and subsequent years, water authorities shall have power to make charges by way of meter or otherwise in respect of water supplied to any such lands and heritages as are specified in paragraph 4 of Schedule 1 to the Local Government (Scotland) Act 1975.

Number of Statutory Instrument of 1978	Act or Measure and how amended
No. 1176 (S.) *Art. 8(3).*	(4B) As respects the year 1978–79 and subsequent years, water authorities shall have power to make charges by way of meter or otherwise in respect of water supplied to any such lands and heritages as are specified in paragraph 3 of Schedule 1 to the Local Government (Scotland) Act 1975.
No. 1174 (S.) *Art. 8(3)*	(4C) As respects the year 1978–79 and subsequent years, water authorities shall have power to make charges by way of meter or otherwise in respect of any such lands and heritages as are specified in paragraph 2(1)(b) and (c) of Schedule 1 to the Local Government (Scotland) Act 1975.
No. 1173 (S.) *Art. 7(3).*	(4D) As respects the year 1978–79 and subsequent years, water authorities shall have power to make charges by way of meter or otherwise in respect of water supplied to any such lands and heritages as are specified in paragraph 5 of Schedule 1 to the Local Government (Scotland) Act 1975".
No. 318	GENERAL RATE ACT 1967 (c. 9)
Reg. 2(2).	In s. 26(3) (a) for the words "one quarter of an acre" in each place where they occur substitute "0.10 hectare".
No. 993. *Art. 3.*	In s. 68(1) (as amended by 1975 c. 5 s. 1(1)) for "1980" substitute "1981".
No. 218 *Art. 3* *(1.4.1977).*	In Schedule 8 at the end of paragraph 6 add:— "with the exception of the permanent private halls of the University of Oxford, that is to say, Campion Hall, St. Benet's Hall, Mansfield College, Regent's Park College and Greyfriars."
No. 616	PARLIAMENTARY COMMISSIONER ACT 1967 (c. 13)
Art. 3.	In Schedule 2, in alphabetical order, insert "Forestry Commission".
No. 244 *Reg. 2(1).*	AGRICULTURE ACT 1967 (c. 22) In s. 51(7)(a) for the word "acreage" in each place where it occurs substitute "area".
Reg. 2(2).	In s. 52(2)(d) for the words "ten acres" in each place where they occur substitute "four hectares".
No. 272 *Art. 11(2), Sch. 5, par. 1.*	In s. 66(3) for the words "the Secretary of State" substitute "the Secretary of State for Scotland and the Secretary of State for Wales".
No. 272	SLAUGHTER OF POULTRY ACT 1967 (c. 24)
Art. 11(2), Sch. 5, para. 1.	In s. 8 for the words "the Secretary of State" substitute "the Secretary of State for Scotland and the Secretary of State for Wales".
No. 382.	DEVELOPMENT OF INVENTIONS ACT 1967 (c. 32)
Art. 2.	In s. 4(2)(b) (as amended by 1975 c. 68 s. 26) for the sum of " £20,000 " substitute " £250,000 ".
No. 739 (local). *Art. 3, Sch.*	MANCHESTER CORPORATION ACT 1967 (c. xl) In Schedule 1 omit the entry relating to s. 11 of the Manchester Corporation Act 1970 c. li.

Number of Statutory Instrument of 1978	Act or Measure and how amended
No. 1817 (S.).	LEGAL AID (SCOTLAND) ACT 1967 (c. 43)
Regs. 2, 4.	In s. 2(1) (as amended by S.I. 1977/1981) for the sums of " £2,400 " and " £1,500 " substitute " £2,600 " and " £1,700 " respectively.
Regs. 3, 5.	In s. 3(1) (as amended by S.I. 1977/1981) for the sums of " £760 " and " £340 " substitute " £815 " and " £365 " respectively.
No. 272.	FARM AND GARDEN CHEMICALS ACT 1967 (c. 50)
Art. 11(2), Sch. 5, para. 1.	In s. 5(1) for the words " the Secretary of State " substitute " the Secretary of State for Scotland and the Secretary of State for Wales ".
No. 272.	SEA FISHERIES (SHELLFISH) ACT 1967 (c. 83)
Art. 11(2), Sch. 5, para. 1.	In s. 17(3) for the words " the Secretary of State " substitute " the Secretary of State for Scotland and the Secretary of State for Wales ".
No. 1057.	ADMINISTRATION OF JUSTICE ACT 1968 (c. 5)
Art. 2.	In s. 1(1)(*b*)(i) (as amended by S.I. 1975/1215) for " sixteen " substitute " eighteen ".
No. 267 (E., W.). *Art. 4, Sch. 1.* No. 360 (S.). *Art. 4, Sch. 1.*	FIREARMS ACT 1968 (c. 27) For s. 32(1) (as substituted by S.I. 1976/2157 (E., W.) and S.I. 1976/2158 (S.)) substitute:— " 32.—(1) Subject to this Act, there shall be payable— (*a*) on the grant of a firearm certificate a fee of £16; (*b*) on the renewal of a firearm certificate or on the replacement of a firearm certificate which has been lost or destroyed, a fee of £13; (*c*) on any variation of a firearm certificate (otherwise than when it is renewed or replaced at the same time) so as to increase the number of firearms to which the certificate relates, a fee of £13; (*d*) on the grant of a shot gun certificate a fee of £7; and (*e*) on the renewal of a shot gun certificate or on the replacement of a shot gun certificate which has been lost or destroyed, a fee of £5."
Art. 5. *Art. 5.* *Art. 6, Sch. 2.* *Art. 6, Sch. 2.*	[S. 32(3A) continued as amended by S.I. 1976/2157 (E., W.) and S.I. 1976/2158 (S.).] For s. 35(1)(3) (as amended by S.I. 1976/2157 (E., W.) and S.I. 1976/2158 (S.)) substitute:— " 35.—(1) Subject to this Act, on the registration of a person as a firearms dealer there shall be payable by him a fee of £30." " (3) Before a person for the time being registered as a firearms dealer can be granted a new certificate of registration under section 33(5) of this Act, he shall pay a fee of £25."
No. 1453 (local). *Art. 3.*	LANCASHIRE COUNTY COUNCIL (GENERAL POWERS) ACT 1968 (c. xxix) In s. 5(2) for " 1978 " substitute " 1988 ".

Number of Statutory Instrument of 1978	Act or Measure and how amended
No. 1847 (E., W.). *Art. 3, Sch.* (*1.5.79*).	GAMING ACT 1968 (c. 65) In s. 48(3)(*a*)–(*c*) (as amended by S.I. 1977/570) for the sums of " £3,000 ", " £600 " and " £450 " substitute " £8,700 ", " £1,740 " and " £1,300 " respectively. In subs. (3)(*d*) for " £48 " and " £24 " substitute " £54 " and " £27 " respectively. In subs. (3)(*e*) for " £24 " and " £12 " substitute " £27 " and " £13·50 " respectively.
Art. 4 (*1.5.79*).	In s. 48(4)(*a*) (as amended by S.I. 1977/570) for " £3,000 " substitute " £8,700 ". In subs. (4)(*b*) (as amended by S.I. 1977/570) for " £600 " substitute " £1,740 ". In subs. (4) last sentence (as amended by S.I. 1977/570) for " £450 " substitute " £1,300 ".
No. 496. *Art. 3.*	HORSERACE BETTING LEVY ACT 1969 (c. 14) In s. 1(2) [for levy period beginning after 1.5.78] for " six months " substitute " eight months ".
No. 272. *Art. 11(2), Sch. 5, para. 1.*	PONIES ACT 1969 (c. 28) In s. 2(1) for the words " the Secretary of State " substitute " the Secretary of State for Scotland and the Secretary of State for Wales ".
No. 1821. *Art. 2(1).*	SEA FISH INDUSTRY ACT 1970 (c. 11) In s. 23(2) (as amended by S.I. 1976/2230) for the sum of " £5 million " substitute " £6 million ".
No. 272. *Art. 11(2), Sch. 5, para. 1.*	AGRICULTURE ACT 1970 (c. 40) In s. 66(1), definition of " the Ministers ", for the words " the Secretary of State " substitute " the Secretary of State for Scotland and the Secretary of State for Wales ".
No. 739 (local). *Art. 3, Sch.*	MANCHESTER CORPORATION ACT 1970 (c. li) In s. 4 omit the definitions of " hackney carriage byelaws " and " private hire vehicle ".
No. 1603. *Reg. 3(1).* *Reg. 3(2).*	HYDROCARBON OIL (CUSTOMS AND EXCISE) ACT 1971 (c. 12) In s. 13(1) after the word " warehousing " insert " in an excise warehouse ". In s. 14 after the word " warehoused " insert " in an excise warehouse ".
No. 318. *Reg. 2(3).*	RATING ACT 1971 (c. 39) In s. 2(4) for the words " five acres " substitute " two hectares ".
No. 651 (*local*). *Art. 3(l).*	EXETER CORPORATION ACT 1971 (c. lxv) In s. 23 omit the words " or a private hire vehicle ".
No. 844 (*local*). *Art. 3, Sch.*	MANCHESTER CORPORATION (GENERAL POWERS) ACT 1971 (c. lxvii) In s. 23(1) for the sums of " five pounds " and " one pound " substitute " £10 " and " £5 " respectively.

Number of Statutory Instrument of 1978	Act or Measure and how amended
No. 1602.	FINANCE ACT 1971 (c. 68)
Reg. 3(2).	In Schedule 1 para. 1(2), after the word " shall " insert " , unless the goods are Community transit goods ".
Reg. 3(3).	In para. 1(7), after the first word of the subpara. (" goods ") insert " of which entry is required under this paragraph ", and for the words " anything in this paragraph " substitute " that requirement ".
No. 44.	BETTING AND GAMING DUTIES ACT 1972 (c. 25)
Art. 3.	In Schedule 4 para. 2 (as amended by S.I. 1976/1925) subpara. (2)(*b*), for " 20p " (in both places) and " 50p " (in both places) substitute " 50p " and " £1 " respectively. In subpara. (3)(*a*)(*b*) for " 50p " (wherever occurring) substitute " £1 ". In subpara. (4) for " 20p " substitute " 50p ".
No. 273.	FINANCE ACT 1972 (c. 41)
Art. 5(5).	In s. 2(1)(2) (as substituted by 1977 c. 36 Sch. 6) for the words " United Kingdom " wherever they occur substitute " United Kingdom or the Isle of Man ".
Art. 5(5).	In s. 5(1) (as substituted by 1977 c. 36 Sch. 6) for the words " United Kingdom " wherever they occur substitute " United Kingdom or the Isle of Man ".
Art. 5(6).	In subs. (2) of s. 5 for the words " United Kingdom " in the second place where they occur substitute " United Kingdom or the Isle of Man ".
Art. 5(5).	In subs. (3)(*a*) of s. 5 for the words " United Kingdom " substitute " United Kingdom or the Isle of Man ".
Art. 5(7).	In s. 8B(1)(*a*) (added by 1977 c. 36 Sch. 6) for the words " United Kingdom " substitute " United Kingdom or the Isle of Man ".
Art. 5(1).	In s. 11(2)(*a*) (as substituted by 1977 c. 36 Sch. 6) for the words " United Kingdom " substitute " United Kingdom and the Isle of Man ".
Art. 5(2)(3).	In s. 12(5) for the words " United Kingdom " (in both places where they occur), and in subs. (6)(*b*), substitute " United Kingdom and the Isle of Man ".
Art. 5(5).	In ss. 12(8) (as amended by 1977 c. 36 Sch. 6), 16(2) and 21(3) for the words " United Kingdom " wherever they occur substitute " United Kingdom or the Isle of Man ".
Art. 5(5).	In s. 24(1) for the words " United Kingdom " in both places where they occur substitute " United Kingdom or the Isle of Man ".
Art. 5(4).	In s. 24(2A) (added by 1973 c. 51 s. 7) for the words " United Kingdom " in the first place where they occur substitute " United Kingdom or the Isle of Man " and in the second place where they occur substitute " United Kingdom and the Isle of Man ".
Art. 5(5).	In s. 46(4) for the words " United Kingdom " wherever they occur substitute " United Kingdom or the Isle of Man ".
Art. 5(8).	In s. 49 for the words " United Kingdom " in the second place where they occur substitute " United Kingdom or the Isle of Man ".
No. 1392 (S.).	HOUSING (FINANCIAL PROVISIONS) (SCOTLAND) ACT 1972 (c. 46)
Reg. 3.	In Schedule 2 for paragraph 8(1)(2) (as amended by S.I. 1977/1581) substitute (13.11.78):—

" (1) Subject to sub-paragraph (2) below, the needs allowance for each week is:—

    (*a*) for an individual person who has no dependent children   £27·25

    (*b*) for a married couple   ...   .   £39·45

    (*c*) for an individual person who has a dependent child or children   ...   .   £39·45

    (*d*) for each dependent child of a tenant or his spouse   ...   £6·55

Number of Statutory Instrument of 1978	Act or Measure and how amended
	(2) The needs allowance for each week is:—
	(*a*) for an individual person who has no dependent children and who is a chronically sick or disabled person ... £30·15
	(*b*) for a married couple, one of whom is a chronically sick or disabled person ... ... £42·35
	(*c*) for an individual person who is a chronically sick or disabled person and who has a dependent child or children ... ... £42·35
	(*d*) for a married couple both of whom are chronically sick or disabled persons ... ... £44·00 "
Reg. 4.	In Schedule 2 for para. 12(1)(1A) (as amended by S.I. 1976/1755) substitute (13.11.78):—
	" (1) The deductions from a rebate or allowance in respect of non-dependants are for each week—
	(*a*) for each person aged 18 years or more, but under 21 years and neither undergoing full-time instruction at an educational establishment (subject in the case of qualifying students to sub-paragraph (1A) below) nor in receipt of supplementary benefit ... ... £1·60
	(*b*) for each person aged 21 years or more, but under pensionable age and neither undergoing full-time instruction at an educational establishment (subject in the case of qualifying students to sub-paragraph (1A) below) nor in receipt of supplementary benefit except in the case mentioned in paragraph (*e*) below ... £2·40
	(*c*) for each person in receipt of supplementary benefit ... £0·95
	(*d*) for each person of pensionable age not in receipt of supplementary benefit, except in the case mentioned in paragraph (*e*) below ... ... £0·95
	(*e*) for a married couple where the husband is of pensionable age and not in receipt of supplementary benefit... £0·95
	(1A) In respect of non-dependants who are qualifying students, the deductions for each week for which (if they were tenants) they would be subject to deductions from rent for the purposes of paragraph 17(3) of this Schedule by virtue of regulations for the time being in force under the said paragraph 17(3) are—
	(*a*) for each person aged 18 years or more, but under 21 years and not in receipt of supplementary benefit ... £1·60
	(*b*) for each person aged 21 years or more but under pensionable age and not in receipt of supplementary benefit ... ... £2·40 "
Reg. 5.	In Schedule 3 para. 3(1) (as amended by S.I. 1977/1581) insert at the beginning " Subject to paragraph 4(1A) below " (13.11.78).
Reg. 6.	In Schedule 3 para. 4(1) (as amended by S.I. 1977/1581) insert at the beginning " Subject to subparagraph (1A) below " (13.11.78).
	After subpara. (1) insert (13.11.78):—
	" (1A) (*a*) Where a rebate or an allowance is first granted in relation to an application made to the authority and:—
	(i) the authority is satisfied that had the applicant made an application for a rebate or an allowance at any time within the 12 months preceding the receipt of the current application he would have been entitled to such rebate or allowance (whether or not he would have been entitled to it continuously until the receipt of the current application); and
	(ii) the authority considers that the personal or domestic circumstances of the applicant are exceptional;
	the authority may allow the rebate period or the allowance period to

Number of Statutory Instrument of 1978	Act or Measure and how amended
	commence at the beginning of any rental period within the 12 months preceding the receipt of the current application:

Provided that the authority shall not grant the applicant a rebate or allowance for any week in the rebate period or allowance period before the rental period in which the current application was received if they would not have done so under their rebate scheme or allowance scheme in operation in that week;

(*b*) where under paragraph (*a*) above a rebate period or an allowance period commences earlier than it would otherwise have done, then:—

(i) the information and evidence which the applicant is required to supply under paragraph 2(1) above may additionally include such information and evidence as to the matters specified in that paragraph and as to the applicant's circumstances in the first part of the period as the authority may reasonably require; and

(ii) the rebate or allowance for any week in the first part of the period shall be calculated, subject to paragraph (iii) below, in accordance with the authority's rebate scheme or allowance scheme in operation in that week; and

(iii) notwithstanding anything in paragraph 3 above, it shall be the authority's duty to assess the income of the applicant and any spouse of his during the first part of the period on such basis as appears to them to be appropriate in the circumstances of the particular case."

Reg. 7. In Schedule 3 para. 4(2)(*b*) (as amended by S.I. 1977/1581) for the words " March or April 1977 " substitute " March or April 1978 ".

No. 1333 (S.). *Art. 3.* In Schedule 4 insert at the end of para. 3 " and the exclusion from the housing revenue account of expenditure on the supply or provision of anything under the said sections 140 and 141 shall not, in respect of the year 1979–80 and subsequent years, extend to such expenditure when incurred in relation to a hostel or a lodging-house ".

No. 34.   HOUSING FINANCE ACT 1972 (c. 47)

Art. 2. In s. 8(3) column 2 of the Table (for the year 1978–79) for " 80% " substitute " 100% ".

No. 1302. *Reg. 3.* In Schedule 3 para. 1(3) for the words " paragraph 4(1) " substitute (13.11.78) " paragraphs 4(1) and 4(1A) ".

Reg. 4. For para. 8 of Sch. 3 (as substituted by S.I. 1977/1467) substitute (13.11.78):—

" 8.—(1) Subject to sub-paragraph (2) below, the needs allowance for each week is—

(*a*) for an individual person who has no dependent children £27·25
(*b*) for a married couple ... ... £39·45
(*c*) for an individual person who has a dependent child or children ... ... £39·45
(*d*) for each dependent child of a tenant or his spouse ... £6·55

(2) The needs allowance for each week is—

(*a*) for an individual person who has no dependent children and who is registered in pursuance of arrangements made under section 29(1) of the National Assistance Act 1948 (welfare arrangements for handicapped persons) ... ... £30·15
(*b*) for a married couple one of whom is so registered ... £42·35
(*c*) for an individual person who is so registered and who has a dependent child or children ... ... £42·35
(*d*) for a married couple both of whom are so registered... £44·00. "

Number of Statutory Instrument of 1978	Act or Measure and how amended
Reg. 5.	In Schedule 3 for para. 12(1)(1A) (as substituted by S.I. 1976/1470) substitute (13.11.78):—

Reg. 5.

In Schedule 3 for para. 12(1)(1A) (as substituted by S.I. 1976/1470) substitute (13.11.78):—

" (1) The deductions from a rebate or allowance in respect of non-dependants are for each week—

    (*a*) for each person aged 18 years or more, but under 21 years and neither undergoing full-time instruction at an educational establishment (subject in the case of qualifying students to sub-paragraph (1A) below) nor in receipt of supplementary benefit ... ... £1·60

    (*b*) for each person aged 21 years or more, but under pensionable age and neither undergoing full-time instruction at an educational establishment (subject in the case of qualifying students to sub-paragraph (1A) below) nor in receipt of supplementary benefit ... £2·40

    (*c*) for each person in receipt of supplementary benefit ... £0·95

    (*d*) for each person of pensionable age not in receipt of supplementary benefit, except in the case mentioned in paragraph (*e*) below ... ... £0·95

    (*e*) for a married couple both of pensionable age and not in receipt of supplementary benefit ... ... £0·95

(1A) In respect of non-dependants who are qualifying students, the deductions for each week for which (if they were tenants) they would be subject to deductions from rent for the purposes of section 25(2)(*c*) of this Act by virtue of section 25(3)(*c*) thereof are—

    (*a*) for each person aged 18 years or more, but under 21 years and not in receipt of supplementary benefit ... £1·60

    (*b*) for each person aged 21 years or more, but under pensionable age and not in receipt of supplementary benefit ... ... £2·40. "

Reg. 6.

In Schedule 4 para. 3(1) insert at the beginning the words " Subject to paragraph 4(1A) below " (13.11.78).

Reg. 7(a).

In para. 4(1) of Schedule 4 insert at the beginning (13.11.78) " Subject to sub-paragraph (1A) below ".

Reg. 7(b).

After sub-para. (1) insert (13.11.78):—

" (1A) Where—

    (*a*) a rebate or an allowance is first granted in relation to an application made to the authority (" the current application ") and:—

        (i) the authority is satisfied that, had the applicant made an application for a rebate or an allowance at any time within the 12 months preceding the receipt of the current application, he would have been entitled to such rebate or allowance (whether or not he would have been entitled to it continuously until the receipt of the current application); and

        (ii) the authority considers that the personal or domestic circumstances of the applicant are exceptional,

the authority may allow the rebate period or the allowance period to commence at the beginning of any rental period within the 12 months preceding the receipt of the current application:

Provided that the authority shall not grant the applicant a rebate or allowance for any week in the rebate period or allowance period before the rental period in which the current application was received (" the first part of the period ") if they would not have done so under their rebate scheme or allowance scheme in operation in that week;

    (*b*) under paragraph (*a*) above a rebate period or an allowance period commences earlier than it would otherwise have done, then—

Number of Statutory Instrument of 1978	Act or Measure and how amended

Reg. 7(b). (cont.)	(i) the information and evidence which the applicant is required to supply under paragraph 2(1) above may additionally include such information and evidence as to the matters specified in that paragraph and as to the applicant's circumstances in the first part of the period as the authority may reasonably require; and
	    (ii) the rebate or allowance for any week in the first part of the period shall be calculated, subject to sub-paragraph (iii) below, in accordance with the authority's rebate scheme or allowance scheme in operation in that week; and
	    (iii) notwithstanding anything in paragraph 3 above, it shall be the authority's duty to assess the income of the applicant and any spouse of his during the first part of the period on such basis as appears to them to be appropriate in the circumstances of the particular case."

No. 217.
 Reg. 2.
	In Schedule 4 for para. 4(2) substitute:—
	    " (2) A rebate period and an allowance period shall end, subject to paragraphs 5 and 6 below—
	    (a) if the tenant is of pensionable age, not later than twelve months after the date on which he was notified that his application for a rebate or allowance was granted; and
	    (b) if the tenant is not of pensionable age—
	    (i) where the date of notification falls during the month of March or April in any year, not later than nine months after that date; and
	    (ii) in any other case not later than seven months after that date:
	Provided that where in any case the period is less than the maximum period specified in paragraph (a) or (b) above, the authority may extend the period, subject to paragraphs 5 and 6 below, so as to end not later than the expiry of the relevant maximum period."

No. 1302. Reg. 8.	In para. 10(4B) of Sch. 4 (as inserted by S.I. 1975/1441) for the words " the exception in paragraph 4(2)(b) " substitute " the proviso to paragraph 4(2) ".
No. 1818 (S.).	LEGAL ADVICE AND ASSISTANCE ACT 1972 (c. 50)
Reg. 2.	In s. 1(a) and the last sentence of s. 1 (as amended by S.I. 1977/1982) for the sums of " £48 " and " £340 " substitute " £52 " and " £365 " respectively.
No. 1564 (S.). Reg. 2(1). Reg. 2(2).	In s. 4(2) (as amended by S.I. 1977/1663) for the sum of " £23 " substitute " £25 ". For Schedule 1 (as amended by S.I. 1977/1663) substitute:— " 1. Exceeding £25 but not exceeding £28 a week ... ... £3 2. Exceeding £28 but not exceeding £30 a week ... ... £6 3. Exceeding £30 but not exceeding £32 a week ... ... £9 4. Exceeding £32 but not exceeding £34 a week ... ... £12 5. Exceeding £34 but not exceeding £36 a week ... ... £15 6. Exceeding £36 but not exceeding £38 a week ... ... £18 7. Exceeding £38 but not exceeding £40 a week ... ... £21 8. Exceeding £40 but not exceeding £42 a week ... ... £24 9. Exceeding £42 but not exceeding £44 a week ... ... £27 10. Exceeding £44 but not exceeding £46 a week ... ... £30 11. Exceeding £46 but not exceeding £48 a week ... ... £33 12. Exceeding £48 but not exceeding £50 a week ... ... £36 13. Exceeding £50 but not exceeding £52 a week ... ... £39."

Number of Statutory Instrument of 1978	Act or Measure and how amended
No. 1176 (S.).	GAS ACT 1972 (c. 60)
Art. 9, Sch.	In s. 34(1) omit the words " and subsection (3) to the rating of the Corporation in Scotland ".
No. 272.	AGRICULTURE (MISCELLANEOUS PROVISIONS) ACT 1972 (c. 62)
Art. 11(2), Sch. 5, para. 1.	In s. 1(8), definition of " the Ministers ", for the words " the Secretary of State " substitute " the Secretary of State for Scotland and the Secretary of State for Wales ".
No. 272.	EUROPEAN COMMUNITIES ACT 1972 (c. 68)
Art. 11(2), Sch. 5, para. 1.	In s. 7(4) for the words " the Secretary of State " substitute " the Secretary of State for Scotland and the Secretary of State for Wales ".
No. 323 (S.).	LAND COMPENSATION (SCOTLAND) ACT 1973 (c. 56)
Art. 2.	In s. 28(1) for the word " six " substitute " two and three quarters ".
No. 474.	POWERS OF CRIMINAL COURTS ACT 1973 (c. 62)
Art. 3.	In s. 2(1) for the words " not less than one year " substitute " not less than six months ".
No. 1568.	LEGAL AID ACT 1974 (c. 4)
Reg. 2.	In s. 1(1)(*a*) (as amended by S.I. 1977/1934) for the [weekly] sum of " £48 " substitute " £52 ".
Reg. 3.	In s. 1(1) (as amended by S.I. 1977/1934) for the [capital] sum of " £340 " substitute " £365 ".
No. 1567. *Reg. 2(1).*	In s. 4(2) (as amended by S.I. 1977/1635) for the sum of " £23 " substitute " £25 ".
Reg. 2(2).	For the table in s. 4(3) (as amended by S.I. 1977/1635) substitute:—

" Exceeding £25 but not exceeding £28 a week £3
Exceeding £28 but not exceeding £30 a week £6
Exceeding £30 but not exceeding £32 a week £9
Exceeding £32 but not exceeding £34 a week £12
Exceeding £34 but not exceeding £36 a week £15
Exceeding £36 but not exceeding £38 a week £18
Exceeding £38 but not exceeding £40 a week £21
Exceeding £40 but not exceeding £42 a week £24
Exceeding £42 but not exceeding £44 a week £27
Exceeding £44 but not exceeding £46 a week £30
Exceeding £46 but not exceeding £48 a week £33
Exceeding £48 but not exceeding £50 a week £36
Exceeding £50 but not exceeding £52 a week   ... ... £39."

No. 1571. *Reg. 2.*	In s. 6(1) (as amended by S.I. 1977/1935) for the [yearly] sum of " £2,400 " substitute " £2,600 ".
Reg. 3.	In s. 6(1)(*a*) (as amended by S.I. 1977/1935) for the sum of " £1,600 " substitute " £1,700 ".
Reg. 4.	In s. 9(1)(*a*) (as amended by S.I. 1977/1935) for the [yearly] sum of " £760 " substitute " £815 ".
Reg. 5.	In s. 9(1)(*b*) (as amended by S.I. 1977/1935) for the sum of " £340 " substitute " £365 ".

Number of Statutory Instrument of 1978	Act or Measure and how amended
No. 272.	DUMPING AT SEA ACT 1974 (c. 20)
Art. 11(2), Sch. 5, para. 1.	In ss. 6 and 12(3) for the words " the Secretary of State " substitute " the Secretary of State for Scotland and the Secretary of State for Wales ".
No. 272.	CONTROL OF POLLUTION ACT 1974 (c. 40)
Art. 11(2), Sch. 5, para. 12(a). para. 12(b).	At the end of s. 39(2) insert " In the application of this section to Wales, the words ' the Secretary of State ' shall be substituted for the words ' the Minister of Agriculture, Fisheries and Food ' and the words ' and the said Minister acting jointly ' shall not have effect.". In s. 51(2) after the word " Scotland " insert " and Wales ".
No. 920.	FRIENDLY SOCIETIES ACT 1974 (c. 46)
Art. 2(a).	In s. 64(1)(c) (as amended by S.I. 1976/86) for the sum of " £10,000 " [relating to gross sums] substitute " £15,000 ".
Art. 2(b).	In s. 64(1)(d) (as amended by S.I. 1976/86) for " £1,000 " substitute " £1,500 ".
No. 993.	GENERAL RATE ACT 1975 (c. 5)
Art. 3.	In s. 1(1) for " 1980 " substitute " 1981 ."
No. 1840.	SOCIAL SECURITY ACT 1975 (c. 14)
Art. 2.	In s. 7(1)(5) (as amended by S.I. 1977/2180) for " £1·90 " and " £950 " substitute " £2·10 " and " £1,050 " respectively.
Art. 3. Art. 4.	In s. 8(1) for " £1·80 " substitute " £2 ". In ss. 9(2) and 10(1) for " £2,000 " wherever occurring, and for " £6,250 " in each of those sections, substitute " £2,250 " and " £7,000 " respectively.
No. 912. *Art. 6. Arts. 2, 3, Sch.*	In ss. 30(1), 45(3) and 66(4) (as amended by S.I. 1977/1325) for " £40 " substitute " £45 ". For Schedule 4 (as amended by 1975 c. 60 s. 22(2), S.I. 1977/1325 and 1978/475) substitute:—

" SCHEDULE 4

RATES OF BENEFITS, GRANTS AND INCREASES FOR DEPENDANTS

PART I

CONTRIBUTORY PERIODICAL BENEFITS (SECTIONS 14–31)

Description of benefit	Weekly rate
1. Unemployment or sickness benefit (section 14).	£15·75
2. Invalidity pension (section 15).	£19·50
3. Invalidity allowance (section 16).	(a) higher rate ... ... £4·15 (b) middle rate ... ... £2·60 (c) lower rate ... ... £1·30 (the appropriate rate being determined in accordance with section 16(2)).
4. Maternity allowance (section 22).	£15·75
5. Widow's allowance (section 24).	£27·30
6. Widowed mother's allowance (section 25).	£19·50

Number of Statutory Instrument of 1978	Act or Measure and how amended

Description of benefit	Weekly rate
7. Widow's pension (section 26).	£19·50
8. Category A retirement pension (section 28).	£19·50
9. Category B retirement pension (section 29).	(*a*) lower rate ... ... £11·70 (*b*) higher rate ... ... £19·50 (the appropriate rate being determined in accordance with section 29(7)).
10. Child's special allowance (section 31).	(*a*) before 2nd April 1979 ... £6·35 (*b*) on and after 2nd April 1979 ... ... £5·35

PART II

MATERNITY GRANT AND DEATH GRANT

Description of Grant	Amount
	£
1. Maternity grant (section 21)	25·00
2. Death grant (section 32), where the deceased was at his death—	
(*a*) under the age of 3	9·00
(*b*) between the ages of 3 and 6	15·00
(*c*) between the ages of 6 and 18	22·50
(*d*) over the age of 18—	
(i) if on 5th July 1948 that person had attained the age of 55 in the case of a man or 50 in the case of a woman	15·00
(ii) in any other case	30·00

PART III

NON-CONTRIBUTORY PERIODICAL BENEFITS (SS. 34–40)

Description of benefit	Weekly rate
1. Attendance allowance (section 35).	(*a*) higher rate ... ... £15·60 (*b*) lower rate ... ... £10·40 (the appropriate rate being determined in accordance with section 35(3)).
2. Non-contributory invalidity pension (section 36).	£11·70
3. Invalid care allowance (section 37).	£11·70
3A. Mobility allowance (section 37A).	£10·00
4. Guardian's allowance (section 38).	(*a*) before 2nd April 1979 ... £6·35 (*b*) on and after 2nd April 1979 ... ... £5·35
5. Category C or Category D retirement pension (section 39).	(*a*) lower rate ... ... £7·05 (*b*) higher rate ... ... £11·70 (the appropriate rate being determined in accordance with section 39(2)).
6. Age addition (to a pension of any category, and otherwise under section 40).	£0·25

Number of Statutory Instrument of 1978	Act or Measure and how amended

PART IV

INCREASES FOR DEPENDANTS (SS. 41–49)

Benefit to which increase applies (1)	Increase for qualifying child (2)		Increase for adult dependant (3)
	before 2nd April 1979 (*a*)	on and after 2nd April 1979 (*b*)	
	£	£	£
1. Unemployment or sickness benefit—			
(*a*) where the beneficiary is under pensionable age	1·85	0·85	9·75
(*b*) where the beneficiary is over pensionable age	6·35	5·35	11·70
2. Invalidity pension	6·35	5·35	11·70
3. Maternity allowance	1·85	0·85	9·75
4. Widow's allowance	6·35	5·35	—
5. Widowed mother's allowance	6·35	5·35	—
6. Category A or B retirement pension	6·35	5·35	11·70
7. Category C retirement pension	6·35	5·35	7·05
8. Child's special allowance	6·35	5·35	—
9. Non-contributory invalidity pension	6·35	5·35	7·05
10. Invalid care allowance	6·35	5·35	7·05

Where unemployment or sickness benefit is payable at a weekly rate determined under section 14(6) of this Act, column (3) of this Part of this Schedule shall have effect subject to section 44(5)(*b*); and where an invalidity pension is payable at a weekly rate determined under section 15(4) of this Act, column (3) shall have effect subject to section 47(2)(*b*).

PART V

RATE OR AMOUNT OF INDUSTRIAL INJURIES BENEFIT

Description of benefit, etc.	Rate or amount
1. Injury benefit under section 56 (weekly rates).	(*a*) for any period during which the beneficiary is over the age of 18 or is entitled to an increase of benefit in respect of a child or adult dependant ... £18·50
	(*b*) for any period during which the beneficiary is not over the age of 18 and not so entitled ... ... £15·75
2. Maximum disablement gratuity under section 57(5).	£2,120

Number of Statutory Instrument of 1978	Act or Measure and how amended

Description of benefit, etc.	Rate or amount
3. Disablement pension under section 57(6) (weekly rates).	For the several degrees of disablement set out in column (1) of the following Table, the respective amounts in that Table, using— (a) column (2) for any period during which the beneficiary is over the age of 18 or is entitled to an increase of benefit in respect of a child or adult dependant; (b) column (3) for any period during which the beneficiary is not over the age of 18 and not so entitled:

TABLE

Degree of disablement	Amount	
(1)	(2)	(3)
Per cent.	£	£
100	31·90	19·50
90	28·71	17·55
80	25·52	15·60
70	22·33	13·65
60	19·14	11·70
50	15·95	9·75
40	12·76	7·80
30	9·57	5·85
20	6·38	3·90

Description of benefit, etc.	Rate or amount
4. Unemployability supplement under section 58 (increase of weekly rate of disablement pension).	£19·50
5. Increase under section 59 of weekly rate of unemployability supplement (early onset of incapacity for work).	(a) if on the qualifying date the beneficiary was under the age of 35, or if that date fell before 5th July 1948 ... ... £4·15 (b) if head (a) above does not apply and on the qualifying date the beneficiary was under the age of 45... £2·60 (c) if heads (a) and (b) above do not apply, and on the qualifying date the beneficiary was a man under the age of 60, or a woman under the age of 55 ... £1·30
6. Maximum increase under section 60 of weekly rate of disablement pension in cases of special hardship.	£12·76 or the amount (if any) by which the weekly rate of the pension, apart from any increase under section 61, 63, 64 or 66, falls short of £31·90 whichever is the less.
7. Maximum increase under section 61 of weekly rate of disablement pension where constant attendance needed.	(a) except in cases of exceptionally severe disablement £12·70 (b) in any case ... ... £25·40

Number of Statutory Instrument of 1978	Act or Measure and how amended	
	Description of benefit, etc.	Rate or amount
	8. Increase under section 63 of weekly rate of disablement pension (exceptionally severe disablement).	£12·70
	9. Increase under section 64 of weekly rate of injury benefit (dependent children).	(*a*) in respect of each qualifying child before 2nd April 1979 ... ... £1·85 (*b*) in respect of each qualifying child on and after 2nd April 1979 ... ... £0·85
	10. Increase under section 64 of weekly rate of disablement pension (dependent children).	(*a*) in respect of each qualifying child before 2nd April 1979 ... ... £6·35 (*b*) in respect of each qualifying child on and after 2nd April 1979 ... ... £5·35
	11. Increase under section 66(2) of weekly rate of injury benefit (adult dependant).	£9·75
	12. Increase under section 66(2) of weekly rate of disablement pension (adult dependant).	£11·70

	13. Widow's pension under section 68 (weekly rates)—
	    (*a*) initial rate ... ...
	    (*b*) higher permanent rate ...
	    (*c*) lower permanent rate ...
		
		£27·30
		£20·05
		30 per cent. of the weekly rate for the time being of a widow's pension as specified in Part I of this Schedule, paragraph 7.

	14. Widower's pension under section 69 (weekly rate).	£20·05
	15. Allowances under section 70 in respect of children— (*a*) weekly rate of allowance at higher rate.	 (i) in respect of each qualifying child before 2nd April 1979 ... ... £6·35 (ii) in respect of each qualifying child on and after 2nd April 1979 ... ... £5·35
	(*b*) weekly rate of allowance at lower rate.	(i) in respect of each qualifying child before 2nd April 1979 ... ... £1·85 (ii) in respect of each qualifying child on and after 2nd April 1979 ... ... £0·85
	16. Maximum under section 91(1) of aggregate of weekly benefit payable for successive accidents.	(*a*) for any period during which the beneficiary is over the age of 18 or is entitled to an increase of benefit in respect of a child or adult dependant ... £31·90 (*b*) for any period during which the beneficiary is not over the age of 18 and not so entitled... ... ... £19·50"

Number of Statutory Instrument of 1978	Act or Measure and how amended
No. 912.	INDUSTRIAL INJURIES AND DISEASES (OLD CASES) ACT 1975 (c. 16)
Art. 4.	In ss. 2(6)(*c*) and 7(2)(*b*) (as amended by S.I. 1977/1325) for " £10·50 " substitute (15.11.78) " £11·70 ".
No. 1102.	MINISTERIAL AND OTHER SALARIES ACT 1975 (c. 27)
Art. 2(1).	In s. 1(2) (as amended by S.I. 1977/1295) for " £20,208 " substitute " £22,228 ".
Art. 4.	In s. 1(3) for " £13,000 " substitute " £14,300 ".
Art. 2(2),	In Schedule 1 Part I (as originally enacted) for " £20,000 " substitute " £22,000 ".
Sch. 1.	In respect of the next three persons listed for " £13,000 " (as originally enacted) substitute " £14,300 ".
	In items (*a*)–(*g*) for " £13,208 " (substituted by S.I. 1977/1295) substitute " £14,528 ".
	In Part II item 1 (as amended by S.I. 1977/1295) for " £7,500–£9,708 " substitute " £8,822–£10,678 ". In items 2, 3 for " £7,500–£9,708 " substitute " £8,250–£10,450 ".
	In Part III for " £14,500 ", " £11,000 " and " £11,000 " (as originally enacted) and (as substituted in last line by S.I. 1977/1295) " £8,270 " substitute " £15,950 ", " £12,100 ", " £12,100 " and " £9,097 " respectively.
	In Part IV (as amended by S.I. 1977/1295 in respect of the first three and fifth persons listed) for " £7,020 ", " £6,020 ", " £5,520 ", " £5,000 " (this figure as originally enacted) and " £5,020 " substitute " £7,722 ", " £6,622 ", " £6,072 ", " £5,500 " and " £5,522 " respectively. In respect of the last four persons listed for " £4,000 " (as originally enacted) substitute " £4,400 ".
Art. 3, *Sch. 2.*	In Schedule 2 Part I (as originally enacted) in reference to the House of Commons, for " £9,500 ", " £7,500 " and " £4,000 " substitute " £10,450 ", " £8,250 " and " £4,400 " respectively. In reference to the House of Lords, for " £4,003 " and " £2,953 " (substituted by S.I. 1977/1295) substitute " £4,403 " and " £3,248 " respectively.
No. 1603.	FINANCE (NO. 2) ACT 1975 (c. 45)
Reg. 3(4).	In s. 16(2)(*d*) for the words " section 80(1)(*e*) " substitute " section 80(1A)(*b*) ". After subs. (2)(*e*) (added by 1978 c. 42 s. 3) of s. 16 insert:—
	" (*f*) permitting goods to be destroyed or abandoned to the Commissioners without payment of customs duty in such circumstances and subject to such conditions as they may determine; ".
No. 273. *Art. 7(1).*	In s. 18(2)(*a*) for the words " Part I of the Finance Act 1972 " substitute " either Part I of the Finance Act 1972 or Part I of the Value Added Tax and Other Taxes Act 1973 ".
No. 912.	SOCIAL SECURITY PENSIONS ACT 1975 (c. 60)
Art. 7.	In s. 6(1)(*a*) (as amended by S.I. 1977/1325) for the sum of " £17·50 " substitute " £19·50 " (13.11.78).
No. 1329.	EMPLOYMENT PROTECTION ACT 1975 (c. 71)
Reg. 2.	In s. 8(2) for the sum of " £21 " substitute " £50 ".
No. 434.	FINANCE ACT 1976 (c. 40)
Art. 2.	In s. 64(2)(*a*) for the sum of " £6,000 " substitute " £8,000 ".
Art. 3.	In Schedule 7 Part I for Tables A, B and C substitute:—

Number of Statutory Instrument of 1978	Act or Measure and how amended

" TABLE A

CARS WITH ORIGINAL MARKET VALUE UP TO £8,000
AND HAVING A CYLINDER CAPACITY

Cylinder capacity of car in cubic centimetres	Age of car at end of relevant year of assessment	
	Under 4 years	4 years or more
1,300 or less	£190	£130
More than 1,300, but not more than 1,800	£250	£165
More than 1,800	£380	£255

TABLE B

CARS WITH ORIGINAL MARKET VALUE UP TO £8,000
AND NOT HAVING A CYLINDER CAPACITY

Original market value of car	Age of car at end of relevant year of assessment	
	Under 4 years	4 years or more
Less than £2,500	£190	£130
£2,500 or more, but less than £3,500 ...	£250	£165
£3,500 or more, but not more than £8,000	£380	£255

TABLE C

CARS WITH ORIGINAL MARKET VALUE MORE THAN £8,000

Original market value of car	Age of car at end of relevant year of assessment	
	Under 4 years	4 years or more
More than £8,000, but not more than £12,000	£550	£365
More than £12,000	£880	£585 "

Number of Statutory Instrument of 1978	Act or Measure and how amended
No. 319.	LAND DRAINAGE ACT 1976 (c. 70)
Reg. 3, Sch., para. 1.	In s. 30(2)(*c*) for the words " £20 for each acre " substitute " £50 for each hectare ".
paras. 2, 3.	In ss. 48(1) and 49(1) for the word " acre " substitute " hectare ".
para. 4.	In s. 51(2) for the word " acre " substitute " hectare " and for " 10p " in each place where it occurs substitute " 25p ".
para. 5.	In s. 52(1) for the word " acre " substitute " hectare ".
para. 6.	In s. 116(1), definition of " agricultural land ", for the words " one quarter of an acre " substitute " 0·10 hectare ".
para. 7.	In Schedule 2 Part I para. 1(1)(*a*)(*b*) and (*d*) for the words " 10 acres ", " 20 acres " and " 10 acres " substitute " 4 hectares ", " 8 hectares " and " 4 hectares " respectively.
No. 913.	SUPPLEMENTARY BENEFITS ACT 1976 (c. 71)
Reg. 2(1) (2).	In Schedule 1 Part II, for paras. 7 and 8 (as substituted by S.I. 1977/1326) substitute:—

" *Normal requirements*

7. Requirements of persons, other than blind persons—

			£
(*a*) husband and wife or other persons falling within paragraph 3(1) of this Schedule	A	...	25·25
	B	...	31·55
	C	...	31·80
(*b*) person living alone or householder not falling within sub-paragraph (*a*) above who is directly responsible for household necessities and rent (if any)	A	...	15·55
	B	...	19·90
	C	...	20·15
(*c*) any other person aged—			
(i) not less than 18 years	A	...	12·45
	B	...	15·95
	C	...	16·20
(ii) less than 18 but not less than 16 years		...	9·55
(iii) less than 16 but not less than 13 years		...	7·95
(iv) less than 13 but not less than 11 years		...	6·55
(v) less than 11 but not less than 5 years ...		...	5·30
(vi) less than 5 years		...	4·40

Blind persons

8. Requirements of persons who are or include blind persons—
(*a*) husband and wife or other persons falling within paragraph 3(1) of this Schedule—

			£
(i) if one of them is blind	A	...	26·50
	B	...	32·80
	C	...	33·05
(ii) if both of them are blind ...	A	...	27·30
	B	...	33·60
	C	...	33·85
(*b*) any other blind person aged—			
(i) not less than 18 years	A	...	16·80
	B	...	21·15
	C	...	21·40
(ii) less than 18 but not less than 16 years		...	10·45
(iii) less than 16 but not less than 13 years		...	7·95

Number of Statutory Instrument of 1978	Act or Measure and how amended

	(iv) less than 13 but not less than 11 years ... 6·55 (v) less than 11 but not less than 5 years ... ... 5·30 (vi) less than 5 years ... ... 4·40."
Reg. 2(3).	In Schedule 1 Part II para. 10(1)(*a*)(*b*) (as amended by S.I. 1977/1326) for " £14·00 " and " £9·30 " substitute " £15·60 " and " £10·40 " respectively.
No. 1939.	ENDANGERED SPECIES (IMPORT AND EXPORT) ACT 1976 (c. 72)

Art. 5.	In Schedule 1 Part I delete:—
	             " Primates
	Macaca rhesus Rhesus monkey
	Macaca nemestrina Pig-tailed monkey "
	In Part II after the words:—
	             " Perch
	Stizostedion vitreum glaucum Blue walleye "
	insert:—
	             " Drumfish
	Cynoscion macdonaldi "
	After the word " Butterflies " insert:—
	   " Ornithoptera
	     Trogonoptera }Birdwing butterflies "
	     Troides
	For the words " Parnassius apollo apollo " substitute " Parnassius apollo ".

Art. 6.	In Schedule 2 after the words:—
	   " Dicksoniaceae Dicksoniaceae "
	insert:—
	   " Didiereaceae Didiereaceae ".
	After the words:—
	   " Palmae Areca ipot "
	insert in second column:—
	                            " Chrysalidocarpus decipiens
	                            Chrysalidocarpus lutescens
	                            Neodypsis decaryi ".

Art. 7.	In Schedule 3 for paras. 5 to 22 substitute:—
	     " 5. The whole or any part, or anything made wholly or partly there-from, of any tusk of any of the following animals, namely
	     (*a*) any animal of the family Elephantidae (elephants)
	     (*b*) any animal of the family Suidae (pigs)
	     (*c*) any animal of the species Monodon monoceros (narwhal)
	     (*d*) any animal of the species Odobenus rosmarus (walrus)
	and powder and waste of any tusk of any of the animals referred to in sub-paragraphs (*a*) to (*d*) of this paragraph.
	     6. The whole or any part, or anything made wholly or partly therefrom, of any tooth of any mammal and powder and waste of any tooth of any mammal.
	     7.—(1) The whole or any part of the horns of any mammal to which Schedule 1 to this Act applies.
	     (2) Anything made wholly or partly from the whole or any part of the horn or waste of the horn of any animal of the family Rhinocerotidae.
	     8. The stuffed head or the skull, together with the skin covering it, of any mammal or reptile to which Schedule 1 to this Act applies.
	     9.—(1) Any furskin, skin or hide of a defined animal, if raw, tanned or dressed.
	     (2) Any piece or cutting (including the head, tail and any paw) of any furskin, skin or hide of a defined animal.
	     (3) Tanned or dressed furskin of a defined animal or defined animals which are assembled in plates, rectangles, crosses, trapeziums or otherwise.

Number of Statutory Instrument of 1978	Act or Measure and how amended

(4) Any rug coverlet coat, jacket, cape or stole or any other item of clothing made wholly or partly of any furskin of a defined animal (except where the furskin is trimming only).

(5) In this paragraph a defined animal means
    (*a*) any animal of the following families, namely
        Felidae (cats) (except Felis catus (domestic cat))
        Ursidae (bears);
    (*b*) any animal of the following sub-families, namely
        Hemigalinae (civets and palm civets)
        Lutrinae (otters)
        Paradoxurinae (palm civets)
        Viverrinae (linsangs, civets and genets);
    (*c*) any animal of the genus Arctocephalus (fur seals);
    (*d*) any animal of the following species, namely
        Canis lupus (wolf)
        Colobus angolensis (Angolan colobus)
        Colobus guereza (guereza)
        Colobus polykomos (western black and white colobus, otherwise known as ursine colobus)
        Crocuta crocuta (spotted hyaena)
        Equus burchelli (Common or Burchell's zebra)
        Equus grevyi (Grevy's zebra)
        Equus zebra (mountain zebra)
        Hyaena brunnea (brown hyaena)
        Lama guanacoe (Guanaco)
        Mungos mungo (banded mongoose)
        Vicugna vicugna (vicuna).

10.—(1) The whole or any part of any raw hide or skin if fresh, salted, dried, pickled or limed and whether or not split and the leather of any animal of the families Elephantidae (elephants) and Macropodinae (wallabies and kangaroos).

(2) Any clothing (including footwear, watch straps and belts) and any wallet, purse, handbag, travelling bag, brief case, toilet case, suitcase or any other similar container made wholly or partly of the hide, skin or leather or any animal of the families Elephantidae (elephants) and Macropodinae (wallabies and kangaroos).

11. The skin and scales of any animal of the family Manidae (pangolins).

12. Hair, whether or not carded or combed, of any animal of the species Vicugna vicugna (vicuna).

13. Yarn made wholly or partly of hair of any animal of the species Vicugna vicugna (vicuna).

14. Fabric made wholly or partly of hair of any animal of the species Vicugna vicugna (vicuna) and any coat or jacket made wholly of partly of any such fabric.

15. Musk derived from any animal of the species Moschus moschiferus (musk deer).

16.—(1) The whole or any part of any raw hide or skin, if fresh, salted, dried, pickled or limed and whether or not split, and the leather of any animal of the class Reptilia (reptiles).

(2) Any clothing (including footwear, watch straps and belts) and any wallet, purse, handbag, travelling bag, brief case, toilet case, suitcase or any other similar container made wholly or partly of the hide, skin or leather of any animal of the class Reptilia.

17.—(1) The whole or any part of the bony shell and its covering scales, if unworked, simply prepared or polished, of any of the order Testudinata (turtles, tortoises and terrapins).

Number of Statutory Instrument of 1978	Act or Measure and how amended

(2) Anything made wholly or partly from the bony shell, its covering scales and the claws, of any member of the family Cheloniidae (sea turtles).

18. The meat and cartilage, including callipee and callipash, of any animal of the family Cheloniidae (sea turtles).

19. The whole shell of any animal of the species Papustyla pulcherrima, otherwise known as Papuina pulcherrima (green tree snail).

20. The casque (whether or not attached to the upper part of the bill) of any bird of the species Rhinoplax vigil (helmeted hornbill), or anything made wholly or partly therefrom.

21.—(1) Plumage, that is to say, any feather or feathers, or any skin or any other part with any feathers on it, of any bird or birds, other than excepted plumage.

(2) In sub-paragraph (1) above, excepted plumage means

(*a*) plumage which is that only of a bird of any of the following species, namely
> Chrysolophus pictus (golden pheasant)
> Gallus gallus (red junglefowl and domestic fowl)
> Phasianus colchicus (common pheasant, otherwise known as ring-necked pheasant)
> Struthio camelus (ostrich)
> Sturnus vulgaris (starling);

(*b*) plumage which is that only of a bird of any domestic form of any of the following species, namely
> Anas platyrhynchos (domestic duck)
> Anser anser (domestic goose)
> Anser cygnoides (Chinese goose)
> Cairina moschata (Muscovy duck)
> Columba livia (domestic pigeon)
> Meleagris gallopavo (turkey)
> Numida meleagris (Guineafowl);

(*c*) plumage which consists only of the down feathers of any adult female bird of the species Somateria mollissima (eider duck);

(*d*) plumage which consists only of the train feathers of any adult male bird of the species Pavo cristatus (Indian peacock);

(*e*) plumage none of which falls outside paragraphs (*a*) to (*d*) above.

22. Anything made wholly or partly of plumage (within the meaning of paragraph 22 above and subject to the exception where stated).

23. Any egg, whether whole or blown, of any bird other than

(*a*) a bird of any of the following species, namely
> Alectoris chukar (chukar)
> Alectoris rufa (red-legged partridge)
> Coturnix japonica (Japanese quail)
> Gallus gallus (red junglefowl and domestic fowl)
> Perdix perdix (common partridge);

(*b*) a bird of any domestic form of any of the following species, namely
> Anas platyrhynchos (domestic duck)
> Anser anser (domestic goose)
> Anser cygnoides (Chinese goose)
> Cairina moschata (Muscovy duck)
> Meleagris gallopavo (turkey)
> Numida meliagris (Guineafowl).

24. The whole or any part of the wings or anything made wholly or partly therefrom of any member of the following genera, namely
> Ornithoptera ⎫
> Trogonoptera ⎬ Birdwing butterflies.
> Troides ⎭

Number of Statutory Instrument of 1978	Act or Measure and how amended
	25. The stem of any plant of any of the families Cyatheaceae and Dicksoniaceae (tree ferns). NOTE: In this Schedule, any common name which appears in brackets after a scientific name is included by way of guidance only; in the event of any dispute or proceedings, only the scientific name concerned is to be taken into account." [NOTE: Sch. 3 of the 1976 Act was also amended by S.I. 1978/1280 but this statutory instrument is revoked and superseded by S.I. 1978/1939.]
No. 489.	NATIONAL HEALTH SERVICE ACT 1977 (c. 49)
Art. 3(a).	For Schedule 4 para. 1(1) substitute:— " (1) The number of members of the Central Council shall be not less less than forty-two, and not more than forty-six, of whom— (*a*) fifteen shall be nominated members in accordance with sub-paragraph (2) below; (*b*) twenty-seven shall be selected members in accordance with sub-paragraph (5) below; and (*c*) the remaining members shall be such persons appointed by the Secretary of State as he thinks fit.";
Art. 3(b).	At the end of para. 1(2)(*a*) of Sch. 4 insert:— " The President of the Royal College of Radiologists; The Dean of the Faculty of Anaesthetists."
No. 1785.	HOME PURCHASE ASSISTANCE AND HOUSING CORPORATION GUARANTEE ACT 1978 (c. 27)
Art. 3.	At the end of Part II of the Schedule insert:— " The Clydebank Municipal Bank Limited Cumnock Municipal Bank Limited Cunninghame District Municipal Bank Limited Kilsyth and Cumbernauld District Municipal Bank Limited Motherwell District Municipal Bank Limited The Stockton-on-Tees Municipal Savings Bank Limited Strathkelvin District Municipal Bank Limited West Lothian District Municipal Bank Limited."
No. 1777.	EMPLOYMENT PROTECTION (CONSOLIDATION) ACT 1978 (c. 44)
Arts. 2, 3. No. 1778.	In s. 15(1) for the sum of " £6·60 " substitute " £7·25 ".
Arts. 2, 3. No. 1777.	In s. 75(1) for the sum of " £5,200 " substitute " £5,750 ".
Arts. 2, 3.	In s. 122(5) for the sum of " £100 " substitute " £110 ". In Schedule 14 para. 8(1)(*a*)–(*c*) for the sum of " £100 " substitute " £110 " in each case.

INDEX

TO THE

PUBLIC GENERAL ACTS

AND

GENERAL SYNOD MEASURES 1978

A

CHRONICALLY SICK AND DISABLED PERSONS (NORTHERN IRELAND) ACT: c. 53
II, p. 1363

§ 1. Information as to need for and existence of social welfare services, II, p. 1363.
2. Provision of social welfare services, II, p. 1364.
3. Duties of Housing Executive, II, p. 1365.
4. Access to and facilities at premises open to the public, II, p. 1365.
5. Provision of public sanitary conveniences, II, p. 1365.
6. Provision of sanitary conveniences at certain premises open to the public, II, p. 1366.
7. Signs at buildings complying with sections 4 to 6, II, p. 1366.
8. Access to and facilities at university and school buildings, II, p. 1366.
9. Advisory committees, etc, II, p. 1367.
10. Co-option of chronically sick or disabled persons by Committees of Health and Social Services Board, II, p. 1367.
11. Co-option of chronically sick or disabled persons to committees of district council, II, p. 1367.
12. Separation of younger from older patients, II, p. 1367.
13. Information as to accommodation of younger and older persons, II, p. 1368.
14. Badges for display on motor vehicles used by disabled persons, II, p. 1368.
15. Special educational treatment for the deaf-blind, II, p. 1370.
16. Special educational treatment for children suffering from autism, etc., II, p. 1370.
17. Special educational treatment for children suffering from dyslexia, II, p. 1370.
18. Power to define certain expressions, II, p. 1371.
19. Regulations and orders, II, p. 1371.
20. Interpretation, II, p. 1371.
21. Short title and commencement, II, p. 1371.

CHURCH OF ENGLAND (MISCELLANEOUS PROVISIONS) MEASURE: No. 3
II, p. 1529

§ 1. Special majorities required for certain Measures, II, p. 1529.
2. Provisions with respect to certain persons in office at commencement of Ecclesiastical Offices (Age Limit) Measure 1975, II, p. 1530.
3. Provision for altering financial year of Church Commissioners, II, p. 1530.
4. Amendments relating to constitution of Church Commissioners, II, p. 1531.
5. Additional member of diocesan boards of finance, II, p. 1531.
6. Restriction on power to charge fees for searches, etc. of certain registers in certain diocesan record offices, II, p. 1532.
7. Extension of power to dispose of land no longer required for purpose for which acquired, II, p. 1532.
8. Church, etc. to be vested in Church Commissioners for certain purposes where fee simple is in abeyance, II, p. 1532.
9. Power to extend Inspection of Churches Measure 1955, II, p. 1533.

D

DOMESTIC PROCEEDINGS AND MAGISTRATES' COURTS ACT—*continued*

PART II

AMENDMENTS OF GUARDIANSHIP⸤OF⸥MINORS⸤ACTS 1971 AND 1973

Amendment of provisions relating to the⸤custody of minors

Amendment of provisions relating to orders for maintenance

General provisions

PART III

AMENDMENTS OF OTHER ENACTMENTS RELATING TO
DOMESTIC PROCEEDINGS

Amendments of Affiliation Proceedings Act 1957

Amendments of Maintenance Orders (Reciprocal Enforcement) Act 1972

Amendments of Matrimonial Causes Act 1973

Amendments of Parts II and V of Children Act 1975

EMPLOYMENT PROTECTION (CONSOLIDATION) ACT—*continued*

EMPLOYMENT PROTECTION (CONSOLIDATION) ACT—*continued*

F

FINANCE ACT—*continued*

CHAPTER II

CAPITAL GAINS

CHAPTER III

PROFIT SHARING SCHEMES

PART IV

CAPITAL TRANSFER TAX

G

H

I

J

PART I
CONSTITUTION OF THE SUPREME COURT OF JUDICATURE OF NORTHERN IRELAND

PART II
THE HIGH COURT
General jurisdiction

L

M

N

NATIONAL HEALTH SERVICE (SCOTLAND) ACT—*continued*

PART I

SCHEDULED OFFENCES

Preliminary enquiries, bail and young persons in custody

§ 1.   Preliminary enquiry into scheduled offences, I, p. 39.
  2.   Limitation of power to grant bail in case of scheduled offences, I, p. 40.
  3.   Legal aid to applicants for bail in case of scheduled offences, I, p. 40.
  4.   Holding in custody of young persons charged with scheduled offences, I p. 41.
  5.   Directions under s. 4, I, p. 41.

Court and mode of trial

  6.   Court for trial on indictment of scheduled offences, I, p. 42.
  7.   Mode of trial on indictment of scheduled offences, I, p. 42.

Evidence, onus of proof and treatment of convicted young persons

  8.   Admissions by persons charged with scheduled offences, I, p. 43.
  9.   Onus of proof in relation to offences of possession, I, p. 44.
 10.   Treatment of young persons convicted of scheduled offences, I, p. 45.

PART II

POWERS OF ARREST, DETENTION, SEARCH AND SEIZURE, ETC.

 11.   Arrest of terrorists, I, p. 46.
 12 and schedule 1.   Detention of terrorists, etc., I, pp. 46, 60.
 13.   Constables' general power of arrest and seizure, I, p. 46.

O

OATHS.   *See also* OATHS ACT (c. 19).

To be taken by Judges (c. 23, s. 13(2)) ...   .   I, p. 375
To be taken by member of Scottish Assembly (c. 51, s. 12)   ...   II, p. 1183
To be taken by member of Welsh Assembly (c. 52, s. 30)   ...   II, p. 1283

OATHS ACT: c. 19   ...   .   I, p. 256

PART I
ENGLAND, WALES AND NORTHERN IRELAND

§ 1.   Manner of administration of oaths, I, p. 256.
  2.   Consequential amendments, I, p. 257.

PART II
UNITED KINGDOM
Oaths

3.   Swearing with uplifted hand, I, p. 257.
4.   Validity of oaths, I, p. 257.

Solemn affirmations

5.   Making of solemn affirmations, I, p. 257.
6.   Form of affirmation, I, p. 258.

Supplementary

7 and schedule.   Repeals and savings, I, pp. 258, 260.
8.   Short title, extent and commencement, I, p. 259.
Schedule.   Repeals, I, p. 260.
        Part I.   Consequential repeals, I, p. 260.
        Part II.   Repeal of an obsolete enactment, I, p. 260.

OFFICIAL SOLICITOR.   *See* JUDICATURE (NORTHERN IRELAND) ACT (c. 23, s. 75).

OVERSEAS INVESTMENT.   *See* EXPORT GUARANTEES AND OVERSEAS INVESTMENT
    ACT (c. 18).

P

PARLIAMENT.

Act of Parliament to approve treaties, required under European Assembly
    Elections Act (c. 10, s. 6)   ...   .   **I, p. 116**

Addresses from both Houses of Parliament required under—

Judicature (Northern Ireland) Act (c. 23, s. 13(1)) ...   ...   I, p. 375
National Health Service (Scotland) Act (c. 29, s. 90(3))   ...   I, p. 640

Orders, regulations, reports etc. to be laid before Parliament under—

Civil Aviation Act (c. 8, ss. 1(3), 3(5)(7))   ...   .   I, pp. 80, 83
Commonwealth Development Corporation Act (c. 2, ss. 6(1), 11(2)(3),
    12(5), 16(5))   ...   .   I, pp. 7, 10, 11, 12
Community Service by Offenders (Scotland) Act (c. 49, s. 11)   II, p. 1160
Consumer Safety Act (c. 38, s. 8(2))   ...   .   I, p. 760
Co-operative Development Agency Act (c. 21, ss. 5(3), 6(2), Sch. 2 para. 3)
                                I, pp. 268, 269, 272
Employment Protection (Consolidation) Act (c. 44, ss. 37(2), 148(5))
                                II, pp. 930, 1023

PARLIAMENT—*continued*

European Assembly Elections Act (c. 10, sch. 1 para. 3(5))   I, p. 121
Export Guarantees and Overseas Investment Act (c. 18, s. 11(7)) I, p. 252
Local Government (Scotland) Act (c. 4, s. 1)   ...   ...   I, p. 31
National Health Service (Scotland) Act (c. 29, ss. 5(4), 11(7), 12(7), 66,
  67, 86(4), 94(4)–(6))   ...   ...   I, pp. 592, 597, 598, 630, 638, 646
Participation Agreements Act (c. 1, s. 1(5))   ...   .   I, p. 2
Scotland Act (c. 51, ss. 51(2), 62)   ...   .   II, pp. 1200, 1205
Suppression of Terrorism Act (c. 26, s. 8(6))   ...   ...   I, p. 528
Wales Act (c. 52, ss. 47(2), 57)   ...   .   II, pp. 1290, 1295

Orders, regulations, reports etc. to be laid before the House of Commons
  under—
Employment Subsidies Act (c. 6, ss. 2(2)(3), 3(3))   ...   ...   I, p. 75
House of Commons (Administration) Act (c. 36, s. 3(1))   ...   I, p. 736

Orders, regulations etc. subject to annulment in pursuance of a resolution of
  either House of Parliament under—
Adoption (Scotland) Act (c. 28, s. 60(2))   ...   .   I, p. 574
Civil Aviation Act (c. 8, ss. 4(3), 9(3), 14(3))   ...   I, pp. 83, 86, 89
Commonwealth Development Corporation Act (c. 2, s. 3(5), sch. 1 para.
  1(2))   ...   .   I, pp. 5, 15
Community Service by Offenders (Scotland) Act (c. 49, s. 10(3))
                                                                                II, p. 1160
Consumer Safety Act (c. 38, s. 7(6))   ...   .   I, p. 759
Co-operative Development Agency Act (c. 21, s. 5(5))   ...   I, p. 268
Domestic Proceedings and Magistrates' Courts Act (c. 22, ss. 2(3), 10(11))
                                                                                I, pp. 274, 284
Employment Protection (Consolidation) Act (c. 44, s. 154(2))   II, p. 1028
European Assembly Elections Act (c. 10, sch. 1 para. 5(6))   I, p. 122
Home Purchase Assistance and Housing Corporation Guarantee Act
  (c. 27, s. 4(1)) ...   .   I, p. 536
Housing (Financial Provisions) (Scotland) Act (c. 14, ss. 11(4), 14, 15)
                                                                                I, pp. 208, 209, 210
Import of Live Fish (Scotland) Act (c. 35, s. 1(5))   ...   ...   I, p. 733
Industrial and Provident Societies Act (c. 34, s. 2(4))   ...   I, p. 731
Inner Urban Areas Act (c. 50, s. 15(2))   ...   .   II, p. 1174
Judicature (Northern Ireland) Act (c. 23, ss. 56(1), 119(2)(3))
                                                                                I, pp. 407, 443
Medical Act (c. 12, ss. 2(6)(8), 4(7), 6(3), 11(13), 27(7), sch. 1 para. 4(3),
  sch. 4 paras. 1(6), 7(6))   I, pp. 136, 138, 139, 147, 161, 165, 170, 172
National Health Service (Scotland) Act (c. 29, s. 105(2))   ...   I, p. 648
Nuclear Safeguards and Electricity (Finance) Act (c. 25, s. 3(3)) I, p. 518
Protection of Children Act (c. 37, s. 8)   ...   .   I, p. 748
Rating (Disabled Persons) Act (c. 40, ss. 4(5), 8(2), sch. 1 para. 12(3))
                                                                                II, pp. 783, 787, 790
Refuse Disposal (Amenity) Act (c. 3, s. 10(5))   ...   ...   I, p. 26
Scotland Act (c. 51, ss. 4(7), 42(6), 72(6), 76(3), 81(4), 82(5))
                                                        II, pp. 1180, 1196, 1209, 1211, 1213
State Immunity Act (c. 33, s. 15(2))   ...   .   I, p. 72
Suppression of Terrorism Act (c. 26, s. 7(4))   ...   ...   I, p. 527
Theft Act (c. 31, s. 6)   ...   .   I, p. 711
Transport Act (c. 55, s. 11(6)) ...   .   II, p. 1384
Wales Act (c. 52, ss. 3(7), 13(3), 37(5), 66(4), 68(3), 77(3), 78(4))
                                        II, pp. 1275, 1279, 1287, 1301, 1303, 1304

PARLIAMENT—*continued*

SCOTLAND ACT—*continued*

SCOTLAND ACT—*continued*

SCOTTISH ASSEMBLY.   *See* SCOTLAND ACT (c. 51).

SEARCH.   Powers of, under—

SERVICE BY POST.

SERVICE THROUGH THE FOREIGN AND COMMONWEALTH OFFICE (c. 33, s. 12)

SHERIFF COURT.   Jurisdiction under—

SHIPBUILDING (REDUNDANCY PAYMENTS) ACT: c. 11   ...   ...   I, p. 127

SOLOMON ISLANDS ACT: c. 15   ...   .   I, p. 227

The new state

Nationality law

T

TRANSPORT ACT: c. 55   ...   .   II, p. 1373

County transport planning (England and Wales)

§ 1. Passenger transport policies in county areas, II, p. 1373.
2. County public transport plans, II, p. 1375.
3. Agreements with operators, II, p. 1377.
4. Concessionary fare schemes, II, p. 1377.

Public service vehicle licensing

5. Community bus services, II, p. 1378.
6. Use of community bus for contract work, II, p. 1380.
7 and schedule 1. Car-sharing for social and other purposes, II, pp. 1380, 1392.
8 and schedule 2. Road service licences and permits, II, pp. 1381, 1393.

Road traffic regulation

9 and schedule 3. Lorries, II, pp. 1382, 1395.
10. Drivers' hours (EEC Rules), II, p. 1382.
11. Control of off-street parking, II, p. 1382.
12. Bicycles, II, p. 1384.

Waterway transport and railways

13. National policy for inland waterway transport, II, p. 1384.
14. British Rail public service obligations, II, p. 1384.
15. Transfer of controlling interest in Freightliners Limited, II, p. 1385.
16. Amendment of Railways Act 1974 s. 8, II, p. 1386.

National Freight Corporation (finance)

17. Reduction of capital debt, II, p. 1387.
18. Capital grants, II, p. 1387.
19. Funding of pension obligations, II, p. 1387.
20. Provisions supplementary to s. 19, II, p. 1388.
21. Travel concessions for transferred employees, II, p. 1390.

General

22. Transport supplementary grant, II, p. 1390.
23. Finance (general), II, p. 1391.
24 and schedule 4. Commencement; interpretation; repeals, II, pp. 1391, 1398.
25. Citation and extent, II, p. 1391.

Schedule 1. Re-statement of Road Traffic Act 1960, Schedule 12, Part II, II, p. 1392.
Schedule 2. Amendments about road service licences and permits, II, p. 1393.
Schedule 3. Amendments about lorries, II, p. 1395.
Schedule 4. Repeals, II, p. 1398.

TRUSTEE SAVINGS BANKS ACT: c. 16   ...   .   I, p. 234

§ 1. Investment powers of trustee savings banks, I, p. 234.
2. Duty to invest with National Debt Commissioners (and description ' ordinary deposits ') confined to certain deposits in savings accounts, I, p. 235.
3. Power of trustee savings bank to borrow, I, p. 236.
4. Application to Isle of Man and Channel Islands, I, p. 236.
5 and schedule. Citation, interpretation, repeals and extent, I, pp. 237, 238.

Schedule. Enactments repealed, I, p. 238.

TUVALU ACT: c. 20 ...   .   I, p. 261

§ 1 and schedule 1. Independence for Tuvalu, I, pp. 261, 264.
2. Consequential modifications of British Nationality Acts, I, p. 261.
3. Retention of citizenship of the United Kingdom and Colonies by certain citizens of Tuvalu, I, p. 262.
4 and schedule 2. Consequential modifications of other enactments, I, pp. 263, 264.
5. Interpretation, I, p. 263.
6. Short title, I, p. 263.

Schedule 1. Legislative powers of Tuvalu, I, p. 264.
Schedule 2. Amendments not affecting the law of Tuvalu, I, p. 264.

V

Value Added Tax.   *See* Finance Act (c. 42, Pt. II).

W

ST